RESEARCH IN PSYCHOANALYSIS:
PROCESS, DEVELOPMENT, OUTCOME

RESEARCH IN PSYCHOANALYSIS: PROCESS, DEVELOPMENT, OUTCOME

EDITED BY

THEODORE SHAPIRO AND ROBERT N. EMDE

INTERNATIONAL UNIVERSITIES PRESS, INC.
Madison   Connecticut

Copyright © 1995, International Universities Press, Inc.

INTERNATIONAL UNIVERSITIES PRESS and IUP (& design) ® are registered trademarks of International Universities Press, Inc.

All rights reserved. No part of this book may be reproduced by any means, nor translated into a machine language, without the written permission of the publisher.

Library of Congress Cataloging-in-Publication Data

Research in psychoanalysis : process, development, outcome / edited by Theodore Shapiro and Robert N. Emde.
    p. cm.
Includes bibliographical references and index.
ISBN 0-8236-5795-7
1. Psychoanalysis—Research. I. Shapiro, Theodore. II. Emde, Robert N.
RC506.R44 1994
616.89'17'072—dc20   94-3704
                                                                                CIP

Manufactured in the United States of America

CONTENTS

Introduction: Some Empirical Approaches to Psychoanalysis
Theodore Shapiro and Robert N. Emde   1

I. RESEARCH ON THE PROCESS

Empirical Studies of the Psychoanalytic Process
Joseph Weiss   7

What Psychoanalysis Needs Is More Empirical Research
Virginia Teller and Hartvig Dahl   31

Mannequins in the Labyrinth and the Couch-Lab Intersect
Joseph Caston   51

Defensive Control of States and Person Schemas
Mardi J. Horowitz   67

How Will Psychoanalysis Study Itself?
Enrico E. Jones   91

Psychoanalytic Process Research: Methods and Achievements
Horst Kächele and Helmut Thomä   109

DISCUSSIONS

New Understandings of Psychoanalytic Process
Donald P. Spence   131

A Clinician's Comments on Empirical Studies of
    Psychoanalysis
Jacob A. Arlow   143

The Clinician and the Scientist
Theodore Shapiro   153

II. PSYCHOANALYSIS AND DEVELOPMENTAL PSYCHIATRY AND PSYCHOLOGY

The Intersubjective Domain: Approaches from
    Developmental Psychopathology
R. Peter Hobson   167

Applied Psychoanalysis: How Research with Infants and
    Adolescents at High Psychosocial Risk Informs
    Psychoanalysis
Joy D. Osofsky   193

Discourse, Prediction, and Recent Studies in
    Attachment: Implications for Psychoanalysis
Mary Main   209

Psychoanalytic and Empirical Approaches to
    Developmental Psychopathology: An Object-
    Relations Perspective
Peter Fonagy   245

DISCUSSION

Can Empirical Studies of Development Impact on
    Psychoanalytic Theory and Technique?
Joseph D. Lichtenberg   261

III. OUTCOME STUDIES

The Columbia Records Project and the Evolution of
    Psychoanalytic Outcome Research
Henry M. Bachrach   279

The Effectiveness of Psychotherapy and Psychoanalysis:
  Conceptual Issues and Empirical Work
Robert S. Wallerstein   299

Outcome Research in Psychoanalysis: Review and
  Reconsiderations
Judy L. Kantrowitz   313

The Era of Measures of Transference: The CCRT and
  Other Measures
Lester Luborsky and Ellen Luborsky   329

Integrating Experientially Based Concepts and
  Behavioral Observations in Developmental and
  Intervention Research
Christoph M. Heinicke   353

DISCUSSIONS

Empirical Research in Psychoanalysis
Otto F. Kernberg   369

On Empirical Research
Arnold M. Cooper   381

The Rewards of Research
Robert M. Galatzer-Levy   393

Epilogue: A Beginning—Research Approaches and
  Expanding Horizons for Psychoanalysis
Robert N. Emde   411

Name Index   425

Subject Index   433

INTRODUCTION: SOME EMPIRICAL APPROACHES TO PSYCHOANALYSIS

Theodore Shapiro, M.D.
Robert N. Emde, M.D.

As we approach the one hundredth year after the birth of psychoanalysis, we take stock of our status as science. Freud was firmly convinced, in a growing positivist world, that he would be remembered as the discoverer of the secret of dreams, and that his unique method of inquiry was the best method to explore human inner life. In these searches, he was a psychic determinist in a world of deterministic physics and growing knowledge about the evolution of natural history. Indeed, Freud sought a parallel place for the science of psychoanalysis.

As we entered the twentieth century, the empirical basis of science became central. Philosophers of science began to explore the limits of our certainties, and statistical duplicative experimental approaches gave rise to a growing faith in probabilistic statements. Science became that body of truths to be held tentatively until newer hypotheses could be tested by accumulated empirical observations designed to select among alternative theories. What was happening within psychoanalysis during this same period?

Psychoanalysis grew as a clinical discipline and as such was for a long time cultivating the technical possibilities that arose in order to help patients change. Nonetheless, Freud's earliest observation during the late nineteenth century, suggested that we change neurotic misery into plain human unhappiness, and at the end of his life, he epigrammatically offered, "Where id was, there ego shall be." These pronouncements and the image of the analytic case as a unique scientific exploration became sufficient reasons for continuing our clinical practices. To some it meant that we were not in need of extraclinical verification or further intraclinical scrutiny.

However, this was not enough for those who sought greater certainty about our findings and our methods. Some few of us were further trained in the methods of empirical science and were determined to try those methods on the psychoanalytic situation itself and on proposals and hypotheses that were generated from the developmental point of view of psychoanalysis. Others sought to test the efficacy of the method as a treatment.

The work of those who took the path outlined above has led to a body of information, gathered over 40 or more years, that is far-reaching and that has had a significant impact on hypothesis generation in other areas, such as developmental psychology, interpersonal processes, cognitive psychology, and psychiatric treatment. This volume is dedicated to summarizing the work of some selected psychoanalytic investigators and psychoanalytically informed researchers who have been laboring to bring our science into parity with other scientific clinical disciplines. The standard research methods they use include the assessment of reliability of observations, the validation of constructs and the testing of hypotheses according to contemporary statistical techniques that identify patterns, estimate probabilities for prediction, and guide inference.

The volume is divided into the study of process, developmental studies, and outcome studies.

Each investigator has devoted a considerable portion of his or her time learning and practicing science in this manner, and collectively the authors have provided us with a large body of work to review. As a complement to this rich broth of science review, we have gathered a number of clinical scientists to offer commentaries in order to bridge the impact of the work on practicing psychoanalysts. Each of the editors also joins with commentary and an epilogue at the volume's end.

A word about style. We asked our authors for the impossible. We asked them to be personal, perspectivistic, and to cover their research programs and the psychoanalytic implications of their work in an essay of one-half the usual length for *Journal* articles. This led to a challenging editorial task for the authors and ourselves, but we believe the essays are remarkably readable, nontechnical, and informative.

It is not certain that Freud would have applauded the intrusion of tape recorders and pre- and post-therapy examinations, but he certainly would have been sympathetic to the breadth of influence and the curiosity of today's psychoanalytic scientists. Their efforts are remarkably creative, and their devotion to single-case methodology and innovation of approach are all part of the psychoanalytic tradition.

Psychoanalysis has a special opportunity in today's world of accelerating advances in molecular genetics and the neurosciences. Psychoanalysis is unique in its commitment to understanding individuality and psychological meaning, as other disciplines, basic and clinical, occupy themselves with general processes and biological mechanisms. The opportunity of psychoanalysis is to discover the meaning of biological variation as it is actively constructed in the course of the transactions of development and as an individual's biography reveals itself in panoramic detail through its activation in the transference relationship. The opportunity to add to our knowledge about individuality and meaning, however, depends on an empirical base wherein methods can be replicated and shared, and wherein concepts and findings can be clearly defined and communicated. The authors of this volume are alike in their dedication to such an empirical base.

Finally, we must acknowledge that there are those who fear that the practice of psychoanalysis will become a historical relic. We believe, in contrast, that the investigations as presented here will keep the clinicians' work alive. The science will not kill the practice, but will give the practice a new meaning and further enhance psychoanalysis for the twenty-first century.

I. RESEARCH ON THE PROCESS

EMPIRICAL STUDIES OF THE PSYCHOANALYTIC PROCESS

Joseph Weiss, M.D.

> *A number of quantitative, empirical studies of the psychoanalytic process have been carried out to test a theory of the mind, psychopathology, and therapy based on concepts derived from Freud's ego psychology. The theory we tested assumes that the patient suffers from unconscious pathogenic beliefs that hinder the pursuit of certain important goals, and that in therapy the patient works in accordance with an unconscious plan to disprove these beliefs by testing them with the therapist. The patient controls his repressions unconsciously, lifting them when he decides unconsciously that he may safely do so.*
>
> *Our research supports the hypotheses that the patient tests his pathogenic beliefs throughout therapy, that he is more insightful immediately after the therapist passes a test or offers him an interpretation helpful in disproving the beliefs, and that he benefits over the long term from interpretations that he may use to carry out his plan. It also supports the hypotheses that the patient works in accordance with an unconscious plan and that he exerts control over his repressions.*
>
> *The research indicates that, in analysis, the patient sets the agenda and benefits from corrective emotional experiences provided him when the therapist passes his tests. Finally, the research supports the idea that the psychoanalytic theory of the mind and therapy may be fruitfully studied by empirical, quantitative methods.*

THE EMPIRICAL STUDIES REPORTED HERE were designed to test a particular theory of the mind, psychopathology, and therapy. This theory, as discussed below, is based on concepts that Freud evolved piecemeal in his late work as part of his

---

Training Analyst, San Francisco Psychoanalytic Institute; Co-Director, San Francisco Psychotherapy Research Group.

This research has been supported by NIMH grants MH-13915, MH-34052, MH-35230, administrative and financial assistance from the Mt. Zion Hospital and Medical Center, and grants from the Fund for Psychoanalytic Research, the Broitman Foundation, and the Miriam F. Meehan Charitable Trusts.

ego psychology. It assumes unconscious cognition, unconscious control, and an unconscious wish for mastery. In assuming these things the present theory contrasts sharply with the theory presented by Freud in the *Papers on Technique*, for Freud's 1911–1915 theory assumes neither unconscious thought, unconscious control, nor an unconscious wish for mastery. In testing the present theory, we tested a theory derived from Freud's late works against the 1911–1915 theory.

The testing of the present theory was carried out over a period of many years by the Mt. Zion Psychotherapy Research Group, which I co-direct with Harold Sampson. The development of the theory was greatly helped by the research findings of the group. In testing the present theory against the theory of the *Papers on Technique*, we first located those areas in which the two theories make different testable predictions. We then carried out studies to determine which set of predictions fit better with our findings.

The Theory

Unconscious Mental Functioning

Our most general hypothesis assumes that a patient unconsciously performs many of the same kinds of functions he performs consciously. He unconsciously thinks, assesses reality, makes decisions, and carries out plans. Moreover, he exerts control over his unconscious mental life in accordance with these decisions and plans. He unconsciously regulates his repressions by the criteria of danger and safety, maintaining the repression of a particular mental content for as long as he unconsciously assumes that he would endanger himself if he experienced it. He brings forth the content when he unconsciously decides that he may safely experience it.

Psychopathology

A person's psychopathology stems from maladaptive beliefs about himself and his interpersonal world. These beliefs may be unconscious. They are usually acquired in early childhood by inference from traumatic experiences with parents and siblings. They are concerned with both reality and morality. Since they give rise to psychopathology, they may be called "pathogenic." They are maladaptive in that they warn the person guided by them that if he attempts to reach certain normal and desirable goals, he will put himself in danger. He may experience this danger as internal or external. He may expect to develop severe guilt, shame, fear, or self-torment, or he may expect to hurt someone he loves or be hurt by him. Here are some examples of pathogenic beliefs: "I do not deserve to be happy," or "If I am assertive I will hurt others or be rejected by them," or "If I become sexually excited I will be punished."

The Analytic Process

The analytic process is a process by which the patient works with the analyst to disprove his pathogenic beliefs. He suffers from his pathogenic beliefs and so is highly motivated unconsciously to disprove them. He works throughout analysis by testing his pathogenic beliefs with the analyst: he carries out trial actions and observes the analyst to determine whether the analyst behaves as the beliefs predict or whether, as the patient hopes, the analyst does not do so. Also, he works, by making use of the analyst's interpretations, to become aware that he is guided by certain beliefs that are false and maladaptive.

After the patient experiences the analyst as passing a test or offering an interpretation he can use in his struggle to disprove his pathogenic beliefs, he may take a small step toward disconfirming these beliefs. He may feel relieved, less anxious, and more secure. Moreover, since he maintains his repressions in obedience to his pathogenic beliefs, he may react to the analyst's passing one of his tests or to his offering him a helpful interpretation by becoming slightly more insightful, less inhibited, and less defensive.

The patient in therapy unconsciously develops a simple plan that tells him which problems to tackle first and which to defer. In making this plan the patient is concerned with avoiding danger. For example, a patient at the beginning of therapy felt threatened by the belief that he must comply with others lest he hurt them. Therefore, during the first phase of therapy, he planned to work by testing the analyst, to disprove the belief that unless he complied with the analyst he would hurt him.

Relation of the Theory We Tested to the 1911–1915 Theory and to Ego Psychology

The theory we tested differs considerably from the 1911–1915 theory, for the latter assumes neither an unconscious wish for mastery, nor unconscious cognition, nor unconscious control. According to the 1911–1915 theory, which is based largely on Freud's (1900) early theory of the mind, the unconscious mind consists of psychic forces, namely impulses and defenses, that are regulated "automatically" by the pleasure principle, without regard for thoughts, plans or beliefs. The impulses seek gratification and the defenses oppose their coming forth. From the dynamic interactions of the impulses and the defenses are derived almost all of the phenomena of psychic life (Freud, 1926, pp. 225–226). The patient in therapy, rather than wishing unconsciously to solve his problems, is highly motivated unconsciously to resist treatment so as to retain the infantile gratifications he obtains in his symptoms.

The 1911–1915 theory, with its assumption of unconscious automatic regulation by the pleasure principle, may be thought of as based on the "automatic functioning hypothesis" (AFH). The concepts of Freud's late work, from which the present theory is derived, assume the unconscious use of higher mental functions, and so may be thought of as based on the "higher mental functioning hypothesis" (HMFH). Concepts based on the HMFH are contained in scattered passages throughout

Freud's late works. For example, in the *Outline* (1940a) Freud indicated that a person unconsciously controls his repressions by the criteria of safety and danger.[1] A person maintains the repression of a particular unconscious mental content as long as he unconsciously assumes that his experiencing it would endanger him, and he brings it forth when he unconsciously decides that he may safely experience it. In deciding whether he may safely carry out an unconscious plan of action, he relies on memories of previous attempts to carry out such a plan, and he conducts "trial actions," that is, tests of the environment.

In certain passages in his late writings Freud postulated that a person has a strong unconscious wish for mastery (1920, pp. 32, 35; 1926, p. 107). Also, he assumed that the patient in analysis works with the analyst to master his problems (1937, p. 235). In the *Outline* Freud (1940a, pp. 146, 199) described the wish for mastery in terms of the ego's task of self-preservation. In carrying out this task the ego strives for control over the demands of the instincts.

In addition, Freud assumed that a patient may suffer from a particular pathogenic belief, e.g., the belief in castration as a punishment. He wrote repeatedly that the fear of castration arises from a belief, as opposed to a fantasy, and that the patient acquires this belief in childhood by normal processes of inference from experience (1940a, p. 190; 1940b, p. 277).

The Research

In carrying out their research studies, the Mt. Zion group uses as data the transcripts of entire analyses and of psychotherapies

[1]Freud (1940a) wrote of the ego: "its constructive function consists of interpolating, between the demand made by an instinct and the action that satisfies it, the activity of thought which, after taking its bearings in the present and assessing earlier experiences, endeavours by means of experimental actions to calculate the consequences of the course of action proposed. In this way the ego comes to a decision on whether the attempt to obtain satisfaction is to be carried out or postponed or whether it may be necessary for the demand by the instinct to be suppressed altogether as being dangerous. (Here we have the *reality principle*.) Just as the id is directed exclusively to obtaining

that have been audiorecorded for research purposes. Our investigators use rating scales to measure a variety of phenomena about both patient and analyst. They use blind judgments to prevent their raters from being biased by expectations, and they use statistics to determine the reliability of measures, to quantify the relations among variables, and to assess the significance of their findings.

Testing the Automatic Functioning Hypothesis Against the Higher Mental Functioning Hypothesis

Few analysts today assume that unconscious mental life is regulated exclusively either automatically or by higher mental functions. Most analysts assume both kinds of regulation. Nonetheless, research studies of the relative explanatory power of the hypotheses are important. This is because the AFH still exerts a powerful, perhaps predominant, influence on psychoanalytic thinking. The perusal of a group of current psychoanalytic journals makes clear that the HMFH is seldom invoked explicitly. Indeed, only a small number of psychoanalytic writers make regular explicit use in their clinical discussions of such concepts as unconscious thought, belief, plan, or goal. In addition, a test of the AFH against the HMFH dramatizes and emphasizes the explanatory power of the HMFH.

Among analysts who do assume unconscious use of higher mental functions are Horowitz (1991) with his concept of unconscious schemas concerning role relationships, and Luborsky (1988) who assumes that the patient works in therapy to master his core conflictual relationships. In addition, Dahl et al. (1980, 1988) have developed a decision theory of emotion.

In testing the AFH against the HMFH we studied certain events that occur regularly in an analysis to determine which hypothesis explains these events better. We used as our data the transcripts of the first 100 sessions of the analysis of Mrs. C.,

---

pleasure, so the ego is governed by considerations of safety. The ego has set itself the task of self-preservation, which the id appears to neglect" (p. 199).

whose analysis had been recorded and transcribed for research purposes.

Spontaneous Emergence of Previously Repressed Mental Contents

The HMFH and the AFH provide different explanations for the emergence of previously repressed mental contents, without their being interpreted. The HMFH assumes that these contents may come forth because the patient unconsciously decides that he may safely experience them. The AFH assumes that they may come forth if they push through the patient's repressions to consciousness or if they are disguised or isolated so that they evade the repressing forces.

The two theories may be tested against each other because they make different predictions about how the patient will feel while unconscious mental contents, which have not been interpreted, are emerging. According to the HMFH the patient will have overcome his anxiety about the contents before they come forth, and so will not feel especially anxious while they are emerging. Also, according to the HMFH, the patient will have no need to be defensively uninvolved with the contents while they are emerging, and so will experience them fully.

The AFH hypothesis assumes that if previously repressed mental contents come forth because they push through the patient's repressions, the patient will come into conflict with them while they are emerging, and so feel increased anxiety. If they come forth because they are disguised or isolated, and so evade the forces of repression, the patient will not feel anxious about them while they are emerging. However, because they are disguised or isolated, he will not experience them vividly.

Gassner et al. (1982) tested the two hypotheses against each other by determining how the patient felt during the coming forth of previously repressed mental contents that had not been interpreted. Gassner located a number of speech segments in the transcripts of sessions 41–100 in which Mrs. C. was becoming conscious of such contents, and which our raters judged to have been warded off during the first 10 sessions of the treatment. Then Gassner had raters determine, by several measures, how anxious the patient felt while these contents were emerging. She found that in these segments Mrs. C. was not especially anxious. By one measure of anxiety, Mrs. C. was no more anxious in these segments than in random speech segments. By another, she was significantly less anxious statistically than in random segments. Gassner also had raters measure Mrs. C.'s level of experiencing in these segments. They found that Mrs. C.'s level of experiencing was sigificantly higher statistically in these segments than in random segments. This finding shows that Mrs. C. was not withdrawn or defensively uninvolved with the previously repressed contents while they were emerging, and indeed was more focused on them than on random contents. This finding was statistically significant.

This combination of findings is the one predicted by the HMFH but not by the AFH. Thus, the findings support our hypothesis.

Patient's Transference Demands on the Analyst—Testing Beliefs versus Seeking Gratifications

The HMFH and the AFH provide different explanations for why the patient in analysis makes transference demands on the analyst. According to the HMFH the patient makes such demands in accordance with an unconscious decision. He does so primarily to test his pathogenic beliefs as part of his working to disprove them. He unconsciously hopes to demonstrate that the therapist will not behave as his pathogenic beliefs predict. According to the AFH, he makes these demands primarily in order to gratify unconscious impulses. We tested the two hypotheses against each other by studying how Mrs. C. felt during the first 100 sessions of her analysis when she made transference demands on the analyst, and he did not yield to them.

We assumed from our understanding of Mrs. C.'s plan that she made such transference demands in order to test the pathogenic belief that she could force the analyst to yield to her demands. She was burdened by this omnipotent belief, and wanted to disprove it. We hypothesized that Mrs. C. would feel anxious while testing the analyst, for she would fear that he would yield to her demands and so fail her tests. However, we assumed she would feel relieved upon observing that the analyst did not yield[2] to her demands, and so would pass her tests. She would feel less anxious and less tense.

Analysts who subscribe to the AFH and who read the same transcripts we did assumed that Mrs. C. was making transference demands on the analyst in an attempt to gratify unconscious impulses. They predicted that when the analyst did not yield to her demands, her impulses would be frustrated so that she would become more tense.

Silberschatz (in Weiss et al., 1986, Chapt. 18) tested the two hypotheses against each other by demonstrating that immediately after the analyst responded to Mrs. C.'s demands by not yielding to them, Mrs. C. became significantly (statistically) less anxious, more relaxed, bolder, and more loving than she had been just before the analyst's responses. These findings support the HMFH and not the AFH. (We assumed that Mrs. C. became more loving after the analyst passed her tests because she was pleased that the analyst was helping her.)

The Gassner and the Silberschatz studies fit well together. Gassner's study indicates that during her analysis Mrs. C. felt safe enough to bring previously repressed mental contents to consciousness without their having been interpreted. Silberschatz's studies show how she may have acquired the sense of safety that permitted her to bring forth these contents. She

[2]Mrs. C. is exceptional in that she experienced the analyst's neutrality as passing her tests. In many instances analytic neutrality, as recommended by the 1911–1915 theory, is not the optimal response to the patient's testing.

may have done this by testing her pathogenic belief that she could force the analyst to yield to her demands, and was relieved when the analyst passed her tests by not yielding. She became more secure with the analyst and able to bring forth previously repressed mental contents. (Gassner found that some of the contents Mrs. C. brought forth without their having been interpreted concerned Mrs. C.'s fear of being in control, and her fear of being aggressive.)

Studies of Patient Working in Analysis to Disprove His Pathogenic Beliefs

From our theory we hypothesized that a patient may benefit from any intervention by the analyst that he can use in his efforts to disprove his pathogenic beliefs and to pursue the goals forbidden by them. That is, he may benefit from any intervention he can use in his efforts to carry out his plan. Moreover, he may benefit immediately after such an intervention, for he may infer from it that the analyst disagrees with the beliefs and is sympathetic to the goals. He may then feel relieved and less anxious, and so may take a small step in the direction of disproving the beliefs and pursuing the goals. Also, since he regulates his repressions in accordance with his pathogenic beliefs and the dangers they foretell, he may, after a proplan intervention, become slightly more insightful and slightly less inhibited.

Since the testing of this hypothesis requires a reliable formulation of the patient's unconscious plan for analysis, our first step was to demonstrate that independent judges could agree reliably on the patient's plan. Caston (1986) demonstrated this. He broke down the patient's plan formulation into four components: (1) the patient's goals, (2) the obstructions (pathogenic beliefs) that impede the patient in the pursuit of his goals, (3) the tests the patient might perform in his efforts to disprove the pathogenic beliefs, and (4) the insights the patient could use in his efforts to disprove these beliefs.

Caston provided independent judges with extensive lists of possible goals, pathogenic beliefs, tests, and insights. These included all such items that Caston considered plausible. He also gave the judges the condensed transcripts of the first 10 sessions of Mrs. C.'s analysis. He asked them to read the transcripts, then rate the items in each of the four categories for their pertinence to the patient's plan. He demonstrated a high level of reliability.[3]

Studies on Immediate Effects of Interpretation During Analysis

Caston used his formulations of Mrs. C.'s plan to study the effects on her of the analyst's interventions during the first 100 sessions of Mrs. C.'s analysis. He tested the hypothesis that during these sessions Mrs. C. would demonstrate an immediate favorable response to pro-plan interventions (that is, to interventions she could use in her efforts to carry out her plan) and that she would not respond favorably to, or would be set back by, anti-plan interventions. In particular, Caston hypothesized that following a pro-plan intervention the patient would immediately become bolder and more insightful, and that following an anti-plan intervention she would become less bold and less insightful. (Mrs. C.'s plan consisted in part of her disproving the belief that she was responsible for the happiness of her parents and siblings.)

Caston found strong confirmation of this hypothesis in his pilot study. However, in his replication study, he found that this hypothesis holds for pro-plan interventions but not for anti-plan interventions. Apparently Mrs. C. responded powerfully to pro-plan interventions but was not set back by anti-plan interventions.

Bush and Gassner (1986), in a study of the last 100 sessions of Mrs. C.'s analysis, tested the hypothesis that Mrs. C. would

---

[3]The reliability coefficients were as follows: immediate goals, .87; eventual goals, .72; obstructions, .91; test power, .85; plan compatibility of interpretations, .92.

demonstrate an immediate beneficial effect from pro-plan interventions and be set back by anti-plan interventions. Mrs. C.'s plan during these sessions, which was to some degree unconscious, was to prepare for termination by working to disprove her belief that if she revealed her wish to leave her analyst she would hurt him. Bush and Gassner hypothesized that Mrs. C. would show a beneficial effect immediately after an intervention, which she could use to reduce her guilt about terminating, and that she would be set back by an intervention she would experience as impeding her efforts to terminate. Bush and Gassner found strong statistical support for this hypothesis.

Immediate Effect of Interpretations on Patients in Brief Psychotherapy

Fretter (1984), Broitman (1985) and Davilla (1992) studied[4] the transcripts of three brief (16-session) psychotherapies using a revised version of Caston's method (Curtis and Silberschatz, 1986; Silberschatz and Curtis, 1986; Rosenberg et al., 1986). In contrast to Caston and to Bush and Gassner, Fretter and Broitman confined their studies to the effects of interpretations, that is, interventions designed to convey insight. Fretter hypothesized that immediately following a pro-plan interpretation the patient would be more involved with what she was saying, and so would demonstrate a higher level of experiencing. Fretter demonstrated this by correlating the planfulness of the therapist's interpretations with the degree to which the patient shifted in her level of experiencing in speech segments from just before to just after his interpretations. When she correlated the mean level of the planfulness of all interpretations in a given hour with the mean level of all the shifts in experiencing in that hour she found significant correlations: .78 in one case, .54 in another, and .57 in a third (Silberschatz et al., 1986a).

[4]Their studies were carried out under the supervision of Curtis and Silberschatz.

Broitman studied the same cases, the same interpretations, and the same speech segments as Fretter had studied. She demonstrated a statistically significant correlation between the planfulness of the therapist's interpretations and immediate shifts in the patient's level of insight as measured by a generic insight scale.

Davilla (1992) studied the same patients, the same interpretations, and the same speech segments as Fretter and Broitman. She demonstrated that in two of the three cases, the patient, after a pro-plan interpretation, moved toward his goals as defined in the patient's plan formulation (and the third patient did not). This finding was statistically significant.

Fretter's, Broitman's, and Davilla's findings support our hypothesis.

Long-term Effect of Interpretation

Fretter (1984) tested the hypothesis that pro-plan interpretations have a lasting as well as an immediate effect. She did this by calculating the percentage of pro-plan and anti-plan interpretations offered to each patient, and then by correlating this percentage with how well the patient was doing six months after the termination of therapy. The treatment outcome at six months was assessed by clinical interviews conducted by an independent evaluator and by a battery of nontheory-based outcome measures completed by the patient (Silberschatz et al., 1986a). Fretter found strong support for our hypothesis. She demonstrated that in the three cases studied, the patient who was offered the highest percentage of pro-plan interpretations did the best, the patient who was offered the second highest did second best, and the patient who was offered the lowest did the worst.

Norville (1989) tested the hypothesis that the mean planfulness of the interpretations a patient received would correlate with the treatment outcome at six months after termination as measured by an independent evaluator and by a battery of nontheory-based outcome studies completed by the patient. She tested this hypothesis using the transcripts of seven brief psychotherapies of sixteen sessions each, which included the three therapies studied by Fretter and Broitman. She had her raters, in each case, rate all of the interpretations in a sample of five sessions, which she obtained as follows: she divided the last 15 sessions of each therapy into five groups of three sessions each; one such group consisted of sessions two, three, and four, another of sessions five, six, and seven, and so forth. She then selected, at random, a session from each group of three. She found that the mean of the ratings for planfulness of the interpretations offered the patient in his therapy correlated with the treatment outcome in six of the seven cases.

Studies of Patient's Testing of Therapist

We carried out a series of studies to determine how the patient in brief psychotherapy reacts when the therapist passes his tests. In a study of two patients, we demonstrated that immediately after a passed test the patient showed a higher level of experiencing than just before the passed test. One of the patients also showed an immediate increase in boldness and relaxation; the other did not (Silberschatz and Curtis, 1993).

In another study we demonstrated that in two out of three cases the patient reacted to a passed test by demonstrating an immediate decrease in tension, as measured by the Voice Stress Measure (Kelly, 1989). In a study of one patient we demonstrated that after a passed test the patient showed more proplan insight (as defined in the patient's plan formulation) than immediately before the test (Linsner, 1987). In another study of one patient we demonstrated that immediately after a passed test the patient showed greater capacity to exert control over regressive behavior (Bugas, 1986).

Changing Levels of Insight in Brief Psychotherapies—Evidence for the Plan Concept

The starting point for this study was our clinical impression that the patient often demonstrates considerable insight into his pathogenic beliefs and goals at the beginning of therapy, then after a short time appears to lose this insight. We hypothesized that the patient makes his problems clear to the therapist at the beginning so as to provide the therapist with the knowledge he needs to help the patient. Then the patient appears to lose insight, and he makes false statements about himself in order to test the therapist. The patient hopes the therapist will supply the missing insights and refute the false statements. He loses insights or makes false statements even though he receives helpful (pro-plan) interpretations.

We tested this hypothesis by studying four brief psychotherapies. In each one the patient knew in advance that the therapy would be limited to 16 sessions (Edelstein, 1992; O'Connor et al., 1993; Weiss, 1992). Of these four patients, three received reasonably good interpretations; the fourth did not. We determined the patient's levels of pro-plan insight in each of the 16 psychotherapy sessions, and in three interviews conducted by an independent evaluator: an intake interview, an interview immediately after the termination of the therapy, and another interview six months after termination. In determining the patient's level of insight in a given session, we first located all the pro-plan insight statements in that session. Then, we had each insight statement rated for the degree to which it was pro-plan. Finally, we added up all the insight ratings in each session.

A striking finding is immediately apparent from graphs of the patients' levels of insight throughout the 16 sessions and the three evaluation interviews. In each case the level of insight throughout the 19 sessions follows a similar pattern: each patient shows high insight at the beginning, low insight at approximately the middle of therapy, and a rise in insight toward the

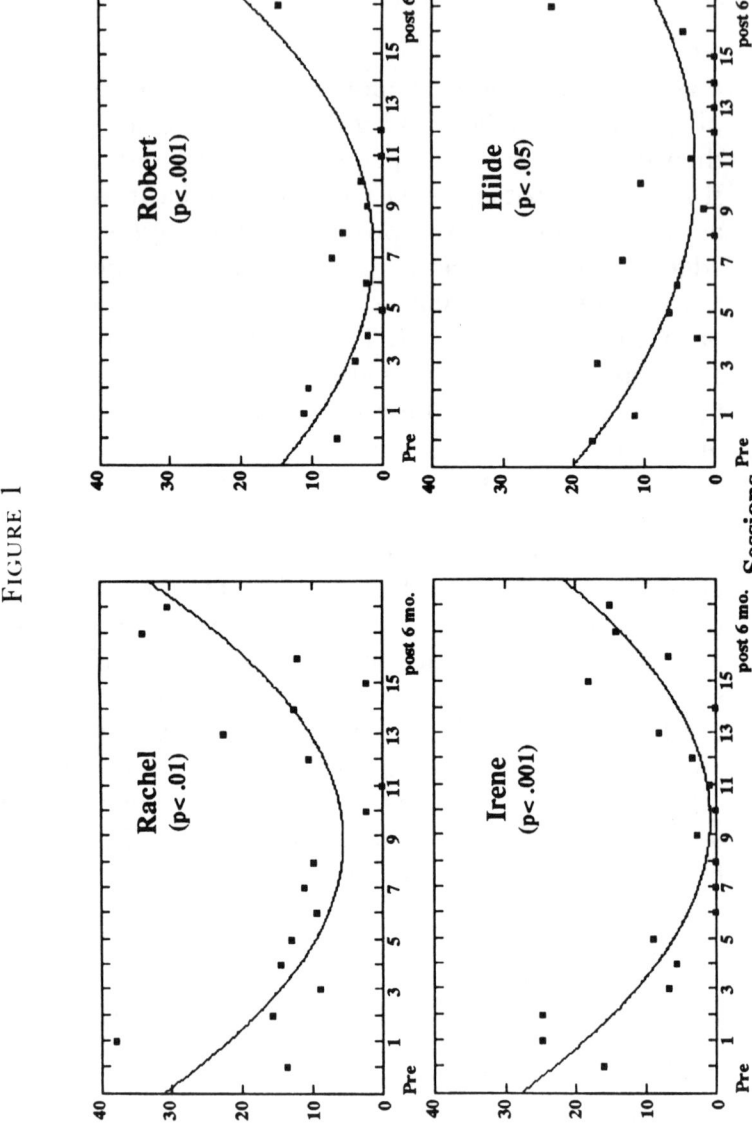

FIGURE 1

end. In each case a parabolic curve fits the data.[5] This curve was the length of the therapy plus the follow-up interviews. This finding was statistically significant (see Figure 1).

These findings support the hypothesis that the patient has an unconscious plan for therapy. He knows in advance that he has only 16 sessions, and according to our hypothesis he unconsciously wishes to use his allotted time as efficiently as he can. He must show insight at the beginning in order to provide the therapist with the knowledge the therapist needs to help him. Then he begins to test his pathogenic beliefs in relation to the therapist. He does so by losing insight and by presenting false ideas about himself in the hope that the therapist will supply the missing insights and refute the false ideas. He tests mildly at first, for he is not sure that the therapist will pass his tests. As he experiences the therapist as passing his tests, he tests more vigorously, until in the middle of therapy he loses all insight. As the patient gets closer to termination, he tests less vigorously because he will soon be left without a therapist to pass his tests. Also, since he does not test his pathogenic beliefs with the independent evaluator in the followup sessions, his level of insight in these sessions is higher in each case than during the middle part of therapy, and in several cases higher than at any point in therapy.

We determined the planfulness of the therapist's interpretations in each therapy. In two of the cases, Rachel and Robert, the interpretations were consistently highly pro-plan. In the case of Irene, they were moderately pro-plan. This shows that in these cases the patient's decreasing levels of insight during the first part of therapy does not reflect the patient's compliance with bad (anti-plan) interpretations. Also, our ratings of the

[5]In a fifth therapy, studied after this paper was written, the patient also lost insight during the course of therapy. However, a parabolic curve did not significantly fit the raw scores due to greater variability in insight throughout the therapy. The plot of smoothed scores, however, indicated that the pattern was also parabolic, though less dramatically so. The quadratic regression closely approached significance ($p = .052$ for the quadratic term in the regression).

therapists' interpretations enabled us to show that patients who receive good interpretations have relatively high insight in the followup interviews. Rachel and Robert received good interpretations and demonstrated relatively high insight in the six-month followup interviews. Irene received moderately good interpretations and showed moderate insight in the six-month followup interview. Hilde's therapist was less skillful than the others. He gave Hilde poor interpretations, and Hilde showed little insight in the six-month followup interview. In the case of Hilde, her low insight during the middle and later parts of her therapy may express not testing, but compliance with false (anti-plan) interpretations.

At this point the reader may ask, "How do you reconcile Fretter's and Broitman's findings, that after a pro-plan interpretation the patient demonstrates an immediate increase in insight and experiencing, with the findings of the present study that, even while receiving pro-plan interpretations, the patient at first appears to lose insight?" According to our explanation the patient (as suggested by the research described above) reacts to a pro-plan interpretation by experiencing an immediate increase in security, and therefore permits a small but measurable increase in insight. However, after a short time he may rely on his greater security not to acquire greater insight—as measured by the Insight Scale (Edelstein, 1992; Grebel, 1993)—but to test the therapist more vigorously. His behavior may be compared to that of a man who is striving to accomplish a major task and who suddenly inherits a moderate sum of money. He feels immediate relief and greater security. However, rather than simply enjoying his greater security, he uses his new capital to work harder than ever to achieve his goals.

Some Implications of the Research

Our research supports the idea that the psychoanalytic theory of the mind and therapy may be studied fruitfully by empirical, quantitative methods. This is so because the behavior of the patient is lawful. For example, within broad limits, all patients suffer from pathogenic beliefs, all test these beliefs regularly in relation to the therapist, and all benefit when the therapist passes the patient's tests. As our research demonstrates, our hypotheses about the patient's behavior give rise to predictions that may be tested and either supported or refuted by quantitative methods. For example, we demonstrated that the patient benefits immediately when the therapist behaves appropriately to his tests.

For another example, in our study of the effects of interpretation, we specified in advance the relation between two variables: the planfulness of the therapist's interpretations and the patient's responses to the interpretations as indicated by changes in his levels of experiencing. We then studied the relation between the two variables, and we demonstrated a statistically significant correlation between them.

Our research throws light on the nature of analysis. It does not support the contention of some theoreticians that the analyst may scarcely understand the patient until he and the patient have explored the patient's problems together for many months or even years or until certain dynamisms have evolved. We found that in the case of Mrs. C. we could make a reliable formulation of the patient's unconscious pathogenic beliefs, goals, and plans from studying the transcripts of the first 10 sessions of her analysis. And Gassner and Bush demonstrated that the plan inferred from these first 10 sessions was applicable to the process of termination, as it was still guiding the patient's behavior during the final 100 sessions of her analysis. Throughout her analysis, Mrs. C. was unconsciously worried about the analyst for whom she felt omnipotently responsible. During the first 100 sessions she tested her belief in her responsibility for the analyst by attempting to demonstrate to herself that she could not push him around. During the last 100 sessions she tested this same belief by attempting to demonstrate to herself that she would not hurt the analyst if she made clear to him her wish to terminate. What I have said about analysis also applies to brief psychotherapy: the therapist may make a reliable plan formulation applicable to the entire therapy by simply studying the transcripts of the intake session and the first two therapy sessions.

Our studies support the higher mental functioning hypothesis and the various propositions derived from it that are outlined at the beginning of this paper. The studies indicate that the patient is not well characterized as continually attempting to gratify repressed impulses. He is better characterized as repeatedly testing the analyst and as demonstrating a high degree of responsiveness to whatever the analyst says or does. He demonstrates immediate reactions to the analyst's interventions, interpretations, and behavior. He lifts his repressions, however slightly, immediately after a pro-plan interpretation.

The research indicates that in analysis it is the patient rather than the analyst who sets the agenda, and that it is the analyst's responsibility to infer where the patient unconsciously wants to go, and to help him get there.

The research also suggests that the patient benefits not just from interpretation but, equally important, from his relationship to the analyst. Indeed the patient may achieve a great deal without benefit of interpretation if the analyst, by his approach, passes the patient's tests. Our research supports the idea that the patient benefits from a particular kind of corrective emotional experience, namely the experience that the patient himself unconsciously is seeking by his testing of the analyst. Our findings are also consistent with the findings of certain social psychologists, for example, those of Brim (1992) with regard to persistent mastery strivings in adults. They are also compatible with Wallerstein's (1986) conclusion that supportive therapy is just as effective as insight therapy in bringing about structural change. Moreover, they fit the observations of self psychologists that the patient may demonstrate progress after the therapist responds to him with appropriate empathy.

Our research provides the therapist with criteria for deciding whether he is on the right track. The therapist may assume he is on the right track if the patient reacts to him by becoming more relaxed and secure, bolder and more insightful, or alternately, by testing his pathogenic beliefs more vigorously.

Our findings should be regarded as tentative until replicated. The ultimate guarantee of freedom from both error and research bias is independent replication of research findings.

REFERENCES

BRIM, G. (1992). *Ambition: How We Manage Success and Failure Throughout Our Lives*. New York: Basic Books.

BROITMAN, J. (1985). Insight, the mind's eye: an exploration of three patients' processes of becoming insightful. Doctoral dissertation, Wright Institute. *Dissertation Abstracts International*, 46(8). Univ. Microfilms 85-20425.

BUGAS, J. S. (1986). Adaptive regression and the therapeutic change process. Unpublished doctoral dissertation, Pacific Graduate School of Psychology. *Dissertation Abstracts International*, 47(7b). Univ. Microfilms 86-22826.

BUSH, M. & GASSNER, S. (1986). The immediate effect of the analyst's termination interventions on the patient's resistance to termination. In Weiss et al. (1986), pp. 299–320.

CASTON, J. (1986). The reliability of the diagnosis of the patient's unconscious plan. In Weiss et al. (1986), pp. 241–255.

CURTIS, J. & SILBERSCHATZ, G. (1986). Clinical implications of research on brief psychodynamic psychotherapy: I. Formulating the patient's problems and goals. *Psychoanal. Psychol.*, 3:13–25.

DAHL, H., HOROWITZ, M. J. et al. (1980). New directions in affect theory. Proceedings of Amer. Psychoanal. Assn. Conference, New York.

——— et al., Eds. (1988). *Psychoanalytic Process Research Strategies*. New York: Springer.

DAVILLA, L. (1992). The immediate effects of therapist's interpretations on patient's plan progressiveness. Unpublished doctoral dissertation, California School of Professional Psychology.

EDELSTEIN, S. (1992). Exploration of the relationship between insight and outcome in four brief psychotherapies. Unpublished doctoral dissertation, The Wright Institute Graduate School of Psychology.

FRETTER, P. (1984). The immediate effects of transference interpretations on patients' progress in brief, psychodynamic psychotherapy. Doctoral dissertation, University of San Francisco. *Dissertation Abstracts International*, 46(6). Univ. Microfilms 85-12112.

FREUD, S. (1900). The interpretation of dreams. *S. E.*, 4.

——— (1905). On psychotherapy. *S. E.*, 7.

——— (1911–1915). Papers on technique. *S. E.*, 12.

——— (1920). Beyond the pleasure principle. *S. E.*, 18.

——— (1926). Psycho-analysis. *S. E.*, 20.
——— (1937). Analysis terminable and interminable. *S. E.*, 23.
——— (1940a). An outline of psychoanalysis. *S. E.*, 23.
——— (1940b). Splitting of the ego in the process of defense. *S. E.*, 23.
GASSNER, S., SAMPSON, H., WEISS, J. & BRUMER, S. (1982). The emergence of warded-off contents. *Psychoanal. Contemp. Thought*, 5:55–75.
——— ——— BRUMER, S. & WEISS, J. (1986). The emergence of warded-off contents. In *The Psychoanalytic Process: Theory, Clinical Observation and Empirical Research.* New York: Guilford Press, pp. 171–186.
GREBEL, J. (1993). Manifestations of insight in brief psychotherapy. Unpublished doctoral dissertation, Pacific Graduate School.
HOROWITZ, M. J. (1991). *Person Schemas and Maladaptive Interpersonal Patterns.* Chicago: Univ. Chicago Press.
——— & STIMSON, C. (1991). Program of stages in conscious and unconscious processes. In *Psychotherapy Research: An International Review in Programmatic Studies*, ed. L. Beutler & M. Crago. Washington, DC: Amer. Psychol. Assn.
KELLY, T. (1989). Do therapist's interventions matter? Unpublished doctoral dissertation, New York University.
LINSNER, J. P. (1987). Therapeutically effective and ineffective insight: the immediate effects of therapist behavior on a patient's insight during short-term dynamic therapy. Unpublished doctoral dissertation, The City University of New York. *Dissertation Abstracts International*, 1988, 48(12b). Univ. Microfilms 88-01731.
LUBORSKY, L. (1988). *Who Will Benefit from Psychotherapy.* New York: Basic Books.
NORVILLE, R. (1989). Plan compatibility of interpretations and brief psychotherapy outcome. Doctoral dissertation, Pacific Graduate School of Psychology, Palo Alto, CA. *Dissertation Abstracts International*, 50(12B):5888. Univ. Microfilms 90-12770.
O'CONNOR, L., EDELSTEIN, S., BERRY, J. & WEISS, J. (1993). The pattern of insight in brief psychotherapy: a series of pilot studies. Unpublished.
ROSENBERG, S., SILBERSCHATZ, G., CURTIS, J., SAMPSON, H. & WEISS, J. (1986). The plan diagnosis method: a new approach to establishing reliability for psychodynamic formulations. *Amer. J. Psychiat.*, 143:1454–1456.
SILBERSCHATZ, G. & CURTIS, J. T. (1986). Clinical implications of research on brief dynamic psychotherapy. II. How the therapist helps or hinders therapeutic progress. *Psychoanal. Psychol.*, 3(1):27–37.
——— ——— (1993). Measuring the therapist's impact on the patient's therapeutic progress. *J. Consult. Clin. Psychol.*, 61:403-411.
——— ——— SAMPSON, H. & WEISS, J. (1991). Research on the process of change in psychotherapy: the approach of the Mount Zion Psychotherapy Research Group. In *Psychotherapy Research: An International Review of Programmatic Studies*, ed. L. Beutler & M. Crago. Washington, DC: Amer. Psychol. Assn.
——— FRETTER, P. & CURTIS, J. (1986a). How do interpretations influence the process of psychotherapy? *J. Consult. Clin. Psychol.*, 54:646–652.
——— SAMPSON, H., & WEISS, J. (1986b). Testing pathogenic beliefs versus seeking transference gratifications. In *The Psychoanalytic Process: Theory, Clinical Observation and Empirical Research.* New York: Guilford Press, pp. 267–276.

WALLERSTEIN, R. S. (1986). *Forty-two Lives in Treatment: A Study of Psychoanalysis and Psychotherapy*. New York: Guilford Press.
WEISS, J. (1992). Studies on the change in the patient's level of insight during brief psychotherapy. Presented at Annual Meeting of Society for Psychotherapy Research, Berkeley, CA.
——— SAMPSON, H. & MT. ZION PSYCHOTHERAPY RESEARCH GROUP (1986). *The Psychoanalytic Process: Theory, Clinical Observation and Empirical Research*. New York: Guilford Press.

WHAT PSYCHOANALYSIS NEEDS IS MORE EMPIRICAL RESEARCH

VIRGINIA TELLER, PH.D.
HARTVIG DAHL, M.D.

The threefold purpose of this paper is to highlight the past accomplishments and survey the present reality of psychoanalytic process research, and to assess the future prospects for empirical research in this field. An overview of the major results of our own interdisciplinary approach to psychoanalytic process research, with abundant pointers to the literature where more detailed accounts can be found, fulfills the first purpose. The second is achieved with a brief, roughly chronological survey of sites in the United States where efforts have been made in the second half of the century to establish settings in which psychoanalytic process research could flourish. A comparison is made between the prevailing model for psychoanalytic research in this country and a substantially different model at the University of Ulm in Germany. We conclude with a discussion of the difficulties and rewards that await anyone interested in pursuing a serious, scientific investigation into the psychoanalytic process.

MORE THAN TWENTY YEARS AGO, Dahl (1972) called for a new approach to psychoanalytic research in order "to redeem the promise of psychoanalysis as a science" (p. 237). At the core of Dahl's proposal lay a commitment to a new form of data collection based on verbatim transcripts of recorded psychoanalytic sessions and to new forms of data analysis based on the then emerging computer techniques for processing natural language text. Dahl argued that such an approach was "essential to attract to psychoanalysis the kind of imaginative and research-oriented young candidates that our field needs" (p. 256).

Only a scattered handful of researchers in the United States and Europe heeded the call for empirical research, and

---

Dr. Teller is on the Faculty of Hunter College and Graduate School, City University of New York. Dr. Dahl is on the faculty of SUNY Health Science Center, Brooklyn, NY.

in some respects the promise of psychoanalysis as a science has not been fulfilled. Although we shall concentrate in this paper on our own contributions to psychoanalytic process research, some of the reasons for the failure of psychoanalysis to develop more fully as a scientific enterprise will also be explored.

The first part of the paper focuses on three areas of research—computer content analysis, emotions, and FRAMES—where our efforts to understand the psychoanalytic process have met with particular success. We then attempt to place our work in historical perspective by presenting a brief chronology of other sites in the United States that have engaged in psychoanalytic research during the postwar decades. The situation in this country is also compared with that in Germany, where the climate for psychoanalytic research is somewhat different. The paper concludes with an assessment of the conditions under which psychoanalytic process research could prosper into the next century.

Three Avenues of Inquiry

An interdisciplinary perspective has been a crucial element in our program of research. A voyage of discovery (Dahl, 1993), which spans more than two decades, has been a search for objective patterns and structures in the free-association discourse of patients in psychoanalysis. The structures we have found have led to a better understanding of the phenomenon of psychoanalytic clinical inference and have helped demystify the process of psychoanalytic therapy. The ultimate goal has been to develop a unified measure capable of identifying psychopathology, assessing the analytic process, and measuring the outcome of psychoanalytic treatment. As Teller (1988) pointed out, because psychoanalysis lacks a basic science of its own, the field must seek in other disciplines ideas that might allow the principles of psychoanalysis to be formalized in a true scientific discipline. We have traveled a great distance, and along the route we have used many navigational aids, borrowing experimental methods from psychology, techniques for analyzing data from computer science, and theory from linguistics, cognitive science, and artificial intelligence, as well as psychoanalysis.

Computer Content Analysis

The saga began with Dahl's pioneering studies using the then new computer content analysis techniques, which depend on computer dictionary categories designed to capture specific kinds of verbal contents. Dahl (1972) was able to summarize the course of two and a half years of a recorded analysis in a graphic figure showing the final downhill course in dramatic fashion. Moreover, clinically interesting computer dictionary categories sharply discriminated "work" from "resistance" sessions, as measured by factor score profiles obtained using multivariate statistical methods. Finally, Dahl (1974) produced a rigorously defined three-dimensional representation of the three most important groups of patient words—clusters that seemed to capture the patient's central conflicts—as tightly knit groupings of words in different corners of a three-dimensional space represented as a cube.

Emotions

A new view of emotions emerged several years later when Dahl noted the similarity between the first three dimensions of de Rivera's (1962) decision theory of emotions and those that Freud (1915) proposed when he wrote that mental life is governed by three polarities, the antitheses: subject (ego)-object (external world), pleasure-unpleasure, and active-passive. Dahl and Stengel (1978) replicated and expanded de Rivera's empirical test of people's ability to classify emotions using these three dimensions. Fifty-eight judges were asked to classify nearly 400 emotion words on each dimension, separately. The results showed wide agreement on the classification of a large number of words on the three dimensions with high reliabilities. Choices on 153 words were significant at p < .001 on all three dimensions, a joint chance probability of less than one in a billion. Moreover, the choices on the dimensions were uncorrelated, supporting the assumption of their independence. Finally, the judges' ages and sex were also uncorrelated with their decisions. Considering the many sources of possible error, this degree of agreement was impressive. Schwartz and Trabasso (1984) showed that children as young as six are also able to make reliable judgments on these three dimensions. The interaction of the three dimensions produces a classification scheme with eight main and four intermediate categories. Figure 1 shows the three-dimensional classification for the eight main categories. This judgment process is formalized into a systematic and reliable method for identifying, classifying, and labeling emotions in transcripts (Dahl et al., 1992).

On the basis of these findings and an extensive review of emotion theories, Dahl (1978, 1979) formulated a new psychoanalytic model of motivation that postulates two basic classes of emotions, one with the characteristics of appetitive wishes and another that functions as feedback about the outcome of those wishes. As described by Dahl (1993), this cognitive theory included three more or less radical ideas. First, emotions are independent of the somatic appetites ("drives"); rather, they share the central properties of appetites such as thirst, hunger, and sex. Second, emotions with objects (IT emotions) function essentially as appetitive *wishes* about those objects, and emotions that index an inner state (ME emotions) function as *beliefs* about the state of fulfillment or nonfulfillment of the wishes. Third, the IT and ME emotions together form the core of an information feedback system that provides basic knowledge of our most fundamental motives and their outcomes.

One of the advantages of the feedback system is that it allows for systematic explanations of much clinical knowledge about addictions, maladaptive personality structures, and the functions of defenses (Dahl, in press). In addition, the feedback

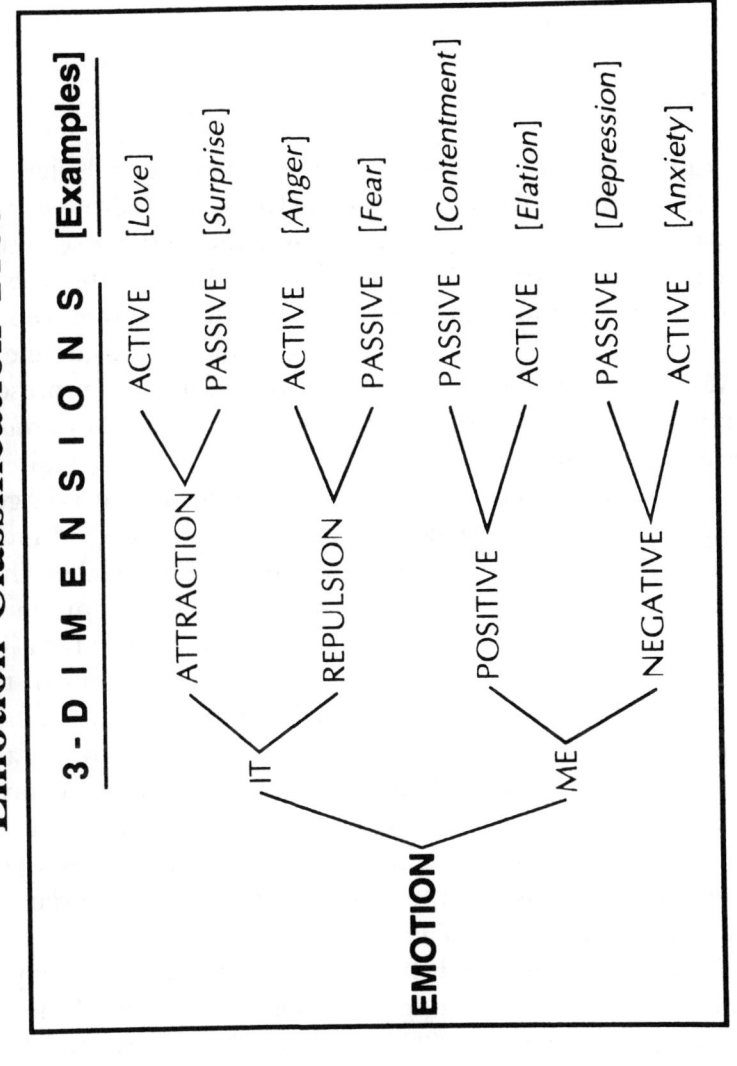

FIGURE 1

system includes the first and third of the three components of Luborsky's (1990) core conflictual relationship themes (CCRT's): the patient's wish, the responses of the other, and the responses of the self.

FRAMES

The discovery of FRAMES was initially reported by Teller and Dahl (1981) and elaborated by them (1986). The acronym now stands for fundamental repetitive and maladaptive emotion structures (Dahl, 1993). Simply put, FRAMES are the *plots* of the stories that patients in psychotherapy tell about their repetitive, maladaptive behaviors. More formally, we define a FRAME as a *recurrent, structured sequence of events* that represent significant *wishes* and *beliefs* manifested in a person's *actions, thoughts, perceptions, and/or emotions*. Our three most basic assumptions are that: (1) *adaptive* behavior, by its nature, is largely transparent, that is, its structure reflects the structure of interaction with the environment in which it occurs rather than merely the structure of the memory of the adapting organism (Simon, 1981); (2) *maladaptive* behavior is more readily visible precisely because it is not adapted to the requirements of the situation and thus reflects the internal memory structure of the organism *and*, by extension, the end result of the history of the experiences that produced the particular memory structures; and (3) these *recurrent maladaptive behavior patterns* are clinically most visible in situations where a person is requested (and permitted) to freely display them, for example, when given the "basic rule" to *free-associate* in psychoanalysis.

Dahl (1988) proposed that FRAMES: (1) are represented in the mind in *nonverbal* code in a dual code system of mental representations (Bucci, 1985); (2) especially as structured sequences of *emotions* and *defenses* (Dahl, 1978, 1979; Dahl and Stengel, 1978); (3) are the *residues of early object relations* (Gedo, 1979); (4) *endure over time* and (5) *across conflicts, objects, and situations*, and (6) *can interact* with each other; (7) *can account for* a wide spectrum of *repetitive, neurotic, maladaptive behavior* and, perhaps, some adaptive behavior; (8) *permit specific predictions* of *wishes* and *beliefs*, and (9) provide the *framework for a theory of change* independent of any particular *theory of how to bring about the change* (Dahl, 1991).

Dahl and Teller (in press) summarize the main characteristics of the FRAMES, including methods for identifying them, the validity and reliability of empirical research findings, and the strengths and weaknesses of the FRAME approach. Hour 5 of a recorded psychoanalysis (specimen hour; in Dahl et al., 1988) has been scrutinized in particular detail because it was in this session that FRAMES were first discovered. Dahl (1988) subsequently documented all of the repetitions in hour 5 of five FRAMES whose prototypes appeared in that hour. Figure 2 shows a simplified representation of one of these, the Critical/Friendly FRAME, and Table 1 lists the repetitions (instantiations), including four with the analyst in the transference. Miller (1990) then traced the fate of these five FRAMES from the early part of the case through a group of middle hours that had been identified by Jones and Windholz (1990) as the height of the transference neurosis to the final hours of the analysis. Miller found that four of the five FRAMES from hour 5 were very much in evidence in the middle hours, but at end of the case all of them had either vanished or the plots had different outcomes.

Davies (1989) found structures similar to FRAMES in the behavior of twelve three-year-old children. From videotapes of their peer play and coded records of twelve mother-child interactions, she identified recurrent patterns in the behaviors that were consistent for each child in his or her interaction with the mother and in peer play separately with two other children. These structured patterns, she argued, were different for each child, and each child's peer play patterns uniquely reflected the patterns of interaction with his or her own mother.

A major step forward came recently with the demonstration, reported by Hölzer and Dahl (unpublished), that most of

TABLE 1
5 Prototype Frames and 19 Instantiations Found in Hour 5

Instance	Frame Structure	Object	E1	E2	E3	E4	E5
Prototype	**Control**	**In a Course**	**56**	**56**	**56**		
I 1	Control	Hus & Tel	12/13	14	12-14		
I 2	Control	Parents	20	21/22	21		
I 3	Control	H & Money	57/58	58	58		
I 4	Control	Assistant	1	2/4	3/9		
I 5	Control	By father	15	15	15		
Prototype	**Critical/Friendly**	**Anybody**	**48**	**48**	**48**		
I 1	Critical/Friendly	Assistant	1	2	1/3		
I 2	Critical/Friendly	*Analyst	47/48	52	61/62		
Prototype	**Delay**	**Boys/Pars**	**19/20**	**20**	**20**	**20**	**20**
I 1	Delay	Husband	19/20	18	18	18	—
I 2	Delay	*Analyst	18-20	18	18-20	19/20	20
I 3	Delay	Buy Clothes	60/62	62	60	60	60
I 4	Delay	Telephone	15	—	15	15	15
I 5	Delay	By father	15		15	15	—
Prototype	**Support**	**Husband**	**18**	**18**	**18**	**18**	
I 1	Support	Boys/Pars	18-20	20	20	20	
I 2	Support	*Analyst	18-20	20	46	52	
I 3	Support	By father	16/17	17	17	17	
Prototype	**Togetherness**	**Boys**	**19**	**19**	**19/20**		
I 1	Togetherness	Professor	55	55	—		
I 2	Togetherness	*Analyst	53/54	53-56	56		
I 3	Togetherness	Father	13/16	16/17	13		
I 4	Togetherness	By father	16	16/17	16		

PROTOTYPE OF THE CRITICAL-FRIENDLY FRAME

FRAME
(Summary Predicates)

SUMMARY OF JUSTIFICATION
(Primary Predicates)

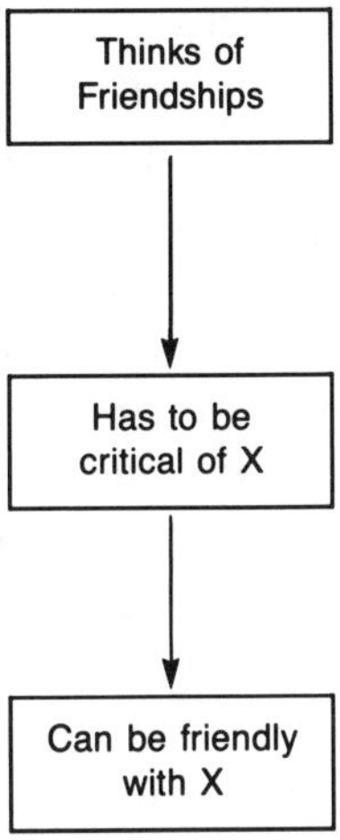

Thinks of Friendships

1. P has friends. [*And this makes me think of friendships I've had with other people...*]
2. People in general want to have friends [group-typical behavior.]

Has to be critical of X

1. *I seem to have to find fault with just about everybody that I'm friendly with to some degree...*
2. *I still have to find fault with them and maybe criticize them to David.*
3. *I always have to openly criticize them.*
4. *If I...can't be critical...then I just can't...be around them...*

Can be friendly with X

1. *...I have to kind've done that and then I can go on to a, re-, a, some kind of friendly relationship with them.*

FIGURE 2

the events in FRAMES are actually expressions of emotions. This insight led to an improved, systematic procedure for finding and representing FRAMES that makes identification of prototypes and their instantiations straightforward and reliable. The new method uses Dahl's emotion classification scheme (Dahl et al., 1992) to identify segments of text that express the same emotion category. The different emotion categories then become the basic events in a FRAME, and their sequence is determined from the story told in the text. All of the prototype FRAMES previously identified have been rediscovered using the new method, and it has been applied to three other psychoanalytic cases with excellent success. A project now underway will use this method to look for FRAME prototypes and instantiations in 15 psychoanalytic cases, and to trace the course of each FRAME from an early to a mid- and a late hour in each sample case.

At this point we believe we are close to achieving the three primary aims of our research (Dahl and Teller, in press), namely, that FRAMES will enable researchers to: (1) provide a detailed description of each patient's recurrent maladaptive structures, i.e., psychopathology, (2) identify the nature of therapist interventions that succeed in changing those structures, and (3) assess the outcome by determining the fate of the FRAMES at the end of treatment.

Not every project has ended in success. Years of work with Benjamin Rubinstein, during which we conducted a pilot study, a main study, and a replication designed to find out how well analysts could agree on evidence for clinical hypotheses independently formulated from transcripts of psychoanalytic sessions, produced limited results. Although we found that clinicians could indeed agree with reasonable reliability, we also discovered a significant "caller bias" in that judges consistently rated evidence they themselves found for a hypothesis higher than the other judges rated the same evidence (Dahl, 1983). Nonetheless, Rubinstein was unable to elucidate the logical reasoning that might link particular pieces of evidence with the hypothesis they had been advanced in support of.

Another lengthy study sought to test whether an analyst's choice of syntax was related to expressions of countertransference (Dahl et al., 1978). A number of syntactic and other linguistic properties of the analyst's interventions correlated significantly with countertransference and accounted for 50% of its variance, but we were unable to extract a stable, robust set of such properties with the various multivariate statistical techniques we used to analyze the data.

Historical Context

Since the early 1950's a number of programs developed throughout the country have devoted at least part of their resources to psychoanalytic research and research training. Several of the most important are mentioned below.

The east coast has been home to three of the earliest programs established. In 1953 George Klein and Robert R. Holt established the Research Center for Mental Health (RCMH) at New York University, and they were co-directors until Klein's untimely death in 1971. Funded largely by federal research and training grants, the faculty members and fellows enjoyed unusual freedom in pursuing their interests. Merton M. Gill and Donald P. Spence were associated with RCMH, and Dahl received his research training there as well. For nearly three and a half decades, Lester Luborsky and his colleagues in the Psychotherapy Research Group at the University of Pennsylvania have studied both short-term and longer-term psychotherapy from a variety of perspectives. Since 1991 this group, headed by Paul Crits-Christoph, has continued its work as the Center for Psychotherapy Research. At the SUNY Health Science Center, Brooklyn (formerly Downstate Medical Center), research training in psychiatry was organized around a Doctor of Medical Science degree that was actively supported from 1956 until funding for the program ended in 1979. After finishing their residencies, psychiatrists admitted to the program spent two additional years taking courses in research methods, and were awarded the degree after completing a dissertation. Teller was a postdoctoral fellow in this program.

On the west coast, Joseph Weiss and Harold Sampson have headed the San Francisco Psychotherapy Research Group for more than 25 years. Associated with the San Francisco Psychoanalytic Institute, the group has, among many studies, extensively investigated the now famous recorded psychoanalytic case of "Mrs. C." Mardi Horowitz established the Program on Conscious and Unconscious Mental Processes at the University of California, San Francisco, with a grant from the John D. and Catherine T. MacArthur Foundation in 1985. The latest computer technology has been used to allow researchers access to multiple measures on a case while sitting at a work station.

An academic psychology department rather than a medical center has been the research site for others, notably Hans Strupp at Vanderbilt University and Wilma Bucci at Adelphi

University's Derner Institute. Both have pursued research and taught in clinical psychology programs for many years.

Since late 1989, Robert S. Wallerstein has led a group of psychoanalysts that convenes regularly at meetings of the American Psychoanalytic Association to plan a collaborative multisite program of psychoanalytic therapy research. This consortium faces several problems, including uneven levels of research experience among its members, the large number of participants (around 20) and their geographic disparity, and the lack of a single, clear focus or methodology for a program of research. However, in 1993 several members met with officials at NIMH to discuss funding prospects, and the American Psychoanalytic Association gave $25,000 in seed money to further their goal of obtaining grants for their proposed research.

A quite different situation exists in Germany, where psychotherapy and psychiatry are separate departments in schools of medicine. One obvious benefit is that psychotherapy does not compete under the same umbrella with other forms of psychiatric intervention for resources. In a significant number of the 25 departments, anchoring psychoanalysis to academic psychotherapy has enabled the establishment of major psychoanalytic research programs. Created in 1967, the Department of Psychotherapy at the University of Ulm was headed by Helmut Thomä until his retirement in 1991, at which time Horst Kächele assumed leadership. Over 25 years the researchers in this department have garnered support, produced major results, and attracted distinguished visitors from around the world. In a number of respects the Ulm department serves as an attractive model for what an ideal setting for psychoanalytic research might be.

Perhaps most important, this department has been able to attract funds since its inception by funding from the German government and long-term grants from *Deutsche Gemeinschaft*, the German Research Foundation. On top of the basic resources funded, research activities are accorded a greater role in the department's function, one equal to that of teaching and clinical responsibilities. In particular, research on long-term treatments such as psychoanalysis is not discouraged. Interest in psychoanalytic therapy is reinforced by the fact that the Ulm Psychoanalytic Institute includes both training analysts and candidates from the Department of Psychotherapy. These features stand in contrast to those at comparable American institutions.

As a more recently established group, Ulm's Psychotherapy Department has been eager to incorporate more than one view of the psychotherapy process. Instead of developing a unique focus and fitting all of their studies into a single mold, the researchers in Ulm have reviewed all major work in the field and have attempted to integrate and elaborate upon the results of others. The Ulm process model (Thomä and Kächele, this volume) has evolved over the years into a set of robust, general methods for investigating the psychotherapy process. Dahl's emotion theory, Teller and Dahl's FRAME method, Luborsky's CCRT model, and Horowitz's Configurational Analyses are among the approaches currently being studied. In 1972, Horst Kächele, inspired by Dahl's (1972) computer content analysis report, began using computer content analysis which led to the development of "the now famous Ulm Textbank, the world's largest collection of transcribed recorded psychotherapy and psychoanalytic cases stored in computer files with many programs to facilitate their study" (Dahl, 1993). This store of over fifteen million transcribed words of data is also available to qualified researchers elsewhere (Mergenthaler and Kächele, 1993).

Junior members of the faculty work in close proximity to their seniors and are encouraged to collaborate. This type of training, which resembles an apprenticeship, works reasonably well. However, unlike in the United States, promotion in German academia usually entails accepting a position at another institution. Consequently there is far less continuity in the Ulm faculty than at a typical American university or medical school. A final ingredient in the Ulm recipe is the contribution that a variety of disciplines have made to the department's development, with a faculty drawn from medicine, psychology, computer science, and statistics.

The Research Enterprise

Innovation and progress in understanding the process of psychoanalysis can only take place in an environment where trained scientists with adequate funding engage in cooperative research. Among the requirements for serious scientific study in any discipline are a thorough grounding in the relevant methodologies, familiarity with computational tools, and access to a standardized body of data. As far as psychoanalytic process research is concerned, these requirements entail commitments to: (1) appropriate investigational methods, especially the design of repeated single-case studies with repeated measures; (2) developing scoring manuals, and training judges in their use; (3) statistics for assessing the reliability of ratings obtained and for the multivariate analysis of results; (4) the latest computer methods for text processing, including storing, retrieving, and analyzing data; and (5) studying verbatim transcripts of recorded psychoanalytic sessions stored in a standardized format in computer-readable form.

This is a tall order, and it has long been recognized that psychoanalysts whose primary pursuit is private, clinical practice are often ill-equipped to meet the rigorous standards for scientific investigation. Moreover, several obstacles confront any aspiring psychoanalytic researcher.

One problem that has diminished the prospects for empirical psychoanalytic research is the gradual deterioration in opportunities for funding. The generous research and training awards from NIMH that were abundant in the 1950's, 60's, and 70's, in particular the Career Development and Research Scientist programs that initially supported many of today's senior researchers, have largely disappeared or are now targeted for other types of psychiatric intervention deemed more effective or amenable to controlled testing. Such sources of funding are unlikely to be restored in the foreseeable future, and isolated grants from private sources, such as the MacArthur Foundation, have done little to stem the flow away from research on long-term treatments. The Fund for Psychoanalytic Research, established by the American Psychoanalytic Association in 1976, has provided a steady trickle of small grants which have helped sustain a few dedicated researchers. The very modest stipends[1] can be used for expenses such as research assistance and data collection, but not for overhead expenses or for salary support for a principal investigator other than a student or postdoctoral fellow. This policy precludes released time from clinical duties or private practice for most psychoanalytic researchers.

Progress has also been impeded in that the groups engaged in process research tend to work in isolation from each other without building on the findings of other groups studying similar phenomena. The result is an enormous redundancy of effort that could be avoided if a spirit of cooperation rather than competition prevailed. For example, there has been a consensus in recent years that repetitive structures in a patient's free-association discourse may hold the key to understanding the psychoanalytic process. Luborsky's CCRT's (this volume), Horowitz's configurational analyses (this volume), Strupp's cyclical maladaptive patterns (Strupp et al., 1988), Weiss and Sampson's higher mental functioning hypothesis (Weiss, this volume), and Gill and Hoffman's PERT's[2] (Hoffman and Gill, 1988) resemble in certain respects the structured event sequences called FRAMES which we have developed. All of these are attempts to represent repetitive structures, yet little systematic work has been done to compare these approaches, and the researchers

---

[1] Until recently, a maximum of $12,000 per year for two years; the limit is now $20,000.

[2] Patient's experience of the relationship with the therapist.

involved often seem to barely acknowledge the existence of alternative conceptions of the data.[3]

A second example of redundancy can be found in the data banks that have been built over the years in Germany, New York, San Francisco, and elsewhere as repositories for recorded psychoanalytic and psychotherapy cases. Each group has adopted a different set of standards, including rules for transcribing and for using codes to maintain confidentiality and procedures for releasing the data for research purposes. This has made it all the more difficult to share data among sites and to share computer programs developed at one site for data analysis elsewhere.

A firm footing for psychoanalytic research is unlikely to be found in any U.S. psychoanalytic training center today. In his comprehensive survey of the country's 28 accredited institutes, Morris (1992) described the typical curriculum as consisting of "four major tracks—theory, development, psychopathology, and practice" (p. 1188), conspicuously omitting a research track! Nor do medical school psychiatry departments provide a suitable home. The widespread emphasis placed on psychopharmacology and short-term psychotherapies, coupled with the teaching and clinical duties of faculty members, forces a low priority for research on long-term psychotherapy. As a remedy, Thomä (in press) has proposed changing the "structure and function" of the International Psychoanalytical Association and converting "Broomhills in London into an institute for psychoanalytic research." However, even he is pessimistic about the possibility of accomplishing so radical a change in the goals of psychoanalysis.

Conclusion

The rewards of research—the joy of discovery or the satisfaction of devising an innovative technique for exploring the psychoanalytic process—are neither guaranteed nor necessarily

---

[3]Two exceptions are Luborsky et al. (1993) and Dahl (1988).

easy to attain. In our case, we believe we have demonstrated that objective patterns and structures are present in the free-association discourse of patients in psychoanalysis; that repetition is the key to understanding free-association discourse; and that, to a large extent, the reasoning process involved in making inferences from free-association discourse appears to be informed, astute common sense. Above all, we hope to have presented ample evidence to refute Eissler's (1969) astonishing claim nearly a quarter-century ago when he wrote: "The decrease in the momentum of psychoanalytic research is due not to subjective factors among the analysts, but rather to historical facts of wider significance: the psychoanalytic situation has already given forth everything it contains. It is depleted with regard to research possibilities, at least as far as the possibility of new paradigms is concerned" (p. 469).

REFERENCES

BUCCI, W. (1985). Dual coding: a cognitive model for psychoanalytic research. *J. Amer. Psychoanal. Assn.*, 33:571–607.

DAHL, H. (1972). A quantitative study of a psychoanalysis. In *Psychoanalysis and Contemporary Science*, ed. R. Holt & E. Peterfreund. New York: Macmillan, pp. 237–257.

——— (1974). The measurement of meaning in psychoanalysis by computer analysis of verbal contents. *J. Amer. Psychoanal. Assn.*, 22:37–57.

——— (1978). A new psychoanalytic model of motivation: emotions as appetites and messages. *Psychoanal. Contemp. Thought*, 1:375–408.

——— (1979). The appetite hypothesis of emotions: a new psychoanalytic model of motivation. In *Emotions in Personality and Psychopathology*, ed. C. E. Izard. New York: Plenum, pp. 201–225.

——— (1983). On the definition and measurement of wishes. In *Empirical Studies of Psychoanalytic Theories*, ed. J. Masling. Hillsdale, NJ: Erlbaum, pp. 39–67.

——— (1988). Frames of mind. In *Psychoanalytic Process Research Strategies*, ed. H. Dahl, H. Kächele & H. Thomä. New York: Springer, pp. 51–66.

——— (1991). The key to understanding change: emotions as appetitive wishes and beliefs about their fulfillment. In *Emotion, Psychotherapy, and Change*, ed. J. Safran & L. Greenberg. New York: Guilford Press, pp. 130–165.

——— (1993). The discovery of FRAMES: fundamental repetitive and maladaptive emotion structures. Charles Fisher Memorial Lecture, New York Psychoanalytic Society, January 26.

―――― (in press). An information feedback theory of emotions and defenses. In *Ego Defenses: Theory and Measurement*, ed. H. Conte & R. Plutchik. New York: Wiley.
―――― HÖLZER, M. & BERRY, J. (1992). *How to Classify Emotions for Psychotherapy Research*. Ulm, Germany: Univ. Ulm Press.
―――― KÄCHELE, H. & THOMÄ, H. (1988). *Psychoanalytic Process Research Strategies*. New York: Springer.
―――― & STENGEL, B. (1978). A classification of emotion words: a modification and partial test of de Rivera's decision theory of emotions. *Psychoanal. Contemp. Thought*, 1:269–312.
―――― & TELLER, V. (in press). The characteristics, identification, and applications of FRAMES. *Psychother. Res.*
―――― ―――― MOSS, D. & TRUJILLO, M. (1978). Countertransference examples of the syntactic expression of warded-off contents. *Psychoanal. Q.*, 47:39–363.
DAVIES, J. (1989). The development of emotional and interpersonal structures in three-year-old children. Doctoral dissertation, Derner Institute for Advanced Psychological Studies, Adelphi University.
DE RIVERA, J. (1962). A decision theory of emotions. *Dissertation Abstracts International*.
EISSLER, K. R. (1969). Irreverent remarks about the present and the future of psychoanalysis. *Int. J. Psychoanal.*, 50:461–471.
FREUD, S. (1915). Instincts and their vicissitudes. *S. E.*, 14.
GEDO, J. E. (1979). Theories of object relations: a metapsychological assessment. *J. Amer. Psychoanal. Assn.*, 27:361–373.
HOFFMAN, I. & GILL, M. M. (1988). A scheme for coding the patient's experience of the relationship with the therapist (PERT): some applications, extensions, and comparisons. In *Psychoanalytic Process Research Strategies*, ed. H. Dahl, H Kächele & H. Thomä. New York: Springer, pp. 67–98.
JONES, E. & WINDHOLZ, M. (1990). The psychoanalytic case study: toward a method for systematic inquiry. *J. Amer. Psychoanal. Assn.*, 38:985–1015.
LUBORSKY, L. (1990). A guide to the CCRT method. In *Understanding Transference: The Core Conflictual Relationship Theme Method*, ed. L. Luborsky & P. Crits-Christoph. New York: Basic Books, pp. 15–36.
―――― BARBER, J.; BINDER, J.; CURTIS., J.; DAHL, H.; HOROWITZ, L.; HOROWITZ, M.; PERRY, J.; SCHACHT, T.; SILBERSCHATZ, G. & TELLER, V. (1993). Transference-related measures—a new class based on psychotherapy sessions. In *Handbook of Dynamic Psychotherapy—Research and Clinical Practice*, ed. N. Miller, L. Luborsky, J. Barber & J. Dougherty. New York: Basic Books, pp. 326–341.
MERGENTHALER, E. & KÄCHELE, H. (1993). Locating test archives for psychotherapy research. In *Handbook of Dynamic Psychotherapy—Research and Clinical Practice*, ed. N. Miller, L. Luborsky, J. Barber & J. Dougherty. New York: Basic Books, pp. 53–61.
MILLER, S. (1990). Structural change in patients: a reliability study. *Twenty-first Annual Meeting of the Society for Psychotherapy Research*.
MORRIS, J. (1992). Psychoanalytic training today. *J. Amer. Psychoanal. Assn.*, 40:1185–1210.
SCHWARTZ, R. & TRABASSO, T. (1984). Children's understanding of emotions. In *Emotions, Cognition and Behavior*, ed. C. Izard, J. Kagan & R. Zajonc. New York: Cambridge Univ. Press, pp. 409–437.

SIMON, H. (1981). *The Sciences of the Artificial.* Cambridge, MA: MIT Press.
STRUPP, H., SCHACHT, T. & HENRY, W. (1988). Problem-treatment-outcome congruence: a principle whose time has come. In *Psychoanalytic Process Research Strategies,* ed. H. Dahl, H. Kächele & H. Thomä. New York: Springer, pp. 1–14.
TELLER, V. (1988). Artificial intelligence as a basic science for psychoanalytic research. In *Psychoanalytic Process Research Strategies,* ed. H. Dahl, H. Kächele & H. Thomä. New York: Springer, pp. 163–177.
——— & DAHL, H. (1981). The framework for a model of psychoanalytic inference. *Proc. 7th Int. Joint Conference on Artificial Intelligence,* 1:394–400.
——— ——— (1986). The microstructure of free association. *J. Amer. Psychoanal. Assn.,* 34:763–798.
THOMÄ, H. (1993). Training analysis and psychoanalytic education: proposals for reform. *Annals Psychoanal.,* 21:3–75.

MANNEQUINS IN THE LABYRINTH AND THE COUCH-LAB INTERSECT

JOSEPH CASTON, M.D.

Matters of psychoanalysis as science and what status clinical work merits within its empirical enterprise are considered here, in the light of several research studies. Summarized, these include empirical investigations of the problems of agreement and stereotypy in psychoanalytic formulation, and a briefly sketched investigation of the effects of psychoanalytic interventions from the viewpoints of two psychoanalytic paradigms.

> Indeed an idea, or a notion, like the physicist's ultimate particles and rays, is only known by what it does.
> I. A. Richards—*Philosophy of Rhetoric.*
>
> With drives as with genes, the initial question is what they do, not what they are.
> J. A. Fodor—*Psychological Explanation.*

WHEN I WAS IN TRAINING, I strove to construct psychodynamic patterns from the stories that patients told in ways that mimicked my teachers' preferences and still made sense in the given case. It was easy to find colleagues who understood a case likemindedly—and just as easy to find an opposing opinion. But how striking that an occasional conference leader might sway everyone away from an otherwise unanimously held formulation, and instead persuade us toward some brilliant, totally idiosyncratic view!

Pragmatically, in order to go on with my work as psychotherapist, I submerged the doubts all this stimulated. These

---

Training and Supervising Analyst, San Francisco Psychoanalytic Institute; Associate Clinical Professor, Department of Psychiatry, University of California, San Francisco.

were: how can we make good our clinical claims, if each of us differently describes the shadow that the clinical object throws on the wall? And to what extent are its stable descriptions a function of the object, and not viewers' expectancy? We move on happy ground if our clinical conception of events and persons derives from the way things *really* are, but it just might be that such observational regularities have arisen from stereotypical templates of how we *expect* things to be.

Unresolved, such matters need trouble our trust in our overall perception of the process, and our belief that apparently therapeutic interventions work *because* they derive from and are grounded in our formulations.

Seitz (1966) actualized these concerns when he published his group's failure to *systematically* demonstrate that senior analysts can agree on formulations relevant to the conduct of a case. His paper generated little alarm. Alarm would have been appropriate. If we cannot build our house on the firm bedrock of reliable observation, we cannot claim to be a "science" at all. My bias was, and is, that psychoanalysis *has* a strong empirical core, and that to demonstrate such has been a problem of method.

Complex Psychoanalytic Formulations: Agreement Studies

I first explored measuring analysts' ability to agree on psychodynamic inferences about an analytic case within the "control mastery" frame of reference (Weiss, Sampson et al., 1986). I later applied the same method to evaluate the reliability of *classical*, i.e., *mainstream psychoanalytic*, formulations. A final and further development of the method allowed me to study stereotypic judgments in mainstream clinical formulations, a very different kind of problem that I coined "the psychoanalytic mannequin."

The opportunity to do this came about when Joseph Weiss and Harold Sampson, who had access to verbatim analytic transcripts, asked me to develop a method to test a hypothesis, to wit, that the efficacy of analytic interventions is a function of their power to disconfirm irrational dangers according to a patient's "unconscious plan." But I did not begin there, considering that such an assessment of interventions *depends* on a control mastery formulation *specific* to the case.

What if, I argued at the outset, the only people able to construct such an unfamiliar formulation—a patient's unconscious plan—were two analysts who lived in San Francisco? Then any finding borne out by their studies could not carry the weight of a causal theory, which demands the replicability and justifiability of its claims. Agreement rests on the ontological suppositions and approach of a given psychoanalytic paradigm, *as operationalized*. If you cannot show that clinicians schooled in a perspective (e.g., Kleinian, Kohutian, mainstream) can reliably identify what *they* regard as key observables, then the context of discovery, which precedes the context of justification, has been tragically disabled. Any warrant for claims that then derive from it, such as how interpretations work, is undermined.

Accordingly, the *prior* step meant assessing the reliability of the entire control mastery formulation of a case. What was daunting was that one dealt, as in all of psychoanalysis, with complex, interwoven clinical inferences; Strupp et al. (1966) had already warned that only low inference, experience-near variables tended to achieve high levels of reliability. Lester Luborsky's CCRT studies had begun to appear, but their format, focus, and specificity did not match what was called for.

The solution I developed and applied did demonstrate agreement for second-order inferences in both control mastery and mainstream psychoanalytic formulations. There are four methodological moves. First, a paradigm's formulation is dissected into its component conceptual domains, and how clinical judgments are scaled within each is described. Second, a clinical team generates a wide array of plausible clinical propositions *about* the case. Third, a *separate* team rates the applicability of these propositions, making particular judgments about specific clinical points in, from, and regarding the verbatim text according to given scales or tasks. The last step applies statistical tests to the latter judges' numerical ratings.

For *mainstream psychoanalysis*, the domains included: (1) conflictedness in the historical moment, and in its telling; (2) defense-impulse configurations; (3) displacement transferences, and "other" transferences; (4) historical linkages; and (5) wish structures. For *control mastery theory*, domains were: (1) the patient's goals; (2) obstructions (later termed "pathological beliefs"); (3) unconscious tests and their "power."

Protocols describe how to rate the observations of the relative presence or intensity of a dimension that each domain involves, on 9-point scales. Mainstream judges rated: (1) *Conflictedness*: how conflicted the patient was/is about an action/state he or she refers to in its historical context and, separately, about telling it to the analyst. A judge would thus doubly evaluate the following rubric, "leading a man on at a party," as located in the actual verbatim text of the hours. (2) *Defense-impulse configurations*: the degree an action/state is used by the patient in the service of "defending against" other target states. The judge is asked, e.g., "To what extent is her inability to respond after her father's request for reassurance used in the service of defending against an array of target behaviors," each with a form such as, "avoiding stimulating her father to greater demands." That these latter items allude to other person(s) sets up the next task. (3) *Transference*: the extent to which the action referred to a displacement transference (major other represents the analyst), and/or other transference variants. The "father" item above, e.g., requires rating the extent of a parallel in which the father stands for the analyst, and/or in which the patient stands for the analyst. (4) *Linkages among (48) historical antecedents and current compromise formations*: how powerful the link is between a historical element (e.g., "father's embarrassment to kiss, as at camp") and current compromise formations (e.g., "the patient's controlling, subduing, toning down her assistant's activities"; "impulsively rubbing her teacher's knobby tie"). (5) *Associations between wishes and historical antecedents or current compromise formations*: the degree a given wish appears associated inferrably with particular instances of either these two elements, as an active or passive wish or a wish to *escape* its active or passive form (using a list of 37 wish types, e.g., "be more powerful than," "impregnate," "merge with").

Control mastery judges rated: (1) *Goals*: the extent to which the patient wants to become able to achieve or renounce activities or states not yet mastered (e.g., "to be firm with her clients"). (2) *Obstructions* (later termed "pathological beliefs"): the degree to which a defensive or dysphoric attitude jeopardizes pursuit of a goal (e.g., "guilt about hurting people if the patient excludes them"). (3) *Tests and test power*: how likely the patient's action or statement is to evoke clarifying information from the analyst's response to confirm how safe a goal is, or not (with reference to passages in the text and a given goal).

By asking independent judges to focus on *fixed* arrays of clinical propositions in each domain, this methodology allows specific features to be assessed from verbatim text in an orderly way. The judgments are otherwise like those we make clinically, except that now quantification allows us to measure agreement. When such judgments are made at many different text-points, they yield an increasingly specific profile about the patient's central concerns and patterns. But the propositions must first have been plausible for the case, since implausible ones will deceptively inflate agreement. Having a prior and different team generate the array of case-specific, plausible propositions helps to resolve this problem, and avoids the later pitfall of idiosyncratic formulations.

Both the classical and control mastery formulation studies yielded high levels for agreement on order, and the classical studies showed modest to good levels for agreement on magnitude. (Ordinal agreement: mainstream domains 1 to 4, half of domain 5 determinations, and control mastery domains 1 to 3, achieved reliabilities at $rho = .69$ to $.96$, at $p < .001$ or better; magnitudinal agreement: all mainstream domains achieved Chi squares at p

< .01 or better; T indices ranged from 15% to 91%.) These findings demonstrate that analysts can reliably identify and evaluate clinical data based on second-order inferences, according to the rubrics of two (related) psychoanalytic paradigms. The methodological creativity of psychoanalytic researchers in the last two decades has further demonstrated our power to agree on different facets of formulation (Caston, 1993).

Is the power of our enterprise diminished because agreement seems only demonstrable by use of guided systems such as these, and "not" in spontaneous clinical settings? I do not think so. To zero in on such controlled details only clarifies the regularity of judgments and distinctions that underlie the craft of clinical work in the first place. It is like asking informed weather observers not for their spontaneous grasp of how the weather is and might be, but for their particular readings of the winds, warmth, and clouds.

The details of undertaking these empirical pursuits, and not solely the findings, have illuminated three points for me. The first is that, *within a given paradigm, there is no such thing as the formulation of a case, but rather, any given psychoanalytic formulation is one of a family of compatible, descriptive schemas about a clinical narrative and context.* Each proposition rated or evaluated within a conceptual domain formulates a clinical or historical moment. A series of such judgments *within* a domain forms a hierarchical profile *about* the patient, thus presents another aspect of formulation. And if one links together all judged propositions that relate to a given *theme* that is represented across domains, then the resulting theme cluster, a complex relational narrative, very much resembles naturally arising clinical ones (see Caston and Martin, 1993, Figures 3 and 4).

Second, that we are able to systematically demonstrate high levels of agreement within each of two different psychoanalytic paradigms validates neither. It only shows that mainstream judges can agree with each other, and control mastery judges, likewise. Such tasks would not serve as a test of the competing views, and the present results represent no basis for their eclectic unification. But each paradigmatic case directs us pragmatically to *some* real feature of the clinical situation, i.e., a phenomenon deriving from an identifiable regularity in the world; and we are behooved to pay attention. But—*are* these things what paradigms assume and call them, e.g., "resistances," "selfobject transferences," or "unconscious plans"? Since Kant, no one has ever seen a thing-in-itself, so we are stuck with developing ideas about what things-as-they-seem *are*—based on what they *do*. Whether the labels are wrongly conceived concerns a different, and not merely empirical, level of argument. Accordingly, rigorous clinical *and* philosophical debate need continue as to whether key observables merit the claims they bear.

Third, even if we establish the reliability of a paradigm-centered formulation, we have not yet ruled out that the agreement merely derives—as an artifact—from the readiness to perceive stereotypic patterns that override the text. What clinicians see may be no more than a psychoanalytic mannequin that eclipses the particularities of the patient. Just this worry seized me while I carried out the control mastery agreement study: The judges, now informed in the no-longer arcane diagnosis of an unconscious plan, typically conceptualized the case in a narrow band of a guilt dynamic. Was it possible that they were stretching this idea, rubber-glovelike, to any clinical text? I had no method or time to test this, but made the "test of the mannequin" the central effort of my later studies on classical psychoanalytic formulations.

Beyond Agreement: Studies of Psychoanalytic Mannequins

In order to show that agreement is *not* based on a prior, overriding interpretive set shared by the observers, one must demonstrate that a *particular* text is necessary to infer a formulation's presence or absence.

Because dynamic formulations name multiple, intertwined causal conditions and effects, they leave us in a labyrinthine predicament. True causes can be proposed along with wrongly inferred, i.e., false ones. A partly false formulation may achieve unmerited validation of its false parts, *just because* these are wedded to the causal elements that are responsible for the effects. We must be careful that mannequins do not crowd us as we find our way through the labyrinth!

The problem is how to discern or construct such stereotypes so that they can be studied. It is of no help to show that rival formulations from *other* cases do not match the target case; people are so different that most formulations are implausible for the case at hand, making such comparisons trivial.

My solution is *to generate a mannequin from the case itself.* By adding a new judge team and varying the method used in the agreement study, mannequins can be studied by the following logic.

Recall that, based on the actual clinical materials, a proposition-generating team has developed lists of plausible clinical items about this case for each domain. All by themselves, these lists contain relevant bits of real and potential information about the patient's dynamics, focus, and history. So that we can assess agreement, these items are then independently rated by each judge member of the next team, who are *also* informed by a reading of the entire five hours, and by knowing exactly *where* the proposition focuses in the text.

But one should note that *if one reads only these propositions, without knowledge of the full clinical text, one may still deduce a picture of a patient.* One can thus, in effect, construct a *stereotypic* view of *this* patient, given this modicum of real information about her, from one's own psychoanalytic formulas and common sense. The third, *new* team does just that, rating the lists of propositions but *without ever reading the verbatim analytic text at all.* Thus, these "mannequin judges" are textless—but not clueless.

To illustrate, the reader himself may begin to construct a putative "mannequin" formulation, *without* benefit of analytic text, if he reviews even the very few items given earlier as domain exemplars. Both mannequin and textwise judges rated 99 such propositions. But because textwise judges read *both* text *and* propositions, they are vastly more informed about the relative presence of *particular* clinical features.

This question is empirically tested by the following logic: if analysts who *do* read the text (i.e., textwise judges) agree with each other significantly *more* in their ratings of the propositions than they do with analysts who *do not* read the text (i.e., mannequin judges) but who rate the *same* clinical propositions, *then* we may infer that reading the text makes a difference. In that case, the particularity of the patient is *not* overridden by stereotypes. One might also put it that the mannequin judges may be guided, in making higher-order inferences, by generalizations about behavior that do not reflect how a particular case unfolds.

Some 62 separate tests for mannequins were done in the five mainstream psychoanalytic domains listed in the agreement studies section, and simplified to 9 comparisons each for magnitude and order (Caston and Martin, 1993, Figure 2). *In most domains, formulations drawn from reading the text passed the "test of the mannequin," i.e., surpass stereotypical assumptions about the patient's dynamics.*

The gross exception is the classic displacement transference, for which mannequins are overwhelmingly operative both ordinally and magnitudinally. That means we are in big trouble here, *epistemically* speaking. The stereotypical transference generalization the mannequin judge is able to make with very little data, we conclude, is not further refined by knowledge of the particular case. Of course, it is possible that these *are* the "real" transferences of the patient, and that both the mannequin and textwise judges are right. It is just that for the moment we have no way to disconfirm that *these* transference observations are the result of stereotypical expectations. In contrast, we are able to make that claim in virtually every other domain (including "other-than-displacement transferences"). *In sum, even if it is in reality true that these displacement transferences apply to the case, we have for the time being lost our epistemic warrant for asserting that clinical distinction and for any inference we derive thereby.*

In other domains, a striking and felicitous finding is that the four textwise judges, judging independently, nonetheless *unanimously agree* significantly more often than mannequin judges on the absolute absence (where relevant) of most wish variables, nondisplacement transference, and defense-impulse configurations. *We may conclude that adequate clinical text is indeed necessary to, and does, establish exclusionary inferences in psychoanalytic work.*

One may wonder whether the studies of other paradigms might survive the test of the mannequin. These findings do not validate mainstream psychoanalysis, but underwrite its hypotheses as testable. They give us good reason to believe that our observational instruments work in a garden variety case, and will work in others.

Testing Hypotheses About Psychoanalytic Interventions

In our field, the dark entanglement of many causal factors and their relative weights creates and complicates the richness of clinical assertion. Once we try to answer a question in a controlled, empirical way, we immediately and sharply face this crowd of competing, coexisting possible causes, and can only study a few at a time. Even within the realm of verbal interventions, there are many variables relevant to outcome and process.

My colleagues and I studied the immediate effects of analytic interventions on the patient's productions in the first 100 sessions (Caston et al., 1986). We tested two hypotheses: (1) for control mastery, that an intervention's efficacy depends on the degree that it is "plan-compatible" or "pro-plan," i.e., helps the patient disconfirm an unconscious danger (here, guilt) with respect to the *patient's* goals (in essence, to be able to be oppositional in order to be close); (2) for classical psychoanalysis, that interventions "work" to the extent they interpret what the patient is warding off (optimally, of moderate depth—"too-deep" interpretations are rare in this sample). Scales assessed an intervention's degree of: (1) its compatibility with the patient's unconscious plan for mastery, and (2) its psychoanalytic interpretiveness in terms of what is warded off.

Two "progressive effects" scales that could satisfy both paradigms were derived from a classical rule of thumb: expansions in the patient's expressiveness and associations represent a progressive, i.e., less pathologically defended, movement. One scale rated degree of the patient's making insight-relevant linkages, and the other, the bold expressive tackling of relevant issues. Random bites of verbatim text were used. Separate judge teams were appropriately blind to each other or to text segments (e.g., effect-rating judges blind to the analyst's interventions, and intervention-rating judges blind to the patient's post-intervention responses, and to each other's ratings). Post-intervention effect ratings were statistically adjusted, as if the patient always began at the same pre-intervention level of insightfulness or boldness. Also, psychoanalytic interpretiveness and plan compatibility ratings were statistically readjusted to remove the segment of interdependence between them. In this way, we could evaluate their *separate* effectiveness.

Our primary findings show zero effects for the control mastery hypothesis, and significantly positive effects for the classical hypothesis. Since we had selected randomly, these results hold for the *general spectrum* of interventions. Scrutiny of findings that do support control mastery, from our early pilot work and others' studies on analytic interventions, lead us to the following conclusion: the control mastery hypothesis *is* borne out when the realm of interventions has been sufficiently *narrowed* in some way (e.g., thematically, as to a guilt dynamic). Silberschatz' early work (1978) illustrates this point. He identified passages of analytic process in which the patient "tests" the analyst with a transference provocation, and evaluated the hypothesis that if the analyst's response is then pro-plan, then progressive effects immediately follow in the patient's productions. But he finds a virtually zero effect in a large pool of such interactional sequences. Only when he *narrows* the realm to "key tests"—those keyed to the theme of the patient's goals (provoking a pertinent analyst's response) are the findings positive and significant (1978, 1986).

Post hoc, we also found that the control mastery hypothesis *was* upheld when, following a pattern clue from another study, we excluded "very anti-plan" interventions, thus limiting the range to "slightly anti-plan to very pro-plan." Anti-plan interventions, i.e., those most likely to confirm belief in the danger of the "goal" toward oppositionalness, had thus *not* led to predicted low ratings for immediate effects on the patient's insight and boldness (Caston et al., 1986). One might have to consider that while "anti-plan" interventions carried meanings that made it less safe to be oppositional, they may well have simultaneously pertained to, even increased the safety of, *other* coexisting dynamic themes or goals in the patient.

To interpret what is warded off, draws from and applies to a wide range of conflict themes in a case. It is not surprising that the mainstream hypothesis is upheld across the entire spectrum of patient-analyst exchanges, in contrast to the relatively monothematic focus of control mastery theory. To put it another way, the interpretable realm of the derivatives of a patient's conflicts must be wider than, *and encompass*, the realm of derivatives that pertain to the patient's "unconscious plan." The wider realm likely consists of responsive, dysphoric relational states *beyond* those that are merely guilt-configured, e.g., shame, envy, loss, anxiety, disgust, despair, narcissistic woundedness. These responsive states in turn are tied to *proactive* relational dispositions in the person toward excitement, vengeance, zeal, lust, affection, domination, restoration, parentiform protection, and so on. The interactions between these two spectra—passionate interest and passionate response—better fulfill and underlie, it seems to me, the complex matrix of narratives of human conflict we study and treat in psychoanalysis.

The Couch-Lab Intersect

What is the place of clinical work as source and context for scientific justification? We must remind ourselves that most of our clinical assertions, published or not, are untested. It is true that the terms "clinical evidence" and "supporting data" can be applied to either discovered or tested hypotheses. But only when we say, for a specified context, that the "data support," or "evidence upholds" a *tested* hypothesis, it means "proven true." If we say the data support a *discovered* hypothesis, on the other hand, it means not more than "have good reason to consider it."

Discovered hypotheses emerge from the chaos as provisional. They have an intermediate status "on the way" to fully establishing a truth claim. That should not prevent us from going forward in the immediate clinical situation, where we make our best, pragmatic gambles as we choose from an array of understandings and timings. The richest syntheses and hypotheses arise from this clinical source.

While research methodologists are enabled to test clinical hypotheses, case study theorists are not excluded from this arena. Solo clinical investigators can also approach the ideal of controlled comparisons within a case based on process notes. *Insofar as they do, they strengthen their arguments thereby*. What clinical authors often do not do is look through their own data randomly in seeking comparison for their hypotheses, instead of only for support.

Well-founded clinical observations also have the deductive power to overturn a universal hypothesis, as when the observation logically contradicts the hypothesis. The best examples include the clinical basis on which Freud jettisoned the topographic theory to favor the structural, and the additional clinical observations by Arlow and Brenner that amplify the grounds for that theory shift, particularly with respect to dreams, establishing powerful deductively *logical* grounds to abandon the topographic theory.

Furthermore, the philosopher Glymour (1974) has characterized the logical and observational convergence that, as in astronomy, tests assertions in clinical psychoanalysis. These logical proofs *do not* depend on statistics or controls. They require that two general psychoanalytic theorems, each separately linked with a current observation, predict a single new observation, that if borne out, substantiates those hypotheses. While so far eluding our investigative application, it demonstrates our underlying clinical logic.

The clinical analyst, the philosopher of science, and the empirical psychoanalytic scientist represent an "intellectual predicament"—three, mutually countering powers, all of whom articulate *good* reasons to criticize the flaws in each others' approaches. Yet all three perspectives are inherently intertwined in the domain of clinical evidence. In the long run, clinical theorists are best served, and serve best, when they assimilate and apply all three.

A guiding principle of the empirical research presented here is that rigor does underlie the clinical understanding of the narratives of human conflict. Because real action and motives have play in a therapy, the number of highly probable interpretations is, simply, not endless. It is pragmatically finite, unlike the hermeneutics of literary texts.

Psychoanalysis is a craft—and a science. At the level of craft, in our everyday work, we take account of a dozen factors at once, and, somewhat like Molière's character who speaks prose without knowing it, we assess and assimilate multiple interacting variables and make patterns of them, without necessarily being aware of it. As science, however, we have to know it and spell it out—so that we can continue our debate.

REFERENCES

CASTON, J. (1993). Can analysts agree? The problems of consensus and the psychoanalytic mannequin. I. A proposed solution. *J. Amer. Psychoanal. Assn.*, 41:493–511.

——— GOLDMAN, R. & MCCLURE, M. M. (1986). The immediate effects of psychoanalytic interventions. In *The Psychoanalytic Process*, ed. J. Weiss, M. Sampson et al. New York: Guilford, pp. 277–298.

———— & MARTIN, E. (1993). Can analysts agree? The problems of consensus and the psychoanalytic mannequin. II. The empirical tests. *J. Amer. Psychoanal. Assn.*, 41:513–548.

FODOR, J. A. (1968). *Psychological Explanation.* New York: Random House.

GLYMOUR, C. (1974). Freud, Kepler, and the clinical evidence. In *Philosophical Essays on Freud*, ed. R. Wollheim & J. Hopkins. Cambridge, Eng.: Cambridge Univ. Press, pp. 12–31.

RICHARDS, I. A. (1936). *The Philosophy of Rhetoric.* London: Oxford Univ. Press.

SEITZ, P. (1966). The consensus problem in psychoanalytic research. In *Methods of Research in Psychotherapy*, ed. L. A. Gottschalk & A. H. Auerbach. New York: Appleton-Century-Crofts, pp. 209–225.

SILBERSCHATZ, G. (1978). Effects of the analyst's neutrality on the patient's feeling and behavior in the psychoanalytic situation. Dissertation, New York University.

———— (1986). Testing pathological beliefs. In *The Psychoanalytic Process*, ed. J. Weiss, H. Sampson et al. New York: Guilford.

STRUPP, H. H., CHASSAN, J. B. & EWING, J. A. (1966). Toward the longitudinal study of the psychotherapeutic process. In *Methods of Research in Psychotherapy*, ed. L. A. Gottschalk & A. H. Auerbach. New York: Appleton-Century-Crofts, pp. 361–400.

WEISS, J., SAMPSON, H. et al., Eds. (1986). *The Psychoanalytic Process.* New York: Guilford.

DEFENSIVE CONTROL OF STATES AND PERSON SCHEMAS

MARDI J. HOROWITZ, M.D.

I have studied psychoanalytic treatments intensively in single case studies, and have developed a method—configurational analysis—that formulates cases according to (1) phenomena, (2) states of mind, (3) person schemas, and (4) analysis of conflict in terms of defensive control of emotion by shifts in topics, states, and schemas. At each of these levels I have developed research tools that lead to reliable and quantitative empirical findings. Here, while summarizing the corpus of my work, I emphasized role-relationship model (RRM) configurations that contain clinically valid qualitative inferences about interactions of wish, fear, and defense.

PSYCHOANALYTIC TECHNIQUE AIMS AT CHANGE through a combination of insight, working through, and new relationship experiences. Psychoanalytic *research and theory* aim to explain character formation, and answer the question of what changes during treatment, and how. Explanations of character involve influences on self-formation of drives, temperament, and early interactions with significant others. Explanations of change during treatment involve the influences of transferences, mourning, and new identifications. All of these deal with enduring, internalized, and slowly changing knowledge structures.

Some of these structures function to preserve continuity of both self-organization and relationships. I shall refer to these as person schemas. Psychoanalytic treatment seeks to formulate what is maladaptively repetitive in such schemas of self and

---

Professor of Psychiatry and Director, Center for the Study of Neuroses, Langley Porter Psychiatric Institute, San Francisco, CA.

This work involved many colleagues, whom I cite, and was supported by NIMH grants, an NIMH CRC award, and two five-year awards for the Program on Conscious and Unconscious Mental Processes from the John D. and Catherine T. MacArthur Foundation.

others, and how to reach more adaptive levels of development. Although maladaptive patterns endure and repeat in neurotic character pathology, they are not easy for the clinician to formulate. Self and relationship schemas are not unitary; an analyst must consider layers and contradictions in self-concepts and role-relationship models.

Any patient with a neurotic character structure is capable of many states of mind. Different transference phenomena occur in different states of mind. Neurotic character usually has contradictions, such as having states of being both too domineering and too submissive, of being too impulsively active and too passively reactive, or of being too greedily mean and too forgivingly kind. Case formulations have to consider multiple enduring schemas of self and others that can evoke such alternative states at different times.

My area of research concerns understanding and formulating multiple states of mind and the enduring person schemas that can organize each state of mind in a single patient. It concerns how processes of defensive control may affect memories, unconscious fantasies, and person schemas. Such research can help us formulate the personality structure of patients in the here-and-now, and from such models, and to reconsider our explanations of how the meaning structure now present developed. We can also project how this meaning structure may change during treatment, or assess actual change processes by examining process notes, transcripts, or videorecorded material from successfully completed cases.

Phenomena

In this paper, I shall discuss states of mind, person schemas, and processes of control that can defensively shift states of mind. I shall specify some salient phenomena these constructs aim to explain, such as transference, identification, and mourning. These phenomena and theories of explanation of their formulation were studied upon a data base of eight intensively studied and 52 extensively studied cases of brief dynamic psychotherapy for pathological grief reactions, and three psychoanalytically treated cases where slow changes in states, schemas, and control processes occurred because of interactions involving transference, identification, and mourning. The psychoanalyses were studied by review of process notes (Horowitz, 1990, 1991a, 1993). The brief therapies were studied by review of videotapes and transcripts (Horowitz et al., 1984a, 1984b, 1993, 1994). Video recording allowed many clinicians to view the same data and discuss theories for classifying phenomena and theories for explaining them.

Phenomena of Transference

These phenomena include cycles of gradually deepening regressions during treatment. At first the patient may act appropriately to the actual ground rules and social structure of the therapy situation. With regression, the patient may express passions based on views of self and other that differ from the current opportunities for actual patient and therapist roles. In the midst of these transference neuroses, cycles of states may occur. For example, the patient may woo the analyst to express an extra-analytic love interest, experience an interpretation of such aims as a rejection, then become vehemently angry, then ashamed, then dull and depressed, then allied in seeking insight, and then repeat the cycle by daydreaming about or covertly promoting an extra-analytic liaison. The cycle can repeat itself many times without gross change, with each repetition emanating from belief systems that unfold like a script based on unconscious and changing roles of self and other. As the patient develops new psychic structure, there may be conscious recognitions and changes in the cycle of states. In addition, states of resistance to enacting or reporting the cycle may arise. These are also based on unconscious schemas, perhaps ones encoding expected criticism from the analyst or scenarios of how to avoid anticipated threats (Horowitz, 1991b).

Identification Phenomena

These include changes in style and belief based on and reflecting behaviors, attitudes, roles the patient sees in the analyst. If the analyst has responded to being wooed for an extra-analytic liaison by being compassionate, noncritical, and abstinent, the patient may change. Instead of the usual state of excoriating self-criticism for "behaving like a fool" or humiliating self-abasement after an intense expression of transference feelings, the patient may reflect on his or her own behavioral pattern from a softened, more compassionate stance of reflective self-appraisal and self-evaluation.

The change process from harsh to soft self-criticism may be based in part on increasing levels of insight and enhanced capacities for self-reflection. The change may also be based on identification with new behavioral models provided by the analyst. That is, the patient learns from observing how the analyst handles situations evoked by the patient. The analyst repeatedly shows how to accept previously derogated aspects of self, teaching the patient a route to more mild self-criticism as well as self-acceptance (Horowitz, 1993).

Mourning Phenomena

Mourning exhibits clear but slow changes in views of self and views of whom and what is lost. Suppose the patient has had a long-cherished belief that someday an ideal parent would replace a lost or deficient parent, who would accept the self, bond in love with the self, and provide a wonderful role model with whom to identify. Because the analyst is actually accepting, the idealized hope is projected entirely onto the analyst. The transference is clarified and interpreted, and the patient is helped to confront and accept that the idealized fantasy will never be realized. Imperfections in the actual parent are recognized, and the hope of restorative childhood, really as a child, is relinquished. The patient weeps or rages over what is lost, and gradually gives up expectations of finding the totality of ideal projections in any real person. The patient then seeks realistically possible new and good-enough relationships rather than waiting and pining for a lost ideal. The patient's self-organization is changed during this mourning process (Horowitz, 1990).

My research has concerned efforts to describe such phenomena in relational-emotional terms and to develop explanations for shifting states of mind in terms of shifts in organizing schemas of self and other. Styles for controlling emotion by shifting these schemas and so shifting the experienced state of relatedness have been described as equally relevant elements in case formulation. Case formulation is the distillation of inferences about how and why the patient developed disruptive symptoms and distorted personality traits, and how and why these traits endure despite opportunities to learn more adaptive alternatives.

Case Formulation

To develop models of the processes of change in character structure, one needs to formulate the way things are at the onset of treatment and then again at subsequent periods. The differences among the assessments are described and then explored in a theory of change processes. In order to develop an explanatory model of change in character, one needs to define how the differences may have come about in terms of patient-analyst transactions. These transactions include interpretation and insight, and trials and repetitions of new modes of relating.

Psychodynamic formulations are constructed from inferences about the interplay of wish, fear, and defense. This interplay can be examined at each step of a simple four-step approach to case formulation developed using the intensively studied cases mentioned earlier (Horowitz et al., 1984a; Horowitz, 1987; Horowitz et al., 1993, 1994).

The configurational analysis approach looks for interactions of wish, fear, and defense at each of four levels. It starts with (1) statement of the *phenomena* to be explained. Phenomena include topics of preoccupation, concern, and emotional conflict as well as maladaptive personality traits and psychiatric signs and symptoms. In addition to these distressing phenomena, clinicians describe desired acts that cannot be achieved and clear signs of defensive avoidance. Then (2) different phenomena that tend to occur simultaneously are examined within a *states-of-mind* analysis. The clinician now considers wish, fear, and defense in terms of desired, dreaded, and defensive compromise states of mind (Horowitz, 1987). Next (3) the clinician infers the internalized self and other schemas of each state in terms of *role-relationship models* (Horowitz, 1987, 1989b; Horowitz et al., 1991c). Once there is some description of the subject's repertoire of states and schemas, (4) the shifts among elements in this repertoire are examined in terms of habitual styles of *defensive control* of states and schemas (Horowitz, 1988).

Phenomena Derived from Unconscious Mental Processes

Freud described deflections from ordinary conscious experience as either intrusions of repressed ideas and feelings, or strange omissions of logically expectable ones (Breuer and Freud, 1895; Freud, 1920). He later broadened the concept of repression to include other defense mechanisms. By linking intrusions and omissions to specific contents, such as discrete stressor life events, it has been possible to show empirical validation of these observations (Horowitz et al., 1993, 1994). Self-report scales (Horowitz et al., 1979), clinician ratings (Horowitz, 1986), and judge-based content analytic procedures (Horowitz et al., 1993) all have been used to quantify such observations, demonstrate the hypothesis that trauma increases conflict in terms of both heightened intrusiveness and heightened avoidances, and clarify diagnoses such as post-traumatic stress disorder (PTSD). Of interest, during PTSD, there may be phases in which more dreaded states of mind occur (intrusive phases) and ones in which defensive compromise states of warding off predominate (denial phases) (Horowitz, 1986).

Periods of intrusion and denial in stress response syndromes indicate deflections from ordinary conscious experience over long periods, such as days and weeks. In shorter periods, such as analytic sessions, there are short-order intrusions and avoidances that are often signs of emergence of a conflictual topic, one in which the person wants both to express and to ward off the ideas and feelings contained in an associational matrix. We have been able to show empirical evidence of this combination, in leakage of emotion, fragmentation of important ideas, and verbal and nonverbal warding-off behaviors such as dyselaboration (the effort to obscure, retract, or give misinformation) and stifling of facial emotional expression (Horowitz et al., 1993, 1994). In microanalysis, by finding coexistence of emotional expression and signs of warding off, one can identify conflictual topics that then require further formulation in terms of schemas that may organize the ideas about self and other within the topics and thus contribute to the emotional coloration of the state of mind in which the topics are contemplated. This combination of expression and warding off is a hallmark of incomplete processing of an idea, and it occurs in incomplete mourning, a prototype of incomplete processing.

States of Mind

We became especially interested in mourning as a prototype of the resolution of stress response syndromes, and pathological grief reactions as a prototype of abnormal responses to stressor events (Horowitz et al., 1984a). Individual cases were examined, and we found that repression and other defensive control processes varied in different states of mind. For example, ideas about a lost relationship that were repressed to avoid guilt in one state of mind were expressed, with guilt resulting, in other states of mind. Warding off was not an either/or phenomenon;

repression was not just lifted and replaced by insight at a specific point in treatment, but rather was cyclical in relation to periods of conscious representation and communication.

For example, a young man lost his brother by suicide and felt guilty that he had not heeded a call for help and paid a visit, but had instead focused upon his own enterprises. Because, four years later, he continued to have both severe avoidances and occasional intrusive images and pangs of sudden, unpleasant sadness and anxiety (Horowitz, 1991b, 1991c), he volunteered for research on pathological grief that utilized psychotherapy as well as research sessions. His presented with a distraught state of sadness characterized by pining for his lost brother and fears for himself as being imperfect like his brother, and so perhaps also vulnerable to future suicidal impulses. To ward off this state, he often attempted to stabilize himself in an unfeeling state in which he was unconcerned with the loss.

He experienced intrusive images in which the brother was entering his presence, alive, as if visiting after a long separation. This was an aspect of a desired state of mind in which he could once again feel calm and safe in spite of the loss event. There was also a dreaded state of shameful worry, in which he felt a complex blend of guilt, anxiety, and shame about being self-seeking rather than brother-helping. His communications in treatment varied in both verbal and nonverbal characteristics of emotion and defensive control of emotion depending on what topic he was talking about and what state he was in; this could be demonstrated with empirical validity and reliable measurement of state characteristics (Horowitz et al., 1993). Such findings were replicated by cluster- and factor-analytic techniques in a second case (Horowitz et al., 1994).

Such state analyses provide the following dynamic configurations at a surface level: the wish for the desired calm and safe state of restoration of the deceased, the dread of feeling guilt and experiencing accusations against self, and the defensive compromise of numbing to the loss.

Internalized Views of Self and Others: Person Schemas as Role-Relationship Models

As suggested by Jacobson (1964), Sandler and Rosenblatt (1962), Kernberg (1975), and others, the person-schematic derivatives of drives can be conceptualized in terms of the sense of self, the object person who is a target of impulse, and the sequence of actions that aim at gratification of wishes. In order to obtain consensus on formulations about these elements, it has been found that systematic approaches foster reliability of inferences (Perry et al., 1989; Caston, 1993; Caston and Martin, 1993; Weiss and Sampson, 1986; Horowitz and Eells, 1993). We found that formats for inferring multiple self schemas and various views of how to relate to the same other person are necessary. To meet these needs we designed the RRM and formatted a configuration of such models into wish, fear, and defense arrangements (Horowitz, 1977, 1987, 1989b; Horowitz et al., 1991c).

A role-relationship models configuration (RRMC) contains inferences about the interactions of wishes, fears, defenses, and quasi-adaptive compromises about the same relationship theme. Wishes are specified in terms of desired roles of self and others, and desired sequences of action. Fears are specified in terms of dreaded views using the same format of roles, actions, and reactions. Defenses are considered as both relatively more symptomatic (problematic compromise) and relatively less symptomatic (adaptive or quasi-adaptive compromise) removals from the impulsive, drivelike, emotional intensity of wish-fear dilemmas. Quasi-adaptive compromises are usually personality configurations that reduce impulsivity and emotionality to achieve safety rather than satisfaction.

The RRMC is a systematic format that can provide for consensual agreements if different people review the same case material. Equally useful for case formulation by the analyst or supervisee, it is a form for general use and is shown in Figure 1. Self schemas are placed in the center, enduring roles and attributes, such as traits or qualities, are entered into these areas. The roles and traits of others are entered in the appropriate areas, as are patterns of transactions between self and other. Three-party relationship patterns may be substituted for these two-party formats.

There are four quadrants in an RRMC. To the right are the relatively more positive affective configurations, to the left, relatively more negative ones. At the bottom are more drivelike, developmentally primitive, and richly passionate role-relationship models, such as a wish-fear dilemma. At the top are more defensive forms that escape from the dilemma of desired and dreaded RRMs. These compromise forms defend by warding off the states of mind in which passions and dreaded consequences would be too fully experienced. An example of an RRM for the example case of pathological grief is presented in Figure 2.

An obligatory script often links the more passionate RRMs. The same wish that may lead to the highly desired state of mind, in the lower right quadrant of an RRMC, can have threatening consequences that lead into the highly dreaded states shown in the lower left quadrant. A person may want to fall in love with another person, but then fear becoming too involved, being abused and/or abandoned, and then growing violently enraged, deeply ashamed, or very depressed.

To avoid the particular patterns of the obligatory script leading from wish to fear, more defensive schemas for transaction are activated, leading to the compromise states shown in the upper part of the RRMC.

RRMCs are too simple to contain a formulation in its entirety. Because their format is graphic, however, they do simultaneously present a great deal that is observed. Empty spaces in the format encourage specific inferences. By following a common format, it is possible to see if there is any consensus about formulation, to compare this method of formulation with other approaches, and to make and compare pre- and post-treatment formulations.

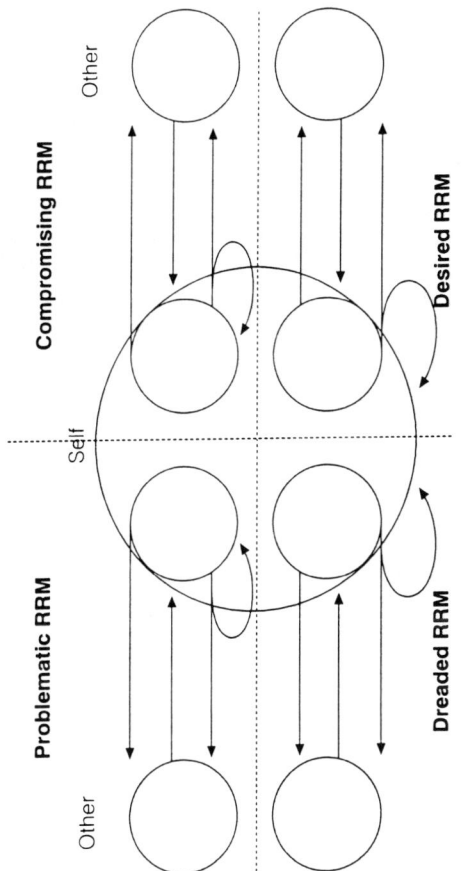

Figure 1. Role-Relationship Models Configuration Format (from Horowitz et al., 1991c).

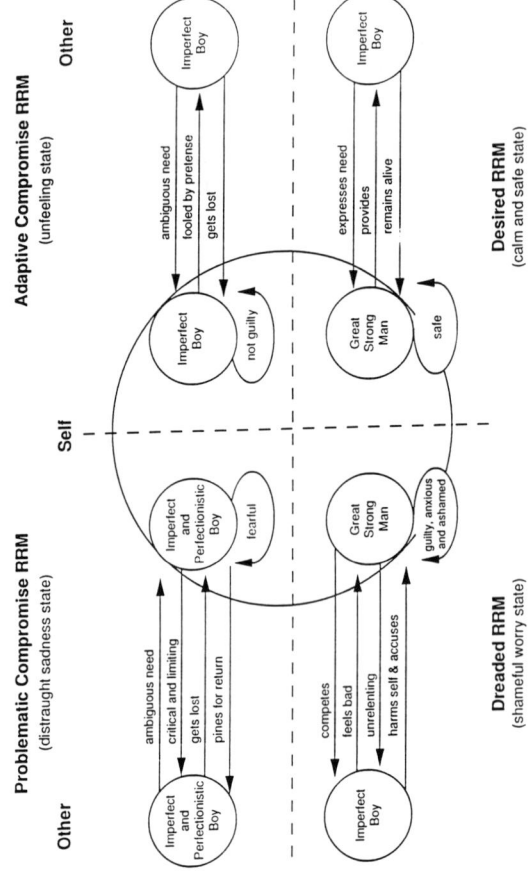

Figure 2. RRMC for the Brother Theme (from Horowitz et al., 1991a).

To determine validity, the RRMC approach was compared and contrasted with other methods, such as the core conflictual relationship theme (CCRT), in both the individualized—case-specific categories (Luborsky et al., 1991)—and the nomothemic—general categories—form of the CCRT (Crits-Christoph and Demorest, 1991), as well as with the social-psychological system of structural analysis of social behavior (Hartley, 1991; Benjamin and Friedrich, 1991). The RRMC method provided a formulation that converged very well with these other methods, and had the advantage of being richer in case specifics about multiple self schemas and defensive layering of RRMs (Horowitz et al., 1991b). The RRMC is better for formulating multiple and shifting transferences (Bird, 1972; Stone, 1967).

I taught the preceptorship course in which psychoanalytic candidates write papers, usually from observing transference and resistance in their analytic cases. This RRMC method helped them to clearly specify varieties of transference reactions in each case. The RRMC has also been useful in training psychiatric residents and postdoctoral fellows in formulation of personality disorders and transferences. First the trainees define transference phenomena. Then they describe states of mind that are involved in transferences (both of the patient and their own countertransferences). Finally, they describe RRMs, script sequences, and configurations of relationship concepts.

RRMCs are comprised of RRMs that are formed on the basis of specific sets of internalized object-relations patterns. One RRMC can be drawn up for a set of strong self schemas, and one for weak ones. Or an RRMC can be drawn up for a set of transferences, or for relationship patterns with mother, father, work supervisor, spouse, child, or friend. Figure 2 shows the relationship with a brother who had committed suicide. Other RRMs for that case were drawn up for conflicts in sexual relationships, and for conflicts in work relationships with superiors, peers, and subordinates. Recurrent patterns noted in transference reactions resembled these RRMCs for external relationships. Once RRMC formulations are clear, the origin of the repetitive patterns can be understood in terms of developmental history. The pattern of the role-relationship models is based on past experiences, both real and fantasy, and will continue to color future relationships until it is altered by the formation of new schemas.

Reliability and Validity of RRMCs

Eells and I undertook reliability studies of the RRMC. We took correct and incorrect RRMCs and had independent judges rate these as related to their observation of video recordings of patients in therapy. Judges were reliable ($r = .6$) in ratings and the goodness of fit of the correct RRMCs to the correct subjects was significantly different from incorrect RRMC-to-case matches.

A second reliability study (Horowitz et al., in press) was then conducted. Independent teams took five transcripts of discourse from each of two subjects and followed RRMC derivation procedures. Teams produced six and eight RRMCs for each case, one for each self-other relationship repeatedly described in the transcripts.

New judges reliably (ICC = .89 for RRMs; .79 for RRMC judgments) agreed in rating contrasts and agreements between the RRMs and RRMCs from the two teams. They had significant differences in the goodness-of-fit ratings between correct and incorrect RRM and RRMC pairings. For example, the Yale-UCSF correct RRMs were rated at a mean of four for similarity as compared to 2.5, 2.6, and 3.5 for a variety of incorrect to correct RRM comparisons ($p = .001$ for all three types). "Incorrect" involved case, relationship, and RRMC quadrant mismatches in separate calculations. The RRMCs of Yale were scored at 3.4 for correct, and 2.6, 2.8, and 3.0 for a variety of incorrect pairings ($p = .001$ for all three types).

Qualitative analysis of RRMCs can lead to categories of contradictions (such as love-hate ambivalence, discrepancies between actual and desired relationship, conflicts between dependence and independence). Such categories can lead to new self-report rating scales and observer ratings of narratives about specific relationships. Analyses of the contents of such contradictions have been reported (Horowitz et al., 1991a, 1991c; Horowitz et al., 1994).

A variety of studies have been done to examine the convergent validity between the multiple self schemas and RRMs assessed in discourse and responses of subjects in experimental situations. The experiments use stimuli of multiple selves and others, ratings of attributes of each, and multidimensional scaling of these responses (Merluzzi, 1991; Tunis et al., 1990). For example, a hierarchical cluster analysis was conducted on a single subject's ratings of herself in nine different "stimulus" contexts. The four-cluster solution of her "response" ratings reveals separate clustering of different "selves" defined by attributes. There was a three-way convergence among (1) this result from a hierarchical cluster-analytic solution, (2) the subject's ratings separately on a modified version of the Structural Analysis of Social Behavior categories of Interpersonal Transaction, and (3) narrative-based formulations of her person schemas (Tunis et al., 1990).

Early formulations in the RRMC format may also predict transference reactions later in treatments. The first five therapy hours of a long-term treatment of a socially phobic patient were studied to form Yale (Singer, Salovey, and others) and UCSF (Horowitz, Eells, and others) RRMCs for her relationship with her therapist. Five therapy-hour sets, one and two years into treatment, were then examined using these two correct and three incorrect RRMCs (from other patients and for the same type of case diagnosis, social phobia). Judges were four clinicians operating to give ratings as two independent teams. Reliability was satisfactory ($r = .6$). They rated the five RRMCs, two correct and three incorrect, for goodness of fit to the observed patient's view of the therapist-patient process for each of 10 sessions watched in entirety. The correct RRMC was rated as a significantly greater fit to the videotapes of these sessions. The average rating of goodness of fit of the correct RRMC was 3.8 in sessions 67 through 71, one-third into the therapy, and 3.7 in sessions 138 through 142, two-thirds into the therapy. In contrast, the mean of the incorrect sessions was 1.6 for sessions 67 through 71, and 1.7 for sessions 138 through 142 (standard deviations between 1.3 and 1.6). The correct RRMC was rated as a significantly better fit than the incorrect RRMCs ($f = 3.6, p < .0001$).

Organizational Level of Self and Other Schematization

Issues of person schemas include inferences about current developmental level of self and other schematization. Several levels (roughly, from normal through neurotic, narcissistic, borderline, and psychotically fragmented) have been defined. The degree of hierarchical nesting of otherwise discrepant self schemas and views of others has been considered in these definitions (Horowitz and Zilberg, 1983) as shown in Table 1.

Formulation of the organizational level of self-and-other schematization is important because it has implications for how schematic learning may occur for change processes, and, hence, for techniques during therapy. Therapist actions that were associated with good outcome of patients when used in neurotic-level cases may be associated with poorer outcome when used for more narcissistically vulnerable cases. We used reliable measures of therapist actions to assess what kind of interventions were used, and how frequently (Horowitz et al., 1984b). Increased levels of therapist actions that tended to deal with more explorations of usually warded-off material, and to focus on less conscious fantasies, were associated with better symptom reduction after therapy in patients at a higher organizational level of self-and-other schematization (i.e., "neurotic" rather than "narcissistically vulnerable" levels of character formation).

TABLE 1
ORGANIZATIONAL LEVEL OF SELF AND OTHER SCHEMATIZATION (OLSOS)*

Mode	Description
Mode 5 Normal	Such persons have a well developed supraordinate self (a schema of several self schemas) and function from a relatively unitary position of self as agent and having values about long-standing issues. They have conflicts and negative moods and own these as "of the self." Conflicts are between various realistic pros and cons or limitations of real relationships. Conflicts tend to be consciously handled well through the use of well modulated restraints, renunciations, sublimations, choices, wisdom, humor, or even resignation. The person is able to achieve intersubjectivity or "we-ness" and to empathically know that another is separate with equivalent characteristics to his or her own, also experiencing wishes, fears, emotional reactions, conflicts, memories, and fantasies.
Mode 4 Neurotic	Such persons have self schemas of a realistic nature. Yet, in some situations, they experience contradictory aims of self as agent of action and self as critic that are not resolved in a reasonable time by rational choices. For example, they may see themselves continually as both intending to express some aim in behavior and opposing such expression on moral grounds, with indecisive repetitive rumination on the theme or repetitive doing and undoing actions. Enduring, unresolved enactments of conflicts about sexuality, love, attention, responsibility, and power indicate this mode.
Mode 3 Narcissistically Vulnerable	These persons are often able to maintain a cohesive and relatively realistic self schema, but there are states of exception; in these situations, they are vulnerable to a sense of self-impoverishment, a loss of a sense of self-cohesion, to grandiosity, or to externalization and internalization of characteristics of self and other at an unrealistic level. For example, a person with enduring grandiose delusions confined to a sphere of creativity or sexuality might be assigned this mode, as would a person who consistently disowned personal aggressive behavior, although it was flagrantly obvious to others. Some others are viewed irrationally as if extensions of self (self-objects).

TABLE 1

Mode	Description
Mode 2 Borderline	These persons are not able to stabilize self-cohesion that includes positive and negative self schemas in a supraordinate schema of schemas. Rather, they have various self schemas that are each only part of the actual self and various schemas of others that include only part of the actual behavior of others. Composites that are all-good may be dissociated from composites that are all-bad.
Mode 1 Fragmented	These persons have a self-and-other differentiation that is only partial andd transitory. At times they display or experience a significant level of confusion of self with other, or they regard self and other merged or interchangeable. Parts of the bodily self may be disowned or dissociated.

*Modes derived and revised from Gedo and Goldberg (1973) and Horowitz (1987).

The reverse was true for the patients assessed at pretherapy evaluation as being at the latter, lower level of self-schematization: in these patients, more therapist actions of the more exploratory sort were associated with lower levels of symptomatic improvement. In this group, therapist actions of a more reality-emphasizing and self-concept bolstering sort were associated with more improvement in symptoms. In the higher, more neurotic and less narcissistically vulnerable patients, increased rates of the more supportive therapist actions were associated with less improvement with symptoms. Without entering into the process-to-outcome equation of the effects of this dispositional variable about level of self-schematization, there would have been a general washout of effect, because there were the crossover effects in the type of patient evoking and receiving the actions of the therapist (Horowitz et al., 1984b).

This effect of a positive association between expressive technique and superior outcome in more neurotic patients, but not in more severely impaired ones, with a reverse effect for more supportive technique in the neurotic patients, has also been found by other investigators, including those in the Menninger Psychotherapy Research Project (Wallerstein, 1986) and a more recent study (Piper et al., 1991). There may be different learning processes available at different levels, and technique may need to follow from what is possible for a given patient at a given time in terms of ability to form new schemas of self and others, especially the ability to develop supraordinate schemas that can contain the contradictions and ambivalences of subordinate schemas.

Control Processes

Issues of control and self-regulation about conflictual and dynamically powerful themes constitute the fourth level of formulation in the configurational analysis method (Horowitz, 1987). I began using lists of defense mechanisms as defined by Vaillant (1992) and Horowitz (1988). Unfortunately, my colleagues and I found it difficult to apply these categories to short, recorded episodes of discourse, and so we developed a finer-grained system of categories of control processes (Horowitz et al., 1992) as shown in Table 2. These in turn led to quantitative and reliable measures for assessing verbal dyselaboration (Horowitz, Milbrath et al., 1994) and nonverbal warding-off behaviors such as emotion-stifling, constrictions of eye and mouth (Horowitz, Stinson et al., 1993 a and b).

TABLE 2
COGNITIVE OPERATIONS IN THE CONTROL PROCESS*

Control of Content

1. *Focus of attention*
   The setpoint for attentional focus determines in part the probabilities for the next topics for conscious representation.
2. *Concepts*
   Shifts in settings at this level may facilitate or inhibit different types of concepts relative to one another. The settings will affect how a chain of concepts on the topic of attention is formed and represented.
3. *Appraisal of importance of a chain of concepts*
   Chains of concepts are weighed for their relative importance in terms of their implications for the motives or intentions of self and others. By shifting the appraisal and valuation of a chain of concepts, a person can alter the emotional consequences of ideas,

memories, fantasies, or plans that are involved.

4. *Threshold for decision or interruption*
One may change the setting of the threshold for shifting attention to a new topic, allowing a point of decision or interruption.

Control of Form

1. *Modes of representation*
These settings determine the ratio of words, quasi-sensory images, and enactions in the sphere of conscious representation.
2. *Time span*
The setting of time span establishes a focus for considering a topic in terms of past, present, or future as well as a temporal range from very short to very long periods.
3. *Quality of logical contemplation*
The setting for type of logic and organization determines in part the forms that will be used for the simultaneous and sequential organization of concepts. The forms used may vary from the logic of rational problem-solving to reverielike rules.
4. *Action planning*
Settings for level of action planning may vary from using thought as nonaction, to thought as trial action, to rehearsals of action, to reflexive actions.
5. *Arousal or vigilance level*
The setting of arousal level involves thresholds for excitation or dampening of how various systems react to input from other systems.

Control of Repertoires of Schematization

1. *Self schemas*
In any state of mind one of several potential self schemas tends to be dominant. Shifting which schema is primed may change the state of mind.
2. *Other-person schemas*
Shifting which schema is primed will affect how the behaviors, intentions, and motives of the other person are interpreted.
3. *Role relationship models*
By shifting which role relationship model is used for interpreting an interpersonal situation a person may change mood, states, plans, and actions, and may alter how a topic is contemplated.
4. *Value schemas (critic roles)*
The appraisal of a topic, chain of concepts, or remembered action sequence includes judgments in relation to values. The judgments can range from harsh to accepting views. Judgments can be experienced in thought as if they were made by critics. By shifting schemas and values, a person may vary the degree of praise and blame.
5. *Executive agency schemas*
A person may view the body and mind as that of an individual (I, me) or as that belonging to another person or larger group (we). Shifts in how topics are viewed may occur with changes in which executive schemas are currently primed.

---

*From Horowitz et al. (1992).

Control-process language allows description of several combined mental activities in a current state of mind. This microanalytic focus may be useful to therapists as they think about how to phrase an intervention aimed at reducing an automatic (unconscious) defensiveness of the patient by encouraging a change in conscious efforts. For example, a therapist may make very brief interventions, such as, "You seem vague," or, "You want to take that idea back." The patient can act on that information by striving to be clear or by reexamining the recently disavowed idea.

Much of psychoanalytic technique works from this point of view, with a focus of the patient's attention on his or her own shifts in affect of topic. These narrow-focus interventions are used as a preliminary technique for subsequent interpretations of what is warded off and of why the ideas, feelings, and self-concepts are so threatening. This sequence fosters development of a self-observing capacity before repressed memories or regressive schemas are interrupted (Horowitz et al., 1992, pp. 334–335).

REFERENCES

BENJAMIN, L. B. & FRIEDRICH, F. J. (1991). Contributions of structural analysis of social behavior to the bridge between cognitive science and a science of object relations. In *Person Schemas and Maladaptive Interpersonal Patterns*, ed. M. J. Horowitz. Chicago: Univ. Chicago Press, pp. 379–412.

BIRD, B. (1972). Notes on transference: universal phenomenon and hardest part of analysis. *J. Amer. Psychoanal. Assn.*, 15:267–301.

BREUER, J. & FREUD, S. (1895). Studies on hysteria. *S. E.*, 2.

CASTON, J. (1993). Can analysts agree? The problems of consensus in the psychoanalytic mannequin: I. A proposed solution. *J. Amer. Psychoanal. Assn.*, 41:493–512.

—— & MARTIN, E. (1993). Can analysts agree? The problems of consensus in the psychoanalytic mannequin: II. Empirical tests. *J. Amer. Psychoanal. Assn.*, 41:513–548.

CRITS-CHRISTOPH, P. & DEMOREST, A. (1991). Qualitative assessment of relationship theme components. In *Person Schemas and Maladaptive Interpersonal Patterns*, ed. M. J. Horowitz. Chicago: Univ. Chicago Press.

FREUD, S. (1920). Beyond the pleasure principle. *S. E.*, 18.

GEDO, J. E. & GOLDBERG, A. (1973). *Models of the Mind*. Chicago: Univ. Chicago Press.

HARTLEY, D. (1991). Assessing interpersonal behavior patterns using structural analysis of social behavior (SASB). In *Person Schemas and Maladaptive Interpersonal Patterns*, ed. M. J. Horowitz. Chicago: Univ. Chicago Press, pp. 221–260.

HOROWITZ, M. J. (1977). Cognitive and interactive aspects of splitting. *Amer. J. Psychiat.*, 134:549–553.

—— (1986). *Stress Response Syndromes*. Northvale, NJ: Aronson, 1992.

—— (1987). *States of Mind*. New York: Plenum.

―――― (1988). *Introduction to Psychodynamics: A New Synthesis.* New York: Basic Books.
―――― (1989a). *Nuances of Technique in Dynamic Psychotherapy.* Northvale, NJ: Aronson.
―――― (1989b). Relationship schema formulation: role-relationship models and intrapsychic conflict. *Psychiat.*, 52:260–274.
―――― (1990). A model of mourning: change in schemas of self and other. *J. Amer. Psychoanal. Assn.*, 38:297–324.
―――― (1991a). Psychic structure and the processes of change. In *Hysterical Personality Style and the Histrionic Personality Disorder*, ed. M. J. Horowitz. Northvale, NJ: Aronson, pp. 193–262.
―――― (1991b). *Person Schemas and Maladaptive Interpersonal Patterns*, ed. M. J. Horowitz. Chicago: Univ. Chicago Press.
―――― (1991c). Introduction to the two cases. In *Person Schemas and Maladaptive Interpersonal Patterns*, ed. M. J. Horowitz. Chicago: Univ. Chicago Press, pp. 105–114.
―――― (1993). Personality structure and change during psychoanalysis. In *Psychic Structure and Psychic Change: Essays in Honor of Robert S. Wallerstein*, ed. M. J. Horowitz, O. F. Kernberg & E. Weinshel. Madison, CT: Int. Univ. Press, pp. 1–28.
―――― COOPER, S.; FRIDHANDLER, B.; PERRY, J. C.; BOND, M. & VAILLANT, G. E. (1992). Control processes and defense mechanisms. *J. Psychother. Pract. Res.*, 1:324–336.
―――― & EELLS, T. (1993). Case formulations using RRMCs: a reliability study. *Psychother. Res.*, 3:57–68.
―――― FRIDHANDLER, B. & STINSON, C. (1991a). Person schemas and emotion. *J. Amer. Psychoanal. Assn.*, 39(Suppl.):173–208.
―――― LUBORSKY, L. & POPP, C. (1991b). A comparison of the role-relationship models configuration and the core conflictual relationship theme. In *Person Schemas and Maladaptive Interpersonal Patterns*, ed. M. J. Horowitz. Chicago: Univ. Chicago Press, pp. 213–220.
―――― MARMAR, C.; KRUPNICK, J.; WILNER, N.; KALTREIDER, N. & WALLERSTEIN, R. S. (1984a). *Personality Styles and Brief Psychotherapy.* New York: Basic Books.
―――― ―――― WEISS, D. S., DEWITT, K. & ROSENBAUM, R. (1984b). Brief psychotherapy of bereavement reactions: the relationship of process to outcome. *Arch. Gen. Psychiat.*, 41:438–448.
―――― MERLUZZI, T. V.; EWERT, M.; GHANNAM, J. H.; HARTLEY, D. & STINSON, C. H. (1991c). Role-relationship models configuration (RRMC). In *Person Schemas and Maladaptive Interpersonal Patterns*, ed. M. J. Horowitz. Chicago: Univ. Chicago Press, pp. 115–154.
―――― MILBRATH, C.; JORDAN, D.; STINSON, C.; EWERT, M.; REDINGTON, D.; FRIDHANDLER, B.; REIDBORD, S. & HARTLEY, D. (1994). Expressive and defensive behavior during discourse on unresolved topics: a single case study. *J. Personal.*
―――― STINSON, C.; CURTIS, D.; EWERT, M.; REDINGTON, D.; SINGER, J. L.; BUCCI, W.; MERGENTHALER, E.; MILBRATH, C. & HARTLEY, D. (1993). Topics and signs: defensive control of emotional expression. *J. Clin. Consult. Psychol.*
―――― ―――― FRIDHANDLER, B., EWERT, M. & REDINGTON, D. (in press c). Pathological grief: an intensive case study. *Psychiat.*, 56:356–374.

———— WILNER, N. & ALAVAREZ, W. (1979). The impact of event scale: a measure of subjective stress. *Psychosom. Med.*, 41:209–218.
———— & ZILBERG, N. (1983). Regressive alterations in the self concept. *Amer. J. Psychiat.*, 140:284–289.
JACOBSON, E. (1964). *The Self in the Object World.* New York: Int. Univ. Press.
KERNBERG, O. F. (1975). *Borderline Conditions and Pathological Narcissism.* Northvale, NJ: Aronson.
LUBORSKY, L.; CRITS-CHRISTOPH, P.; FRIEDMAN, S. H.; MARK, D. & SCHAFFLER, P. (1991). Freud's transference template compared with the core conflictual relationship theme (CCRT): illustrations by the two cases. In *Person Schemas and Maladaptive Interpersonal Patterns*, ed. M. J. Horowitz. Chicago: Univ. Chicago Press, pp. 167–196.
MERLUZZI, T. V. (1991). Representation of information about self and other: a multidimensional scaling analysis. In *Person Schemas and Maladaptive Interpersonal Patterns*, ed. M. J. Horowitz. Chicago: Univ. Chicago Press, pp. 155–166.
PERRY, J. C., AUGUSTO, F. & COOPER, S. H. (1989). Assessing psychodynamic conflicts: I. Reliability of the ideographic conflict formulation method. *Psychiat.*, 52:289–301.
PIPER, W. E., AZIM, H. F. A., JOYCE, A. S. & MCCALLUM, M. (1991). Transference interpretations, therapeutic alliance, and outcome in short-term individual psychotherapy. *Arch. Gen. Psychiat.*, 48:946–953.
SANDLER, J. & ROSENBLATT, B. (1962). The concept of the representational world. *Psychoanal. Study Child*, 17:128–145.
STONE, L. (1967). The psychoanalytic situation and transference. *J. Amer. Psychoanal. Assn.*, 15:3–55.
TUNIS, S. L., FRIDHANDLER, B. & HOROWITZ, M. J. (1990). Identifying schematized views of self with significant others: convergence of qualitative and clinical methods. *J. Personal. Soc. Psychol.*, 59:1279–1286.
VAILLANT, G. E. (1992). *Ego Mechanisms of Defense: In Clinical Practice and in Empirical Research.* Washington, DC: Amer. Psychiat. Press.
WALLERSTEIN, R. S. (1986). *Forty-two Lives in Treatment: A Study of Psychoanalysis and Psychotherapy.* New York: Guilford Press.
WEISS, J. & SAMPSON, H. (1986). *The Psychoanalytic Process: Theory, Clinical Observation and Empirical Research.* New York: Guilford Press.

HOW WILL PSYCHOANALYSIS STUDY ITSELF?

ENRICO E. JONES, PH.D.

> *Psychoanalysis has been slow in responding with formal research to challenges to the validity of its diverse and sometimes competing theoretical constructs. Among many psychoanalysts there is continued uncertainty about whether experimental and quantitative studies can contribute significantly to psychoanalytic knowledge, and resistance to introducing research procedures into analytic treatment. The methods and findings of a Berkeley research program are summarized, and implications for psychoanalytic theory and practice are drawn. A model for single-case quantitative research is described that uses information derived from the analyst-analysand interaction over the course of an analysis, and offers the potential for planned, systematic research through the replication of findings over a succession of analytic cases.*

SINCE THE MID-1970'S, A RESEARCH program based at Berkeley's Psychology Department has carried out a series of studies on the processes and outcomes of a variety of psychologically mediated interventions. Treatments of diverse type and length have been studied, including crisis intervention (Jones et al., 1986), brief psychodynamic psychotherapies (Jones et al., 1988; Jones et al., 1992), and cognitive-behavioral treatments (Jones and Pulos, 1993). More recently, we have directed our efforts toward the study of process in psychoanalysis (Jones and Windholz, 1990; Spence et al., 1993) and in analytic therapy (Jones et al., 1993). I attempt here to summarize our research experience, and to draw its implications for the increasing interest in generating a formal scientific and research base for psychoanalytic theory and practice. The emphasis of this overview is on the development of a research methodology, and the explication of my view of process research.

Professor of Psychology, University of California at Berkeley.
I wish to thank Dr. Cheryl Goodrich for her helpful critical readings of earlier versions of this paper.

Early Studies

The early focus of the Berkeley Psychotherapy Research Project was on the impact of demographic and social factors on psychotherapy, particularly on the effect of therapist-patient match. Patient-analyst match has recently become the subject of inquiry for a group of psychoanalytic investigators (Kantrowitz et al., 1989, 1990). Our own research has lead us to conclude that such patient characteristics as socioeconomic status, sex, age, or race do not inform sufficiently about psychological status. Samples of patients so defined include individuals with the widest possible range of pathologies, and psychological conflicts and capacities (Jones, 1974, 1985; Jones and Thorne, 1987). Matching patient and therapist, at least in terms of demographic characteristics, has not been strongly predictive of patient outcome in a series of studies (Jones, 1978, 1982; Jones and Zoppel, 1982; Jones et al., 1987). The limited discoveries yielded by this work led to a shift in the research from the more external focus to one that was more psychoanalytic in orientation and concentrated on the nature of the therapist-patient interaction itself.

How Should Psychoanalysis Be Studied?

Since the 1940's there have been perhaps as many as 2,000 controlled experiments, mostly conducted by psychologists, attempting to determine the validity of psychoanalytic concepts (Hornstein, 1992). Although a good deal of this research seems to support psychoanalytic constructs, much of the content of these laboratory-based, experimental studies bears only a distant similarity to what psychoanalysts have demonstrated in clinical work, e.g., the use of subliminal stimuli to evoke libidinal and aggressive wishes in study subjects (Silverman, 1976). Field research that has attempted to assess the effectiveness of analytic treatments through statistical means has similarly seemed removed from important psychoanalytic questions.

After an exhaustive review of systematic research studies on the effectiveness of psychoanalysis, Bachrach et al. (1991) conclude, "The quantitative studies, in particular, have not contributed fresh insights into psychoanalysis, nor have they demonstrated findings with substantially greater rigor than previous clinical investigations" (p. 911). There lingers, then, an understandable skepticism about the value of formal scientific research within the psychoanalytic tradition and its potential for meaningful contribution to psychoanalytic theory and practice.

If psychoanalytic research is to move forward, it must be firmly grounded in the phenomena considered important to the clinical psychoanalyst. Although Grünbaum (1984) has asserted that clinical evidence derived from the consulting room is not useful for establishing the validity of psychoanalytic ideas because it is likely "contaminated" by suggestion, circular reasoning, and theoretical preference, he has more recently conceded (Grünbaum, 1988) the potential of acquiring valid data by means of audiorecording analytic sessions. If the testing of psychoanalytic hypotheses occurs outside the treatment situation, and is limited to controlled clinical trials and experimental studies, only "those parts of the theory can be tested that do not need a special interpersonal relation as a basis of experience and whose statements are not immediately related to clinical practice" (Wallerstein, 1986, p. 444). Psychoanalytic practice is the crucial place in which proof of its explanatory ideas must be derived. There is an emerging consensus about the central importance of clinical data, or data derived from the psychoanalytic process, for the study of psychoanalytic hypotheses because they are the necessary, ecologically valid context for meaningful inquiry.

Studying the Analytic Process

In order to use clinical data to test psychoanalytic constructs, it is necessary to first establish that certain kinds of observable phenomena co-occur, and then assess the strength of their relation. Clinical phenomena must be intersubjectively observable, which is to say that different judges can agree independently about whether they occur and their characteristics. Disagreements about the interpretation or meaning of the same case material are commonplace in clinical work, and constitute important grounds for criticism about the scientific status of psychoanalytic methods for acquiring knowledge. It is crucial that any research methodology establish the extent of consensus, or reliability, among judges about the presence and nature of a clinical phenomenon. It seemed that the direct study of the analytic process would be aided by a comprehensive classification system, a method that would describe and define process that would form the basis for an observationally grounded research. After much thought about what should constitute such a system, and according to what principles it should be constructed, I developed a Psychotherapy Process Q-set (PQS) which is designed to provide a basic language for the description and classification of intervention processes in a form suitable for quantitative analysis.

The method is designed to be applied to an audio- or videotaped record or verbatim transcript of actual treatment hours. In clinical data recorded by conventional means (process notes and case reports), what is retained is selective, and it is often impossible to discern what the data are and what in fact are inferences based on data. Accurate and reliable records of the psychoanalyst's and analysand's utterances are essential in attaining intersubjective agreement about processes that require inference. Recordings also have the enormous advantage of opening the door of "privileged access" to psychoanalytic data and fulfilling the cardinal requirement of science: publicly verifiable data.

The PQS comprises 100 items describing patient attitudes, behaviors, or experience; the analyst's actions and attitudes; and the nature of their interaction. Two examples of Q-items are: "Patient resists examining thoughts, reactions or motivations related to problems" and "Therapist interprets warded-off or unconscious wishes, feelings, or ideas." A manual (unpublished) provides the items and their definitions, to minimize potentially varying interpretations. After studying a record of a treatment hour, clinical judges proceed to the ordering of the 100 PQS items, each printed separately on cards to permit easy arrangement and rearrangement. The items are sorted into nine piles ranging on a continuum from Least Characteristic (category 1) to Most Characteristic (category 9). The number of cards sorted into each pile (ranging from 5 at the extremes to 18 in the middle or "neutral" category) conforms to a normal distribution, which requires judges to make multiple evaluations among items, thus avoiding either positive or negative halo effects. The special value of the Q-method is that it provides a way of quantifying the qualities of the analytic or therapeutic process, and can capture the uniqueness of each analytic hour while also permitting the assessment of the similarities or dissimilarities among hours and among patients (see Block, 1961). The instrument addresses key questions concerning unit of analysis, content and coverage, questions of sampling, the use of inference, and the role of theoretical perspective (Jones et al., 1991). Q-methodology (among other sophisticated techniques now available) addresses the long-standing problem of how to achieve agreement about the nature of clinical phenomena, and judgments requiring relatively high levels of inference can now be made reliably by trained clinical judges.

The Q-Technique and Time Sampling

In process research, the question arises as to what time frame or segment should be studied. A self-evident characteristic of the ongoing analytic process is that it has a temporal sequence, or "stream" that consists of the interdependent and meaningful relation between the actions and intentions of analyst and analysand. The usual approach for taking into account time and rendering it amenable to study is to restrain it through some form of sampling. The sampling may consist of arbitrary time periods, such as 10-minute segments, or specific behaviors or events, or a theoretically linked phase. It has become increasingly clear that aggregate data analyses that use rates, frequencies or ratios of units across time segments (e.g., five-minute segments within a session or across several sessions) without consideration of meaningful factors of context and timing cannot capture change processes. Aggregations obliterate the context; it is more the patterning of variables than their simple concurrence that indicates their significance as analytic process. With the Q-technique, an entire hour, not just a small segment, is rated. The analytic hour might be termed a "natural" time frame; it is a segment of time that has practical utility for researchers as well as inherent meaning for analysts and patients.

The Q-Technique and Unit of Observation

What should be the unit selected for study—interpretations, dreams, or turns of speech? In process research there are potentially as many different units of observation as there are theoretical or empirical constructs, and each may require a different kind of measurement. The choice of level or unit of analysis refers to the degree of generality or specificity. If one selects a grain of analysis that is too fine, there is a risk of separating variables that function together, or the "artificial untying of variables"; likewise, too global a level of analysis may lead the investigator to make the error of the "artificial tying of variables," where variables are clumped together that do not occur together in the phenomenon under study. The unit chosen, whether a symptom, e.g., Luborsky's (1967) "momentary forgetting," or a "patient test" (Weiss and Sampson, 1986) depends on the construct or the particular research question being investigated. The "therapeutic alliance" construct, for example, refers to a wide range of therapist and patient behaviors and is at a general level of analysis, while a turn of speech or a transference interpretation is more specific.

Most observational systems use ratings of relatively narrow dimensions of process that are tied to particular constructs, e.g., transference interpretations. Our own studies have shown the value of measuring multiple interventions and interactions of the kind contained in the PQS in revealing clinically meaningful patterns or configurations. In one study of brief psychotherapy of patients suffering from post-traumatic stress responses and pathological grief reactions, a therapeutic process emphasizing evocation of the patient's feelings, the linking of memories with current experience, the examination of views of the self in relation to others, and the frequent use of transference interpretations was associated with successful outcomes in less disturbed patients. In contrast, patients who suffered greater psychological distress were helped more by therapists who provided encouragement, reassurance, advice about reality-based problems, and supported patients' defenses (Jones et al., 1988). In another study comparing brief psychodynamic and cognitive therapies, we demonstrated that the extent to which *each* of these very different treatment approaches contained elements of *psychodynamic* technique (e.g., emphasis on affective experience, the interpretation of unconscious wishes and ideas and of defenses, and attending to the patient-therapist interaction during treatment sessions) was consistently associated with positive outcome in *both* therapy modalities (Jones and Pulos, 1993). The PQS has been able to provide difficult-to-obtain confirmation of the usefulness of technique derived from psychoanalytic principles by studying the patterning of many different aspects of process.

The Q-Technique and Single-Case Research

Research strategies relying on group data have significant limitations as a means for informing us how patients change. Process research that derives its data from samples of patients and therapists rests on two assumptions: (1) that the interpersonal processes that occur have fixed meanings that are context-independent, and (2) that such processes discretely and uniquely contribute to outcome (Jones et al., 1992). An illustration will help clarify this problem. It has been argued by some theorists (e.g., Malan, 1976) that the frequency of transference interpretations in brief, psychodynamic psychotherapy is related to outcome. This is a classic example of a "decontextualized" conception of process, in which all transference interpretations are assumed to have a fixed meaning, i.e., the same significance for process regardless of accuracy, timing, or importance, and that they contribute to patient change in a direct way regardless of what else is occurring between therapist and patient. There are clearly problems with framing the hypothesis in this fashion, since it assumes that an isomorphism exists between outcome and the relative *frequency* of a particular therapist intervention. However, a therapist may interpret the transference relatively infrequently, but when he or she does, it may have an important impact. In this case, simply counting the relative frequency of specific therapist actions in samples of treatments will not allow us to detect any relation to patient change. Each therapeutic technique or action derives its meaning only from the impact it has on the ongoing patient-therapist interaction. The context-determined meaning of events makes it difficult to identify simple, direct associations between particular therapist actions or patient behaviors and treatment outcomes in group data or samples of treatments (Jones et al., 1988).

Studies of the psychoanalytic process, which remain closer to the subjective experience of analyst and analysand and retain a complexity of context, are more likely to yield useful findings. The PQS, which can be effectively applied in single-case research designs as well as in studies of samples of patients, can take into account the interaction of multiple influences in psychoanalytic treatments. Specific processes are conceptualized as simultaneously and conjointly defining the meaning of an event; one element becomes more fully understood in relation to others. Within this framework any given interaction is best understood when viewed within a sequence of actions that extend over time. A longitudinal approach, i.e., one that takes into account time, context, and the effect of previous hours on subsequent events in therapy, then becomes a natural framework for the study of process. Analytic process is then studied as interrelated configurations or patterns of relationships (or Q-items) along temporal dimensions (e.g., Jones and Windholz, 1990).

It is here that single-case research, which more naturally captures the context in which analyst and patient actions occur, has important advantages. The primary means of clinical inquiry, teaching, and learning has been, and still remains, the case study method, grounded in the tradition of naturalistic observation. Statements about psychotherapy that are derived from group data typically have little direct relevance for the clinical problems that are presented to the psychotherapist. In fact, many analysts implicitly view their clinical work as scientific, as a form of single-case research, and are not fully aware of its limits as a methodology. There are, however, long-recognized difficulties in using data from the clinical psychoanalytic method for hypothesis-testing or the verification of clinical constructs: the problem of assessing the reliability of case study data, i.e., the manner in which observations are selected and recorded; the difficulty in choosing among alternative interpretations of the same observations; the sources of uncontrolled variation; the problems in comparing one case study to another; and the difficulty in replication (Jones et al., 1993). Although Edelson (1988) has argued to the contrary, these limitations have led to a widely shared view among researchers that the single-case study is important primarily as a source of new information, or as the basis of a new principle and as an illustration of an approach; in short, for hypothesis-generation rather than testing.

Advances in quantitative methodology in single-case research has led to a resurgence of interest in single-case designs

(Jones, 1993; Kazdin, 1982). In fact, almost all of the research on psychoanalytic process has used one or another kind of single-case methodology (Luborsky, 1967; Dahl, 1974; Weiss and Sampson, 1986; Jones and Windholz, 1990). Most criticisms of single-case research apply to the uncontrolled, informal case study, and it is important to distinguish between these and the more formal and systematic study of the individual case. Single-case research can be considered a subclass of intrasubject research that avoids averaging across cases. A variable or dimension (e.g., the analyst's interpretive activity) will fluctuate; such a variable can only take one value or score at a specific point in time, and repeated measures of the variable(s) over time are conducted. This approach, then, involves the repeated measure of a set of variables over time within the individual case, and focuses on the temporal unfolding or change of these variables and the attempt to understand this change as a function of other variables. The Berkeley Project has developed methodologies which might be termed "single-case quantitative analysis" (Hilliard, 1993) that use longitudinal analyses of data derived from observer-based ratings of audio- and videorecorded process.

In an initial study of psychoanalytic process using the PQS (Jones and Windholz, 1990), the analytic hours of the oft-studied six-year analysis of "Mrs. C." were audiorecorded and transcribed, and blocks of ten sessions were selected at regular intervals throughout the course of the analysis. Transcripts of these hours were then rated in random fashion by clinical judges with the Q-set. The resulting Q-data provided a chronicle of the course of the analysis based on reliable descriptive categories, and showed striking changes over time on different sets of Q-sort ratings. Over the years the patient's discourse was less intellectualized and dominated by rationalization, and increasingly reflected greater access to her emotional life and a developing capacity for free association. The data also allowed us to characterize particular stages in the analysis, and in the later phase captured the resolution of transference resistances, signaled by the patient's greater openness about her desires and fantasies, including sexual desires and the need for intimacy, as well as alleviation of the patient's long-standing feelings of inadequacy, guilt, and anxiety.

Single-Case Research and Causal Effects

A limitation of this initial study was that it did not provide evidence of causal relations. The data did not reveal to what these evident changes in the analytic process and in the patient might be attributed. A skeptic could argue that these changes could have resulted simply from the passage of time. One of the crucial problems for psychoanalysis as scientific endeavor is identifying causal relations. Testing hypotheses about causal relations in analytic process can contribute to verifying or refuting broad psychoanalytic principles. Edelson (1988), for example, points out that the efficacy of interpretive interventions is a major argument in psychoanalysis for the existence of the unconscious ideas it postulates as causal, and that establishing this efficacy in studies of the analysand's responses to interpretation should have a high priority in psychoanalytic research.

Q-sort ratings of the analytic process in the single case can be studied *over time* in ways that begin to identify causal relations. Establishing the facts of chronology is especially important in demonstrating causal effect (Edelson, 1988). Quantitative analyses that make use of temporal sequence include time-series analysis, or sequential analysis (e.g., Moran and Fonagy, 1987; Grünzig, 1988; Jones et al., 1993b). In a second study of the Mrs. C. case (Spence et al., 1993), time-series analysis was used to attempt to identify causal relations. The transcripts of the analytic hours were scored by computer with a measure of free association based on the co-occurrence of words that are highly associated in normal language usage. Findings showed that the analyst's interpretations had a greater influence on the associative structure of the patient's language in the latter phase of treatment. Using the Q-items that scored the analyst's activity, it could then be demonstrated that particular categories of intervention, i.e., the interpretation of defenses, identifying a recurrent theme in the material, and discussion of dream or fantasy material led to an increase in the patient's associative freedom, and that this effect carried over into at least the following three analytic sessions. Using time-series analysis, it is possible to look at delayed effects. Such findings may be relevant to the question of whether more frequent sessions are more effective than fewer, since the former tends to facilitate continuity in treatment, and provide for greater delayed effects (Spence et al., 1993).

Time-series analysis stands in contrast to the more usual procedure in therapy process research of segmenting a record of the process, usually transcripts of therapy hours, into sections of comparable length. In that method, the conjunction of two purportedly causal events is identified. Luborsky's (1967) "symptom context method," for example, identifies the relation of the occurrence of a symptom and its determinant; Weiss and Sampson (1986) use the "critical events" approach, selecting patient transference "tests," and the patient's subsequent reaction to the therapist's response to such tests. Silberschatz et al. (1986) identified instances of transference interpretations and nontransference interpretations during the course of therapy sessions. Ratings of patients' immediate responses to interpretations of either type were made and then compared to baseline scores to determine whether either category of intervention was more effective in fostering patients' insight, involvement, and capacity for free association. The idea is to identify the co-occurrence of two phenomena of interest (e.g., interpretations and insight or involvement) by extracting samples of segments representing the two events. If a time-bound association between the two can be demonstrated by contrasting these to randomly selected or control segments, this may constitute evidence for a causal relationship. This strategy of replication through segmentation has the difficulty of missing processes that change at a slower rate. It has the additional limitation of overlooking reciprocal influence, i.e., the patient's influence on the therapist's attitude and behavioral response. Time-series approaches preserve the sequential dependencies in the analytic process and can identify relations over a long period of time.

Time-series analysis can be used to study the relations between many kinds of variables within a single analyst-patient dyad. An example of the application of this method is the study of a psychoanalysis of a diabetic teenager who mismanaged her blood glucose levels (Fonagy and Moran, 1990). Time series was used to demonstrate that improvement in the patient's ability to control her diabetes was predicted by the emergence of certain unconscious themes concerning oedipal conflict during analytic hours. Briefly summarized, a time series examines the causal relation between one series of data points (e.g., scores on a dimension of therapy process, such as a class of interventions, or series "A") and a second series (e.g., a measure of the patient's affective state, or series "B") that have been collected over a period of time, say during the course of an analysis. Time series requires data extracted at equal intervals over a relatively large number of measurement occasions (minimum $N = 50$). The essential idea is to first control for the correlation inherent in the repeated measure of any variable, and then apply a model to determine whether series "A" can predict series "B." The time-series analysis of single-case data could then provide evidence of causal relations in the therapy process by demonstrating that we can reduce the uncertainty in predicting the patient's affective states ("B") from a knowledge of the therapist's past activity ("A"), over and above our ability to predict simply from the patient's past affective states (see Gottman, 1981, for a discussion of the more technical aspects of this approach).

In a further application of time-series analysis in single-case research, we have begun to study bidirectional effects. The conventional manner of studying process attempts to identify the ways in which therapist actions or techniques influence patient change. Causal influences are assumed to flow principally in one direction. In a recent study (Jones et al., 1993b), a patient suffering from a severe depression was seen in twice-weekly psychoanalytic therapy for two and one-half years. Each session was audio- and videotaped, and assessments of patient change were obtained at regular intervals; videotapes of therapy hours were Q-sorted in random order. We applied a form of sequential analysis that can also capture processes in which causality is reciprocal rather than unidirectional. This analysis of causal effects in therapy showed that therapist and patient mutually influenced one another. During the beginning phase of therapy, our data showed that the therapist was more nonjudgmental, facilitative, and neutral, and that the patient's severely depressive affect seems to have gradually drawn the therapist toward a more actively challenging and emotionally reactive and involved posture. This change in the nature of the process was predictive of the gradual abatement of the patient's symptoms.

Newer theories about the psychoanalytic process have begun to emphasize an interactional perspective, i.e., an appreciation of mutual influence processes between analyst and patient. The recognition of reciprocal influence in research models would allow the study of contemporary interactive conceptions of process which emphasize the subjective experience of the analyst and related notions about enactments (McLaughlin, 1991). It is consistent, too, with the current greater attentiveness to countertransference and the role of the analyst's emotional interaction with the patient, unconscious as well as intentional, in the change process. In time series and other sequential models, the influence of patient characteristics and behavior on the analyst, on the analytic relationship, and on the evolving analytic process can also be identified and assessed, offering a more adequate research model of the analytic process. Such findings may begin to provide formal evidence for the validity of contemporary interactive conceptions of analytic process.

Single-Case Research and the Problem of Generalizability

An important criticism of single-case research is that its results are not generalizable. This view reflects a lack of understanding about the inferential possibilities offered by single-case data. Chassan (1979), among others, has argued that the intensive study of the single case can provide more operationally meaningful information that has more direct implications for analysis and psychotherapy than observations extended over a relatively large number of patients. The heterogeneity of characteristics in larger samples and the reliance on averages result in a lack of specificity, a vagueness about patient characteristics and other variables from which inferences are drawn. Applying findings derived from group data directly to the individual case violates the logic of inference.

A single-case research model, based on frequent observations of the individual patient over longer periods, addresses some of these limitations. It attempts to establish the generality of its findings through replication on a case-by-case basis rather than through group averages. A focus on the variability within the analytic dyad is the very core of process research. Establishing the presence of certain patterns or configurations of variability across a series of cases would begin to form the basis for generalizability. The scientific base for clinical psychoanalysis would be greatly strengthened by a programmatic research effort that would attempt to replicate findings over a succession of studies of individual cases.

Conclusions

The complex processes of psychoanalysis are more validly and usefully captured in the formal, quantitative study of the single case than in experimental or other means that do not derive data from the consulting room. Sophisticated descriptive coding systems, such as the Psychotherapy Process Q Set, now make it possible to achieve agreement among clinical judges about the nature of clinical phenomena. Accurate and reliable records of the psychoanalyst's and analysand's utterances, in the form of verbatim recordings, are essential in attaining agreement about clinical processes that require inference. This makes necessary, of course, the introduction of research procedures into psychoanalytic treatments.

Single-case quantitative research has the unique potential for studying change and variability in the individual patient. Single-case research models are closer to traditional methods of psychoanalytic investigation, and are likely to have more direct relevance to theoretical questions as well as to clinical practice. Research on the single case is more scientifically persuasive if certain features are included in its design. First, such studies should use methods like the PQS that can track and quantify various aspects of the interaction, so that the effect of multiple influences in analytic process can be taken into account. Second, they should be longitudinal, following the process over longer periods of the analysis, so processes that change slowly can be identified. In addition, if such models are interactive, they can potentially identify reciprocal influence processes between patient and analyst. Finally, such research should be programmatic, i.e., represent an organized, systematic attempt to replicate findings over a number of individual cases. Intensive, quantitative studies of individual psychoanalytic treatments, particularly the analysand's responses to interpretation, are more likely to permit the uncovering of causal links that could verify or refute competing theories about how the analytic process effects change.

REFERENCES

BACHRACH, H. M., GALATZER-LEVY, R., SKOLNIKOFF, A. & WALDRON, S. (1991). On the efficacy of psychoanalysis. *J. Amer. Psychoanal. Assn.*, 39:871–916.

BLOCK, J. (1961). *The Q-sort Method in Personality Assessment and Psychiatric Research*. Springfield, IL.: Charles C Thomas.
CHASSAN, J. B. (1979). *Research Design in Clinical Psychology and Psychiatry* (2nd ed.). New York: Wiley.
DAHL, H. (1974). The measurement of meaning in psychoanalysis by computer analysis of verbal contexts. *J. Amer. Psychoanal. Assn.*, 22:37–57.
EDELSON, M. (1988). *Psychoanalysis: A Theory in Crisis*. Chicago: Univ. Chicago Press.
FONAGY, P. & MORAN, G. S. (1990). Studies on the efficacy of child psychoanalysis. *J. Consult. & Clin. Psychol.*, 58:684–695.
GOTTMAN, J. M. (1981). *Time Series Analysis*. New York: Cambridge Univ. Press.
GRÜNBAUM, A. (1984). *The Foundations of Psychoanalysis: A Philosophical Critique*. Berkeley, CA: Univ. California Press.
——— (1988). The role of the case study method in the foundations of psychoanalysis. *Canad. J. Philos.*, 18:623–658.
GRÜNZIG, H. (1988). Time series analysis of psychoanalytic treatment processes: sampling processes and first findings in a single case. In *Psychoanalytic Process Research Strategies*, ed. H. Dahl, H. Kächele & M. Thöma. New York: Springer.
HILLIARD, R. (1993). Single-case methodology in psychotherapy process and outcome research. *J. Consult. Clin. Psychol.*, 61:373–380.
HORNSTEIN, G. A. (1992). The return of the repressed: psychology's problematic relations with psychoanalysis, 1909–1960. *Amer. Psychol.*, 47:254–263.
JONES, E. E. (1974). Social class and psychotherapy: a critical review of research. *Psychiat.*, 37:307–320.
——— (1978). The effects of race on psychotherapy process and outcome: an exploratory investigation. *Psychotherapy: Theory, Research, Practice*, 15:226–236.
——— (1982). Psychotherapists' impressions of treatment outcome as a function of race. *J. Clin. Psychol.*, 38:722–731.
——— (1985). Psychotherapy and counseling with black clients. In *Handbook for Cross-cultural Counseling and Therapy*, ed. P. Pederson. Westport, CT: Greenwood, pp. 173–179.
——— (1993). Introduction to special section on single-case research in psychotherapy. *J. Consult. Clin. Psychol.*, 61:371–372
——— CUMMING, J. D. & HOROWITZ, M. J. (1988). Another look at the nonspecific hypothesis of therapeutic effectiveness. *J. Consult. Clin. Psychol.*, 56:48–55.
——— ——— & PULOS, S. M. (1993). Tracing clinical themes across phases of treatment by a Q-set. In *Psychodynamic Treatment Research: A Handbook for Clinical Practice*, ed. N. Miller, L. Luborsky, J. Barber & J. Docherty. New York: Basic Books, pp. 14–36.
——— GHANNAM, J., NIGG, J. T. & DYER, J. F. (1993). A paradigm for single case research: the time series study of a long-term psychotherapy for depression. *J. Consult. Clin. Psychol.*, 61:381–394.
——— HALL, S. A. & PARKE, L. A. (1991). The process of change: the Berkeley Psychotherapy Research Group. In *Psychotherapy Research: An International Review of Programmatic Studies*, ed. L. Beutler & M. Crago. Washington, DC: American Psychological Association, pp. 99–106.

―― Krupnick, J. L. & Kerig, P. K. (1987). Some gender effects in a brief psychotherapy. *Psychother.*, 24:336–352.

―― Parke, L. A. & Pulos, S. M. (1992). How therapy is conducted in the private consulting room: a multidimensional description of brief psychodynamic treatments. *Psychother. Res.*, 2:16–30.

―― & Pulos, S. M. (1993). Comparing the process in psychodynamic and cognitive-behavioral therapies. *J. Consult. Clin. Psychol.*, 61:306–316.

―― & Thorne, A. (1987). Rediscovery of the subject: intercultural approaches to clinical assessment. *J. Consult. Clin. Psychol.*, 55:488–495.

―― & Windholz, M. (1990). The psychoanalytic case study: toward a method for systematic inquiry. *J. Amer. Psychoanal. Assn.*, 38:985–1015.

―― Wynne, M. F. & Watson, D. D. (1986). Client perception of treatment in crisis intervention and longer-term psychotherapies. *Psychother.*, 23:120–132.

―― & Zoppel, C. L. (1982). Impact of client-therapist gender on psychotherapy process and outcome. *J. Consult. Clin. Psychol.*, 50:250–272.

Kantrowitz, J. L.; Katz, A. L.; Greenman, D. A.; Morris, H.; Paolitto, F.; Shashin, J. & Solomon, L. (1989). The patient-analyst match and the outcome of psychoanalysis: a pilot study. *J. Amer. Psychoanal. Assn.*, 37:893–919.

―― ―― & Paolitto, F. (1990). Followup of psychoanalysis five to ten years after termination: III. The relation between the resolution of the transference and the patient-analyst match. *J. Amer. Psychoanal. Assn.*, 38:655–678.

Kazdin, A. E. (1982). *Single-Case Research Designs: Methods for Clinical and Applied Settings*. New York: Oxford Univ. Press.

Luborsky, L. (1967). Momentary forgetting during psychotherapy and psychoanalysis: a theory and research method. In *Motives and Thought: Psychoanalytic Essays in Honor of David Rapaport, Psychol. Issues* Monogr. 18/19, ed. R. R. Holt. New York: Int. Univ. Press, pp. 177–217.

Malan, D. H. (1976). *The Frontier of Brief Psychotherapy*. New York: Plenum.

McLaughlin, J. T. (1991). Clinical and theoretical aspects of enactment. *J. Amer. Psychoanal. Assn.*, 39:595–614.

Moran, G. S. & Fonagy, P. (1987). Psychoanalysis and diabetic control: a single case study. *Brit. J. Med. Psychol.*, 60:357–372.

Silberschatz, G., Fretter, P. B. & Curtis, J. T. (1986). How do interpretations influence the process of psychotherapy? *J. Consult. Clin. Psychol.*, 54:646–652.

Silverman, L. H. (1976). Psychoanalytic theory: "the reports of my death are greatly exaggerated." *Amer. Psychol.*, 31:621–637.

Spence, D. P., Dahl, H. & Jones, E. E. (in press). Impact of interpretation upon associative freedom. *J. Consult. Clin. Psychol.*

Wallerstein, R. S. (1986). Psychoanalysis as a science: a response to new challenges. *Psychoanal. Q.*, 55:414–451.

Weiss, J. & Sampson, H. (1986). *The Psychoanalytic Process*. New York: Guilford.

PSYCHOANALYTIC PROCESS RESEARCH: METHODS AND ACHIEVEMENTS

Horst Kächele, M.D.
Helmut Thomä, M.D.

This paper describes the basic achievements of many years of systematic research on the psychoanalytic process. The basic aims of this research are first dealt with in terms of their embeddedness in the intensive discussions of the methodology of clinical and empirical validation of psychoanalytic clinical propositions. From then on, the four-level strategy of the Ulm project on psychoanalytic process research is unfolded. This strategy implies starting from extensive clinical case formulations and moving to systematic time-sampled descriptions of selected segments in treatments. From there on, a further refined level of observation consists in the application of rating scales for a diversity of clinical concepts. The introduction of technologically sophisticated computer-based analysis of the various texts opens up a wide array of perspectives for study of the psychoanalytic process, which are illustrated.

I. Psychoanalytic Rationale of the Ulm Research Program

WE HAVE BEEN INVOLVED IN A long-standing endeavor to study the "homeland" of psychoanalysis, i.e., the "psychoanalytic situation." We are convinced that only the careful investigation of the exchange between patient and psychoanalyst can be used to probe essential aspects of psychoanalytic theory and to develop an empirically based theory of the process.

Interpretation was the topic of our first attempts to study aspects of the process clinically. Thomä and Houben (1967) identified important aspects of an analyst's technique and its theoretical foundations by examining interpretations, and by studying the therapist's reactions to estimate their therapeutic

From the Department of Psychotherapy, University of Ulm.
The Ulm group has been generously supported by the German Research Foundation from 1970–1988.

effectiveness. While conducting these studies, we slowly became aware of problems concerning the effectiveness of interpretations and the truth of theories. These problems remain in the center of current controversies (Strenger, 1991). In order to study interpretations systematically, we followed a recommendation made by Isaacs (1939) and designed a schema, in 1963. It required that the psychoanalyst locate interpretations while preparing the protocol (see Thomä and Kächele, 1992, pp. 22–23). While working on this project, we became aware that the question of validation can only be addressed by empirical process and outcome research. All our later investigations are based on the rationale of single-case methodology (Schaumburg et al., 1974) which corresponds best to Meissner's (1983) dictum of psychoanalysis as the science of subjectivity.

The shortcomings of studies that are based even on formalized protocols by the treating analyst were commented on by Spence (1986), who pointed out that analytic narratives are constructed according to concealed psychodynamic assumptions. Often it is impossible to recognize the analyst's contribution; furthermore, it is insufficient to selectively describe only a few interpretations. There is no way to know what has been omitted. For scientific investigations, it is not enough to rely on the memory of the analyst. Therefore, psychoanalysts introduced audiorecording of sessions as a means to get as close as possible to the psychoanalytic dialogue.

While this technical tool is routine among research-minded psychoanalysts (Thomä and Kächele, 1992, p. 24), we agree with Colby and Stoller (1991) that a transcript "is not a record of what happened" but "only of what was recorded' (p. 42). Our answer to this warning has been to find out empirically what can be reconstructed of the "true" psychoanalytic process on the basis of such transcripts. The major progress brought about by this tool is that independent observers are able to study the analytic process from the dialogue. In addition, methods developed in other fields, such as content and discourse analysis, can be applied to the material.

In order to find out what psychoanalysts do, it is not enough to rely on their personal definition and presumed application of concepts (Sandler, 1983; Sander et al., 1991). The analysts' implementation of their concepts as interpretive tools can only be studied in the analytic interaction. We sought to provide a systematic description of what analysts say and how patients participate in the dialogue. Tape recordings provide a sufficient data base. Nonetheless we had to deal with many epistemological and methodological problems with regard to extra- or intraclinical testing of hypotheses (Thomä and Kächele, 1975). In spite of difficulties, we have become convinced that many of the crucial concepts of psychoanalysis relate to domains that surface in verbal manifestations. Though unconscious processes can also be investigated within experimental conditions (Kächele et al., 1991), we sought to achieve ecological validity by working on natural samples. In the course of a treatment, data are produced that confirm or disconfirm clinical hypotheses (Hanly, 1992).

Process models are not a theoretical, abstract matter; they are in fact a part of every analyst's day-to-day practice. The conceptions of process handed down from one generation of analysts to the next, often expressed only in metaphorical terms, contain unspoken theories. Sandler (1983, p. 43) correctly demands that the private dimensions of the meaning of concepts be brought into the open. If these studies are done, we shall be surprised by diversity of meanings of "psychoanalytic process" in the field (Compton, 1990).

We have outlined a process model that is designed to be broad enough to include other process models based on a "focal concept" (Thomä and Kächele, 1987). Focus refers to "the major interactionally created theme of the therapeutic work, which results from the material offered by the patient and the analyst's efforts at understanding" (p. 350). As the individual focuses are linked to one another via a central conflict our model can be applied to both short- and long-term therapies.

The concept of the Ulm process model of the course of psychoanalytic treatment is the result of our confrontation with the developing field of research in psychotherapy. We feel strongly that psychoanalytic process research has to move beyond a subjective perspective in which all theoretical positions are equal in their therapeutic potency, as argued by Pulver (1987). We think that his conclusion that analysts working with different theoretical orientations obtain equally good results (p. 289) has not been substantiated. What psychoanalysis needs is to move from story-telling to a contemporary empirical science (Meyer, 1990). We need descriptive investigations of the process of interaction, of what goes on in the analyst and in the patient, and how their unconscious fantasies are expressed verbally and nonverbally (see section III).

In the explanation of the interactive foundation of the process approach, we allow for the analyst's personal involvement in the material presented by the patient. In clinical language we also argue that countertransference and transference are interconnected; in the language of research we could say that the cognitive and affective conceptions of the analyst determine the semantic space that is possible for the patient. The true degree of this involvement is made more obvious by tape recordings. They betray what one can easily overlook, namely, that there can be a significant discrepancy between one's professional ideal and daily routine (Kubie, 1958).

As Dahl (1983) has demonstrated, a selective factor operates in the psychoanalyst's perception of the patient's productions; the demand to exercise evenly suspended attention precludes the integration at the level of everyday expectancies but may even further the involvement at the level of unconscious role expectancies (Sandler, 1976). These various comments on judgment and evidence formation tend to confirm the bipersonal understanding of the analytic situation, where real relationship and transference issues are not dissected along lines of what is real and what is fantasy, but have to be looked at as constructions in social space (Gergen, 1985; Gill, 1991; Hoffman, 1991).

For these reasons in the transference neurosis intrapsychic conflicts are expressed at least partially in the interaction. The way the transference neurosis develops is a function of the dyadically negotiated process (Thomä and Kächele, 1975, 1987). This form is unique to each therapeutic dyad initially conferring on each psychoanalytic treatment the status of a singular history.

Freud's model of the psychoanalytic process, comparing it with the game of chess, implies rules that constitute the game and exist independently of particular circumstances; after all, chess is played by the same rules all over the world. Then there are the strategies and tactics applicable to the various phases of the game, e.g., opening and end-game strategies; these differ in accordance with the individual techniques of each player and are also regulated interactively, in that the individual player takes account of the presumed strength of his opponent in working out his strategies. Does psychoanalysis have something like a fixed set of game rules that can be specified in isolation from each concrete situation (Thomä and Kächele, 1987, p. 215)? Many psychoanalysts still believe that the psychoanalytic method has the status of the chess game which can be determined in isolation from concrete objectives. Such a belief could be justified by Freud's statement about the independence of the transference neurosis from the influence of the analyst:

> The analyst . . . sets in motion a process, that of the resolving of existing repressions. He can supervise this process, further it, remove obstacles in its way, and he can undoubtedly vitiate much of it. But on the whole, once begun, it goes its own way and does not allow either the direction it takes or the order in which it picks up its points to be prescribed for it [Freud, 1913, p. 130].

This statement contains many ambiguities. Although the rules were designed to prevent social interaction between analyst and patient, such interaction is inevitable (de Swaan, 1980, p. 405). It has never been possible to produce the social null situation in concrete form, although it became a central utopian fantasy of psychoanalysis.

In our view it is impossible to agree with the often-made assumption that, in general, in each process, the sequence of phases is organized in the form of a linear working over of ontogenetic development (e.g., Fürstenau's [1977] process model). In terms of the ideas set out above on the interactive generation of a focus—i.e., from the interaction of the patient's topic and the analyst's scheme—we regard psychoanalytic therapy as a focal therapy without limitation of time and with a changing focus. Rather than naturally linear, we consider the sequence of foci to be the result of an unconscious bargaining process between the needs or wishes of the patient and the possibilities of handling those of his analyst (Thomä and Kächele, 1987, pp. 34–65).

Our research has been couched in a descriptive mode of the psychoanalytic process. Most of clinical psychoanalytic research has been based on subjective reports from an unspecified population of observations and an unspecified procedure of selection (Kächele, 1986). We believe systematic investigation, however, is necessary whether psychoanalysis is regarded as hermeneutic or as a natural science. Independent of the empirical findings and their impact, a systematic approach in itself has definite consequences for psychoanalytic theory. Any empirical approach includes a critical attitude and presupposes operational considerations. One has to ask what kind of empirical data refer to particular psychoanalytic concepts.

II. Research Approach and Findings

The Ulm Textbank (UTB)

We set out to establish a data base for repeated observation and measurement, independent of the two parties involved.

Taking up the encouraging lead of Gill et al. (1968) tape-recording of sessions became the *via regia* for establishing the object of investigations. At present the Ulm Textbank offers a most diverse collection of texts gathered since 1967 (verbal data) on psychotherapy/psychoanalysis and speech/text samples from neighboring fields (Kächele and Mergenthaler, 1983; Mergenthaler, 1985). Mergenthaler (1986) developed rules for transcription, now available in English (Mergenthaler and Stinson, 1992).

At present we can provide potential users with about 40 different sorts of speech, about 1,000 different speakers, and about 5,000 sessions (see Table 1). Two-thirds of the material has been supplied as a result of scientific contacts and joint research projects with other institutions. In most cases these contributions were tied to actual uses of the UTB services. While the donations were primarily from the field of psychotherapy, other users were also often linguists who did not require services of the UTB other than the provision of recordings and transcripts along with word and line counts. At present, we maintain contact with about 30 institutes in Germany, four in the United States, two in Sweden, two in Switzerland and one in Austria. All together, the electronically stored texts include a vocabulary of 155,000 German and 20,000 English words and total tokens of more than 10 million.

Thus far, 22 psychoanalytic treatments of eight analysts and 22 patients have been totally or partially recorded, and large samples of the recorded sessions have been transcribed. Many of them are not yet as systematically investigated as the cases of Amalia X., Christian Y., Franziska X., and Gustav Y.—which we have placed in the center of our multidimensional studies. Those other analytic cases have been used for clinical, linguistic, philosophical, and theological studies by a host of analysts and scientists from other disciplines.

We focused on four psychoanalytic process research cases on which systematic time series of recorded sessions were transcribed and stored in the UTB. Amalia X. and Christian Y.

TABLE 1

Text type	Number of Units		
	Patients	Therapist	Sessions
1. Counseling	1	1	4
2. Short-term Therapy (1 × a week)	16	8	170
3. Psychoanalytic Therapy (2 × a week)	29	24	170
4. Psychoanalysis (4 × a week)	22	8	110
		3	
5. Marital Therapy	1*	1	2
6. Family Therapy	32*	5	32
7. Group Therapy*			
9. Group Work	3*	1	3
11. Behavior Psychotherapy	2	1	1
12. Initial Interview	349	31	374
13. Initial Interview Report	232	13	378
14. Psychotherapy Case Notes	3	2	19
15. Psychoanalysis Case Notes	2	1	158
18. Balint Group Work	2	1	53
19. Self-experiential Group	4	1	4
20. Dreams	2	2	123
22. Psychological Testing	84	5	227
23. Catamnestic Interview	55	3	57
24. TAT (Thematic Apperception Test)	72	6	72
25. "Narrative"	72	6	72
26. Genetic Counseling	29	4	29
29. Individual Reports	1	19	19
30. Scientific Report	1	40	40
32. Cognitive-behavioral therapy	1	1	20
33. Supervision	6	5	15
34. Psychiatric Interview	24	5	24
36. Family Interview	2	1	1
37. Interactional Schema-analytic Therapy	1	1	28
39. Semi-standardized Interview	11	1	11
99. Other Total	45	8	72
Total	882	162	3211

*Couple, family, group.

were treated by a senior analyst (H. T.); Franziska and Gustav were treated by an analyst in training (H. K.). The clinician, of course, is an important figure in this kind of psychoanalytic research and should not remain anonymous even if this puts an additional burden on the recording. We feel strongly that he or she has a special contribution in the evaluation of the empirical findings (Thomä, 1985). However, the inclusion of uninvolved third parties is essential and decisive in the testing of theories. The contemporary version of Freud's inseparable bond thesis consists not only in the psychoanalyst's double role as clinician and researcher, but also in the integration of scientists (Thomä and Kächele, 1987, p. 370). The fantasied presence of third persons in the psychoanalytic situation has repercussions on the process; our studies on this subject support our clinical experience (Kächele et al., 1988).

The Empirical Approach of a Multilevel Observational Strategy

Our aim was to establish ways to systematically describe long-term psychoanalytic processes in various dimensions and to use descriptive data to examine process hypotheses. This also entails the generation of both general process hypotheses as well as single case process assumptions. Hypothesis generation needs to specify, for each patient, what kind of material had to be worked on in order to achieve change in various dimensions of specified theoretical relevance for each particular case—be it structural properties or symptomatic (speech) behavior. Our approach at first did not include the recording of external measures that would limit the intrusions on the clinical process (Kächele et al., 1988); in a later collaborative study with Meyer on the thought processes of the analyst we have modified this stance (Meyer, 1988).

Our methodological conception consists of a four-level approach: A-level—clinical case study; B-level—systematic clinical descriptions; C-level—guided clinical judgment procedures; D-level—computer-assisted text analysis. This multilevel approach reflects our understanding that the tension between clinical meaningfulness and objectification cannot be solved creatively by using a single approach.

A-Level—Clinical Case Study. The clinical case study, based on the good memory or accurate process notes of the analyst, fulfills an important communicative function within the profession. However, the use of vignettes to illustrate a point is not a convincing means for explaining, for example, why Mr. Z. in Kohut's (1979) first treatment did not reach the goals he is claimed to have reached in the second treatment. Instead of vignettes there is a need for carefully prepared case studies. More should be published (Meyer, 1992) in our view.

B-Level—Systematic Clinical Description. Systematic clinical descriptions from structured points of view based on tape recording of the whole treatment and verbatim transcripts of adequate samples ($1/5$ of all sessions: 10–5, 26–30, 5401–505) is another important step that is close to clinical reasoning. Verbatim records of the sessions are used. This clinical-descriptive step allows for an evaluation that is under some constraints: not all sessions will be available, as we work with a systematic time sample. Still, the assumption is made that systematic analysis in first-time intervals can capture the decisive change processes. We prepared a fairly extensive report on our first case, Christian Y., by a joint endeavor of the treating analyst, a second analyst, and a clinical psychologist, using group discussion (Thomä and Kächele, 1973). We used the following points of description for each of five sessions that were sampled over the treatment span from hour one to 505 at regular intervals of 25 sessions: (1) external situation of the patient and treatment; (2) transference/countertransference situation; (3) relations of the patient to important persons outside the treatment, present and past perspectives; (4) working alliance; (5) important episodes within the five sessions. A similar systematic description was prepared for patient Amalia X., by two medical students who focused on a descriptive study of changes in the patient's body image: she was suffering from hirsuitism as part of her neurotic difficulties (Kächele et al., 1991).

The material made available by such an effort can serve many purposes. It provides easy access to the whole case, being

TABLE 2.
Systematic Description of Amalia X.'s Analysis:
Focal Issues (Transference)

Sessions

- 1–5   : The analysis as confession.
- 26–30 : The analysis as an examination.
- 51–55 : The bad, cold mother.
- 76–80 : Submission and secret defiance.
- 101–105: Searching her own rule.
- 116–120: The disappointing father and the helpless daughter.
- 151–155: The cold father and her desire for identification.
- 176–180: Ambivalence in the father relationship.
- 201–205: The father as seducer or judge of moral standards.
- 226–230: Does he love me—or not?
- 251–255: Even my father cannot change me into a boy.
- 276–280: The Cinderella feeling.
- 301–305: The poor girl and the rich king.
- 326–330: If you reject me, I'll reject you.
- 351–355: The powerless love for the mighty father, and jealousy.
- 376–380: Separation for not being deserted.
- 401–405: Discovery of her capacity to criticize.
- 426–430: I'm only second to my mother, first-borns are preferred.
- 451–455: Hate for the giving therapist.
- 476–480: The art of loving consists in tolerating love and hate.
- 501–505: Be first in saying goodbye.
- 513–517: Departure—Symphony

more detailed and more systematic than a case history, which tends to be novella-like. The systematic descriptive record also marks out the orderly progress of treatment. One can rearrange the qualitative data, concatenating all transference descriptions one after the other and thereby gain a good view of the development of major transference/countertransference issues. Such a view is illustrated by Table 2.

When more rapid access to the distribution of major themes was desired, we used the method of Topic Index (Simon et al., 1968). Accordingly, in the second case, a list of salient topics was based on an overview of the whole case. The presence of each topic was assessed, and the resulting graphic matrix provided a good overview of where and when patient and/or analyst talked about what topic.

C-Level—Guided Clinical Judgment Procedures. Clinical description, even when performed by two or more observers, keeps the nature of the data on a qualitative level. The necessary step from transforming the rich qualitative and unsystematic knowledge into quantitative assertions has barely started. The tool for achieving this transformation consists of a simple representation of a dimensional aspect of the concept under study. A scale is an elaborate version of a basic "yes" or "no distinction" that marks the beginning of any measurement operation (Knapp et al., 1975). Luborsky (1984) aptly calls these operations "guided clinical judgment procedures," which catches the process of narrowing down the clinician's capacity for recording complex data. When we began the project we felt obliged to move beyond the descriptive statements and work on the development of judgment procedures for specifying conceptual dimensions such as transference, working alliance, anxieties, emotional insight, suffering. Various studies were performed at this level: (1) transference, anxiety and working alliance (Kächele et al., 1975; Grunzig and Kächele, 1978); (2) phrasing the process (Kächele, 1988); (3) suffering (Neudert and Hohage, 1988); (4) emotional insight (Hohage and Kübler, 1988); (5) cognitive changes (Leuzinger-Bohleber, 1987, 1989; Leuzinger-Bohleber and Kächele, 1985, 1988).

The first two were done on the Case Christian Y., the third, fourth and fifth, on Mrs. Amalia X. The sixth study used five analytic cases, one diary-based case, and four from our stock of which larger data bases are available as verbatim protocols.

D-Level—Computer-Assisted Text Analysis. The fourth level in our research consists in supplementing the rating of clinical concepts according to a manual by introducing computer-based text analysis as a tool to tackle the manifold problems that are tied up with rating systems.[1] Since then, the use of the computer

---

[1] We acknowledge that the installation of this approach is directly influenced by Dahl's seminal papers (1972, 1974) and Kächele's attending Spence's summer course in programming and computational linguistics, in Pisa, in 1973 (see also Spence, 1968, 1969).

as tool has been developed from content analysis to text analysis and has been described in detail elsewhere (Kächele and Mergenthaler, 1983, 1984; Mergenthaler and Kächele, 1988, 1991). The computer-based text analysis has been used in quite a few investigations on psychoanalytic material: (1) long-term transference trends (Kächele, 1976, 1988, 1990); (2) verbal activity of psychoanalysts in four psychoanalytic treatments (Kächele, 1983); (3) redundancy in patients' and therapists' language (Kächele and Mergenthaler, 1984); (4) classification of anxiety themes (Grünzig and Kächele, 1978); (5) emotive aspects of therapeutic language (Wirtz and Kächele, 1983); (6) themes of anxiety as psychotherapeutic process variables (Grünzig, 1983); (7) interactional style of four therapists (Lolas et al., 1983); (8) change in body concepts in psychoanalysis (Schors and Kächele, 1982); (9) cognitive changes during psychoanalysis (Leuzinger-Bohleber, 1987, 1989; Leuzinger-Bohleber and Kächele, 1985, 1988); (10) changes of latent meaning structures in psychoanalysis (Mergenthaler and Kächele, 1985); (11) vocabulary measures for evaluation of therapy outcome (Holzer et al., 1992a); (12) personal pronouns in psychoanalytic processes (Schaumburg, 1980).

The host of diverse studies points to the richness of language as a datum for evaluating change processes during treatment. Though it is not possible to summarize the individual findings of the studies, it seems evident to us that this research tool merits further development of computational linguistics—and broader application of the facilities provided by the UTB.

We have concluded that phases of treatment are empirically identifiable. However, the temporal extension of these phases is dependent on the variable under study. Some formal variables, such as speech activity, demonstrate systematic long-term trends reflecting changes in the patient's capacity to use the analytic space provided for him (Kächele, 1983). Other variables, such as computer-assisted measurement of anxiety themes, show rapid session-to-session fluctuations, but mean averages point to moves that correlate with clinically rated transference patterns (Kächele, 1988). There are other variables that demonstrate a cyclical pattern around a slowly moving average line, such as redundancy of the patient's speech, while the analyst's redundancy remains on a stable level (Kächele and Mergenthaler, 1984). There are still other grammatical variables, such as voice construction modes that exhibit quite idiosyncratic patterns within each of the four analytic cases, though all cases move from more passive to more active voice in the course of treatment (Beermann, 1983). We are able to identify patterns of vocabulary assimilation that discriminate between good and poor treatment outcomes (Hölzer et al., 1992a). In a similar manner, we also are able to study the subtle moves in interpersonal regulations as they become obvious by the use of personal pronouns (Schaumburg, 1980).

The integration of findings of the diverse levels of our research model demands caution because there is no one-to-one relationship among the diverse levels. Still, we feel that breakdown of the complex clinical constructs into more easily measurable components of observation leads to refinement of clinical theories. This has been demonstrated in the study of Leuzinger-Bohleber and Kächele (1988) which demonstrated the change in diverse cognitive modules that were derived from Clippinger's (1977) artificial intelligence model. Compiling the changes on diverse planes, we could demonstrate how subtle change can be measured on a pivotal psychoanalytic concept, on patients' capacity to freely associate to their dreams (Leuzinger-Bohleber, 1987, 1989; Leuzinger-Bohleber and Kächele, 1985, 1988).

III. New Directions and Questions

Although we have tried quite a few ways of analyzing transference, it remains a major desideratum to improve on the measurement of this key concept of psychoanalysis. Having implemented a German version of Luborsky's CCRT measure

(Luborsky and Kächele, 1988), we did a preliminary data analysis of a case of short-term therapy (Kächele et al., 1990). Recently we modified the method by using a statistical contingency analysis on a very large sample of relationship episodes, which allowed us to identify seven "repetitive relationship patterns" (Dahlbender et al., in press). As a result, we are now ready to take up the analysis of transference in long-term analytic cases by measuring the contingent distribution of the triangular "wish, response of the other, and response of the self" conception of transference. Based on our recent work, we expect that the concept of multiple "central relationship patterns" is a more appropriate model for long-term treatment transference development than the notion of a single CCRT.

Parallel to this work, we continue to work on the stabilization of the frame method as a more demanding and theoretically more satisfying variant of the widely shared core principles methodology (Teller and Dahl, in press; Dahl et al., 1992). With this approach, we hope to demonstrate the usefulness of the frame method for testing the structural congruence hypothesis between early childhood memories and dreams during psychoanalytic treatment (Holzer et al., 1992b). We likewise hope to improve our modeling of thematic foci.

Research on countertransference still lies ahead. Though enacted countertransference has been identified by linguistic correlates (Dahl et al., 1978) nonverbalized counterreaction may be undetectable on a tape. Therefore, new tools for tapping these affective involvements are needed. The analyst's mood may be detectable in the prosodic features of analyst's speech, a promising field which we believe has not yet found its appropriate methodology. It is clear that these phenomena can be approached only by high-powered computer-assisted tools. By recording the analytic structure dialogue one is able to capture major thematic and structural developments as they surface in the verbal exchange. With regard to the recording of the covert processes in the analyst's and in the patient's mind during and in between the sessions, we still have a long way to go.

A methodological avenue has been opened by Meyer's method of capturing the analyst's feelings and thoughts during the sessions by immediate retroreporting and recording in a freely associative manner after the session (Meyer, 1988). This line of work is also being pursued by means of a tape-recorded interview by a colleague analyst who reviews line by line. We hope to detect the psychology of interpretation as a sequential strategy (H. König and Kächele, in preparation).

Final Remarks

Research findings have to be replicated in order to prove their value. So far, we know only about the effects of our investigations on our own psychoanalytic thinking and actions and on those who are close to our work. It is also true that nothing has changed our psychoanalytic thinking and actions more than the public exposure to friendly critics and critical friends. We say this in order to encourage other psychoanalysts to open the privacy of their clinical work by letting it be scrutinized by others. We recommend the training of researchers who are also trained as clinicians and are able to identify with both tasks (Bowlby, 1979). Reform of psychoanalytic training is needed and in demand (Thomä, 1993). We need analysts and researchers with the ability to support long-term commitment with slow progress. Systematic investigations are dependent on teams supported by institutions which promote cooperation between analysts in practice and full-time researchers. Implementation of such research will move psychoanalysis out of its contemporary crisis.

REFERENCES

BEERMANN, S. (1983). *Linguistische Analyse psychoanalytischer Therapiedialoge unter besonderer Berücksichtigung passivischer Sprechmuster.* Universität Hamburg, Diplom-Arbeit.

BOWLBY, J. (1979). Psychoanalysis as art and science. *Int. Rev. Psychoanal.*, 6:3–14.
CLIPPINGER, J. (1977). *Meaning and Discourse: A Computer Model of Psychoanalytic Speech and Cognition.* Baltimore, MD: Johns Hopkins Univ. Press.
COLBY, K. M. & STOLLER, R. J. (1991). *Cognitive Science and Psychoanalysis.* Hillsdale, NJ: Analytic Press.
COMPTON, A. (1990). Psychoanalytic process. *Psychoanal. Q.*, 59:585–598.
DAHL, H. (1972). A quantitative study of psychoanalysis. In *Psychoanalysis and Contemporary Science*, ed. R. R. Holt & E. Peterfreund. New York: Macmillan, pp. 237–257.
—— (1974). The measurement of meaning in psychoanalysis by computer analysis of verbal context. *J. Amer. Psychoanal. Assn.*, 22:37–57.
—— (1983). On the definition and measurement of wishes. In *Empirical Studies of Psychoanalytic Theory*, Vol. 1, ed. J. Masling. Hillsdale, NJ: Erlbaum, pp. 39–67.
—— HÖLZER, M. & BERRY, J. W. (1992). *How to Classify Emotions for Psychotherapy Research.* Ulm, Germany: Ulmer Textbank.
—— TELLER, V., MOSS, D. & TRUJILLO, M. (1978). Countertransference examples of the syntactic expression of warded-off contents. *Psychoanal. Q.*, 47:339–363.
DAHLBENDER, R., ALBANI, C., POKORNY, D. & KÄCHELE, H. (in press). Central relationship pattern—a structural version of the CCRT. *Psychother. Res.*
DEWALD, P. A. (1972). *The Psychoanalytic Process: A Case Illustration.* New York: Basic Books.
FREUD, S. (1913). On beginning the treatment. *S. E.*, 12.
FURSTENAU, P. (1977). Praxeologische Grundlagen der Psychoanalyse. In *Klinische Psychologie*, ed. L. J. Pongratz. Zurich: Hogrefe, pp. 847–888.
GERGEN, K. J. (1985). The social constructionist movement in modern psychology. *Amer. Psychol.*, 40:266–275.
GILL, M. M. (1991). Indirect suggestion: a response to Oremland's *Interpretation and Interaction*. In *Interpretation and Interaction, Psychoanalysis or Psychotherapy*, by J. D. Oremland. Hillsdale, NJ: Analytic Press, pp. 137–163.
—— SIMON, J., FINK, G., ENDICOTT, N. A. & PAUL, I. H. (1968). Studies in audio-recorded psychoanalysis: I. General considerations. *J. Amer. Psychoanal. Assn.*, 16:230–244.
GRÜNZIG, H. (1983). Themes of anxiety as psychotherapeutic process variables. In *Methodology in Psychotherapy Research*, ed. R. Minsel & W. Herff. Frankfurt: Lang, pp. 135–142.
—— & KÄCHELE, H. (1978). Zur differenzierung psychoanalytischer Angstkonzepte. Ein empirischer Beitrag zur automatischen Klassifikation klinischen Materials (On the automatic differentiation of clinical material). *Z. Klin. Psychol.*, 7:1–17.
HANLY, C. (1992). Inductive reasoning in clinical psychoanalysis. *Int. J. Psychoanal.*, 73:293–301.
HOFFMAN, I. Z. (1991). Toward a social-constructivist view of the psychoanalytic situation. *Psychoanal. Dialog.*, 1:74–105.
HOHAGE, R. & KÜBLER, J. C. (1988). The emotional insight rating scale. In *Psychoanalytic Process Research Strategies*, ed. H. Dahl, H. Kächele & H. Thomä. New York: Springer, pp. 243–255.
HÖLZER, M., KÄCHELE, H., MERGENTHALER, E. & LUBORSKY, L. (1992a). Vocabulary measures for the evaluation of therapy outcome: studying

the transcripts from the Penn Psychotherapy Project (PPP). *Psychother. Res.*, unpublished.

―――― ZIMMERMANN, V. & KÄCHELE, H. (1992b). The frame method and structural congruence hypothesis between early childhood and dreams during psychoanalysis. Presented at the Annual Meeting of the Society for Psychotherapy.

ISAACS, S. (1939). Criteria for interpretation. *Int. J. Psychoanal.*, 20:853-880.

KÄCHELE, H. (1976). *Maschinelle Inhaltsanalyse in der psychoanalytischen Prozessforschung* (Computerized content analysis in psychoanalytic process research). Medizinische Habilitationsschrift, Universität Ulm: PSZ-Verlag Ulm, 1986.

―――― (1983). Verbal activity level of therapists in initial interviews and longterm psychoanalysis. In *Methodology in Psychotherapy Research*, ed. R. W. Minsel & W. Herff. Frankfurt: Lang, pp. 125-129.

―――― (1986). Validating psychoanalysis: what methods for what task. *Behav. Brain Sci.*, 9:244.

―――― (1988). Clinical and scientific aspects of the Ulm process model of psychoanalysis. *Int. J. Psychoanal.*, 69:65-73.

―――― (1990). From clinical investigation to systematic empirical research. The Ulm Psychoanalytic Process Research Program—a twenty-year review. *Psychother. Res.*, 2:1-15.

―――― DENGLER, D., ECKERT, R. & SCHNEKENBURGER, S. (1990). Veränderung des zentralen Beziehungskonfliktes durch eine Kurztherapie. *Psychother. Med. Psychol.*, 40:178-185.

―――― EHLERS, W. & HÖLZER, M. (1991a). Experiment und Empirie in der Psychoanalyse. In *Perspektiven der Psychiatrie. Forschung—Diagnostik—Therapie*, ed. F. Schneider, M. Bartels, H. Gaertner & K. Foerster. Stuttgart: Gustav Fischer, pp. 129-142.

―――― & MERGENTHALER, E. (1983). Computer-aided analysis of psychotherapeutic discourse. In *Methodology in Psychotherapy Research*, ed. R. Minsel & W. Herff. Frankfurt: Lang, pp. 116-161.

―――― ―――― (1984). Auf dem Wege zur computerunterstützen Textanalyse in der psychotherapeutischen Prozessforschung (On the way to computer-assisted text analysis in psychotherapeutic process research). In *Psychotherapie: Makro/Mikroperspektive*, ed. U. Baumann. Göttingen: Verlag für Psychologie Dr. Hogrefe, C. J., pp. 223-239.

―――― SCHMIEDER, B. & SCHINKEL, A. (1991b). *Fokus und Übertragung* (Focus and Transference). University of Ulm, Dept. Psychotherapy, unpublished manuscript.

―――― & SCHAUMBERG, C. (1975). Veränderungen des Sprachinhaltes in einem psychoanalytischen Prozess. *Schweiz. Arch. Neurol. Neurochirugie Psychiat.*, 116:197-228.

―――― RUBERG, W. & GRÜNZIG, H. (1988). Audio-recordings of the psychoanalytic dialogue: scientific, clinical and ethical problems. In *Psychoanalytic Process Research Strategies*, ed. H. Dahl, H. Kächele & H. Thomä. New York: Springer, pp. 179-194.

KNAPP, P. H.; GREENBERG, R. P.; PEARLMAN, C. H.; COHEN, M.; KANTROWITZ, J. & SASHIN, J. (1975). Clinical measurement in psychoanalysis: an approach. *Psychoanal. Q.*, 44:404-430.

KOHUT, H. (1979). The two analyses of Mr. Z. *Int. J. Psychoanal.*, 60:3-27.

KUBIE, L. (1958). Research into the process of supervision in psychoanalysis. *Psychoanal. Q.*, 27:226–236.
LEUZINGER-BOHLEBER, M. (1987). *Veränderung kognitiver Prozesse in Psychoanalysen. Vol. 1: Eine hypothesengenerierende Einzelfallstudie.* Berlin: Springer.
────── (1989). *Veränderung kognitiver Prozesse in Psychoanalysen. Vol. 2: Eine gruppenstatistische Untersuchung.* Berlin: Springer.
────── & KÄCHELE, H. (1985). Veränderte Wahrnehmung von Traumgestalten im psychoanalytischen Prozess. In *Perspektiven der Psychotherapieforschung*, ed. D. Czogalik, W. Ehlers & R. Teufel. Freiburg: Hochschulverlag, pp. 94–119.
────── (1988). From Calvin to Freud: using an artificial intelligence model to investigate cognitive changes during psychoanalysis. In *Psychoanalytic Process Research Strategies*, ed. H. Dahl, H. Kächele & H. Thomä. New York: Springer, pp. 291–306.
LOLAS, F., MERGENTHALER, E. & KÄCHELE, H. (1983). Interactional style of four therapists. In *Methodology in Psychotherapy Research*, ed. W. Minsel & W. Herff. Frankfurt: Lang, pp. 142–149.
LUBORSKY, L. (1984). *Principles of Psychoanalytic Psychotherapy. A Manual for Supportive-Expressive Treatment.* New York: Basic Books.
MEISSNER, W. W. (1983). Values in the psychoanalytic situation. *Psychoanal. Inq.*, 3:577–598.
MERGENTHALER, E. (1985). *Textbank Systems. Computer Science Applied in the Field of Psychoanalysis.* New York: Springer.
────── (1986). *Die Transkription von Gesprächen.* Ulm: Ulmer Textbank.
────── & KÄCHELE, H. (1985). Changes of latent meaning structures in psychoanalysis. *Sprache und Datenverarbeitung*, 9:21–28.
────── ────── (1988). The Ulm Textbank management system: a tool for psychotherapy research. In *Psychoanalytic Process Research Strategies*, ed. H. Dahl, H. Kächele & H. Thomä. Berlin, Heidelberg, New York: Springer, pp. 195–212.
────── ────── (1991). The Ulm Textbank Research Program. In *International Psychotherapy Research Programs*, ed. L. Beutler & M. Crago. New York: Pergamon Press, pp. 219–225.
────── & STINSON, C. H. (1992). Psychotherapy Transcriptions Standards. *Psychother. Res.*, 2:58–75.
MEYER, A. E. (1988). What makes psychoanalysts tick? In *Psychoanalytic Process Research Strategies*, ed. H. Dahl, H. Kächele & H. Thomä. New York: Springer, pp. 273–290.
────── (1990). Psychoanalytische Forschung für das Ende des Jahrhunderts. In *Empirische Forschung in der Psychoanalyse*. Frankfurt: Sigmund-Freud Institut, pp. 8–26.
────── (1992). Nieder mit der Fallgeschichte / es lebe der Behandlungsbericht. In *Die Kunst der Fallgeschichte*, ed. F. Denecke & U. Stuhr. Heidelberg: Asanger.
NEUDERT, L. & HOHAGE, R. (1988). Different types of suffering during a psychoanalysis. In *Psychoanalytic Process Research Studies*, ed. H. Dahl, H. Kächele & H. Thomä. New York: Springer.
PULVER, S. E. (1987). Epilogue to "How theory shapes technique: perspectives on a clinical study." *Psychoanal. Inq.*, 7:289–299.
SANDLER, J. (1976). Countertransference and role-responsiveness. *Int. Rev. Psychoanal.*, 3:43–47.

—— (1983). Reflections on some relations between psychoanalytic concepts and psychoanalytic practice. *Int. J. Psychoanal.*, 64:35–45.
—— DREHER, A. U. & DREWS, S. (1991). An approach to conceptual research in psychoanalysis illustrated by a consideration of psychic trauma. *Int. Rev. Psychoanal.*, 18:133–142.
SCHAUMBURG, C. (1980). *Personal pronomina im psychoanalytischen Prozess*. Doctoral Dissertation, University of Ulm.
—— KÄCHELE, H. & THOMÄ, H. (1974). Methodische und statistische Probleme bei Einzelfallstudien in der psychoanalytischen Forschung. *Psyche*, 28:353–374.
SCHORS, R. & KÄCHELE, H. (1982). Computer-aided content analysis in the study of body concepts. Presented at European Congress of Psychosomatic Research, Noorwijkerhout, Holland.
SIMON, J.; FINK, G.; ENDICOTT, N. A.; PAUL, I. & GILL, M. M. (1968). *Psychoanalytic research and the concept of analytic work*. Unpublished Manuscript, Brooklyn, New York: Department of Psychiatry, Brookdale Hospital Center.
SPENCE, D. P. (1968). The processing of meaning in psychotherapy: some links with psycholinguistics and information theory. *Behav. Sci.*, 13:349–361.
—— (1969). Computer measurement of process and content in psychoanalysis. *Trans. N.Y. Acad. Sci.*, 31:828–841.
—— (1986). When interpretation masquerades as explanation. *J. Amer. Psychoanal. Assn.*, 34:3–22.
STRENGER, C. (1991). *Between Hermeneutics and Science. An Essay on the Epistemology of Psychoanalysis, Psychol. Issues*, Monogr. 59. Madison, CT: Int. Univ. Press.
SWAAN, A. DE (1980). On the sociogenesis of the psychoanalytic situation. *Psychoanal. Contemp. Thought*, 3:381–413.
TELLER, V. & DAHL, H. (in press). The characteristics, identification, and application of FRAMES. *Psychother. Res.*
THOMÄ, H. (1985). The role of the clinician in psychoanalytic process research. Presented at International Workshop for Empirical Research in Psychoanalysis, Ulm.
—— (1993). Training analysis and psychoanalytic education: proposals for reform. *Annual Psychoanal.*, 21:3–75.
—— GRÜNZIG, H. J. & KÄCHELE, H. (1976). Das Konsensusproblem in der Psychoanalyse. *Psyche*, 30:978–1027.
—— & HOUBEN, A. (1967). Uber die Validierung psychoanalytischer Therien durch die Untersuchung von Deutungsaktionen. *Psyche*, 21:664–692.
—— & KÄCHELE, H. (1973). *Psychoanalytische Verlaufsforschung, Teil B*. DFG-Bericht, unpublished.
—— —— (1975). Problems of metascience and methodology in clinical psychoanalytic research. *Annual Psychoanal.*, 3:49–119.
—— —— (1987). *Psychoanalytic Practice. Vol. 1: Principles*. New York: Springer.
—— —— (1992). *Psychoanalytic Practice. Vol. 2: Clinical Studies*. New York: Springer.

WIRTZ, E. M. & KÄCHELE, H. (1983). Emotive aspects of therapeutic language: a pilot study on ver-adjective-ratio. In *Methodology in Psychotherapy Research*, ed. W. R. Minsel & W. Herff. Frankfurt: Lang, pp. 130–135.

DISCUSSION: NEW UNDERSTANDINGS OF PSYCHOANALYTIC PROCESS

DONALD P. SPENCE, PH.D.

As PSYCHOANALYSIS PREPARES to enter its second century, our biggest task, it would seem, is to turn our clinical wisdom—largely stored in the soft tissue of living analysts—into accessible knowledge. As Teller and Dahl make clear, we have no fundamental knowledge of underlying patterns and structures. We are at the same point as the medical establishment found itself at the turn of the century: we need to develop a basic science of psychoanalysis that can be used as a foundation for our clinical wisdom. When wisdom is turned into knowledge in this manner, it stands apart from the clinical moment and carries a truth that is not conditioned by the specific needs of the patient and analyst in the midst of a particular clinical encounter. Just as medicine now rests on hundreds of chemical and biological facts that apply equally to all forms of life, so we need to ground psychoanalysis on a set of principles that go beyond the specific clinical happening. We need to build bridges between the analytic "conversation" and other kinds of two-person discourse; put another way, we need to study the characteristics of this conversation as a particular genre, and learn the details of its landscape and the particular properties of speech that obtain when one of the speakers is largely out of sight, relatively silent, and does not seem to conform to conventional conversational rules. Moving to more clinical issues, we need to translate the many properties of the analytic surface into more usable language so that we can identify which features of the patient's speech cause the analyst to respond; which feature of an interpretation can bring about structural change; what kinds of hours seem to implement good analytic work, and what kinds of hours stand in the way. Above all, we need to move from metaphor—our favorite language—to something less ambiguous and more ostensive—that is, to pointer words which have a more specific meaning than *analytic surface* or *Monday crust.*

Against this background, we can read the papers in this section and question: (1) What do they contribute to the basic science of psychoanalysis that seems to be free of the immediate clinical moment? (2) What evidence do they summarize to support these findings?

The Recorded Case of Mrs. C.

Before either of these questions is addressed, we need to describe a piece of data-gathering which, although not reported in this volume, stands as the touchstone for more than half the studies described in this section. It is probably no exaggeration to say that had this case not existed, these studies would not have been possible and this section could not have been written. What makes Mrs. C. a landmark case is that (1) it is a complete, naturally terminated, clinically successful, supervised analysis running some 1000 hours with the patient being seen five times a week (supervision normally took place on Monday morning, before the Monday hour); (2) it was conducted by an experienced analyst; (3) all hours have been recorded and a small sample of these have been computer-coded; (4) the transcribing has been painstakingly carried out with the result that all proper names and identifying information have been disguised and a uniform convention used to designate pauses, laughter, crying, and other paralinguistic markers.[1] Seventy hours of the case, sampled from each of the six years of treatment, have been scored on the Jones Psychotherapy Q-Set (see below). Because they are computer-readable, they have also been scored

[1]Of particular importance is the fact that the coding conventions have been *systematically* applied; thus *every* instance of a sigh is enclosed in parentheses, every pause greater than a certain length is indicated by a number indicating elapsed time, etc. Computer analysis of the case would not have been possible without this uniformity which reflects an inspired devotion to detail, largely hidden from view.

on a variety of measures of the patterns of the patient's speech (Spence et al., 1993, 1994). Other investigators have studied these and other parts of the case and some of these findings will be described below. Long overdue is a complete accounting of the many studies of Mrs. C. which would bring together the separate findings and weave an integrated story of how they fit with our clinical understanding of the case.

Mrs. C. was a married social worker in her late twenties who had sought treatment because of lack of sexual responsiveness, difficulty in experiencing pleasurable feelings, and low self-esteem. She was the second of four children from a professional family. At the start of the analysis, she had been married less than two years to a successful businessman. Partway through treatment (during the third year), she gave birth to her first child, a daughter; during this period, the analysis was interrupted for about six weeks. This fortuitous event gives investigators a chance to search the patient's associations for early derivatives of conception and pregnancy, her later reactions to the experience of childbirth, and how these events become transformed into such other aspects of the clinical material as dreams and transference fantasies.

When hours are coded by days of the week, it becomes possible to carry out sophisticated studies of sequence (using time-series analysis and related measures) and learn something about the clinical parameters of the five-day analytic week. Spence et al. (1994) found that in a subset of 70 hours, sampled across the life of the case, the number of interventions made by the analyst was increasingly correlated with a measure of patient-analyst interaction (CORtrans) as the case progressed toward termination. This measure indexes the co-occurrence of such pronoun pairs as you/me, you/I, etc., and reflects the extent to which the patient is including references to the analyst in her associations. As co-occurrence rate increases, so does the number of interventions. When this correlation was examined across the five-day week, it was found to rise from a nonsignificant level (near zero) on Monday, to a peak on Wednesday, and then fall to zero again on Friday, suggesting that analytic work seems to follow a natural rhythm during the conventional five-day week. Other studies need to be directed to the way in which the Monday hour (which always followed a two-day interruption) differs from other sessions; the way in which the Friday hour evokes the threat of separation; and other ways in which the natural rhythm of the week is expressed in the form and content of the patient's associations and the analyst's interventions. As five-day-a-week treatments become ever more difficult to arrange, this case and its unexplored sequential information takes on increasing significance.

More generally, the case makes possible a comparison of different models of treatment. Weiss and his colleagues have claimed that what they term the "higher mental functioning hypothesis" (HMFH) provides a more complete account of the clinical facts than conventional theory, which is supposed to rest on the "automatic functioning hypothesis" (AFH). Comparisons have been made of limited sections of Mrs. C. (hours 41–100). On the other hand, Caston and his colleagues, also looking at the early hours of the case (sessions 1–100), claim that AFH is superior to HMFH. It should be noted that although Caston takes pains to tell us that while the interventions under study were selected randomly, it is still possible that the hours actually studied were not the same as the hours studied by Weiss and his team.

What is needed to reconcile this apparent contradiction is a more exhaustive comparison which would apply both measures to the full set of hours of the case. Is there evidence for the superiority of one hypothesis over the other, or does each provide its own particular account, with the effects conditioned by such local variables as the nature of the transference, the place of the hour in the course of treatment, the nature of the preceding hour, and its recency in real time? Before too long, it should be possible to assemble a master chart of the complete course of Mrs. C. that includes all the studies to date and illustrates which findings are specific to local effects and which findings apply equally to all hours. Different phases of the case could be illustrated with relevant clinical vignettes to bring out more clearly the traditional dimensions of the treatment and provide a context for the newer measures. When and if the full case becomes computer-readable, it would then be possible for an interested investigator to identify those portions of the treatment that meet his or her particular interests, and study the hours in question using his or her preferred tools, adding the new findings to the master chart.

When all measures have been applied to all hours, it will be possible to pose a series of comparative questions. Is there evidence that some of the Teller and Dahl FRAMES, for example, also serve as Weiss-style "tests"? Do FRAMES and Weiss tests tend to be correlated with the specific patient and analyst variables scored in the Jones Q-set? When the patient "passes a test," what is the flavor of the therapeutic alliance and the shape of the resistance, in traditional clinical terms? To date, each investigator has tended to cultivate his or her own garden, pretty much ignoring formulations from other camps, and even though a single analysand (Mrs. C.) is the common subject of many studies, it is often hard to tell, from the different descriptions, that it is always the same patient being examined. In similar fashion, it is often hard to tell that the concepts being suggested (for example, "passing a test") have much in common with the average analyst's understanding of his or her day-to-day activity. Not only do bridges need to be built between researchers, but links have to be reestablished between the researcher's conception of analytic process and the average clinician's understanding of what happens during treatment. We shall return to this question in a later section.

Stand-Alone Findings

Several discoveries stand out as candidates for matters of fact that are not tied to any particular clinical moment. Teller and Dahl hypothesize that FRAMES "are the plots of the stories that patients in psychotherapy [and presumably analysis] tell about their repetitive, maladaptive behaviors." We are told that FRAMES (an acronym for Fundamental Repetitive and Maladaptive Emotional Structures) can be reliably identified by first charting an initial prototype and then tracking the subsequent instantiations or exemplars across the course of treatment. A close analysis of Mrs. C. revealed a set of five FRAMES in Hour 5 which continued to appear during the middle section of the case (a section identified by Jones and Windholz, 1990, as the height of the transference neurosis), but then disappeared before the end of treatment was reached. This finding suggests that FRAME evolution may be closely related to such conventional concepts as analytic work and analytic surface, transference and resistance, and that these new measures may provide us with more specific tools for analyzing the development of a case. But despite the frequent use of this tool, it is far from clear how FRAMES are established in practice or where the interested researcher can go to learn how to discover them. The procedure is not systematically described in the paper published in this volume, nor is reference made to a complete account of the procedure.

Another stand-alone finding has been identified by Weiss and his co-workers—namely, the patient's tendency to continuously test his or her pathogenic beliefs in specific interactions with the therapist according to an organized (but unconscious) plan of attack. Weiss hypothesizes that if such a test is "passed successfully," the patient will feel less anxious and more secure, more insightful and less inhibited, although what is meant by *passing* is not immediately obvious. Tests of this kind have been reported in the case of Mrs. C. by at least four different investigators (Gassner, Silberschatz, Bush, and Caston; for references, see Weiss, this volume) and in three different psychotherapies (but to date, in no other analyses). The exact nature of a test and how it can be extracted from the clinical material is not clear from the description, nor are we told anything very useful about measurement reliability or the training of the judge. It may well be that for Weiss and other workers in the field, the ability to spot a test of this kind and decide whether or not it succeeds is a relatively simple matter of clinical judgment, but this ability tends to be projected onto the reader where it clearly does not belong. Once again, the interested investigator has no way of knowing how to put this new knowledge to immediate use, either in his or her clinical work or in the service of further research.

Significantly more accessible to the average clinician/investigator is the measurement instrument called the Psychotherapy Process Q-set (PQS), developed by Jones and already featured in a number of studies of both analytic and psychotherapy cases. The Q-set is user-friendly, first of all, because it applies standard clinical terms to the measurement of the therapy hour or smaller subsection; as a result, findings from this instrument can be quickly translated into more conventional clinical formulations. The 100 items in the PQS are divided equally among patient behavior, therapist behavior, and their interaction; moreover, the items are intentionally worded in highly specific language (e.g., "patient has difficulty understanding the therapist's comments") which appreciably improves reliability.

Have any context-free findings emerged from this instrument? Some early data suggest that certain interventions, identified by the PQS, may bring about an increase in associative freedom, and that the effect can be tracked across consecutive hours in the treatment (Spence et al., 1993). More recent studies, still unpublished, divided the Mrs. C. case into blocks of shared and unshared hours (on the basis of pronoun co-occurrence) and found that when a given intervention was made during the shared hours, it had significantly more impact on the patient, resulting in a significant increase in certain markers of patient distress, than when it occurred during the unshared hours. Could this be an approach to the understanding of when interpretations are mutative and when they are not? It was largely the usability and reliability of the PQS (and the recorded analysis of Mrs. C.) that made these studies possible.

The report from the Ulm research team (Kächele and Thomä) focuses more on goals and procedures than on findings. More than most groups, they are sensitive to (a) the need to relate the more fine-grained analyses (what they refer to as C- and D-level studies) to clinical descriptions (called A- and B-level studies), (b) the growing necessity to use the computer to manage the huge amount of data present in a complete analysis. "The tension," as they put it, "between clinical meaningfulness and objectification cannot be creatively solved by using one approach only"; nevertheless, their report largely fails to bring together the findings from the different approaches. Granted their caution that there is no one-to-one correspondence across the different levels, it would still be of interest to know the clinical context for such measures as high redundancy in patient and therapist language, change in body concept, and change in use of personal pronouns. To what extent are the D-level measures also monitored—perhaps outside awareness—by the listening analyst? To what extent do the long-term trends detected by computer correspond to important turning points in the case under study? The curious clinician needs to know how to fit the more specific findings into a more conventional psychoanalytic point of view; without this attempt, they run the risk of being seen as the highly reliable outpourings of a research machine that has lost sight of the patient.

Caston's paper presents us with the surprising finding—briefly noted above—that data from the first 100 hours of Mrs. C. can be explained more readily by the classical hypothesis (AFH) than the control mastery hypothesis (HMFH). Does this apparent contradiction with Weiss rest on the fact that different hours were sampled? Other studies (e.g., Jones and Windholz, 1990; Spence et al., 1993) have shown the importance of time factors in process research; if Caston's sample of hours came either earlier or later in the case than Weiss's sample, the difference in findings might be easily explained. Whatever the cause, the difference between the two sets of findings marks one of the rare occasions of direct conflict in psychoanalytic research, and it should be a cause for celebration (not the reverse) because it suggests that different groups are starting to converge on similar issues—a sign that we may be approaching the status of a real science.

Stand-alone findings from the Horowitz group are hard to evaluate because, first, they rest on process notes—not the best source of data—of only three analytic cases (Mrs. C., evidently, was not among them); and second, because it is not clear how many of the psychotherapy findings—the bulk of their results—will also apply to analytic cases. One clue that bridges might be found appears when we are told that the RRMC method (an acronym for Role-Relationship Models Configuration) "helped [psychoanalytic candidates] to clearly specify varieties of transference reactions in each case." The Horowitz group now needs to apply their method to all or part of Mrs. C. In the process, they could build on their current multimedia data acquisition system, presently tailored to process psychotherapy data, which allows them to look simultaneously at audiorecordings, videorecordings, and physiological measures. If part or all of this system could be extended to the study of Mrs. C., we would have a better idea how much their theory and method add new insights to our understanding.

Overview

What can the busy clinician or the curious researcher learn from this array of findings? Long-term prospects seem more promising than short-term results. Convergence on the same body of data is beginning to take place, but not until all researchers begin to focus on the same case or at least the same set of hours, shall we have a way of evaluating the comparative contributions of each method and its supporting rationale. But by the same token, many investigators now seem ready to take such a step, and we can anticipate an almost exponential increase in understanding once we see connections made between the different approaches.

Also disappointing is that argument by authority (or by conviction) is still the prevailing means of persuasion: we are *told*, not *shown*, that FRAMES can be reliably discovered, that "tests" of the analyst follow unconscious plans, and that RRMC can be identified in some systematic manner. These claims may be true, but they can hardly qualify as research findings until the underlying procedures enter the public domain and give the interested reader a chance to try out the new recipe. The acid test is: can an independent group, using the appropriate procedures and instruments, discover the same five FRAMES in Hour 5 of Mrs. C. as were reported by the Dahl team? Can an independent group, looking at the first 100 hours of Mrs. C., discover the same pattern of testing as was reported by the Weiss team or the Caston team? The prevalence of acronyms tempts the reader into thinking that the underlying procedures are objective, reliable, and travel easily from group to group, but there may be no correlation between a catchy label and the test it represents. It would be tragic if the acronym were nothing more than a rhetorical trick—a piece of word-magic that implies more than it can deliver.

Even when reliability is established and the procedures prove their claim to being useful tools, readily administered by any interested researcher, they will probably never enter the clinical *Zeitgeist* until they become integrated with the more usual run of clinical observations. Here is another reason to converge on Mrs. C.: as the clinical history of the case becomes better understood, the connection between traditional formulations and the newer methods will become easier to explain. If, for example, it is found that FRAMES change in some significant way after the birth of Mrs. C.'s baby, the new concept can be fitted into the traditional literature on ways in which pregnancy and childbirth change the analytic surface and the climate of the transference. If FRAMES are tracked across the five-day week, it becomes possible to understand how the sequence of the working week tends to shape the material and bring its own constraints to bear on the patient's associations.

When the analyst is found to "fail" a test, do some FRAMES tend to appear more than others, and do they relate in some manner to central problems of countertransference?

Until the research literature begins to include more traditional clinical language and speak to present-day clinical concerns, there is no reason why even the more curious clinician would want to read it. And although research-minded clinicians may be more tolerant of its special vocabulary, they tend to be impatient with arguments by authority, the failure to fully document procedures, and the tendency to let rhetoric (and acronyms) substitute for reliability. Particularly telling would be the report of an empirical finding that was not only reliable, but had significantly influenced an analyst's approach to a case—allowing him or her, for example, to find a more systematic way of judging when to make an intervention or how to frame an interpretation. Findings of this kind cannot so easily be ignored and would improve our claim to being both a real and a meaningful science.

REFERENCES

JONES, E. E. & WINDHOLZ, M. (1990). The psychoanalytic case study: toward a method for systematic inquiry. *J. Amer. Psychoanal. Assn.*, 38:985–1015.
SPENCE, D. P., DAHL, H. & JONES, E. (1993). Impact of interpretation on associative freedom. *J. Clin. Consult. Psychol.*, 61:395–402.
——— MAYES, L. C. & DAHL, H. (1994). Monitoring the analytic surface. *J. Amer. Psychoanal. Assn.*, 42:43–64.

DISCUSSION: A CLINICIAN'S COMMENTS ON EMPIRICAL STUDIES OF PSYCHOANALYSIS

JACOB A. ARLOW, M.D.

AT FIRST GLANCE IT WOULD appear that, for a psychoanalytic clinician like myself to comment on empirical research into the analytic process represents an exercise in temerity. I must confess to little or no training in the rigors of experimental design, and I have in the past made only a peripheral and methodologically constricted contribution to some empirical research into the psychoanalytic process. But as a practitioner I have been interested in the issue of validation of interpretation and of basic concepts of psychoanalysis. This interest, I am certain, I share with many colleagues who would welcome empirically founded, scientifically secure validation of fundamental psychoanalytic propositions as well as of technical procedures.

To be sure, not a few analysts look askance at research of this kind. Many regard such concerns as evidence of persistent doubt concerning the "truth" of psychoanalytic findings, and they feel that interest in such research represents an effort on the part of the researchers to repudiate some unacceptable knowledge about their own motivation, conscious or unconscious.

In addition, there are special features of the analyst's inner experience while he is at work processing the patient's material that tend to render issues of empirical confirmation irrelevant or at least peripheral to his interests. In previous communications (Arlow, 1979; 1993[1]), I delineated two aspects of the analyst's mental functioning as he proceeds from listening to interpretation. One part of the process, which I call the aesthetic

---

Professor of Clinical Psychiatry, New York University College of Medicine.
[1]Discussion of paper by M. Baranger on "The Mind of the Analyst: From Listening to Interpretation," presented at International Psychoanalytical Congress, Amsterdam, July 27.

phase, depends on empathy, intuition, and introspection. The other aspect is a cognitive one, which depends on rationally assembled, methodologically disciplined conclusions from the data of observation. Scientifically, what is intuitively apprehended should be cognitively validatable, but for the most part the analyst at work functions like an artist at the empathic and intuitive level. Every analyst has had the experience of some moment of seemingly clairvoyant intuition, an experience which engendered in him that aesthetic sense of awe which Keats described *On First Looking into Chapman's Homer*:

Then felt I like some watcher of the skies
When a new planet swims into his ken.

or that Greenson (1967), in less elegant terms, described as the "ah-ha" reaction. Many analysts are ready to accept such experiences as self-validating confirmation of the truths of their particular insights, as well as of the fundamentals of psychoanalysis. Even in the physical sciences, in those areas where theory building is difficult and methodology uncertain, some scientists will support certain theories because these theories appeal to their aesthetic sense, because they are "elegant."

On the other hand, there are many analysts who despair of any possibility that empirical studies can establish the validity of psychoanalytic concepts. Especially for those who have received intensive training in the physical sciences, the obstacles to authentic empirical validation seem insurmountable. Many observers, within and outside of psychoanalysis, have long challenged the scientific status of psychoanalysis, but even Waelder (1962), who elucidated the scientific fundamentals on which psychoanalysis is based, did not consider the possibility of empirical research studies into the psychoanalytic process. For him, as for many others, it would appear, the psychoanalytic situation was laboratory enough to test and establish the principles of psychoanalysis.

If empirical investigators in psychoanalysis aspire to the certainty characteristic of the results of research in the physical sciences, they are bound to be disappointed. Physicists start with a number of advantages. They share a common language and they subscribe to agreed-upon standards of measurement of the essential ingredients with which they deal. Analysts, on the other hand, do not share a common language, and all too often, in international and even national scientific exchanges, the individual has to translate the concepts of other analysts into terms that are comprehensible to him. We are rather fortunate in this respect, therefore, that the empirical studies that form the core of this volume emanate from a group of disciplined researchers, who more or less communicate with each other in a language of common concepts and terms, and who share with each other the basic observations, the raw data of their work.

In psychoanalysis, life events change the context and therefore the meaning of observations. Such variables are impossible to control. In designing his research methods, the physical scientist is in a better position to manage this difficulty, the problem of multiple variables. Investigators in the biological sciences are less able to do so and this problem of methodology becomes increasingly difficult in the social sciences, in psychology, and, above all, in psychoanalysis. Thus, it behooves the psychoanalytic researcher to limit the dimensions of the issues under investigation, to reduce them to manageable proportions.

In any empirical investigation, methodology is paramount, and this constitutes the severest challenge to psychoanalytic research. The distinction between observations and data must be kept clear. Observations are a record of experience; data are elements of experience that relate to a specific hypothesis, to the questions posed to the observations. As we all know, the records of analytic experience are notoriously uneven and unreliable. In clinical practice, record-keeping is as a rule haphazard. Even when meticulously written down, process notes constitute only a partial record of the experience, a record that has been consciously and unconsciously edited. In the psychoanalytic literature, most clinical reports are based on relatively current material, and it is rare for the practicing analyst to refer back to notes that were put down, however carefully, months or years back. In the meantime, the context of the material has changed and the analyst, inevitably influenced by the goal of therapeutic progress, may attend selectively to certain specific elements when evaluating the data. It must have been an intuitive appreciation of these factors that influenced Freud to warn against formulating one's understanding of a case prematurely; he recommended waiting until the treatment had been completed before doing so. This does not mean, however, that there are not certain questions of a specific or restricted nature that may be addressed during the course of treatment.

The solution to some of these problems now has become possible by virtue of two technological developments that seem indispensable for empirical studies of psychoanalysis. They are instruments for recording sessions and the computer. In themselves, they do not solve any problems concerning psychoanalytic principles or technique. What they do, first of all, is make available a data base that can serve as a common experience, a common set of observations for independent observers to study. For many analysts the introduction of recording instruments into the treatment situation may seem an assault on the fundamental aspects of the psychoanalytic experience, a violation of confidentiality, privacy, intimacy, and spontaneity. Some analysts have even challenged whether a psychoanalytic process can eventuate under such circumstances. One may be reassured that certain specific safeguards may be instituted, particularly concerning the issue of confidentiality, but conviction about the authenticity of the analytic nature of a treatment that has been recorded, I believe, can come only to those who have had the experience of listening to such records over a long period of time.

The primary virtue of the computer in this research resides in its ability to store vast amounts of information, e.g., the complete record of an analysis, and to be able on command to retrieve those segments of the record the researcher requires to do his work. The computer cannot think. It follows the commands of the investigator to pick up relevant sequences, common facts, configurations of components, patterns of relationships, and other elements in keeping with certain markers delineated by the investigator. Accordingly, each investigator's concept of the psychoanalytic process gets built into the programming of the computer. The questions posed to the computer have to be clearly delineated and unambiguous. These considerations behoove the investigator once again to consider problems for study that can be sharply delineated, i.e., that fall into the realm of manageability.

To what extent the several accounts of work described in this volume have proved successful in this regard remains a subject for closer study. What is notable is that, in practically every instance, the researchers have attempted to design their methodology in terms of some basic concept, an organizing theme for the specific issues to be addressed. For purposes of convenience, some of the investigators have labeled their organizing themes with appropriate acronyms. Thus, Dahl concentrates on Functional Repetitive and Maladaptive Emotional Structures, yielding the acronym FRAMES. Luborsky emphasizes Core Conflictual Relationship Themes (CCRT). For Weiss it is Automatic Functioning Hypothesis versus Higher Mental Functioning Hypothesis (AFH/HMFH). Strupp deals with Cyclical Maladaptive Patterns (CMP), while Horowitz emphasizes configurational analysis conceptualized as Role Relationship Model Configurations (RRMC). Some of the other researchers content themselves with less formalized but nonetheless methodologically appreciated emphasis on basic themes, such as the structural analysis of social behavior. Yet, as Dahl notes, "all of these are attempts to represent repetitive structures, yet no systematic work has been done to compare these approaches, and the researchers involved often seem to barely acknowledge the existence of alternative conceptions of the data." A volume of this nature, which brings together the work of several independent empirical investigators, could mark a first and important step toward a systematic study of the various approaches and their results. It is important, at this stage in the evolution of empirical investigation into the psychoanalytic experience, that some shared-in-common investigative approach should be agreed upon. Such a development is necessary in order to make possible comparative judgments.

From the very beginning of objective studies of the psychoanalytic process, reaching a consensus on the interpretation of the same clinical data has been difficult and often proved to be impossible. In a somewhat rueful spirit, several of the contributors to this volume recall their disappointment and confusion when as students they observed how their distinguished and experienced teachers saw the same objective data each in a different light. The crucial judgments about the meaning of clinical observations cannot be made by the computer. For this task, human beings must be enlisted to serve as interpreters, as judges. Concretely, they are asked to rate specific formulations of the meaning of certain texts or experiences. Accordingly, the same material must be available to the different raters and in standardized form. Critics may take exception to such an approach, arguing that this constitutes an attempt to study mental phenomena in isolation, to seek out constants or patterns independent of conflict, and to objectify the process of investigation to the study of conscious phenomena, independent of the intuitive and empathic factors so characteristic of human communication. Paradoxically, such criticisms seem to underplay the power of unconscious mental influences. After all, both conscious and unconscious influences operate when one reads a text, watches an audiovisual segment of an analysis, or listens to a patient. The raters are not automatons. Much depends on how the data are presented and on the nature of the specific questions posed to the raters.

Here one can raise the question that any attempt to establish the validity of intepretation on the basis of a high statistical indicator of probability represents a hidden form of verification by consensual validation. Sometimes in daily life spontaneous concatenations of events create situations in which consensual validation of unconscious tendencies seems absolutely reliable. Experiences of that sort may create a bias favoring verification by consensual validation. In a research setting, this is not permissible. There is an inherent challenge in the use of raters. The fact that they may agree unanimously or by a large majority on the significance of certain relationships by no means validates the conclusions reached. It may be more of a commentary on the nature and the selection of the raters. In one way or another, almost all of the authors who contributed to this volume were aware of this problem. Some took special pains to devise procedures to counteract such influences.

It should also be noted that in any ordinary experimental situation, the variables are manipulated in connection with the object to be observed, while the observers are considered to be the constant factors. When raters are part of the research design, they become the variables, and the texts of the recorded analysis or the analytic fragments are treated as the constants. In this regard, the contribution by Jones is notable insofar as his research design attempted to minimize the range of variability by narrowing the decisions the raters were called upon to make to a standard set of relevant choices. The use of the Q-sorting technique in this regard seems to be particularly felicitous.

Other investigators, like Caston, were well aware of the tendency for analysts to foist a favorite paradigm upon the data of observation and to interpret according to that paradigm. Caston and others took no exception to this tendency, but tried to use it instead as a base for determining the efficacy of certain favored technical procedures and their underlying rationale. Still others, e.g., Horowitz, formulated their own paradigm, built it into the research design, and are in process of devising measures to determine its applicability and validity.

What struck me as a clinician and as a teacher of psychoanalysis was that in these investigations, dominated by the pursuit of objectivity, no one suggested asking the judges or the raters how they arrived at their conclusions. What criteria did they use? Were their standards comparable? For example, Caston states, ". . . even if we establish the validity of a paradigm-centered formulation, we have yet not ruled out that the agreement merely derives—as an Artifact—from the readiness to perceive stereotypic patterns that override the text." I would reemphasize the last three words of that quotation. Override the text? The implications of that statement are clear, i.e., the meaning of certain texts may be unmistakable as well as unambiguous when the usual criteria for processing communication are applied to them. This may happen when one deals with simpler issues, lower levels of interpretation or conceptualization. Higher-level concepts, the more complicated ones, involve more complex, hierarchically ordered levels of observation. In empirical studies that use judges to interpret the data, the methodology of interpretation used by the judges must receive major attention in the research design. Some of the difficulties originate in that psychoanalytic treatment is based primarily on verbal communication, i.e., through language. Communication by speech can be notoriously ambiguous, and language is inherently metaphoric. Neither the computer nor physical science can tolerate ambiguity or appreciate metaphor. We can thus appreciate the efforts made by some of the researchers to overcome these daunting challenges.

The computer makes available a vast array of observable facts, culled in the course of a psychoanalysis. The question becomes: How can one use the information available to answer specific questions? It would be almost an impossible task to retrace step by step the course of a specific treatment. Several of the investigators have designed innovative approaches aimed at standardizing the various samplings of the data which are possible. These range from random samplings to standard samplings of fixed amounts at definite intervals in the course of the treatment, from segments of one session to segments of three or four contiguous sessions. Already it would seem that objective evidence has been accumulated to demonstrate the efficacy of therapeutic interventions, to measure the progress of treatment, and even to predict changes in the patient's psychic functioning, improvement in his general condition, and perhaps even the outcome of therapy. These segments of such reports are impressive, as well as promising. An interesting sidelight of one set of observations tends to illuminate one of the controversial issues in psychoanalytic training and standards, namely, the relative advantages of a greater number of sessions per week. Perhaps the Board on Professional Standards of the American Psychoanalytic Association might encourage more extensive and repeated empirical studies of this question.

Since a complete record of any single analysis confronts the investigator with an overwhelming quantity of material, the question naturally arises of how effectively a single case study can serve as the basis for generalizing about any psychoanalytic proposition. In his contribution, Jones makes a very cogent defense of the inferential possibilities offered by the data of a single case study, as opposed to studies on larger samples. He states, "The heterogeneity of characteristics in larger samples and the reliance on averages result in a lack of specificity, a vagueness about patient characteristics and other variables from which inferences are drawn.... A single case research model ... attempts to establish the generality of its findings through replications on a case-by-case basis rather than through group averages. A focus on the variability within the analytic dyad is the very core of process research. Establishing the presence of certain patterns of configuration of variability across a series of cases would begin to form the basis for generalizability. The scientific basis for clinical psychoanalysis would be greatly strengthened by a programmatic research effort which attempts to replicate findings over a succession of studies of individual cases." To this statement, any analyst, no matter how closely wedded to the experience within the psychoanalytic situation, would give hearty assent.

Empirical studies represent a field of investigation that is slowly making its impact on psychoanalytic thought. In many respects, it is a discipline in the earliest stages of development, but it is a discipline, it seems to me, that the clinician should be ready to respect, to question, and to learn from.

REFERENCES

ARLOW, J. A. (1979). The genesis of interpretation. *J. Amer. Psychoanal. Assn.*, 27(Suppl.):193–206.
GREENSON, R. (1967). *The Technique and Practice of Psychoanalysis.* New York: Int. Univ. Press.
WAELDER, R. (1962). Psychoanalysis, scientific method, and philosophy. *J. Amer. Psychoanal. Assn.*, 10:617–637.

DISCUSSION: THE CLINICIAN AND THE SCIENTIST

THEODORE SHAPIRO, M.D.

FREUD DISCOVERED A METHOD to systematically explore the human mind, its contents, and its mechanism. His discoveries were made in the historical context of a romantic revolution in middle Europe, and his findings of conflicting agencies within were consonant with such a vision of the human condition. However, at *fin de siècle* there was a new ferment of empirical observation that approached data from the vantage of systematic observation and replicative science, that also sought to reduce observer bias. Behavioral psychology and experimental psychology were only a glimmer away. Many medically trained neurologists and neuroanatomists were pursuing firm empirical descriptions of disease and symptoms based on Virchow's anatomic pathology. Indeed, Freud's early work in Brucke's laboratory was conducted in this spirit. This new breed of physician-investigator sought to discover the laws of regularity that would pinpoint how heterogeneity could be analyzed into uniform concepts that would serve as generalizations of what they saw.

Freud was influenced by both the romantic and empirical scientific vision as he invented the few rules of transformation that accounted for the large array of symbolic representations which he saw clinically. He also developed paradigms that could reduce his observations to essentials, and explored the possibilities and limits of a unique new method of observation, psychoanalysis.

The conflictual mental structures that evolved into compromise behaviors were thought to support repetitive neurotic symptoms and were seen as derivatives of more or less universal unconscious fantasies, all of which obeyed postulated rules governing mental processes. However, as Freudian psychology took root in the twentieth century, and more rigorous, positivistic rules of science were introduced into other areas of inquiry, many critics thought that Freud's psychoanalysis did not fit the canons of the new science. In fact, psychoanalysis became a type of treatment for neuroses, and psychoanalytic practitioners, until the 1950's, by and large, discussed their "science" only in case conferences.

Some philosophers of science, using the model of physics, railed that the rules of verification and reliability that characterized other sciences—yes, even the behavioral sciences—did not apply to the data that were reported as privileged and private (Hook, 1959). (A more recent critique has been offered by Grünbaum [1985].) By contrast, empirical science claimed that there were explicit guides for reliable observation, that there had to be tests of validity which more or less guaranteed that statements made about observations could be verified and cross-validated by other investigators and methods. Moreover, there had to be some way in which the material that was elicited and elaborated could be subjected to statistical tests and the laws of probability.

The papers reviewed in this section on process research all approach their body of data, the case (many of them the same case), from the vantage point of the reliability of their observations and the validity of the measures, and use recorded analyses as an interactional system, as their raw data. Insofar as they approach the data in this manner, more will agree that they achieve the appellation of scientific inquiry. They no longer can be accused of starting from the privileged view of a single clinician/observer who is doing the treatment with all the baggage that that biased position implies.

Teller and Dahl state that "The ultimate goal has been to develop a unified measure capable of identifying psychopathology, assessing the analytic process, and measuring the outcome of psychoanalytic treatment." The Ulm group, under the leadership of Thomä and Kächele, indicates that they are studying the psychoanalytic situation, examining "the exchange between patient and psychoanalyst to probe psychoanalytic theory and to develop an empirically based theory of the process." While they agree that psychoanalysis is "the science of subjectivity," they also, and perhaps contrariwise, wish to render the subjective, idiosyncratic idiom into more centrally observable public language. Horowitz addresses the psychoanalytic treatment process itself, noting that psychoanalytic treatments seek to formulate what is "maladaptively repetitive" in the mental schemas of self and others. He further states, "Such research can help formulate the personality structure of patients in the here-and-now, and from such models, begin to reconsider our explanations of how the meaning structure now present developed." Jones, in parallel fashion, offers that he would like to "provide a basic language for the description and classification of intervention processes," and "open the door of privileged access."

Thus, there is a unity of purpose for all of our investigators who attempt to give us a *new look* at the process formerly observed as a private interchange between analyst and analysand. They all offer the opportunity to look at firsthand recorded data from the analytic situation, and as such they have already accepted the controversial idea that psychoanalytic treatments should be tape-recorded so that the subjectivity of the analyst is circumscribed. Moreover, they all are devoted to single case studies designed to look at a process in its ecological format and in *statu nascendi* to determine its progress and to attempt to extract the essentials of the interaction between analyst and patient that make for progress and change. They seek a meta-description at a basic level designed to apply to psychoanalytic therapy in general, and to extract the basic paradigms that guide our work. In this sense they observe surface to infer deep, organizing, lawful structures.

There is remarkable overlap in the language of the authors who, though they start from different premises, have certainly been influenced by each other over the years. It is clear that the CCRT (Luborsky), the RRM (Horowitz), and the FRAMES (Dahl and Teller) are all related concepts. Indeed, the FRAME concept is better stated in its fullest form—fundamental repetitive and maladaptive emotional structure. Luborsky's core critical relationship theme, too, is more illuminating when the acronym is swept away. Each system partakes of a subject and an object in interaction. Horowitz, too, by studying the role-relational model, again is designating the parties involved in the conflicted interaction as elaborated within. Each of these investigators looks at the psychoanalytic process and its vicissitudes, but they each must concentrate on small units of observation to do so. They take us more intensely into various phases of the treatment in order to arrive at certain generalizable statements that will help us to understand the repetitive interactions in an analysis, and perhaps, at some juncture, they help to formulate a more modal concept of what has transpired. This process falls into a central tenet of any science—the need for composite regularities that characterize any series of surface behaviors into lawlike propositions. If this is not achieved, we become lost in a mire of heterogeneity, where each moment is a unique surprise.

By utilizing case studies as their unit of observation, they obviate, as Jones states, "the error of averaging," and also give us an opportunity to look at cases in depth. On the other hand, the paradigms derived for each case must then be further studied, to see if they predict future relationships throughout the course of one case or if the model derived from the case fits a new case. In the language of the clinician, these studies offer an opportunity to determine how unconscious fantasies operate to dictate current modes of interaction, including transferences, at different points in the same case and across cases. They further offer the opportunity of finding out whether the analyst's interventions and interpretations make a difference and what kinds of difference they make. However, I shall register an important cautionary shibboleth. Each investigator requires that we be able to have access to the interaction in order for their studies to work. Thus, in order to have some kind of valid observational frame, we also require an opportunity to introduce reliable judges trained in a specific rating scale who may look at these data repeatedly from the standpoint of an outsider and not as a subjectively involved therapist.

Caston notes in his paper how troubled he was when Seitz (1966) demonstrated that senior analysts could not agree on formulations relevant to the conduct of the case, and how pleased he was when Weiss and Sampson (1986) offered the control mastery model and tested it against the classical model as an empirical testing ground using external observers as a condition of their work. We, too, should applaud the incursion of such empirical methods in order to secure some of our claims within a community where psychoanalysis was looked at either as a religion, or an art form, or as a subjective encounter used for altering one's life without benefit of any demonstration of its validity.

Although there is much that is similar among our authors, we should notice that each has approached his subject from a somewhat different viewpoint in an attempt to achieve the earlier mentioned stability and validity of observation. This is salutary because even with diverse approaches, and even with different conclusions, as in the case studied by Caston and Sampson and Weiss, the final models are consonant in their stress on interaction within, and lead to our sense that psychoanalysts have been validly focusing on remnants and residua of experiences that are internally structured and then projected outward. The elephant finally emerges from the blind man's descriptions. Indeed, the language of object relations begins to show through even in those areas where the individual investigator does not claim that this is a theoretical feature of his or her initial intent.

One cannot talk about role relationship models or FRAMES, or CCRTS or even control mastery without looking at how people think they habitually interact with each other, either in the transference or in life dialogue. It is these habitual interactions that receive our most careful scrutiny in both transference responses and in the hope held out for the patient that maladaptive encounters at the beginning of analysis will change as the result of the analytic work.

The Ulm data bank is a remarkable study resource, providing investigators with a large library which many interested in the empirical aspects of psychotherapy can visit and linger longer to use if German is spoken. This is a testimony to another effect of scientific scrutiny—the openness of the keepers of the cache of data to serious observers who promise to work diligently to advance our knowledge. Science in the best sense should be open and public.

When Freud encouraged analysts to write up their cases, he was seeking similar openness, *but* did not require the same full disclosure; nor did he fully realize the distorting effect of the author on the product; nor did he know about the future technology that would permit direct access to data via recording. The Ulm group too has permitted open exposure to the English-speaking world and influenced it by interacting generously. The essence of Thomä and Kächele's work, however, is stated in the opposition to the untested ecumenical notion that each method will yield comparable results when followed with sincerity. Contrariwise, they try to demonstrate how each method *may work* and how the outcome is "a result of an unconscious bargaining process" (1987). They thus formulate their proposals, as do Weiss and Sampson, as scientific propositions to be tested for their validity and to determine whether criteria of difference satisfy the null hypothesis, not as tacit political stabs at ecumenism. The array of data sets in the Ulm text bank should provide us with very precise understanding of *how* analyses take place, and *what* kind of data are necessary to apply an external test. They also show us the possibilities of utilizing techniques derived from computer technology that can be applied to systematic individual study. The latter, of course, were not available in Freud's lifetime.

We owe to Weiss and Sampson a format in which a hypothesis about specific models of changes is tested. They systematically pitted one model against another—the control mastery model (CM) versus the automatic functioning model (AF)—and demonstrated in the 106 sessions of the classic case of Mrs. C. that when the anxiety following an interpretation is measured, it does not increase as the automatic functioning hypothesis would predict. Because the anxiety abates, the authors concluded that the patient is seeking a setting in which he or she "works with the analyst to disprove [the patient's] pathogenic beliefs." Using the criteria for safety and danger, as repression is lifted, anxiety lessens. We see in this model a method to test two proposals by evidence of generation of anxiety, and a firm belief by the investigators that the response of the patient is lawful and repetitive. I would submit, parenthetically, that even if their finding does not hold up (and it does not in Caston's work), their method is admirably scientific in its spirit and use. To account for the discrepancy in findings we may have to posit that the model is wrong, or that the observers were differently trained, or that the sessions observed were different. Whatever the case, this is a resolvable problem within the canons of science.

Just as Weiss and Sampson provide an example of empirical testing of alternative hypotheses, Horowitz, too, uses his configurational analysis to study the phenomena, the state of mind of the patient, the person schemas, and to understand the shift from one to another mode of representation to test hypotheses. He approaches his task from the standpoint of the analysis of conflict in terms of defensive control of emotions by empirical observations of shift in topic, state, or schema. This represents a highly sophisticated method and technique used to look at relationship configurations that are not only valid clinically, but also sound ecologically. Horowitz uses real dynamic therapies in real time to seek the repetitive behaviors that derive from unconscious belief systems.

He, also, finds results worth noting, namely, that "repetitive behavior from belief systems unfolds like a script" and that the RRMCs predict transference, responses, and reactions later in the therapy. These observations have been verified in various programs set in motion by Horowitz's group throughout the country. Moreover, neurotic cases do differently from narcissistically vulnerable cases when treated in the same way. This is a finding that makes sense clinically and has face validity as well.

The latter finding is highly salutary because it suggests that we must modify our treatment approaches in accord with the descriptive diagnosis, the stage of development and phase of therapy of the patient. All of these have face validity, but empirical approaches sometimes lead to surprises that fly in the face of what we predict. Parenthetically, I also applaud the use of dynamic psychotherapy as a data source, for I have always thought that psychoanalysis, the prime source of dynamic therapies, should espouse research on such approaches rather than concentrate on our differences.

Jones provides us with a unique opportunity to see the power of an ingenious method of understanding what has happened in a case by exposing material to a court of judges: The Q-sort technique employs statements on cards which the observer is asked to sort into nine piles ranging from most like to least like what was heard. It provides a set of observations using the natural observational frame of a therapeutic hour. It also helps us to diminish the hazard of using artificially derived abstract variables imposed on a case which are too global or general as compared to the patient's own comments, which naturally fit into a particular frame of reference. The statements used in the sort are very close to surface descriptions and therefore easier to discriminate among. He, too, finds that there is a split in the outcome of his studies. The disturbed individual needs encouragement, and the less disturbed needs interpretation. This dichotomy leads me to reemphasize that the data suggest that we must tailor our treatments. It also should make us doubt that a uniform method of treatment is warranted for all comers.

Jones also brings us to the possibility that we may be able to discover *causal effects* over time in single case studies by doing time series analyses. This would be most salutary in our current state of theoretical flux within psychoanalysis. I espouse a view that we dare not settle for a hermeneutic solution rather than a scientifically probing attitude with such reinforcement.

Dahl's broad program of work has spanned a large array of techniques from computer content analysis using linguistic variables, through the study of emotions, and most recently FRAMES. De Rivera's decision theory model of emotion fits nicely into Dahl and Teller's FRAME idea insofar as Rivera's model includes directionality and disposition of affect as well as intensity and quality of affect. We may be pleased that so many roads do lead to Rome, or should we say, FRAMES. He proposes that FRAMES are a nonverbal code in a dual code system that represents a structured sequence of emotions and defense. They are residues of enduring early object relations that run across conflicts, interact with each other, and account for a wide spectrum of repetitive, neurotic, maladaptive behaviors. Teller and Dahl and their coworkers have sought to find the underpinnings of the meaning of experience as viewed from the vantage point of psychoanalysis.

Even as our authors seek greater certainty through methodologically sound work, they have noticed the fly in the ointment. Caston asks the question in the following way: Are they all shielding a mannequin hiding behind the heterologous clothing that covers the form? Are they simply and repetitively finding what they wish, because that is the model of our understanding? Caston distrusts high reliability as simply a problem of model indoctrination. He notes, "any given psychoanalytic formulation is a family of compatible descriptive schemas about a clinical narrative and context." Therefore, high levels of agreement for different psychoanalytic paradigms may only reveal a well propagandized group of observers. His test of the mannequin is a very important guard against such rigidity of interpretation, and it was helpful to find when tested that the mannequin did not overlap exactly with the observations made.

But there was one area—that of displacement transference—where the mannequin seemed to be operative. It may be that we impose the idea of transference all too readily on our observations, and therefore find it to be ubiquitous. We do not want to, as he suggests, "lose our epistemic warrant."

As I review this rich array of research, I find that there are questions about their relevance for my practice. The findings are interesting and enrich my grasp of the problems of science when applied to human interaction in a specific format. Yet we all must admit that there are no clean results that say this is the way to work, except in a few instances to be cited below. This attests to another scientific tenet—we must distrust 100 percent agreement. Science works on a set of tentative statements that can be tested by one or another method and can be looked to in order to open the way for future criticism and reassignment of understanding. The existing models are exactly that, *currently popular models*. They should be looked at as *working hypotheses*, but hypotheses remain as vague as any subjective comment, unless they are subjected to repeated verifying observational tests. Science should protect us from premature closure, from dogmatism, and from zealotry. I am pleased the results are tentative. It would be equally harmful to our aims if we accepted the science and ignored the clinic as another dogmatic authoritarian pronouncement.

A second problem results from this kind of review because most of the investigators have used single case studies. They offer the case as its own control, and they can test the operations of what has transpired over time. This satisfies the analyst's quest for in-depth knowledge. However, the question of generalizability has plagued the single-case study designers over the years. Nonetheless, if such studies give us any possibility of finding causal relations within the individual over the time span in regard to emergent behaviors and actions and thought processes, and also in the transference, it is worth doing such work 40 times over in order to be able to suggest that meaningful structures are not simply related to entailment propositions, where what we claim to have found is merely a feature of the original definition. For example, it is no significant finding to discover that a bachelor is unmarried. It would be news if we found that bachelors all come from broken homes. The result must also be related to causal formats brought to interactions by unconscious processes. We shall ultimately be able to say that patient X did A or B because he was driven by fantasy V and Q, formulated some time in childhood around a set of configurations in relation to his primary objects. Indeed, these will become the proving grounds, not so much of historical or narrative truths, but will show us that there is continuity within the individual in regard to his reaction patterns as described in the here-and-now.

Not only do we have the CCRTs to work with, but we also have the longitudinal observations that come from scientifically constructed work with children. I shall expand my discussion here to briefly include the data from our developmental investigators. Certainly the configurations that adults tell us about their views of their past relationships in their current descriptions of their past as in the Main work (this volume, section II) is relevant. If the Main work stood just alone, we would have a narrative that has some truth function in regard to repetitive patterns. However, when seen in the light of Fonagy's work (this volume, section II), we can now aver that the parental vision also has predictive value in regard to how roles are played out in new situations of toddlerhood. While analytic data give us some further information about how roles are played out in interactions with the analyst as paradigmatic for the past, parents, and oedipal constellations, the prospective strength of successful prediction in childhood bears testimony to the prescience of some psychoanalytic developmental proposals. Again, I would rather have some psychoanalytic proposals trashed if only we could "verify" others.

Psychoanalysis has used a rich array of clinical findings to make sweeping generalizations. We should welcome the empirical thrust of these studies to put our discipline further in the realm of the "doable," rather than the artful. Psychoanalysis is not an arcane treatment method that only has a short temporal span. I think that the contribution of psychoanalysis is served immensely by the empirical investigations presented in this volume. Future work of this sort will further help us endure as a clinical science.

REFERENCES

GRÜNBAUM, A. (1985). *The Foundations of Psychoanalysis.* Berkeley, CA: Univ. California Press.

HOOK, S., Ed. (1959). *Psychoanalysis, Scientific Method and Philosophy.* New York: New York Univ. Press.

SEITZ, P. (1966). The consensus problem in psychoanalytic research. In *Methods of Research in Psychotherapy,* ed. L. A. Gottschalk & A. H. Auerbach. New York: Appleton-Century-Crofts, pp. 361–400.

THOMÄ, H. & KÄCHELE, H. (1987). *Psychoanalytic Practice: Vol. 1, Principles.* New York: Springer.

WEISS, J. & SAMPSON, H. (1986). *The Psychoanalytic Process: Theory, Clinical Observations, and Empirical Research.* New York: Guilford Press.

II. PSYCHOANALYSIS AND DEVELOPMENTAL PSYCHIATRY AND PSYCHOLOGY

THE INTERSUBJECTIVE DOMAIN: APPROACHES FROM DEVELOPMENTAL PSYCHOPATHOLOGY

R. Peter Hobson, Ph.D., F.R.C. Psych.

The purpose of this paper is to consider how nonanalytic research might complement psychoanalytic investigations into the nature and developmental implications of intersubjective psychological processes. Theoretical and empirical studies of early childhood autism and borderline personality disorder illustrate the potential relevance of such research in the field of developmental psychopathology.

Psychoanalysis has a primary concern with intersubjective psychological processes. The study of transference and countertransference affords insight into the ways that one individual can maintain psychic equilibrium through influencing and being influenced by the mental states of someone else. Such study also reveals the potential significance of interpersonal transactions for fostering change in a patient's psychological functioning, not least with regard to his or her capacity to care for others and to maintain self-reflective and coherent thought.

My purpose in stating these unremarkable observations on the nature and yield of psychoanalysis is to assert the uniqueness of psychoanalytic research. There are certain things one can learn about relationships only from within relationships. Correspondingly, much that is special to psychoanalytic understanding about mental functioning can be derived only from

---

From the Developmental Psychopathology Research Unit, Adult Department, Tavistock Clinic, London.

I offer my grateful acknowledgment to Dr. Matthew Patrick, both for his collaboration as a research colleague and for his help in the preparation of this paper. I thank Drs. Robert N. Emde and Theodore Shapiro for their editorial advice.

Sections of this paper have been adapted and modified from a chapter by R. P. Hobson and M. Patrick, titled "Perspectives from Developmental Psychopathology," to be published in *New Perspectives on Psychoanalytic Research*, edited by P. Fonagy and O. F. Kernberg (in preparation).

within the analytic situation. It follows that we should not expect extra-analytic studies to capture the essence of psychoanalysis. On the other hand, we might reasonably hope that such research could illuminate the significance of intersubjective mental functioning for normal and pathological development. I should like to illustrate how colleagues and I at the Developmental Psychopathology Research Unit of the Tavistock Clinic have been pursuing certain lines of research in the hope of furthering our understanding of these matters.

One focus of our research is the condition of early childhood autism. A reason for this is that autism seems to exemplify the profound significance of personal relations for early child development, and in particular for a child's growing understanding of the nature of other people with minds. At the time I first encountered autistic children in the mid-1970's, there were few researchers who paid heed to Kanner's (1943) thesis that autism is fundamentally a disorder of affective relatedness. In the circles of academic psychology and psychiatry, "cognitive" and "linguistic" theories of autism held sway (e.g., Churchill, 1972; Hermelin and O'Connor, 1970; Rutter, 1972). It seemed to me that something was awry. On an intuitive level, one's own experience of being in relation with autistic individuals, the unearthly "feel" of such relative nonengagement, must surely hold the key to this unique disorder. From the perspective of philosophical psychology, it appeared plausible that autism illustrates the force of Wittgenstein's (1953) arguments that human beings need to share a "form of life" rooted in noninferential awareness of and reactivity to bodily anchored meanings in other people's appearances and expressions, if they are to understand minds and use language appropriately.

From my vantage point as a trainee psychoanalyst, I felt that autism might reveal a great deal about the biological bases for and/or the earliest vicissitudes of the object-relational structuring of mind, and perhaps confirm and extend psychoanalytic insights into the affective and interpersonal dimensions of the capacity for creative symbolization. A major thesis of object-relations theory is that from early infancy, a human being is biologically predisposed to engage with other people in ways that effect psychological connectedness and primitive modes of interpersonal sharing and conflict. Our studies of autism are intended to explore basic processes of affect perception and responsiveness, and to investigate the implications of disruption in intersubjective experience for cognitive (and especially symbolic) development.

In the early 1980's, my research interests were shaped by a further influence. My position as a psychotherapist within the increasingly neuroscientific *Zeitgeist* of British psychiatry fueled my desire to make a scientific statement about the significance of psychoanalytic developmental psychology for understanding the pathogenesis of adult psychiatric disorder. Together with my collaborator Dr. Matthew Patrick and other colleagues, I settled upon a disputed border territory between organic and psychodynamic psychiatry, that of so-called borderline personality disorder, as suitable terrain for psychoanalytically inspired and developmentally oriented exploration. At this different level of clinical science, we wished to investigate how individuals who are endowed with the usual building blocks of object-relational psychology might nevertheless acquire structures of thinking, feeling, and defensive organization that underpin disturbed patterns of relationship and states of mind. If early caregiving is inadequate and/or an infant's constitution is so disposed, defensive processes such as splitting and projective identification may be deployed in such a way that the individual's capacity to assimilate and "contain" conflictual experiences in relationships, and to think and feel about such experiences in a coherent way, may be compromised (Bion, 1962a; Kernberg, 1976). With such ideas in mind, we designed a study of borderline personality disorder to examine the relation between configurations of "mental representation" and the particular qualities of relatedness, mood, and self-experience that characterize individuals with this diagnosis (Patrick et al., 1994).

Early Childhood Autism

One of the most perplexing things about early childhood autism is that the syndrome comprises a relatively consistent constellation of seemingly diverse disabilities. Autism is characterized not only by a certain quality of impairment in social relations and interpersonal communication, but it is also regularly associated with marked deficits in creative symbolic thinking and play (see *DSM-III-R*; Rutter and Schopler, 1987). The question is: how do these impairments relate to one another?

I have already noted how until the early 1980's, "linguistic" and "cognitive" theories of autism dominated academic thinking. Once it had become established that autistic individuals do have a characteristic and somewhat unusual profile of scores on standardized IQ tests and other specially designed intellectual tasks, with marked difficulty on language-related rather than visuo-spatial tasks, this was taken as hard evidence that a cognitive disability is in some way primary to the disorder. The prevailing view was that somehow the cognitive deficits made it difficult for autistic individuals to process complex and shifting "social stimuli."

What was missing was a kind of intellectual commitment to examine whether in *normal* development, interpersonal-affective exchanges between very young children and others might have an essential role to play in the acquisition of higher cognitive functions. If this proved to be the case, and if autistic individuals have a profound deficit in their own capacity for affective relatedness with others, then we might find a *developmental* explanation for the perplexing mixture of deficits so characteristic of autism.

In some ways it is surprising that this idea took so long to dawn. On the one hand, there were already eminent developmental psychologists such as Werner and Kaplan (1963) and Vygotsky (1962) who were emphasizing (although not quite explaining) how young children's capacities for creative symbolic thinking were founded upon irreducibly social relations.

For years psychoanalysts had been writing about the complex interrelations between social experience and symbolic functioning (e.g., Ferenczi, 1913; Jones, 1916; Klein, 1930; Rycroft, 1956; Segal, 1957). Mahler (1968) had suggested that there is "a most striking inability, on the part of a psychotic child, even to see the human object in the outside world, let alone to interact with him as with another separate human entity" (p. 3). Yet such potentially illuminating insights were more or less dismissed by academic psychologists and child psychiatrists.

This situation may be changing with the advent of a newly conceived research domain, that of developmental psychopathology. Indeed, psychoanalysis is a founding discipline for this perspective (Cichetti, 1984). From its inception, the psychoanalytic attitude has been to adopt a developmental stance toward such obscure yet revealing conditions as autism, in order to learn about normal development as well as about "abnormality" itself. At the same time, an adequate account of normal development is thought to be essential for our understanding of psychopathological states. I shall now try to highlight the potential value of this approach.

The Capacity to Symbolize

Here are some tentative propositions about the social-developmental origins of the capacity to symbolize. Crudely put, a symbol refers to something for someone. How does a child come to relate to something in such a way that this something has a referring relation to another object or event so that, as Langer (1957) expressed it, a particular conception of the object is carried by the symbol? For example, a two-year-old boy at play might take a matchbox to stand for a car; the child sustains the dual attitude of conferring a self-selected psychological meaning on the matchbox, namely the conception of "carness," alongside his recognition of a given ("matchbox") meaning (e.g., Leslie, 1987). The thesis I should like to explore is that a very important step in this development occurs when the infant relates to *another person's* observable psychological relatedness to visually shared objects and events (Hobson, 1990a; in press). Consider "social referencing," for example: A one-year-old infant who is confronted by a disconcerting "visual cliff" proceeds across the cliff if the caregiver looks on happily, but freezes if the caregiver looks at the cliff with fear (Sorce et al., 1985). The point to note is that a single, visually shared circumstance—the visual cliff—evokes a reaction of anxiety in the infant, but this emotional state can be modified by the infant's reaction to the caregiver's reaction as this "refers to" the environmentally situated source of anxiety. The infant relates not only to the world as perceptually specified, but also to someone else's psychological relation to that same world.

Such instances of social referencing are usually interpreted from the viewpoint of the infant acquiring "information" about the world (see Feinman, 1992). It may be even more significant that this configuration of experience affords an infant the opportunity to learn that *given* objects and events can have multiple, person-related meanings. The meaning-for-me is not necessarily the meaning-for-her. A way is open for the infant to recognize the distinction between the world-as-given, on the one hand, and the nature of persons who have potentially *different* psychological orientations to that world, on the other. Here is a beginning distinction between "thought" (or at least "psychological attitude") and "thing." Before long, and perhaps as a result of recognizing this very distinction, the child comes to exercise his or her own powers as a "meaning-conferring" person, imparting new person-dependent meanings to objects in creative symbolic play (Hobson, 1990a).

Against this background, consider the case of autism. Suppose that because of constitutional abnormality or very early disruption in their capacity for intersubjective coordination with others, autistic children lack the kinds of affective engagement necessary for their growth in understanding that people *have* psychological attitudes (Hobson, 1989a, 1989b). If this is so, then they will be deprived of a "way in" to seeing how different individuals' differing attitudes toward the world reveal the central distinction between thought and thing. Accordingly, autistic children's manifest limitation in creative symbolic play (Wing et al., 1977), as well as their "concrete" one-track modes of thought (Scheerer et al., 1945), may turn out to be developmental sequelae to impairments in specifically interpersonal relatedness. If this proves to be the case, or even if it becomes the most plausible account of the cooccurrence of certain central clinical features of autism, then this will certainly strengthen the argument for the significance of social-developmental processes for the normal child's developing capacity to symbolize.

En passant, I might mention one further set of studies that seems to dovetail with the above account. Much social referencing entails that an infant see—literally—the directedness of other people's psychological attitudes toward a visually specified world. Vision helps the child to triangulate self-in-relation-to-object, self-in-relation-to-other, and other-in-relation-to-object. From this triangulation, an understanding of the respective notions of self, other, and "objects with person-specified meanings" are distilled out. Congenitally blind children also lack this visually based source of knowledge concerning the directedness of psychological attitudes from people to a shared world. Therefore one might expect such children to have autisticlike difficulties with creative symbolic play and perspective-sensitive personal pronoun (I/you) usage (Fraiberg and Adelson, 1977; Keeler, 1958; Hobson, 1990a). As Selma Fraiberg expressed it, blind children may have difficulty in "representing the self as an 'I' in a universe of 'I's' " (Fraiberg and Adelson, 1977, p. 249). Fraiberg also emphasized how incipient autistic features in blind children may be obviated by enlarging and enriching the children's interpersonal experiences, and by thus providing an environment that "lures the child into discoveries of himself and the external world" (p. 282). My colleagues Rachel Brown and Maggie Minter have been investigating these matters by interviewing teachers of congenitally blind and sighted children. They have found that well over 50 percent of congenitally blind children have had problems with symbolic play and confusions in the use of personal pronouns up to their fourth birthday.

The evidence I have cited is provisional and suggestive, but the promise of these convergent lines of research seems clear. Such studies might prompt a reorientation in thinking about the *various* psychological processes or pathologies that influence the forms of self-other connectedness and differentiation which are needed for the emergence and maintenance of the capacity to symbolize.

On Personal Relatedness

There are few psychoanalysts who would dispute that autistic children's profound abnormality in personal relatedness is somehow fundamental to their disorder. However, there is a spectrum of opinion on the nature of the children's interpersonal relations, and corresponding divergences in viewpoint concerning the degree to which a more or less standard object-relational account is applicable or adequate to characterize their structure of mind. As I have described elsewhere (Hobson, 1990b), others, such as Klein (1930), Mahler (1968) and Tustin (1981, 1983) have wrestled with this problem, and each has acknowledged autistic children's constitutional abormalities as well as their propensity to deploy defensive maneuvers that restrict affective contact with others. Mahler (1968) gives a vivid description of the autistic child's inability "to utilize the auxiliary executive ego functions of the (symbiotic) partner, the mother, to orient himself in the outer or inner world" (p. 67), or to perceive her as a "beacon of emotional orientation" (p. 69). Such an account dovetails with my own emphasis on the importance of the child's difficulties in perceiving emotional meanings expressed by other persons—difficulties that might well extend to registering containment *as* containment—and in social referencing. Tustin (1981) has stressed the unintegration (rather than disintegration) of autistic children of the type described by Kanner (1943), such that they live in a predominantly inanimate, sensation-dominated world and have limited responsiveness to people as people. At this level of explanation, if not at other levels, there is considerable convergence in psychoanalytic perspectives on autism.

My contribution here is to suggest that a severe disruption in intersubjective coordination is not only pathognomonic of autism, but also an essential factor in the pathogenesis of autistic children's failure to develop creative symbolic imagination, to evolve a mature awareness of self and other as separate centers of consciousness, and to acquire a full understanding of the forms and functions of language (Hobson, 1993). At *this* level of theory, such a thesis would seem to be in harmony with the psychoanalytical perspective. A formulation of autism in terms of the children's "deficient experience of intersubjectivity" does not preclude a range of additional possibilities about the source of such abnormality. Indeed, the very notion of autism as a disorder of *inter*personal relations points to the possibility that a heterogeneous set of conditions in the child *vis-à-vis* others might eventuate in the "final common pathway" of autistic relatedness.

Let me approach these matters from a different direction. A starting-point is to suppose that an innate biological constitution affords human beings the capacity for intersubjective engagement, and for the *experience* of affective connectedness with and differentiation from others. These kinds of experiential linkage among "selves" are essential to infants' dawning understanding that they and other people have different psychological orientations toward the world (Hamlyn, 1974; Hobson, 1990c, 1990d). One ultimate outcome is that young children acquire *concepts* about the minds of others. They come to know about the ways people are a special class of "thing" in having feelings, thoughts, beliefs, and so on. Such concepts have profound implications for cognitive and linguistic as well as social development (Hobson, 1989a; Baron-Cohen, 1988).

The above line of reasoning opens up the possibility that by studying older autistic children's *concepts* of mental life, and more specifically, their relative incapacity to recognize "meaning" in the diverse emotional expressions of other people, one might establish that there are specific group differences between autistic and nonautistic individuals in precisely that realm of interpersonal understanding which is normally the outcome of developmentally prior, interpersonal-affective relatedness. We have now conducted a program of experimental studies in this regard (Hobson, 1991a), testing autistic and nonautistic individuals who are pairwise matched for chronological and verbal mental age in order to define what is specific to "autism."

I shall give a few examples to illustrate our research strategies. In one study (Hobson et al., 1988a), autistic and matched nonautistic children and adolescents were asked to select which of six photographs showing standardized facial expressions of emotion was the one to "go with" audiotaped vocal expressions, either in the form of humming, groans, or gasps, or in the form of emotionally toned passages of prose. Because such task materials involve stylized and in some ways "degraded" representations of what should have been alive, dynamic, expressive *people*, it was important to devise control tasks in order to pinpoint whether any observed group differences were attributable to subjects' differential sensitivity toward emotion-related meanings in the materials presented. Therefore we also presented a range of nonemotion sound-to-picture matching tasks with items selected from relatively homogeneous categories of sound-generating objects or events (six kinds of vehicles, of birds, of electrical appliances, of gardening tools, of moving water, and of walking, respectively). The results were that when compared with control subjects, the autistic individuals performed less well on the emotion *vis-à-vis* nonemotion conditions. So, too, when asked to name a subset of these task materials, autistic subjects were relatively poor at naming feelings *vis-à-vis* naming nonpersonal objects (Hobson et al., 1989). A subsequent study (Hobson and Lee, 1989) revealed that even on a standard test of choosing pictures for words, the British Picture Vocabulary Scale (the British version of the Peabody Picture Vocabulary Scale [Dunn et al., 1982]), autistic children were specifically impaired on items related to emotion in some way (e.g., "delighted," "greeting," "disagreement").

Another of our studies (Weeks and Hobson, 1987) was an attempt to see whether autistic children were unusual in their propensity to *notice* expressions of emotion. Matched groups of subjects were presented with a pair of target photographs of the faces of individuals who differed in three, two, or one of the following respects: sex, age, facial expression of emotion, and type of hat they were wearing. The task was to notice any one feature that distinguished the targets, and to sort a pile of photographs of new individuals accordingly. There were no "right" or "wrong" responses here, and almost all subjects were consistent in sorting according to some criterion. Whereas the majority of nonautistic children sorted according to people's facial expression (happy versus unhappy) before they sorted according to type of hat (floppy versus woollen), most autistic children gave priority to sorting by type of hat, and only a minority sorted by expression even when this was the only distinguishing feature. Even with such a crude and indirect test of attentiveness to emotion, therefore, there was a group difference in the way predicted from a hypothesis concerning "real-life" unresponsiveness to bodily expressions. A further study (Hobson et al., 1988b) suggested that even among those autistic individuals who *do* discriminate among photographs of facial expressions, the perceptual processes by which they do this are highly abnormal.

I shall cite a final study to illustrate how we are trying to move beyond the level of "emotion recognition," to investigate autistic individuals' probably deficient sense of self (Hobson et al., 1990d; in press). One technique has been to ask subjects to name the individuals depicted in photographs which have included snapshots of their peers, themselves, and the experimenter conducting the task. Compared with matched nonautistic subjects, a subgroup of autistic individuals were more inclined to refer to photographs of themselves and the experimenter by proper names than by personal pronouns, even when these pronouns were comprehended and used adequately in other contexts. Our own tentative interpretation is that the autistic subjects were adopting a relatively detached, almost "third-person" attitude toward the photographs of themselves, and also toward the experimenter within the testing situation. In contrast, nonautistic subjects seemed to identify with the photographs of themselves, and see and care about the photographed person as "me" or "you."

Thus the evidence is highly suggestive that autistic individuals are indeed specifically impaired in their emotional sensitivity, emotion perception, and emotion understanding. Some readers might justifiably remark that there is nothing like proving the obvious; others may diagnose a serious case of reductionism. It is certainly open to question whether social-perceptual deficits are *primary* in autism—indeed, I hope that this illustrates the potential value of experimental research in establishing a framework for psychoanalytic debate. *If* it proves to be the case that the only developmental theory that "works" is one that pinpoints the essence of autism to be a relative failure in intersubjective contact (Hobson, 1991b, 1993), then here we have a body of research that might seem a long way from psychoanalytic concerns, at least in its methodological aspects, but may yet prove to have significance for psychoanalytic thinking.

Borderline Personality Disorder

I shall move on to our research on the nature of borderline personality disorder. Once again, we adopt a developmental perspective. Previous empirical studies have suggested that borderline personality disorder may be associated with a history of early maternal separation (Bradley, 1979), childhood physical and sexual abuse (Bryer et al., 1987; Herman et al., 1989) and neglectful yet overprotective parental care (Zweig-Frank and Paris, 1991). Our own focus is on the ways in which such individuals mentally represent their own early relationships with significant parenting figures. Our starting-point is the psychoanalytic proposition that failures of "containment" in the parent-infant relationship may contribute to the development of severe borderline disturbances of personality (Bion, 1962b; Kernberg, 1976; Kohut and Wolf, 1978). Associated with impaired capacities to reflect on and assimilate their own early experiences, borderline patients may manifest a proneness to idealization and devaluation of others, self-damaging impulsiveness, affective instability, outbursts of anger, suicidal threats and self-mutilating behavior, identity disturbances, chronic feelings of emptiness and boredom, and efforts to avoid real or imagined abandonment. The very concept of borderline personality is only slowly becoming acceptable to British psychiatrists, who are inclined to draw a radical demarcation between what they see as biologically based psychotic disorders and partly psychogenic neurotic disorders. The concept of a personality disorder manifesting a "stable instability" that can involve transient psychotic states is provocative enough; the idea that this is predominantly psychogenic, arising out of disturbed parent-infant relations, is anathema to many. Not least, it represents a serious psychoanalytic challenge to the European traditions of phenomenological and "biological" psychiatry. The question therefore arises: how might we uncover scientific evidence for or against the claim that borderline personality disorder reflects a characteristic form of mental organization, one that pertains to representations of a person's early experience?

Our own research (Patrick et al., 1994) has focused not on the putative causal link from early childhood experience to adult psychopathology, although this certainly figures in our thinking, but instead on the relation between the psychiatrically (and largely behaviorally) defined syndrome of borderline personality disorder and these individuals' current psychological functioning. In a sense, therefore, we are employing the defined syndrome *itself* as a simple (and simplified) index of the constellation of personality attributes and psychological mechanisms for which we believe a psychoanalytic explanation will prove to be most adequate and comprehensive. If diagnosis was to be our independent variable, therefore—and as I shall explain, we compared borderline with nonborderline dysthymic patients—then what we required as our dependent variable on the "intrapsychic" side of the equation was a simple index of the complexities of psychopathology in personality disorder. Here we selected two different instruments, both of which aim to evaluate patients' ways of representing their own early relationships: the Adult Attachment Interview (AAI) of George, Kaplan and Main (1985, unpublished), and the Parental Bonding Instrument (Parker et al., 1979). Each of these yields relatively simple measures of patients' styles of mental representation. It is perhaps especially apt that the more elaborate of these approaches has emerged from the tradition of empirically grounded and psychoanalytically informed thinking about attachment inspired by Bowlby (1969).

The AAI is a semistructured interview in which a person is asked to reflect on aspects of his or her childhood relationships with caregivers. As a part of the interview, subjects are asked to give adjectives describing each parent, and then to back these up with specific memories; to recall specific experiences of parental responsiveness to upset, accidents and illness; and to relate how these relationships have changed over time and how they have influenced their adult personality. Transcribed interviews are classified on the basis of scales that evaluate an individual's state of mind with respect to early relationships. In all, seven scales are normally considered. Examples of these are scales that concern idealization of a parent, where the patient gives a very positive view at a general level that is either unsupported or contradicted by actual memories; persistence of not remembering, reflected in repeated failure to recall supporting memories for generalizations made about the parent-child relationship; and, perhaps most important, coherence of discourse across the interview as a whole, which encompasses how far the individual is able to acknowledge and integrate contradictory experiences and memories. Thus the emphasis is on the "how" rather than the "what" of the individual's memories and attitudes.

Transcripts are ultimately classified into three major categories (with a total of 12 subcategories): free to evaluate attachments, where patients talk coherently and objectively about their early relationships; dismissing of attachments, characterized by a dismissiveness toward the likelihood that early attachment experiences have affected personal development; and preoccupied (or enmeshed) in attitudes toward attachment, where the influence of parents or attachment-related experiences can neither be coherently described nor dismissed, and where such relationships seem to preoccupy attention. In these latter transcripts, patients may also oscillate between good and bad evaluations of the past or of their parents (Main and Goldwyn, 1991). More recently, a further group, "unresolved/disorganized/disoriented" with respect to loss and trauma has been described. Unresolved status is considered on separate scales, based primarily on the notion of cognitive disorganization and disorientation as signs of a particular kind of unresolved experience. This is shown most often in lapses in reasoning, unfounded fear or guilt, or irrational thought processes when the individual is talking about loss or trauma. In other areas such accounts may be quite coherent (Main and Goldwyn, 1991).

I hope this skeletal description will be sufficient to illustrate how we employ the AAI as a simple index of complex processes, in that it yields a small number of categories of styles of mental representation. It is also a psychoanalytically relevant instrument in that it evaluates styles of discourse in a way that bears a close relation to psychoanalytic descriptions of mental organization.

Our second instrument, the Parental Bonding Instrument (Parker et al., 1979), is less subtle in approach. It comprises a 25-item self-report questionnaire that focuses on an individual's judgments concerning the parental contribution to parent-child attachment (e.g., the mother or father is rated on a scale of 0 to 3 for the degree to which she or he invaded the subject's privacy). Subjects complete one questionnaire with respect to mother and one with respect to father. The instrument yields scores on two broad dimensions of care and overprotection. The concept of care involves at one extreme, parental affection, warmth and empathy, and at the other coldness, indifference and rejection. The concept of overprotection involves overprotection, intrusion, and infantilization at one extreme, and the promotion of independence and autonomy at the other. We adopted the measure for three reasons. First, it contrasts with the AAI in format, but is complementary in content insofar as subjects attempt to rate their experiences according to specified aspects of childhood relationships. Second, it has been used in previous studies of borderline and dysthymic patients, so it allowed us to cross-check our results with those from independent investigations. Third, there is evidence that on this instrument, individuals' ratings of their parents correspond with ratings made on those same parents by other informants (Mackinnon et al., 1991).

I would like to emphasize a hazard of employing "simple indices of complex processes." The intention of our strategy is to highlight in as clear and even dramatic a way as possible, how complex intersubjective processes need to be accorded an appropriate place in our theorizing about human psychology. The hazard is that others may take the indices to be the essential factors at work. There is a constant pull toward oversimplification and away from an appreciation of what intersubjective and/or psychoanalytic processes in context actually mean. For example, Adult Attachment Classifications are not the endpoints of scientific investigation, merely signposts on the way.

Most of our studies have involved small groups of closely matched index and control subjects, tested with a view to confirming or disconfirming specific predictions. In the case of the quasi-experimental studies of borderline personality disorder, we selected a small group of 12 female patients who met *DSM-III-R* criteria for this disorder. The control group comprised 12 female patients who met the *DSM-III-R* criteria for dysthymia, a form of chronic mild depression, but none of those for borderline personality. All these individuals had been referred and assessed for psychodynamic psychotherapy at a London teaching hospital, and all had been accepted for treatment and placed on the waiting list. We assessed the possible impact of patients' current depressive state on their interview and questionnaire responses, by administering the Beck Depression Inventory (Beck, 1984): there were no group differences. We determined that the two groups were comparable in their intellectual achievements, age and socioeconomic status. We ensured that ratings of the AAI's were made by someone "blind" to patient diagnoses and to the aims of the study, by sending off the transcripts to a trained nonpsychiatrist who knew nothing of our research undertaking.

The study was intended to investigate one of the basic tenets of object-relations theory and attachment theory, namely that the way in which people represent their early social experience is linked to styles of adult interpersonal functioning in close relationships. More specifically, we wished to examine the hypothesis that particular kinds of abnormality in mental representation may be associated with specific forms of interpersonal psychopathology. As we had predicted, there was a significantly higher prevalence of preoccupied classifications amongst borderline than dysthymic patients, in that all 12 of the borderline but only four out of 12 dysthymic patients were classified as preoccupied. Of the borderline patients, 10 out of 12 fell into one particular preoccupied subcategory, appearing "confused, fearful and overwhelmed" in relation to past experiences with attachment figures. Not one dysthymic patient was classified in this way.

There were also significantly more borderline individuals classified as "unresolved" in relation to trauma and loss. This result was the more striking and interesting because the overall rates of trauma and loss did not differ between the two groups: 9 out of 12 borderline subjects and 10 out of 12 dysthymic subjects reported episodes that met the criteria for significant trauma or loss set out in the AAI rating schedule. The differences arose because every single one of the 9 borderline subjects were classified as unresolved with respect to the trauma or loss they reported, as compared with only 20% (2) of the 10 dysthymic patients who did so. When we focused more specifically on early trauma, we found that 6 borderline patients reported such experiences, ranging from frightening beatings from parental figures to childhood sexual abuse. Five patients from our dysthymic group reported traumata of comparable severity. However, all 6 of the borderline patients were classified as unresolved with respect to these traumatic experiences, while none of the 5 dysthymic patients was classified as in this way. This finding highlights the contrast between our groups in the capacity to assimilate their early conflictual experiences.

With respect to the data from the Parental Bonding Instrument, the borderline group reported significantly lower maternal care and significantly higher maternal overprotection than the dysthymic group. Clearly one cannot jump to the conclusion that the mothers of our borderline patients were actually cold and rejecting yet intrusive and controlling in relation to their offspring in early childhood, since the judgments may have been influenced by a number of factors, both current and past. Nevertheless, it is appropriate to recall Bowlby's hypothesis that powerful interpersonal experiences in early childhood may be particularly potent sources of "multiple models" of interpersonal relationships, and to acknowledge that this pattern of results is what most psychoanalysts would have anticipated.

In summary, the study has yielded evidence that at least in certain patient groups, adults' modes of representing early experience are intimately related to styles of interpersonal functioning. In our sample of patients with borderline personality disorder, their typical preoccupied style of representation characterized by marked yet unexplained oscillations of viewpoint concerning the nature and significance of their past experience, bears an intimate relation to the pattern that characterizes these patients' current interpersonal relatedness. Ten of the 12 borderline patients were unable to locate or contain significant early experiences within a coherent mental framework, or indeed to think about the significance or implications of particular experiences. These findings complement evidence for a correspondence between adults' styles of mental representation and these adults' observed interactions with their own infants and children (Crowell and Feldman, 1988; Main and Goldwyn, 1984; Main and Hesse, 1990), a correspondence that may be responsible for intergenerational influences in the patterning of attachment relationships (Fonagy et al., 1991). While the origins of interpersonal disturbances remain open to debate, there is an obvious case for considering psychoanalytic propositions such as those of Bion (1962a, 1962b), Kernberg (1976), Kohut and Wolf (1978) and more recently Fonagy (1991), that failures of emotional containment or emotional sensitivity and empathy in early infancy may lead to a disruption in the capacity for thinking about the contents of one's own mind.

Discussion

I hope that as well as giving the gist of some empirical studies, I have managed to convey the kinds of attitude and thinking that lie behind our research. Whether investigating issues of "basic science" in psychological experiments with autistic individuals, or studying matters of more widespread clinical relevance in the work on borderline personality disorder, colleagues and myself are attempting to apply conventional scientific methods to aspects of interpersonal development that lend themselves to varieties of "numbers research." We hope that these endeavors fulfill at least two purposes. First, we wish to draw attention to the (often neglected) developmental significance of personal relatedness and relationships for cognitive as well as social development, and to support psychoanalysts and others who have long advocated a social-developmental account of human psychology. Second, we wish to approach important social-developmental issues with novel methodologies in order to gain knowledge and perhaps open theoretical perspectives that will be of value for psychoanalysts and nonanalysts alike.

I shall conclude this contribution by trying to illustrate what I mean. First I consider the work on autism, together with the reseach on normal infancy with which our studies of autism are intimately related. There are a number of investigators who have managed to maintain their identities as psychoanalysts while pursuing analytically informed but methodologically nonanalytic investigations into social-developmental issues of childhood. Perhaps most relevant to our concerns have been the empirical and theoretical contributions of Emde (1983, 1992; Emde et al., 1992) and Stern (1985). Emde's programmatic research has documented the biologically prepared social-regulatory and affective structures that ground an infant's one-to-one relationships with caregivers. The research has also highlighted the significance of social referencing and a caregiver's emotional availability for the one-year-old's capacity to discover and negotiate "meanings" in the world, and to evolve an increasingly elaborated awareness of self. Stern, too, has advanced clear formulations on the importance of infant-caregiver intersubjective transactions and affective attunement for the development of an infant's representations of self *vis-à-vis* other. Correspondingly, in the field of autism, Shapiro and his colleagues (Shapiro, 1977; Shapiro and Hertzig, 1991; Shapiro et al., 1987) have pioneered studies not only on autistic children's unusual use of language, but also on their abnormal affective expressiveness and their sometimes muted but nevertheless observable reactions to separation from and reunion with familiar caregivers. Cohen (1980) and his colleagues (Volkmar et al., 1987) have complemented sensitive descriptions of individual autistic patients with formal studies of the children's central handicaps in social development and adjustment.

On the one hand, psychoanalysis is without parallel as a method of investigation into intersubjective psychological processes. On the other hand, the issues raised and sometimes addressed by formal research may include facets of psychological development that are sometimes tangential to or even beyond the reach of purely psychoanalytic studies. For example, what are the biological bases for and irreducible characteristics of object-relations psychology? How much and in what ways might neurological impairment alter the representational structures of mind? To what extent are there forms of innate understanding and representation, and to what extent do a child's experiences of interpersonal coordination provide a formative influence on the structuring of mind, including the emergent capacity for symbolic representation? How do the organic and/or psychological factors that *disrupt* (say) intersubjective contact or symbolic functioning relate to the processes required to establish such contact or such cognitive abilities in the first place? Infancy research has already proved its value for promoting thinking and debate on such issues, both within and outside psychoanalysis. Both psychoanalytic and nonanalytic research on autism may do the same. The peculiarities of autism may challenge us to rethink how biologically based and coherently organized capacities for emotional sensibility, responsiveness, and experience are necessary for or closely allied to primitive forms of object representation and psychological defense.

Finally, I come to the work on adults' mental representations. Here there is an exciting convergence of perspectives from psychoanalysis and developmental research. The work on young children's attachment-separation reactions inspired by Bowlby (1969, 1973, 1988a, 1988b) has had such an impact for many good reasons, but one of the most important is that Ainsworth's simple and replicable "strange situation" assessment technique (Ainsworth and Wittig, 1969; Ainsworth et al., 1978) managed to capture easily measurable expressions of complex and important individual differences among infant-caregiver dyads. The AAI (George et al., 1985, unpublished) has direct linkage with these studies insofar as the AAI categories were derived by noting how styles of maternal discourse at interview corresponded with direct observations of those same mothers with their infants during the brief separations and reunions of the strange situation. It is no coincidence that this research strategy has led to observations on styles of representation in adults which bear a close correspondence to psychoanalytic perspectives on mental functioning, perspectives that also developed through the study of the mind as reflected in a person's interpersonal as well as intrapsychic relationships.

I believe that over the next decade, we face the prospect of a change in the standing of psychoanalytic thinking within developmental psychology and psychiatry. The change will be propelled by the force of research findings that reflect or coordinate with psychoanalytic thinking, and that cannot simply be dismissed. The findings themselves will not establish the validity of psychoanalytic study, but they will provide new opportunities for rapprochement and mutual enrichment between psychoanalytic and nonanalytic disciplines. From a deepening concern with the processes that underpin and shape an individual's representational world, and with increasing refinement in observing and measuring the interpersonal as well as intrapersonal coordination of social experience in the earliest years of life, there will arise a pressing need to map the intersubjective domain. This has long been the province of psychoanalytic investigation and theory. I anticipate that academic psychologists and psychiatrists will find that psychoanalytic propositions concerning the object-relational foundations of mind and the formative potential of defensive psychological processes are neither so speculative nor so superfluous as many have supposed. At the same time, psychoanalysts will find that conventional research becomes more attuned to and relevant for their own preoccupations—and with this, increasingly illuminating and challenging. I think there are already signs of such changes in attitude within the field of developmental psychopathology.

REFERENCES

AINSWORTH, M. B. & WITTIG, B. A. (1969). Attachment and exploratory behavior of one-year-olds in a strange situation. In *Determinants of Infant Behaviour, Vol. 4*, ed. B. M. Foss. London: Methuen, pp. 111–136.
——— BLEHAR, M., WATERS, E. & WALL, S. (1978). *Patterns of Attachment*. Hillsdale, NJ: Erlbaum.
BARON-COHEN, S. (1988). Social and pragmatic deficits in autism: cognitive or affective? *J. Autism Devel. Dis.*, 18:379–402.
BECK, A. (1984). The Beck Depression Inventory. In *The Psychological Treatment of Depression: A Guide to the Theory and Practice of Cognitive Behavioral Therapy*, ed. M. Williams. New York: Free Press.
BION, W. R. (1962a). A theory of thinking. *Int. J. Psychoanal.*, 43:306–310.
——— (1962b). *Learning from Experience*. London: Heinemann.
BOWLBY, J. (1969). *Attachment and Loss. Vol. 1: Attachment*. New York: Basic Books.
——— (1973). *Attachment and Loss. Vol. 2: Separation*. New York: Basic Books.
——— (1988a). *A Secure Base: Clinical Applications of Attachment Theory*. London: Routledge.
——— (1988b). Developmental psychiatry comes of age. *Amer. J. Psychiat.*, 145:1–10.
BRADLEY, S. (1979). The relationship of early maternal separation to borderline personality in children and adolescents. *Amer. J. Psychiat.*, 136:424–426.
BRYER, J., NELSON, B., MILLER, J. & KROL, P. (1987). Childhood sexual and physical abuse as factors in adult psychiatric illness. *Amer. J. Psychiat.*, 144:1426–1436.
CHURCHILL, D. W. (1972). The relation of infantile autism and early childhood schizophrenia to developmental language disorders of childhood. *J. Autism Child. Schiz.*, 2:182–197.
CICCHETTI, D. (1984). The emergence of developmental psychopathology. *Child Devel.*, 55:1–7.
COHEN, D. J. (1980). The pathology of the self in primary childhood autism and Gilles de la Tourette syndrome. *Psychiat. Clin. N. Amer.*, 3:383–402.
CROWELL, J. A. & FELDMAN, S. S. (1988). Mothers' internal models of relationships and children's behavioral and developmental status: a study of mother-child interaction. *Child Devel.*, 59:1273–1285.
DUNN, L. M., DUNN, L. M. & WHETTON, C. (1982). *British Picture Vocabulary Scale*. Windsor, Eng.: NFER—Nelson.
EMDE, R. N. (1983). The prerepresentational self and its affective core. *Psychoanal. Study Child*, 38:165–192.

———— (1992). Social referencing research: uncertainty, self and the search for meaning. In *Social Referencing and the Social Construction of Reality in Infancy*, ed. S. Feinman. New York: Plenum, pp. 79–94.
———— PLOMIN, R.; ROBINSON, J.; CORLEY, R.; DEFRIES, J.; FULKER, D. W.; REZNICK, J. S.; CAMPOS, J.; KAGAN, J. & ZAHN-WAXLER, C. (1992). Temperament, emotion, and cognition at fourteen months: the Macarthur longitudinal twin study. *Child Devel.*, 63:1437–1455.
FEINMAN, S., Ed. (1992). *Social Referencing and the Social Construction of Reality in Infancy*. New York: Plenum.
FERENCZI, S. (1913). The ontogenesis of symbols. In *First Contributions to Psycho-analysis*. London: Hogarth Press, 1952, pp. 276–281.
FONAGY, P. (1991). Thinking about thinking: some clinical and theoretical considerations concerning the treatment of a borderline patient. *Int. J. Psychoanal.*, 72:639–656.
———— STEELE, H. & STEELE, M. (1991). Maternal representations of attachment during pregnancy predict the organization of infant-mother attachment at one year of age. *Child Devel.*, 62:891–905.
FRAIBERG, S. & ADELSON, E. (1977). Self-representation in language and play. In *Insights from the Blind*, ed. S. Fraiberg. London: Souvenir Press, pp. 248–270.
GEORGE, C., KAPLAN, N. & MAIN, M. (1985). *The Attachment Interview for Adults*. Unpublished manuscript, University of California, Berkeley.
HAMLYN, D. W. (1974). Person-perception and our understanding of others. In *Understanding Other Persons*, ed. T. Mischel. Oxford, Eng.: Blackwell, pp. 1–36.
HERMAN, J., PERRY, J. & VAN DER KOLK, B. (1989). Childhood trauma in borderline personality disorder. *Amer. J. Psychiat.*, 146:490–495.
HERMELIN, B. & O'CONNOR, N. (1970). *Psychological Experiments with Autistic Children*. Oxford, Eng.: Pergamon Press.
HOBSON, R. P. (1989a). Beyond cognition: a theory of autism. In *Autism: Nature, Diagnosis and Treatment*, ed. G. Dawson. New York: Guilford Press, pp. 22–48.
———— (1989b). On sharing experiences. *Devel. Psychopathol.*, 1:197–203.
———— (1990a). On acquiring knowledge about people, and the capacity to pretend: response to Leslie. *Psychol. Rev.*, 97:114–121.
———— (1990b). On psychoanalytic approaches to autism. *Amer. J. Orthopsychiat.*, 60:324–336.
———— (1990c). Concerning knowledge of mental states. *Brit. J. Med. Psychol.*, 63:199–213.
———— (1990d). On the origins of self and the case of autism. *Devel. Psychopathol.*, 2:163–181.
———— (1991a). Methodological issues for experiments on autistic individuals' perception and understanding of emotion. *J. Child Psychol. Psychiat.*, 32:1135–1158.
———— (1991b). What is autism? *Psychiat. Clin. N. Amer.*, 14:1–17.
———— (1993). *Autism and the Development of Mind*. Hillsdale, NJ: Erlbaum.
———— (in press). Through feeling and sight to self and symbol. In *Ecological and Interpersonal Knowledge of the Self*, ed. U. Neisser. New York: CUP.
———— & LEE, A. (1989). Emotion-related and abstract concepts in autistic people: evidence from the British Picture Vocabulary Scale. *J. Autism Devel. Dis.*, 19:601–623.

―――― ―――― & CHIAT, S. (in press). I, you, me and autism: an experimental study. *J. Autism Devel. Dis.*
―――― OUSTON, J. & LEE, A. (1988a). Emotion recognition in autism: coordinating faces and voices. *Psychol. Med.*, 18:911–923.
―――― ―――― ―――― (1988b). What's in a face? the case of autism. *Brit. J. Psychol.*, 79:441–453.
―――― ―――― ―――― (1989). Naming emotion in faces and voices: abilities and disabilities in autism and mental retardation. *Brit. J. Devel. Psychol.*, 7:237–250.
JONES, E. (1916). The theory of symbolism. In *Papers on Psycho-analysis* (5th ed.). London: Ballière, Tindall & Cox, 1948, pp. 87–144.
KANNER, L. (1943). Autistic disturbances of affective contact. *Nerv. Child*, 2:217–250.
KEELER, W. R. (1958). Autistic patterns and defective communication in blind children with retrolental fibroplasia. In *Psychopathology of Communication*, ed. P. H. Hoch & J. Zubin. New York: Grune & Stratton, pp. 64–83.
KERNBERG, O. F. (1976). *Object Relations Theory and Clinical Psychoanalysis.* Northvale, NJ: Aronson.
KLEIN, M. (1930). The importance of symbol-formation in the development of the ego. In *Love, Guilt and Reparation and Other Works 1921–1945.* London: Hogarth Press, 1975, pp. 219–232.
KOHUT, H. & WOLF, E. S. (1978). The disorders of the self and their treatment: an outline. *Int. J. Psychoanal.*, 59:413–425.
LANGER, S. K. (1957). *Philosophy in a New Key.* Cambridge, MA: Harvard Univ. Press.
LESLIE, A. M. (1987). Pretence and representation: the origins of 'theory of mind.' *Psychol. Rev.*, 94:412–426.
MACKINNON, A., HENDERSON, A. & ANDREWS, G. (1991). The Parental Bonding Instrument: a measure of perceived or actual parental behaviour? *Acta Psychiat. Scand.*, 83:153–159.
MAHLER, M. S. (1968). *On Human Symbiosis and the Vicissitudes of Individuation.* New York: Int. Univ. Press.
MAIN, M. & GOLDWYN, R. (1984). Predicting rejection of her infant from mother's representation of her own experience: implications for the abused-abusing intergenerational cycle. *Child Abuse and Neglect*, 8:203–217.
―――― ―――― (1991). *Adult Attachment Rating and Classification System.* Unpublished scoring manual, Department of Psychology, University of California, Berkeley.
―――― & HESSE, E. (1990). Parents' unresolved traumatic experiences are related to infant disorganized attachment status: is frightened and/or frightening parental behavior the linking mechanism? In *Attachment in the Preschool Years: Theory, Research and Intervention*, ed. M. Greenberg, D. Cicchetti & M. Cummings. Chicago: Univ. Chicago Press, pp. 161–182.
PARKER, G., TUPLING, H. & BROWN, L. (1979). A Parental Bonding Instrument. *Brit. J. Med. Psychol.*, 52:1–10.
PATRICK, M., HOBSON, R. P. & MANGHAN, B. (1994). Personality disorder and the mental representation of early social experience. *Devel. Psychopathol.*, 6:375–388.
RUTTER, M. (1972). Childhood schizophrenia reconsidered. *J. Autism Child. Schiz.*, 2:315–337.

———— & SCHOPLER, E. (1987). Autism and pervasive developmental disorders: concepts and diagnostic issues. *J. Autism Devel. Dis.*, 17:159–186.

RYCROFT, C. (1956). Symbolism and its relationship to the primary and secondary processes. *Int. J. Psychoanal.*, 37:137–146.

SCHEERER, M., ROTHMANN, E. & GOLDSTEIN, K. (1945). A case of "idiot savant": an experimental study of personality organization. *Psychol. Monogr.*, 58(4):1–63.

SEGAL, H. (1957). Notes on symbol formation. *Int. J. Psychoanal.*, 38:391–397.

SHAPIRO, T. (1977). The quest for a linguistic model to study the speech of autistic children. *J. Amer. Acad. Child Psychiat.*, 16:608–619.

———— & HERTZIG, M. E. (1991). Social deviance in autism: a central integrative failure as a model for social nonengagement. *Psychiat. Clin. N. Amer.*, 14:19–32.

———— SHERMAN, M., CALAMARI, G. & KOCH, D. (1987). Attachment in autism and other developmental disorders. *J. Amer. Acad. Child Adol. Psychiat.*, 26:485–490.

SORCE, J. F., EMDE, R. N., CAMPOS, J. & KLINNERT, M. D. (1985). Maternal emotional signaling: its effect on the visual cliff behavior of one-year-olds. *Devel. Psychol.*, 21:195–200.

STERN, D. N. (1985). *The Interpersonal World of the Infant.* New York: Basic Books.

TUSTIN, F. (1981). *Autistic States in Children.* London: Routledge & Kegan Paul.

———— (1983). Thoughts on autism with special reference to a paper by Melanie Klein. *J. Child Psychother.*, 9:119–131.

VOLKMAR, K. R.; SPARROW, S. S.; GOUDREAU, D.; CICHETTI, D. V.; PAUL, R. & COHEN, D. (1987). Social defects in autism: an operational approach using the Vineland Adaptive Behavior Scales. *J. Amer. Acad. Child Adoles. Psychiat.*, 26:156–161.

VYGOTSKY, L. S. (1962). *Thought and Language.* Cambridge, MA: MIT Press.

WEEKS, S. J. & HOBSON, R. P. (1987). The salience of facial expression for autistic children. *J. Child Psychol. Psychiat.*, 28:137–152.

WERNER, H. & KAPLAN, B. (1963). *Symbol Formation.* New York: Wiley.

WING, L., GOULD, J., YEATES, S. R. & BRIERLY, L. M. (1977). Symbolic play in severely mentally retarded and in autistic children. *J. Child Psychol. Psychiat.*, 18:167–178.

WITTGENSTEIN, L. (1953). *Philosophical Investigations.* Oxford, Eng.: Blackwell.

ZWEIG-FRANK, H. & PARIS, J. (1991). Parents' emotional neglect and overprotection according to recollections of patients with borderline personality disorder. *Amer. J. Psychiat.*, 148:648–651.

APPLIED PSYCHOANALYSIS: HOW RESEARCH WITH INFANTS AND ADOLESCENTS AT HIGH PSYCHOSOCIAL RISK INFORMS PSYCHOANALYSIS

JOY D. OSOFSKY, PH.D.

Psychoanalysis has provided an influential framework for understanding infants, children, and adolescents. Research over the past two decades with families at high psychosocial risk has allowed us to understand some of the important dynamics affecting such families. This paper describes major aspects of our programmatic research, with an emphasis on new directions in both theory and research using psychoanalytic theory relevant to that research. Theoretical areas addressed are: self development for infants and parents at high psychosocial risk, the salience of negative emotions, intergenerational repetition of maladaptive patterns of behavior, and the effects of chronic traumatic experiences in the context of community violence. The need for a dynamic interactional model in psychoanalytic theory is discussed. It is proposed that intrapsychic and interpersonal development must be included in such a model in order for clinicians to understand infants and adolescents at high psychosocial risk.

OUR RESEARCH PROGRAM HAS focused on socioemotional development in adolescent mothers and their infants. Our early studies (Osofsky, 1976; Osofsky and Danzger, 1974; Osofsky and Eberhart-Wright, 1988, 1992; Osofsky et al., 1988; Ware et al., 1987) found that teenage mothers have more difficulty relating to and parenting their infants at some points during the infants' development than they do at other times.

From the Louisiana State University Medical Center.

Appreciation is expressed to Drs. John Stocks and Martin Drell as well as to the editors for their helpful comments on an earlier version of this paper. Research reported in this paper was supported by grants from the Early Childhood Transitions Network of the John D. and Catherine T. MacArthur Foundation, the Spencer Foundation, and the Institute of Mental Hygiene, New Orleans.

For example, in the first year of life, when infants are naturally dependent on their mothers, many adolescent mothers want their infants to hold their own bottles and take care of themselves. In contrast, in the second year, as their infants become more independent, many adolescent mothers have difficulty with assertion of autonomy and tease their babies, seemingly wanting them to remain dependent. Subsequently, we found (Osofsky et al., 1993a) that difficulties adolescent mothers experience in their current development contribute to problems in being sensitive to their infants' needs (Osofsky et al., 1993a). Adolescent mothers as compared with high-risk but nonpregnant adolescents had more difficulties in the areas of identity formation, sense of basic trust, and intimacy. They were unable to resolve early and midadolescent struggles which appeared to contribute to problems in parenting their infants.

In addition to problems with adolescent personality development, adolescent mothers manifested problems with affect regulation. As compared with nonparenting adolescents, such mothers scored much higher on self-report measures of depressive mood. In two studies, over 60 percent of our samples scored above the clinical cutoff for depression (Radloff, 1977). Mother-infant interaction patterns observed in such dyads indicated that they showed less overall affect, fewer positive affective exchanges, and more negative affect than is typically observed in lower-risk and older mother-infant pairs.

We have focused on emotional availability in the parent-child system in our studies of populations at high psychosocial risk. This work has involved the study of dyadic patterns of behavior and affect that manifest a sense of sustained pleasure and range of emotional expressions if all is going well, and a deficit of pleasure, a "turning-off" if development is not going well (Emde, 1980, 1981; Osofsky and Eberhart-Wright, 1988; Osofsky et al., 1992). This concept reflects an interaction process involving the infant, parent, and dyadic interaction system and expands the familiar concept of maternal sensitivity and responsivity to infant needs as used in attachment research

(Ainsworth et al., 1978). In our studies, we have noted that sensitive, responsive, and positive interactions lead to the development of regulated patterns of affective interactions, including those that provide the child with experiences that change with and adjust to the child's needs. In contrast, caregiving interactions that were overcontrolling, overstimulating, and unstimulating led to more negative or dysregulated affective experiences that interfered with the child's attempts to control the environment. The child learns through the latter interactive experiences that he or she will have little influence or control over the experience.

Dyadic interactions of adolescent mothers and infants showed more negative and less positive affect than those of lower psychosocial-risk older mothers. Both research and clinical work support the notion that the lessening of negative and enhancing of positive affective experiences (affect regulation) are important to promote optimal development. Indeed, these experiences are viewed as core processes in self-regulation and self-development (Emde, 1991; Gianino and Tronick, 1988; Sroufe, 1989; Stern, 1985). On the other hand, affect dysregulation, where there is greater preponderance of negative, and fewer positive affects, communicates the affective unavailability of the caregiving environment and interferes with the child's adaptive development (Emde, 1980; Greenspan and Porges, 1984; Gianino and Tronick, 1988; Sroufe, 1989). The notions of affect regulation, dysregulation, and emotional availability are important processes for a dynamic interactional understanding of theory that places less emphasis on either a drive model to explain aggression or a deficit model of self pathology that includes problems in self-object experience.

Another feature of our research program has involved studying individuals from a variety of ethnic and cultural groups. We have come to realize that without taking into account the context of cultural and ethnic diversity in which infants and children are socialized, we cannot appreciate the potential strengths and vulnerabilities that characterize development. Our work with different ethnic groups in diverse contexts has included studies of adolescent mothers and their infants, work on intergenerational family influences on adolescent development, and studies of children and families living in environments characterized by chronic community violence. We have learned that aspects of development and family patterns often assumed to be normative may not characterize families coming from different ethnic and cultural traditions or those raised under conditions of poverty and stress.

Positive and Negative Emotions and Aggression

Before focusing on the importance of negative emotions for understanding both parent-infant interactions and self development in high-risk groups, we shall elucidate what is understood better—the role of positive emotions in development. Positive emotions, which are organized separately from negative emotions, are adaptive processes that mediate sociability and encourage exploration (Emde, 1988, 1991). While they are part of an infant's biological repertoire, positive emotions need to be activated in the context of caregiving interactions, and are vulnerable to the effects of environmental circumstances. Interactions need to be sensitive and responsive for positive emotions to be prominent and mediate sociability.

In contrast to positive affect sharing, such as reciprocal looking and smiling, which occurs frequently in low-risk groups, adolescent mothers and their infants seldom show such activity. Instead, we observe more negative affect exchanges or "sharing." For example, it is common to see repeated angry exchanges between mother and infant during play, as well maternal teasing and frustration responses from the infant. Further, we have observed six-month-old babies who smile very little, often showing bland, expressionless faces. Many of these infants are raised by mothers who report high levels of depressive mood. As we studied affective patterns of interaction in high-risk infants and their adolescent mothers, we have gained insight into the negative side of the interaction. Because the healthy development of self and emergence of the affective core of self depend on a balance of positive and negative affective experiences reflecting reciprocity in the relationship (Emde, 1983, 1991), we might expect that the development of self for infants raised in primarily negative affective environments would be more problematic.

Our work with high-psychosocial-risk adolescent mothers and their infants provides the opportunity to study infants who are experiencing aversive stimulation. Problems of dysregulation and hostility in the parent-child relationship under such circumstances result in negative experience, and we have found little evidence that this experience can be attributed to differences in innate characteristics. Instead, we have found evidence that problems with aggression and negative affects result from adverse relationship experiences in the family.

Parens (1992) has stated that "hostile destructive affects . . . develop progressively during the first three years of life. Whereas pleasurable experiences are core determiners of the degree to which positive emotions develop, excessive unpleasure experiences are the central determiners and ingredients of the negative emotions" (p. 102). Several psychoanalytic theorists, including Bowlby, Kernberg, and Kohut, from different conceptual perspectives, come to a similar conclusion that hostile destructiveness is not innate but is provoked in the self by negative experiences. Our observations are consistent with those of Bowlby (1980) and Parens (1992), that displays of aggression and negative affect in infants and children at high psychosocial risk seem to be related to variations in adverse experience, rather than to variations in intrinsic features with respect to impulses (Osofsky and Eberhart-Wright, 1988, 1992; Osofsky et al., 1992).

Fraiberg (1987) provides a framework for understanding how these behavioral changes may come about in high-psychosocial-risk children, through her discussion of pathological defenses in infancy between three and eighteen months of age that develop in the face of abuse and neglect in the early environment. Such children had been raised by parents who showed serious personality problems and were unable to nurture their children appropriately. The children, in response, used defenses of avoidance, freezing, fighting, affective transformations, and reversal in order to ward off painful affects associated with the adverse parenting experiences. Fraiberg noted a deviant course of aggressive behavior at the beginning of the second year of life when aggression was discharged in wild outbursts one moment, and then turned back upon the self. Galenson (1986) also described physically abused or neglected infants who displayed at least one of the types of behaviors noted by Fraiberg. Further, she emphasized that children showing these defensive reactions were frequently raised by mothers who were chronically depressed and showed infantile behaviors. The mothers were disorganized and erratic in their behavior, and their infants repeated in their behaviors parentallike outbursts of rage and aggression. The behaviors described by Fraiberg and Galenson are seen commonly in our observations of adolescent mother-infant interactions. The behaviors may be related in part to the unpredicability of adolescents; however, more of the pattern of behaviors seems to result from continual negative interactive experience and a stressful, hostile environment.

Fonagy, Moran, and Target (1992, unpublished) explored the idea of aggression as a defense against threats to the psychological self and the potential outcomes for children raised in non-nurturant environments. They suggest that the defensive protection of the self through aggressive acts by children may be a successful short-term strategy, but one that is inadequate to the severity of the threat and the fragility of the structure it is attempting to defend (Osofsky et al., in press).

This theoretical research contributes insights into the negative side of affective experience in the midst of stressful environments. In the next section, we shall consider how early adverse experiences may influence both the interpersonal and intrapsychic development of the infant and young child.

Self Development for Infants and Parents at High Psychosocial Risk

The internalization of affective experience may be problematic for infants brought up in high-psychosocial-risk environments. Certain aspects of the relationship process are central for the healthy development of the self that depends on both intrapsychic and interpersonal experience. Dyadic affect regulation and dysregulation experienced through the relationship process have important implications for traditional notions of drive theory as well as for more recent ideas of self psychology (Kohut, 1977; Kernberg, 1990). The caregiver needs to be consistently available in order to reflect, mirror, or respond empathically to the needs of the infant.

Through emotional availability and appropriate affect regulation, Fonagy et al. (1991a) emphasize that the caregiver must be sensitive to the child's inner (mental) world in addition to the physical world. Thus, the parent will help contain the infant's overwhelming affects and bind the child's anxiety so that the child can use fantasy to play out conflicts and express fears symbolically. Without this capacity, a child may experience faulty ego functioning with an ego that is unusually tolerant of drive and impulse expression (see case presented in Osofsky et al., 1992). According to adult attachment theory and to Fonagy and his colleagues (1991b), if the parent's capacity to understand the infant is interfered with by incoherent mental representations or the parent's poor relationship history (Main and Solomon, 1990), the infant may experience problematic ego development and may have difficulty developing a good sense of self. At the same time, because of chaotic and dysregulated affective experiences, the child may not be able to maintain impulse control in interaction with others.

Emde (1983, 1991) has proposed an "affective core of self" which provides an individual with a sense of consistency about others in the environment. Organized and patterned affective experience is crucial for an infant to be able to relate and to share feelings with an emotionally available caregiver who is responsive and self-regulatory. Moreover, the caregiver's availability and responsiveness to the infant's affective states, or "mirroring," are sometimes necessary in order for the infant to develop a sense of coherence reflected in the affective core of self (Kohut, 1977; Emde, 1991). With dysregulation of affective experience, which is so common in high-psychosocial-risk groups, this necessary dyadic experience is unlikely, and the coherent organization required for the affective core of self may be in jeopardy.

Intergenerational Repetition of Maladaptive Patterns of Behavior

Our research with a high-psychosocial-risk group of adolescent mothers and their infants also provides an opportunity to consider intergenerational repetition since adolescent pregnancy and parenthood often repeat themselves generation after generation. The dynamic construct of the repetition compulsion can be seen as a process that functions as a bridge between the inner and outer worlds. The process may act as a mediator between healthy and problematic developmental outcomes as past representations confront current perceptions in order to reduce pain. While development continues, the tendency to repeat is uncontrolled. In order to overcome the compulsion to repeat, which involves internalized intrapsychic relationship aspects as well as interpersonal conflicts, the individual may need to experience correction within the context of a new interpersonal relationship experience.

From a psychoanalytic perspective in therapeutic work, early developmental data are often used retrospectively to inform the current ongoing process. Developmental psychoanalysts use a prospective approach to understand present functioning which includes direct observations and actual data in addition to intrapsychic material. Fraiberg and her colleagues (1975) describe the potentially devastating effects of a parent's earlier negative life experiences that have been unresolved and may impact on the current relationship with her child interfering with her ability to parent effectively. In recent research done across several generations, it has been shown that the attachment relationship the mother had with her own mother plays an important part in the relationship she subsequently develops with her child. If the mother had a difficult relationship with her mother and was able to resolve it successfully, then she will be better able to form a positive relationship with her own child. In contrast, if the mother continues to struggle with a past difficult relationship in the present, it is more likely that parenting will be a conflictual experience for her (Main and Solomon, 1990; Main and Goldwyn, 1984). Theoretical explorations based on observations of infants, children, and caregivers raised in very high-risk environments describe the intrapsychic and interpersonal struggles accompanying the development of these children that are verified by observations.

Chronic Traumatic Experiences in the Context of Community Violence

Psychoanalysis as well as other developmental theories assumes a certain consistency in the development of relationship patterns across the generations. However, for groups at high psychosocial risk marked by instability and variability, inconsistencies are more common. Schaer (1988, unpublished) and his colleagues have studied the effects of sustained and unremitting actual trauma on the psychic structure of young children, including physical and sexual abuse, deprivation, neglect, and chronic community violence. Observations of children growing up in poverty environments in the inner city indicated that they displayed a range of problematic behaviors, including impulsive and action-oriented behaviors rather than verbalization, verbal and physical aggression, and little frustration tolerance or future orientation. In such children, object relations were primitive, reflecting, at best, ambivalent interactions with others. Adults were frequently experienced as interchangeable. Similar to our observations, such children lacked the ability to develop basic trust. Their defenses were rigid and archaic, which interfered with adaptive functioning. It should be noted that what is of central importance in such observations is the state of chronic strain and the ego's adaptation to it (Sandler, 1967). With chronic community violence, the trauma is often continuous, which may overwhelm the child and contribute to difficulties with ego organization.

In a study of emerging developmental psychopathology in a subgroup of forty-four-month-old children of adolescent mothers drawn from a larger sample, we found similar traumatic themes revealed in narrative stories told in response to open-ended conflict situations presented symbolically through doll play (Osofsky et al., in press). The children in this study had been exposed to chaotic, unprotected environments where aggression was rampant. Children told stories that contained incoherent aggression and what seemed like inappropriate negative responses. In some, ego organization seemed to be insufficient to meet the task of following and enforcing moral demands, and aggression was idealized. For some children living under conditions of chronic violence, it was as if their intrapsychic structure reflected mental images that were consistent with their experiences, images that were quite different from more expectable or normative patterns of behavior.

Our observations of children exposed to early negative affective interaction experiences and significant affect dysregulation clearly indicate, along with the research of others, that more work, including careful followup studies, is needed to understand their later development (Osofsky et al., 1992; Osofsky et al., in press; Gianino and Tronick, 1988).

Need for a Dynamic Interactional Model

We believe psychoanalytic theory needs to have a dynamic interactional model to account for our findings. Neither a self psychology deficit model for understanding problems with self-object experience nor a drive model for understanding problems with aggressive impulses seems sufficient to organize data from our research experience. To encompass both intrapsychic and interpersonal development for infants and children at risk, a theoretical system is needed that integrates biological givens, early experience, and the reciprocal management of affects within the early relationship. We need to take into account the exchanges between caregiver and child during which affects are not just "mirrored," but actively co-constructed and shared.

A more extensive model would allow for an integration of internalized intrapsychic experience and interpersonal exchanges involving mutual influences of infant and caregiver as well as their variations in situational and cultural contexts. Our empirical data (Osofsky and Eberhart-Wright, 1988, 1992; Osofsky et al., in press), and that of others (Parens, 1992; Fonagy et al., unpublished), in a variety of contexts and from different perspectives, has shown that the development of aggression cannot be understood solely in terms of drives and intrapsychic processes. The changing, reciprocal interactive process between caregiver and infant plays a role in the emergence of aggressive behaviors, e.g., adverse experiences within the family affect the emergence of aggression and negative affects. A meaningful understanding of the development of relationships requires a cultural and ecological context for the development of each individual child, resting on expectations and experiences within that context. The relationship that a child is able to form with another in a highly violent environment, for example, may depend as much or more on being raised by an extended supportive family than by the child's biological makeup or the child's having experienced an insensitive relationship with the mother.

Several domains of psychoanalytic theory have provided background for the development of our dynamic interactional model. Bowlby (1969) proposed the idea of a goal-directed partnership that involves the infant or young child's growing insight into the attachment figure's (or mother's) motives and plans, including infant initiative and sensitive maternal responding (Bretherton, 1992). Sandler's idea of the wished-for response of the object also is relevant to our conceptualization of the early relationship between parent and infant. Sandler and Rosenblatt (1962) linked the expression of an instinctual need with the shape of an object representation where needs become transformed into wishes involving self- and object representation. Our dynamic interactional model extends and modifies existing theoretical perspectives to include various risk groups, family structures, and cultural variations. Further, a dynamic interactional model would consider more than psychoanalytic drive or deficit models, in that intrapsychic components as well as the infant's affective processing of relationship experiences would be included.

Studying affect regulation and emotional availability in high-risk samples has uncovered dimensions of the interaction process that are seen less often in studies of normative groups, that is, the occurrence of negative affect sharing and affect dysregulation. The theoretical issues discussed above, i.e., the development of the self, negative affect sharing, intergenerational repetition, and chronic trauma, coming from our research program, would be interrelated, interconnected, and integrated in a dynamic interactional model. Negative affect sharing, intergenerational repeating, and chronic traumatic experiences disrupt effective reciprocal management of affect (affect regulation). In order for an infant to develop a healthy sense of self, positive experiences are needed that involve affect attunement (Stern, 1985), empathy (Kohut, 1977), and the ability symbolically to assimilate and internalize positive relationship experiences.

An overarching conceptualization is needed to model reciprocal affect regulation or dysregulation in caregiving dyads and the internalization of such processes in the developing child. Long-term prospective studies are required to understand outcomes for infants and children raised under conditions of risk. Based on our knowledge to date about early development and retrospective information, it is likely that such children will have difficulties in developing a healthy sense of self and a capacity for later relationships. In addition, more information is needed about factors that lead to resilience as well as vulnerability for children raised in high-risk environments.

REFERENCES

Ainsworth, M. D. S., Blehar, M. C., Waters, E. & Wall, S. (1978). *Patterns of Attachment: A Psychological Study of the Strange Situation*. Hillsdale, NJ: Erlbaum.

Bowlby, J. (1969). *Attachment and Loss. Vol. 1: Attachment*. New York: Basic Books.

——— (1980). *Attachment and Loss. Vol. 3: Attachment and Loss, Sadness and Depression*. New York: Basic Books.

Bretherton, I. (1992). The origins of attachment theory: John Bowlby and Mary Ainsworth. *Devel. Psychol.*, 28:759–775.

Emde, R. N. (1980). Emotional availability: a reciprocal reward system for infants and parents with implications for psychosocial disorders. In *Parent-Infant Relationships*, ed. P. Taylor. Orlando, FL: Grune & Stratton, pp. 87–115.

——— (1981). Changing models of infancy and the nature of early development: remodeling the foundation. *J. Amer. Psychoanal. Assn.*, 1:179–219.

——— (1983). The prerepresentational self and its affective core. *Psychoanal. Study Child*, 38:165–192.

——— (1988). Development terminable and interminable: II. Recent psychoanalytic theory and therapeutic considerations. *Int. J. Psychoanal.*, 69:283–296.

——— (1991). Positive emotions for psychoanalytic theory: surprises from infancy research and new directions. *J. Amer. Psychoanal. Assn.*, 39:5–44.

Fonagy, P.; Steele, M.; Moran, G.; Steele, H. & Higgitt, A. (1991a). Measuring the ghost in the nursery: a summary of the main findings of the Anna Freud Centre-University College London Parent-Child Study. *Bull. A. Freud Cntr.*, 14:115–131.

——— ——— Steele, H., Moran, G. S. & Higgitt, A. C. (1991b). The capacity for understanding mental states: the reflective self in parent and child and its significance for security of attachment. *Infant Ment. Health J.*, 13:200–217.

Fraiberg, S. (1987). Pathological defenses in infancy. *Psychoanal. Q.*, 51:612–635.

―――― ADELSON, E. & SHAPIRO, V. (1975). Ghosts in the nursery: A psychoanalytic approach to the problems of impaired infant-mother relationships. *J. Amer. Acad. Child Psychiat.*, 14:387–421.

GALENSON, E. (1986). Some thoughts about infant psychopathology and aggressive development. *Int. Rev. Psychoanal.*, 13:349–354.

GIANINO, A. & TRONICK, E. Z. (1988). The mutual regulation model: the infant's self and interactive regulation and coping and defensive capacities. In *Stress and Coping*, ed. T. Field, P. McCabe & N. Schneiderman. Hillsdale, NJ: Erlbaum, pp. 47–68.

GREENSPAN, S. I. & PORGES, S. N. (1984). Psychopathology in infancy and early childhood: clinical perspectives on the organization of sensory and affective-thematic experience. *Child Devel.*, 55:49–70.

KERNBERG, O. F. (1990). New perspectives in psychoanalytic affect theory. In *Emotion: Theory, Research, and Experience*, ed. R. Plutchik & H. Kellerman. New York: Academic Press, pp. 115–131.

KOHUT, H. (1977). *The Restoration of the Self*. New York: Int. Univ. Press.

MAIN, M. & GOLDWYN, G. (1984). Predicting rejection of her infant from mother's representation of her own experience: implications for the abused-abusing intergenerational cycle. *Child Abuse & Neglect*, 8:203–217.

―――― & SOLOMON, J. (1990). Procedures for identifying infants as disorganized-disoriented during the Ainsworth Strange Situation. In *Attachment in the Preschool Years: Theory, Research, and Intervention*, ed. M. Greenberg, D. Cicchetti & E. M. Cummings. Chicago: Univ. Chicago Press, pp. 121–161.

OSOFSKY, J. D. (1976). Neonatal characteristics and mother-infant interaction in two observational situations. *Child Devel.*, 47:1138–1147.

―――― & DANZGER, B. (1974). Relationships between neonatal characteristics and mother-infant interaction. *Devel. Psychol.*, 10:124–130.

―――― & EBERHART-WRIGHT, A. (1988). Affective exchanges between high risk mothers and infants. *Int. J. Psychoanal.*, 69:221–231.

―――― ―――― (1992). Risk and protective factors for parents and infants. In *Human Development: Future Directions in Infant Development Research*, ed. G. Suci & S. Robertson. New York: Springer, pp. 5–39.

―――― ―――― WARE, L. M. & HANN, D. M. (1992). Children of adolescent mothers: a group at risk for psychopathology. *Infant Ment. Health J.*, 13:119–131.

―――― HANN, D. M. & PEEBLES, C. D. (1993a). Adolescent parenthood: risks and opportunities for mothers and infants. In *Handbook of Infant Mental Health*, ed. C. Zeanah. New York: Guilford, pp. 106–119.

―――― HUBBS-TAIT, L., EBERHART-WRIGHT, A. & WARE, L. M. (in press). Vulnerabilities in preschool children of adolescent mothers: a narrative approach. In *The Vulnerable Child*. Madison, CT: Int. Univ. Press.

―――― WEWERS, S., FICK, A. & HANN, D. M. (1993b). Children's exposure to chronic community violence: what are we doing to our children? *Psychiat.*, in press.

PARENS, H. (1992). A view of the development of hostility in early life. *J. Amer. Psychoanal. Assn.*, 39(Suppl.):75–108.

RADLOFF, L. S. (1977). The CES-D Scale: a self-report depression scale for research in the general population. *Applied Psychol. Meas.*, 1:385–401.

SANDLER, J. (1967). Trauma, strain, and development. In *Psychic Trauma*, ed. S. S. Furst. New York: Int. Univ. Press, pp. 154–173.

———— & ROSENBLATT, B. (1962). The concept of the representational world. *Psychoanal. Study Child*, 17:128–145.
SROUFE, L. A. (1989). Pathways to adaptation and maladaptation: psychopathology as developmental deviation. In *The Emergence of a Discipline: Rochester Symposium on Motivation*, Vol. 1, ed. D. Cicchetti. Hillsdale, NJ: Erlbaum, pp. 13–40.
STERN, D. (1985). *The Interpersonal World of the Infant*. New York: Basic Books.
WARE, L. M., OSOFSKY, J. D., EBERHART-WRIGHT, A. & LEICHTMAN, M. L. (1987). Issues in designing a preventive intervention program for adolescent mothers and infants. *Infant Ment. Health J.*, 8:418–428.

DISCOURSE, PREDICTION, AND RECENT STUDIES IN ATTACHMENT: IMPLICATIONS FOR PSYCHOANALYSIS

MARY MAIN, PH.D.

The study of human attachment organization is founded upon the work of John Bowlby and Mary Ainsworth, and takes among its topics the role of early trauma (Bowlby) and early parent-child interaction patterns (Ainsworth) in the development of anxiety and defensive processes. The infant's behavioral response to separations from and reunions with the parent in the Ainsworth Strange Situation has been found to reflect patterns of infant-mother interaction, and permits the classification of infant-mother relationships as secure, avoidant, ambivalent, and disorganized/disoriented. Recently, children's narratives, representations, and fantasies at six have been found predictable from these four categories of attachment to the mother. In addition, an Adult Attachment Interview has been devised in which individuals are asked to describe and evaluate early relationships and experiences. Interview transcripts are classified on the basis of the transcript's discourse characteristics rather than the speaker's apparent history. Four "states of mind with respect to attachment" have been identified, and in infant-parent samples each has been found predictive of the infant's Strange Situation response to the parent. Most strikingly, parents who are coherent, consistent, and plausible in describing and evaluating their own attachment histories, whether favorable or unfavorable, have infants whose Strange Situation response to them is judged secure. These studies are discussed in terms of their implications for the hermeneutic/constructivist controversy in psychoanalysis.

THE STUDY OF HUMAN ATTACHMENT organization is founded on the work of John Bowlby and Mary Ainsworth, and takes among its topics several issues central to psychoanalysis,

---

From the Department of Psychology, University of California, Berkeley.

This paper is dedicated to the memory of Ellen Richardson (1958–1993), a graduate student at Berkeley and its intended co-author. One objective of her doctoral thesis had been the joint consideration of attachment and hermeneutics. I gratefully acknowledge the Kohler-Stiftung Foundation in its support of this project.

including the role of early trauma (Bowlby) and early parent-child interaction patterns (Ainsworth) in the development of anxiety and defensive processes. This article begins with a history of the field of attachment, and emphasizes tentative analogies between insecure patternings of attachment and early ego modifications. I discuss the contribution recent work in attachment may make to considerations of the "linguistic turn" in psychoanalysis, and specifically to queries regarding the status of psychoanalysis as a natural science.

In the opening sections of this article I trace three phases in the development of the field. The lines of study to which these phases refer have not replaced one another in this sequence; rather, each continues to be carried forward from the time of its initiation. In the first, drawing on evolutionary theory and observations of nonhuman primates, Bowlby (1969) called attention to the functioning of an "attachment behavioral system" which, having primary and immediate responsibility for regulating infant safety in man's original "environment of evolutionary adaptedness," unavoidably still acts to lead the infant to continually monitor the physical and psychological accessibility of attachment figure(s). The development and organization of this instinctively guided system was used to explain the child's behavioral and emotional responses to separation and loss.

A second phase in the development of the field centered on individual differences in the one-year-old infant's behavioral response to separations from and reunions with the parent in an unfamiliar laboratory environment (Ainsworth et al., 1978). Infant responses to the parent in the Ainsworth Strange Situation were categorized as secure (Group B), insecure/avoidant (Group A), ambivalent/resistant (Group C) and more recently, as disorganized/disoriented (Group D, Main and Solomon, 1986, 1990). Precursors to each of these "patterns of attachment" were sought in mother-infant interaction, with secure infants repeatedly being found to have had the most sensitive and responsive mothering. Behavioral sequelae to Strange Situation behavior were observed in other settings, with children secure with mother in infancy exhibiting the most favorable outcomes to fifteen years of age.

The most recent phase in the study of individual differences in attachment organization has been described as a "move to the level of representation" (Bretherton and Waters, 1985; Main et al., 1985). In this phase, children's discourse, representations, and fantasies have been found significantly related to early attachment to the mother, with children exhibiting fearful, bizarre, or catastrophic fantasies being drawn almost exclusively from a newly discovered disorganized/disoriented category of infant Strange Situation behavior. There has also been considerable focus upon a semistructured, hour-long Adult Attachment Interview administered to adults. In this interview, individuals are asked to describe early relationships with parents, and to evaluate the effects of these relationships and experiences upon their present functioning (George et al., 1985). The interview is transcribed verbatim, then classified as representative of one of four "states of mind with respect to attachment." Classification rules are based on the transcript's discourse characteristics rather than its contents (the speaker's apparent experiences, see Main, 1991). The central finding of these studies has been that, as administered to parents (including first-time prospective parents), each state of mind as determined from this interview tends reliably to predict[1] a particular, corresponding pattern of infant response to the parent in the Ainsworth Strange Situation. Most strikingly, parents who are coherent, consistent, and plausible in describing and evaluating their own attachment histories, whether favorable or unfavorable, have infants whose response to them in this semistressful situation is judged secure.

---

[1] Here and elsewhere in this manuscript the term "predict" is used to describe our ability to anticipate, e.g., the yet-to-be-born infant's Strange Situation attachment classification from the adult's interview-based attachment classification, at highly statistically significant levels. The terms refers

The concluding section of this article includes a discussion of some tentative similarities between patterns of insecure infant attachment and early ego modifications. I then discuss the notable if somewhat complex implications of our work for constructivist/hermeneutic issues in psychoanalysis. As discussed above, our system of interview analysis relies not upon the speaker's apparent experiences, but rather upon coherence versus three specific forms of incoherence in the discussion of those experiences to predict infant attachment classification. We do not, in other words, need to know what in fact happened during the speaker's childhood in order to (1) reliably analyze a text and (2) predict favorable versus three specific kinds of unfavorable outcomes. This appears initially as a plus for the argument that what is important in text is coherence of narrative, and as a strike against the argument that the adequately interpreted text will be known only as it tallies with the speaker's actual experience. However, the fact that we have developed a set of readily agreed-upon rules for discourse/text interpretation which anticipate the speaker's behavior toward an infant bodes well for the status of text analysis as a type of natural science.

Bowlby's Ethological-Evolutionary Theory of Attachment

Bowlby (1969) proposed that maintenance of proximity to protective adult figures represents the primary mechanism for the regulation of infant safety and survival. In Bowlby's theory, behavior patterns having the predictable outcome of increasing proximity between infant and caregiver (such as crying, calling, pursuing, and clinging) are ascribed to the activity of a complex, instinctively guided but environmentally influenced control system termed the "attachment behavioral system." This system is presumed to have evolved to serve the biological function of ensuring the protection of younger and/or weaker members of

---

to probabilistic prediction across groups rather than deterministic prediction at the individual level.

ground-living primate troops. Once an attachment figure has been selected (usually but not necessarily the infant's biological mother) the infant closely monitors her whereabouts, preserving proximity even under nonstressful conditions. If threatening conditions arise, the attachment behavioral system becomes highly activated, and the infant is led immediately to seek close proximity and contact. Bowlby frequently refers to the infant's "primary" attachment figure, but two or three other attachment figures may also be selected.

Like other systems that serve survival and reproduction, the attachment system is closely coordinated with other behavioral systems, such as exploration, escape, and feeding. It is presumed to be activated and terminated by "signals" from the internal or external environment, as by illness, weakness or injury, or by indications of danger or safety appearing in the environment. No buildup of psychic energy is presumed necessary to the activation of the system, nor is energy (other than physical energy) released or spent following behavioral displays. While most readily activated in younger individuals, the attachment behavioral system is presumed to remain influential throughout an individual's lifetime, and to account for central aspects of an individual's mental state.

Although Bowlby originally proposed that the biological function of the attachment behavioral system was primarily protection from predation, the full import of the system is probably best understood by considering that it serves multiple survival functions (Main, 1981). In addition to protection from predation, proximity provides protection from unfavorable temperature changes, from natural disasters, from the attacks of conspecifics, and from the risk of separation from the group.

The reader should note the following further points:

1. The development of specific or "focused" attachments appears by the third quarter of the first year of life in human infants, and is presumed to be based on social/contingent interactions. There is no evidence that these interactions need be

positive, and infants unquestionably take maltreating parents as attachment figures.

2. As must necessarily be the case if attachment represents the infant's chief mechanism for ensuring survival, the attachment behavioral system is conceived as continually active. This means that, whether or not attachment behavior is displayed at a given time, the attached individual is at some level attending to (monitoring) the physical location and accessibility of the attachment figure(s).[2]

3. This continual monitoring (attention) cannot always be conscious. It is now widely recognized, however, that we have the capacity for attending to, processing, and drawing inferences from input that does not reach the usual levels of awareness (see Kihlstrom, 1987; Eagle, 1987; Clyman, 1991).

4. The concept of a biologically guided attention, which, while continually active, only occasionally reaches levels of conscious awareness, has implications for the development of defensive processes and is in keeping with analytic theory.

5. The formation of an attachment to a specified individual signals a qualitative change in infant behavioral (and no doubt also brain) organization. This given, quantitative terms (such as "strongly" or "weakly" attached) are not used in describing differences among individuals (Ainsworth et al., 1978). Infants who have become attached to maltreating or simply insensitive attachment figures are presumed no "less" attached than others, and attachments are formed by the end of the first year of life in all but extremely anomalous rearing conditions. Strong, continuing displays of attachment behavior in relatively safe circumstances or, conversely, the absence of attachment behavior in threatening situations in which it is expected are believed to signal interferences from other processes rather than quantitative differences in the "strength" of attachment.

[2]In further consideration of the relation between attachment and danger, Bowlby noted that for many mammals the mother provides nourishment and opportunities for learning, while separately a den, burrow, or other special location provides the haven of safety in times of alarm. For the primate

6. In sum, in Bowlby's theory, the infant's insistent concern with maintenance of relations to potentially protective attachment figures represents not the working of a set of "quiet" instincts (see Modell, 1975), but rather the *sine qua non* of infant survival. The attachment behavioral system in primates is therefore highly responsive to danger, intimately related to fear, and activated by frightening conditions of any kind.

Individual Differences in Attachment in Infancy

Ainsworth designed the Strange Situation procedure with the intention of illustrating the way in which attachment behavior would gradually increase in one-year-old infants responding to two separations from, and reunions with, the mother in a strange environment. The procedure constituted the final step in an extensive study of infant-mother interaction conducted in Baltimore. In this study, each infant-mother dyad was observed in the home for four hours every three weeks, with interactions being recorded in the form of narrative record (66 to 80 hours of observation per dyad). Despite observing stable differences in patterns of infant-mother interaction in the home, Ainsworth expected that during the Strange Situation the infants would use mother as a "secure base" for exploration when present, exhibiting attachment behavior during separation and at the initial moments of reunion.[3] Unexpectedly, striking individual differences in response to this 15–20 minute procedure were observed in the Baltimore study, and the following discoveries were made: (1) while 13 of the 23 infants

---

infant, in contrast, it is a specific individual rather than a specific static location that the infant seeks in alarm.

[3] The Strange Situation consists of seven episodes each, apart from the separation episodes (terminated within 30 seconds or less if the infant is distressed) being three minutes long. In the two opening episodes, the mother sits quietly as the child responds to an unfamiliar environment and to the toys, and then to the entrance of a stranger. In the first separation, the infant is left alone with the stranger; mother then returns, and then leaves the infant entirely alone. The stranger returns, attempting to comfort the infant if distressed; the mother returns for the final reunion episode.

exhibited the expected pattern, in six infants attachment behavior was absent, while in four others attachment appeared completely preoccupying; (2) when attachment behavior was absent, it was replaced by exploratory behavior throughout the situation as a whole, and active avoidance of the parent upon reunion; (3) where attachment behavior was continually focused on the parent, angry behavior was also present, exploration was absent, and the infant failed to settle on the parent's return; (4) each pattern exhibited was linked to a specific pattern of infant-mother interaction during the preceding year.

The link between specific kinds of interaction in the home and the infant's response to the mother in a stressful situation suggests that differing internal structures may be developing out of differing patternings of dyadic regulation (see Sander, 1987), and that in the absence of major alterations in life circumstances these structures may have stability and some predictive power. The reader will therefore want to be informed regarding the stability of these categories, and their power to predict behavior in other settings. First, using the full ABCD system (pattern D is described below), a majority of infants in low-risk samples are secure (B) with mother, with about equal numbers falling into patterns A and D and a minority in pattern C. When the infant is seen twice with the same parent attachment classifications have about 80 percent stability between twelve and twenty months of age; however, the same infant is often categorized differently with the two parents, e.g., being secure with mother but avoidant with father.[4] Main and Cassidy (1988) discovered that ABCD classifications with mother in infancy are predictive of four specific patterns of reunion behavior with mother at six years (a finding replicated in Germany by Wartner and her colleagues, in press). Children secure with mother as infants in both middle-class and poverty samples show greater concentration in play, more positive affect,

---

[4]Although fathers are not completely neglected in attachment research, many more investigations have been conducted with mothers.

greater social competence, and greater ego resilience than insecure children in peer settings, and differences favoring children secure with mother at age one are being found to continue to ten years of age (Grossmann and Grossmann, 1991; Suess et al., 1992; Urban et al., 1991).

At the conclusion of the description of each attachment category I describe partial results from a followup study of 40 six-year-olds classified A, B, C, or D with mother in infancy (Kaplan, 1987; Kaplan and Main, 1986; Main et al., 1985). In this study we attempted to access representational processes with respect to attachment, through presenting a photograph of the child and family, seeking a drawing of the family, and interviewing the child regarding what a pictured child might feel and do regarding parent-child separations. Representational processes were presumed by us to play a role in accounting for and maintaining the stability and predictability of behavior. Precisely because the predictive power of several of the assessments described in this paper are remarkable, however, the reader should remain aware that such predictions are probabilistic group predictions and do not refer to individuals.

Group B: Secure

Infants are described as secure when they show the following, notably simple, behavioral patterning. In the opening episodes of the Strange Situation (before the mother's first departure) the infant actively explores the laboratory room and plays with the toys provided. By the end of the first separation (when the infant is left alone with the stranger), the infant shows signs of missing the mother, often going to the door and engaging in search behavior. The mother is actively greeted on reunion, following which the infant happily returns to play. On being left alone entirely during the second separation episode, the infant calls for the mother. The stranger's return is clearly disappointing, and the infant continues to actively indicate a desire for the mother's return, often (but not always) by crying.

On reunion the infant scrambles to the mother, clings, and may endeavor to maintain contact should mother attempt to put him down too quickly. Displays of distress cease rapidly, however, and by the end of this final episode the infant has returned to play.

Ainsworth's narrative records showed that the mothers of B infants had been "sensitive to the signals and communications" of their infants during the first year of life (Ainsworth et al., 1971, 1978). Greater sensitivity to infant signals in the mothers of B (versus A and C) infants has continued to be noted in succeeding studies (see Bretherton, 1985, for review).

At age six, family drawings made by children who had been secure with mother as infants tended to show well individuated, well grounded figures with open arms: the drawings often also included real-world elements, such as a bicycle or a car (Kaplan and Main, 1986). Offered a photograph of themselves with their parents, these children remained casual, smiling or making a comment and then returning it to the examiner. Children secure as infants described a pictured child as probably feeling sad during separations, and offered constructive ideas regarding what the pictured child might "do" (as, try to persuade the parents to stay, or find another relative to stay with). Both in a study of sand-box play (Rosenberg, 1984) and a study of responses to doll-play separations (Solomon and George, 1991), secure children were distinguished from insecure children in that they (a) invented a crisis in mid-story, and (b) then devised a happy ending.

Group A: Insecure/Avoidant

Infants are considered insecure/avoidant when they show little or no distress during the Strange Situation (exploring throughout separations and reunions), and indeed on mother's return avoid and ignore her efforts to attract attention by turning away, looking away, and subtly refusing contact. Picked up by mother, they lean out from mother's body, pointing away to light fixtures or to toys. Put down, they again attend to the environment.

Avoidance of the mother in the Strange Situation was linked to mother's rejection of the infant's attachment behavior in the home. Several mothers described themselves as disliking tactual contact, and behavior records showed them actively pushing the infants away in response to bids for access (Ainsworth et al., 1971, 1978). Further studies continued to link the parent's aversion to physical contact with the infant to the infant's avoidance of the parent under stress (Main and Stadtman, 1981). In interactions in a free play setting, mothers of Group A infants withdrew from the infant when the infant seemed sad (Grossmann and Grossmann, 1991).

Elsewhere, we have suggested that physically rejected infants may be able to refrain from exhibiting distress and other forms of attachment behavior in this mildly stressful separation-and-reunion procedure by minimizing responsiveness to fear-eliciting conditions. This may be accomplished through an "organized shift of attention" away from the mother and/or her absence (and toward the inanimate environment). Such behavior has the advantage of permitting continued organization, and possibly also of permitting the maintenance of whatever proximity to the mother is possible (Main and Weston, 1982). The continual exploration of these infants in the Strange Situation may then be seen as a "diversionary activity" enabling the infant to maintain the "deactivation" or repression of attachment behavior (Bowlby, 1980).

The proposal that, despite appearances to the contrary, experiences of distress are in some sense still active in Group A infants has been borne out in two studies investigating physiological responses. In the first (Sroufe and Waters, 1977), the heart rates of avoidant infants were found at least as elevated as those of secure infants during the separation episodes of the Strange Situation. Recently, pre-to-post Strange Situation rises in cortisol were found substantially (although not significantly) greater for A as opposed to B infants (Spangler and Grossmann, 1993). In this context, it is interesting to note that Ainsworth's most avoidant infants had exhibited marked distress during even minor separations inside the home environment, where they also initiated unpredictable and unprovoked aggressive attacks upon the mother (Ainsworth et al., 1978). In the Strange Situation, then, it seems that not only attachment behavior, but also angry behavior was being repressed or deactivated.

At six, children who avoided mother in infancy tended to draw floating, smiling, nonindividuated family figures, often lacking arms (Kaplan and Main, 1986); frequently turned away from or refused the photograph of the family, or else, accepting it, turned it backwards or dropped it; and, while describing the pictured child as sad during parent-child separations, insisted that they had no idea what the child might do ("I don't know," "Run away"). Some offered magical solutions.

Group C: Insecure—Ambivalent/Resistant

Infants are considered ambivalent/resistant when they appear preoccupied with the mother throughout the Strange Situation, mixing subtle to open resistance in the reunion episodes with continuing expressions of distress and proximity-seeking. Behavior is also marked by heightened emotionality (some exhibit fear at entering the unfamiliar room), little exploration, and an inability to be settled by the parent. To the observer, the Strange Situation behavior of Group C infants can be puzzling—essentially because distress is displayed at length in the presence of a natural clue to safety, i.e., mother's presence.

Ainsworth's home records showed that mothers of C infants were not rejecting of attachment behavior, but were unpredictable in responsiveness and discouraging of autonomy. A review of more recent studies concludes that mothers of Group C infants are distinguished for low, and probably unpredictable, involvement (Cassidy and Berlin, in press). I have suggested that the infants of parents who are unpredictable, and therefore potentially undependable in an emergency, may need to maximize the display of attachment behavior in circumstances normally indicative of safety (Main, 1990).

Few children classified ambivalent/resistant with mother in infancy were available for our sixth-year followup study. Responding to pictured parent-child separations at six, one former Group C infant suggested tossing a bow and arrow at the parents; the other suggested buying the parents flowers, but then hiding their clothing. Both showed some behavioral disorganization at presentation of the photograph. Group C children (taken from our own and succeeding samples) tend to draw very large or very small family figures, placed close together. Some emphasize vulnerable body parts, such as round bellies with belly-buttons.

Group D: Disorganized/Disoriented

Some infants cannot be classified in accordance with Ainsworth's original directions, and are currently termed "cannot classify" (or else unclassifiable, see Main and Solomon, 1990). In our Bay Area study, for example, some infants called for mother during her absence, attempted to open the door (behavior fitting the B or C categories), then fell silent and sharply avoided and ignored her immediately upon reunion (behavior fitting the A category). Reviewing a set of 200 hard-to-classify Strange Situation videotapes taken from both normal and maltreatment samples, we found that what the great majority of unclassifiable (CC) infants shared in common was disorganization and/or disorientation in behavior, exhibited in the parent's presence. These "unclassifiable" infants were observed, for example, rocking on hands and knees with face averted following an abortive approach to the parent; moving away from the parent to lean head on wall when apparently frightened by the stranger; raising hand to mouth in an apprehensive gesture immediately upon reunion; and rising to greet the parent on reunion, then falling prone to the floor. Some infants were observed to freeze all movement with a trancelike expression (e.g., standing immobile with arms in air). Because D behavior represents an interruption in organized behavior as opposed to a new form of organization, the D category is assigned together with a best-fitting, alternate A, B, C, or CC classification (such as, D/B or D/CC). Children unclassifiable (CC) without also being disorganized/disoriented are extremely rare in infancy and will not be discussed further (Main and Solomon, 1990). In the Spangler and Grossmann study (1993), Group D infants showed statistically significant, sharp rises in cortisol succeeding the Strange Situation. Almost all D infants in this sample had been alternatively assigned to Group B, underscoring the import of these brief bouts of disorganized/disoriented behavior (sometimes lasting just 10″–30″ in total).

We have proposed that A and C infants have developed indirect or "conditional" strategies for dealing with frightening situations in the company of a parent who has historically been either rejecting or unpredictably responsive (Main, 1990). Disorganized/disoriented behavior, in contrast, seems to reflect a collapse of behavioral (as well as attentional) strategy which should be expected if the attached infant is *frightened by the parent, rather than simply by the external situation*. Because the infant inevitably seeks the parent when alarmed, frightening behavior on the part of the parent should place an attached infant in an irresolvable paradox in which the infant can neither approach (the B and C "strategies"), shift its attention (the A "strategy"), or flee (Main and Hesse, 1990, 1992). In keeping with this hypothesis, the great majority of maltreated children (80 percent) have been found to fit to the D category (Carlson et al., 1989; Lyons-Ruth et al., 1991). We believe that in some circumstances frightened parental behavior may also be frightening to the infant, especially when the parent additionally appears dissociated. In this case the infant may be in no way maltreated, but may simply be frightened by strange (e.g., occasional trancelike) behavior on the part of the parent associated with the parent's own history of loss or maltreatment. Under such conditions, infant D attachment status may appear as a *second-generation effect of the parent's own traumatic experiences.*

At six, children who had been disorganized/disoriented with mother in infancy frequently scratched out parts of their family drawings, restarted a figure in another place, or asked to begin the drawing again on another page. Most also added ominous or over-bright elements to the drawings (e.g., a family standing on a row of hearts; dismembered body parts; or skeletons). Group D children frequently seemed depressed at presentation of the photograph, and some seemed to become lost in it. One bent silently over the photograph for 12 seconds; another murmured "Where are you, mama?" In response to the pictured separations, some fell silent; some spoke in whispers; some became verbally disorganized ("yes/no, yes/no, yes/no"); and some exhibited directly frightening or frightened ideation, as, the parent might die, or the child might lock himself in a closet (Kaplan, 1987). Succeeding studies continue to show fearful/violent and catastrophic fantasies (as well as frozen silences) in these children when asked to participate in play involving parental figures (e.g., Solomon and George, 1991). These representational responses stand in sharp contrast to the seemingly well-organized, if inappropriate, controlling and role-inverting reunion behavior exhibited by former D infants toward mother at six, which appears in the form of either punitive or caregiving behavior (Main and Cassidy, 1988; Wartner et al., in press).

The Adult Attachment Interview: Parental States of Mind with Respect to Attachment as Predictive of Infant Attachment Classifications

The Adult Attachment Interview is a structured, semiclinical interview focusing on early attachment experiences and their effects. Subjects are asked for five adjectives to describe their relationship to each parent during childhood, and then asked for memories that support their choice of each adjective. They are asked whether they felt closer to one parent, and why; whether they have ever felt rejected during childhood; whether parents had been threatening with them in any way; why parents may have behaved as they did during childhood; and how these experiences may have affected the development of their personality. In addition, they are asked about any major loss experiences. The technique has been described as one of "surprising the unconscious" (George et al., 1985), and a quick review of the interview format shows that it provides ample opportunities for a speaker to contradict, or else simply fail to support, earlier or succeeding statements.

The hour-long interview is transcribed verbatim, and judges work exclusively from the speech (discourse) record. Several scoring systems assist judges in reaching a final classification describing an individual's current state of mind with respect to early experiences and their effects. The subject's presentation of his or her "experiences" is considered relevant only as it is judged to adhere to or violate coherent discourse. Grice (1975) has identified coherent discourse as following a cooperative principle, and requiring adherence to the maxims of *quality* ("be truthful, and have evidence for what you say"), *quantity* ("be succinct, yet complete"), *relation* ("be relevant or perspicacious"), and *manner* ("be clear and orderly").

In our original sixth-year followup study, four adult classifications were devised, each being found to match the infant's Strange Situation classification with the parent five years previously. Thus, secure/autonomous parents had had secure infants; dismissing parents had had avoidant infants; preoccupied parents had had ambivalent/resistant infants; and unresolved/disorganized parents had had disorganized/disoriented infants (Main et al., 1985; Main and Goldwyn, 1993; Main and Hesse, 1990). These results were replicated immediately in Charlottesville (Ainsworth and Eichberg, 1991). As the reader will see from the descriptions of interview classifications provided below, the parent's response to the interview task strongly resembles the infant's response to that parent in the Strange Situation.

Hesse (unpublished) has recently conceptualized the Adult Attachment Interview in terms of two central tasks. In essence, the interview presents the subject with the task of (1) producing and reflecting upon memories involving early relationships as well as any potentially traumatic experiences while (2) simultaneously maintaining coherent discourse with the interviewer. To participate most effectively in the interview, the speaker must respond to each question as relevant and then return the conversational turn to the interviewer. Discourse is judged coherent when a subject is able to both access and evaluate memories while simultaneously remaining truthful (consistent) and collaborative. This is difficult for the parents of insecure infants, and many meet the task with some resistance.

Transcripts are classified *secure/autonomous* when the subject's presentation and evaluation of attachment-related experiences is internally consistent, and responses are clear, relevant, and reasonably succinct. Many individuals with histories of difficult, or even traumatic (as well as positive) experiences are found to fit these criteria. While overall coherence is all that is required for placement in this category, many transcripts also leave the reader with the impression of an active and lively consciousness. We note a tendency for sentences to be placed in the active voice, and a related general willingness to examine the evidence afresh even when the interview is in progress. This is shown in "fresh" or lively speech in which wishes and facts may be spontaneously separated: "I know—and I, I also wish—that there is a special place in his heart where he remembers me." We have also noted corrective ("metacognitive") monitoring of statements just previously made: "No. I never felt rejected. Even if I had, I wouldn't have admitted it to myself. Well, actually, yes. I did feel rejected." Finally, more than other speakers, secure/autonomous individuals appear to me to take a "constructivist" position with respect to past interactions and their influences. During the interview, they may indicate that their memories might be in error; that the person being discussed might have a different viewpoint; and that their present beliefs may later undergo, or may presently be the product of, representational change (Main, 1991).

Individuals are classified *dismissing* when discourse appears aimed at minimizing the import of attachment-related experiences. The interview responses of these individuals are superficially collaborative, but internal contradictions render them apparently untruthful. Frequently, Grice's maxim of quality (*be truthful, and have evidence for what you say*) is violated in that the parents tend to be described in highly positive terms ("excellent mother, a wonderful, caring relationship"), which are unsupported or actively contradicted by episodes later recounted ("I didn't tell her I broke my arm; she would have been really angry"). These contradictions appear to go unnoticed by the speaker, as though isolated. In part because of a frequently stated inability to recall childhood, responses to questions often violate the maxim of quantity by being excessively succinct ("I don't remember"). On the whole, individuals classified dismissing seem to be guided by an effort to appear to answer the questions without actually making linkages to memories. Whether such memories are in fact available at the moment is an open question: a study of physiological responses to the Adult Attachment Interview showed marked increases in skin conductance levels in dismissing subjects when asked to recall experiences of rejection, separation, and threat from parents (Dozier and Kobak, in press).

Individuals are classified *preoccupied* when they exhibit a confused, either angry or passive preoccupation with attachment figures or (very rare) a fearful preoccupation with traumatic experiences. Once started on a particular topic, these speakers frequently have difficulty—evidenced, e.g., in long, grammatically entangled sentences—in "moving on" in a timely way through the interview format. Violations of manner include use of psychological jargon ("I have a lot of material around that issue"); nonsense words ("She was just caring dadadada so much"); addressing the parent as though present in recounting a childhood episode ("She was really mental, I mean, she just started crying when she saw my clothes on the floor, and why did you do that, why can't you ever act like the mother?"); childlike speech ("So I, I hided from the grownups at dinner"); and repetitive use of nebulous phrases ("I would sit on his lap, and that"; "I phoned her, sort of a thing"). These speakers are also identified by violations of the maxim of relevance (as when questions about past relations with parents are met with discussions of recent interactions) and of quantity (interviews with these subjects are often excessively long).

In sum, for preoccupied subjects, interview questions appear to serve the purpose of stimulating memories, but the speaker is often unable to retain a focus on the interview queries. Hence, in many cases, the memories aroused, rather than the intent of the question itself, seem to draw the subject's attention and to guide the subject's speech (Hesse, unpublished).

Interviews are placed in the *unresolved/disorganized* category on the basis of indications of mental disorganization and disorientation occurring specifically during discussions of potentially traumatic events, such as loss of important persons, or physical or sexual abuse. These indices are identified as lapses in the monitoring of reasoning (". . . and so, I've always thought that he died because I forgot to pray for him") and/or discourse (e.g., sudden alteration in discourse into eulogistic speech, such as, "she was young, she was lovely, and she was taken from us by that most dreaded of diseases, tuberculosis"). Lapses of this kind are usually brief and, as in the case of the infant D system, transcripts assigned to unresolved attachment status are also assigned to a second, best-fitting category, and an alternative secure/autonomous assignment is by no means infrequent (unresolved/secure). Not a few highly functioning individuals are assigned to this category.

We have suggested that lapses in the monitoring of reasoning or discourse may in various ways represent either interference from normally dissociated memory systems or unusual absorptions involving memories triggered by the discussion of traumatic events, and may be mediated by associated lapses in working memory (Main and Hesse, 1992). Specifically, lapses in reasoning—e.g., indications that a speaker believes a deceased person is both dead and not dead (in the immediate, physical sense)—may indicate parallel, incompatible belief and memory systems regarding a traumatic event which have become dissociated. Lapses in the monitoring of discourse, such as sudden changes into eulogistic speech, suggest the possibility of "state shifts" where the individual has entered a peculiar, compartmentalized state of mind involving a particular traumatic experience (Hesse, unpublished). Shifts of state involving intrusions from frightening, dissociated memories may result in frightened/frightening behavior on the part of the parent, and hence be the mechanism linking the parent's unresolved state of mind to disorganized/disoriented behavior on the part of the infant. We have recently found that lapses in the monitoring of reasoning or discourse during the Adult Attachment Interview are in fact correlated with indications of dissociative states (Main et al., 1993).

Psychometric Properties of the Interview Classification and Scoring System

Investigators in five countries have reported on the psychometric properties of the Adult Attachment Interview. In low-risk samples, about 16 percent of subjects are judged dismissing, 56 percent secure/autonomous, 10 percent preoccupied, and 18 percent unresolved/cannot classify[5] (Van IJzendoorn and

---

[5] As is the case in infancy, some individuals are unclassifiable with respect to the dismissing, preoccupied and secure criteria, but not substantially disorganized with respect to discussions of trauma. These are placed in the "cannot classify" category, which has been developed too recently for comparison with infant outcomes.

Bakersman-Kranenburg, in press). The dismissing, preoccupied and secure/autonomous categories have been found stable across two- to three-month periods in Britain, Holland, Israel and the USA and across a 15-month period in Canada (78 to 90 percent), but stability including the difficult-to-code unresolved/disorganized category is considerably lower. Interjudge agreement ranges around 80 to 85 percent, and category placement is not affected by interviewer. Waters has demonstrated that the state of mind being assessed is not reducible to a general style of discourse (Waters et al., 1993). In four out of five studies, adult state of mind with respect to attachment has been found unrelated to tests of general intelligence, memory, or verbal fluency (Van IJzendoorn and Bakersman-Kranenburg, in press).

Continued Prediction of Infant Strange Situation Behavior from the Adult Attachment Interview as Conducted with the Parent

The adult-to-infant correspondence described above has now been tested across more than a dozen further samples. The results, consistent across samples, are highly significant, as a recent meta-analysis of Adult Attachment Interview studies demonstrates (Van IJzendoorn, unpublished). Across studies, the parent-to-child secure versus insecure match is about 78 percent. The match across the four categories is about 68 percent (and higher when coders have had more extensive training).

So long as the Adult Attachment Interview is conducted following the Strange Situation, we might infer that the parent's state of mind with respect to attachment is being affected by the infant. However, the Adult Attachment classification of a prospective, first-time parent three months prior to birth predicts the infant's Strange Situation behavior to that parent 15 months later equally well as studies in which the interview has been conducted following the birth of the child. These prebirth studies have been conducted in four countries, and include a study of middle-class London mothers (Fonagy et al., 1991); a poverty sample of African-American and Hispanic adolescents in inner-city New York (Ward and Carlson, in press); a study of Australian fathers (Radojevic, 1992); and a study of Ontario mothers (Benoit and Parker, in press). In this latter study, mothers and adult daughters were found as well matched in Adult Attachment Interview classification as daughters and their infants: using the dismissing, preoccupied and secure/autonomous classifications, the match was 75 percent.

It appears, then, that the overall coherence of an adult's discourse during discussions of early relationships and their effects predicts the security of the unborn child, while specifiable kinds of incoherence in discourse predict specific manifestations of insecurity with respect to the parent, as displayed in avoidant, ambivalent/resistant, and disorganized/disoriented behavior. Several studies have now shown that secure attachment status in mothers is directly associated with sensitive responsiveness to infants and young children. In the future, given the development of adequate systems of observation, it seems likely that we may discover further associations between specific forms of incoherence as manifest in the parent's discourse, and parental insensitivity to selected infant signals.

Conclusions: Attachment and Psychoanalysis

The opening sections of this article have had a necessarily empirical and descriptive focus. My concluding remarks are primarily speculative, and focus upon (1) the relations between "conditional strategies" and the development of defensive processes, (2) the maintenance of steady attentional/representational states as related to signal anxiety and the intergenerational transmission of attachment patterns, and (3) implications of the Adult Attachment Interview for the hermeneutic/constructivist controversy in psychoanalysis.

Conditional Strategies, Control of Attention, and Development of Defensive Processes

In emphasizing the immediacy of the tie between proximity-maintenance and survival in the environment of evolutionary adaptedness, Bowlby drew attention to two conditions of danger: (1) environmental or internal changes directly and immediately threatening to the infant's continuing survival (Freud's [1926] realistic danger), and (2) any conditions intimating separation from the attachment figure, even in the absence of immediate threats from the environment (Bowlby's second realistic danger, and Freud's neurotic danger, to which the infant was expected to respond with learned, or signal, anxiety). Both conditions were expected to activate attachment behavior, while proximity to the mother was expected to terminate it. Exceptions were noted in two- to three-year-old children undergoing prolonged, stressful separations from the parents. Separated for a long enough period, children of this age were observed to enter a state of detachment in which signs of concern with the mother were finally absent (Bowlby, 1969, 1973). Detachment was considered indicative of the onset of repression; repression was considered a result of traumatic experience; and experiences of this kind were considered anomalous in terms of man's evolutionary environment. The onset of detachment had been signaled by avoidance of the mother upon her visit to the toddler in the separation setting.

In this light, we can well understand the initial impact of Ainsworth's discoveries regarding the Strange Situation behavior of twelve-month-old, home-reared infants who had no experiences of major separation. As the reader will remember, only (that majority of) infants whose mothers had been "sensitive and responsive to infant signals and communications" in the home showed the expected behavioral patterning. For infants whose attachment behavior had been consistently rejected, threatening conditions failed to activate attachment behavior. For infants whose mothers had been unpredictable, mother's presence failed to terminate it. Insecure infants, then, either failed to exhibit attachment behavior in threatening conditions, actively avoiding the mother upon reunion, or, remaining preoccupied with mother throughout the separation, failed to explore in conditions of safety. It appeared that behavior bearing a phenotypic resemblance to defensive processes could develop out of patterns of everyday interaction as well as in response to traumatic separations.

Let us now consider these somewhat anomalous or unexpected findings in the light of modern evolutionary biology, and specifically in light of the concept of the "conditional behavioral strategy" (see Maynard-Smith, 1979). Drawing on primate studies, Hinde (1982) questioned whether mothers will be optimally "sensitive" to their infants in all circumstances, or whether variability in circumstances could produce substantial variability in maternal sensitivity and responsiveness. Specifically, he utilized the concept of the conditional behavioral strategy to suggest that "natural selection must surely have operated to produce conditional maternal strategies, not stereotypy," i.e., to produce lability of the response repertoire. In certain environments, then, the mother's reproductive success may be optimized through behavior patterns which violate maximally sensitive caregiving: under these conditions, she may be, e.g., somewhat rejecting (perhaps promoting early infant independence) or somewhat unpredictably responsive (perhaps promoting a prolonging of dependence). There is no implication that the mother's (or infant's, see below) selection of a particular strategy need be conscious. Moreover, as opposed to primary caregiving (or proximity-seeking) strategies, which are presumed to be based on the activities of instinctively biased behavioral systems, conditional behavioral strategies are not presumed to rely on the operation of any particular "conditional behavioral system"—as, for example, a "rejecting" or an "avoidance" behavioral system—but may instead simply involve manipulations of the output of the primary system utilizing coexisting mechanisms (Main, 1990).

I have suggested that infants may also utilize conditional behavioral strategies. Specifically, avoidant and ambivalent/resistant infants may be conceived as having developed conditional behavioral strategies for maintaining proximity and/or behavioral organization under conditions of maternal rejection or unpredictable responsiveness. As the reader is already aware, however, the attachment behavioral system is conceived of as being continually active and context-sensitive. In this conceptualization, then, the conditional behavioral strategy (avoidance or preoccupation) is understood to be imposed on a still-active primary strategy, imposed on aspects of memory, and imposed on awareness of surrounding conditions. Maintenance of the "minimizing" (A) or "maximizing" (C) behavioral strategy is then dependent on the control or manipulation of attention—specifically, an organized shift of attention away from conditions activating attachment behavior in Group A infants, and a heightened vigilance maximizing responsiveness to even minimal clues to danger in Group C infants. It seems inevitable that a continuing "minimization or maximization of the display of attachment behavior relative to the naturally occurring output of the behavioral system" (Main, 1990) will eventually also involve the defensive exclusion or defensive distortion of certain memories and perceptions, as suggested by the Bay Area followup study described above.

Intergenerational Transmission of Insecure/Avoidant and Insecure/Ambivalent Attachment Patterns: Maintenance of Organized Attentional/Representational States as Related to Signal Anxiety

We have now arrived at a proposal regarding the origins of defensive processes *as related to attachment*. Specifically, I have proposed that infants whose mothers are either rejecting or unpredictably responsive must learn to either limit the exhibition of attachment behavior in the presence of activating conditions, or heighten the exhibition of attachment behavior in the presence of terminating conditions. It seems possible that the manipulation of attentional patterning plays a substantial role in the control of behavior for young infants, and that the continuing control of behavior will involve distortions or limitations placed on memory and perception. Thus, defensive processes with respect to attachment are seen as serving to control or manipulate behavior in the service of permitting the infant to maintain proximity to a rejecting, or else inconsistently responsive, parent. Note that what is "repressed" or defensively excluded in this conceptualization is not the memory of any particular traumatic experience, but rather an alternative attentional and behavioral patterning.[6]

If the above conceptualization of the origins of defensive processes with respect to attachment are correct, we can make the following further observations:

1. The avoidant and ambivalent/resistant patterns are conceived as ultimately being held in place by maintenance of a steady attentional/representational state. Violations of these attentional states—specifically, circumstances forcing shifts in attention toward threatening conditions and attachment figures in avoidant/dismissing individuals, and conditions forcing attention away from attachment figures in ambivalent/preoccupied individuals—may eventually in themselves promote feelings of anxiety. Maintenance of these states may therefore subjectively be experienced as a kind of secondary felt security, originating in the conditional strategy which the individual has utilized for maintaining proximity to the parent. Feelings, memories, attentional patterning or interactions threatening to violate these states may then be controlled by signal anxiety.

2. Freud (1926) identified feelings of anxiety as tied to expectations; as having a quality of indefiniteness and lack of object; and as referencing a danger "still to be discovered." In

---

[6]Defense is, of course, organized. Disorganized/disoriented behavior is not defensive in the traditional sense, and indeed Freud had conceptualized disorganization as the state to which defense is the alternative. Following a suggestion made by Liotti (in press), we have recently conceptualized both unresolved adult attachment status and disorganized/disoriented infant at-

keeping with Bowlby's early insistence on the "primary" nature of the anxiety displayed by infants undergoing separation, the response to maternal leavetaking exhibited by infants whose mothers have been sensitively responsive to their signals and communications would not seem indicative of feelings of anxiety (see also Spangler and Grossmann, 1993). Avoidant and ambivalent/resistant infants, however, may experience a kind of learned or signal anxiety in keeping with the complexity and indefiniteness of their situation (see Main, 1990).

3. The similarities uncovered between the behavior of avoidant and ambivalent/resistant infants in the Strange Situation and the discourse of dismissing and preoccupied adults during the Adult Attachment Interview are extraordinary. Considered solely from the viewpoint of discourse, both dismissing and preoccupied adults may be said to exhibit forms of resistance to the interviewer's insistent requests for a description of their attachment-related experiences, and for an evaluation of the relation between those experiences and their present state of mind.

4. In the case of some insecure speakers, we may draw an analogy to the patient who does not *remember* anything of what he has forgotten and repressed, but *acts* it out (Freud, 1914, p. 150). By action, we may refer to behavior toward the infant.

5. Like their infants, then, dismissing and preoccupied adults seem to seek to preserve their own particular attentional/ representational states of mind. During the interview, these states may be preserved in part through violations of Grice's principles of coherence and collaboration. In interaction with the infant, the parent's state of mind with respect to attachment is likely to be preserved by failure to perceive, accurately interpret, or respond to infant behavior which threatens to alter that state. The infant's "conditional behavioral strategy" may then be conceived as a response to parental blocking, distortion,

---

tachment status in terms of dissociative, as opposed to more traditionally defensive processes (Main and Hesse, 1992).

or failures in responsiveness to selected infant signals. The development of a "conditional (A or C) behavioral strategy" on the part of the infant then ultimately assists the insecure parent in preservation of a particular state of mind.

6. With respect to the above, Sander (1987) notes that "Each infant-caregiver system constructs its own unique configuration of regulatory constraint on the infant's access to awareness of his own states" (p. 344). The work of Sander and his colleagues suggests that dyadic adjustments begin in the earliest weeks of infant life, and are potentially supportive of the above proposal.

7. Writing in 1937, Freud notes, "It is easy, then, to accept the fact, shown by daily experience, that the outcome of an analytic treatment depends essentially on the strength and on the depth of root of these resistances that bring about an alteration of the ego" (pp. 239–240). Further, modifications of the ego were understood to be "either congenital or acquired. . . . If they are acquired, it will certainly have been in the course of development, starting from the first years of life" (p. 235). The development of alterations in attentional patterning in the service of control or manipulation of behavior may constitute one important form of early ego modification. Ultimately, these alterations serve protection.

Implications of Recent Work in Attachment for the Hermeneutic/ Constructivist Controversy in Psychoanalysis

The work in attachment described above has implications for the hermeneutic/constructivist controversy in psychoanalysis. Briefly, this controversy has arisen in conjunction with the recent "linguistic turn" in psychoanalysis, in which psychoanalysis is either considered nonscience, or else is reconceptualized as a linguistic/historic science working by criteria differing from the correspondence/prediction criteria of the natural sciences (Wallerstein, 1986). The call for different criteria has originated in part in recognition of two difficulties: that of establishing correspondence between interpretation and history, and that of developing criteria for selecting between conflicting interpretations (Grünbaum, 1984; Eagle, 1984). In keeping with the linguistic turn in psychoanalysis, some have suggested that analysts should abandon the "discourse of energics" (roughly, instinct theory) for the "discourse of meanings" (as expressed in language; see Ricoeur, 1970).

Philosophers have traditionally differentiated between two theories of truth: a *coherence* theory of truth which relies on consistent internal coreference and a *correspondence* theory of truth which relies on the plausibility of statements in terms of correspondence to the real state of affairs in the external world (Main, 1991). As a discipline founded in text interpretation, hermeneutics emphasizes a coherence/consistence form of truth as opposed to correspondence. The distinctive method of the hermeneutic "dialogue" between part and whole allows the interpreter to approach an understanding of text which eventually meets the test of internal coherence, consistency, and configuration (Steele, 1979). Ricoeur (1977) concludes that in psychoanalysis, as in text analysis, truth resides in establishing a "confirmatory constellation" which meets the joint criteria of coherence, inner consistency, and narrative intelligibility.

To those taking a constructivist position, the search for internal coherence and consistency in narrative is frequently (but, I believe, not necessarily) contrasted to the search for external correspondence. First, as Wallerstein points out, the coherence/consistence language of Ricoeur and of Steele is still a "language of evidence and of proof, albeit by hermeneutic-interpretive canons" (Wallerstein, 1986). In addition, Wallerstein notes that tests for predictive correspondence may be ultimately conceptualized as unusually broad tests for consistency in which the externally correspondent existence of some phenomenon yet to be observed will be regarded as either consistent or inconsistent with theory. Finally, all "theorizing or generalizing" sciences, natural as well as social, advance through the method of hypothesis (Blight, 1981).

The methodology and findings surrounding the Adult Attachment Interview stand in a complex and somewhat ironic relation to hermeneutics, to Wallerstein's response to the hermeneutic "challenge" to psychoanalysis, and to contemporary controversies regarding the scientific status of studies of the mind. This statement may be elaborated as follows:

1. Our general approach to developing methodologies has been at once dialectical and in keeping with the canons of normal science. Thus, in developing and refining each new method, we have worked between a known behavior pattern (often, infant Strange Situation response to a given parent) and behavior or language of one or the other individual in a second situation.

In first developing the Adult Attachment classification system across a sample of 44 interview transcripts of parents seen five years previously with the infant in the Ainsworth Strange Situation, we used both the "dialectical" method and the "method of hypothesis." On reading each transcript, we formed a hypothesis regarding likely infant Strange Situation response to that parent as speaker. The hypothesis was specified through a description of those characteristics of the text which led us to believe it would belong to a speaker in a particular "state of mind with respect to attachment" as expressed in caregiving. In each case the hypothesis was "tested" against the infant's Strange Situation behavior in the company of the speaker, and feedback regarding errors was used to refine and test our further hypotheses. A transcript hypothesized to belong to the parent of a secure infant, and in fact belonging to the parent of a secure infant, left the rule system unchanged: should the transcript hypothesized to belong to the parent of a secure infant in fact belong to the parent of an avoidant infant in ways *not* inconsonant with theory (the latter suggests a true miss, or lack of concordance), we altered the rule system for identifying both dismissing and autonomous transcripts. Thus we used feedback from each transcript to develop a rule system discriminating responses to the interview for parents of infants fitting to each category. Note that this system acknowledges mismatches in its development, and leaves open the possibility of studying new mismatches within succeeding samples.

As required by scientific method, (a) this rule system was then immediately tested against a sample of 66 further transcripts for which the coder had no information regarding infant Strange Situation behavior and (b) was shortly thereafter found readily communicable to, hence reliable across, coders. Finally (c), the association between secure vs. insecure interview transcript and secure vs. insecure infant Strange Situation behavior described by this dialectical method of system development has been replicated in over a dozen studies (Van IJzendoorn, in press).

2. As Wallerstein had noted, while the "hermeneutic circle" involves a search for internal consistency, a broad interpretation of consistency includes predictive correspondence (Holt, 1961). We broadened the "hermeneutic circle" by *stepping outside the text* to find consistency with behavior observed several years previously in an entirely different setting. What was considered informative in furthering our understanding of the text was not simply existing relations between parts of the text, but behavior that was externally correspondent. Although the "behavior" observed in this case was that of the infant toward the speaker, the mediating variable is of course the speaker's behavior toward the infant, i.e., the speaker's caregiving.

3. As the reader is aware, some texts were found more coherent than others, and incoherent texts suggested to us that a speaker retained "multiple, incompatible models" of his or her attachment history (Main, 1991). For constructivists, one implication of our findings would be that not all texts are equally in need of being "disambiguated" (i.e., not all texts are ambiguous). At a psychological level, highly ambiguous texts may in fact reflect the speaker's confused and multiple meanings/intentions. The reader should further note that what we attempt to "disambiguate" is not a speaker's history, but rather a speaker's current state with respect to his or her history. Finally,

insofar as it renders the history of an insecure speaker incoherent or noncollaborative, the language form may, again, be compared to resistance.

4. From the strict hermeneutic standpoint, consistency/coherence of text is all we can hope to achieve: figuratively, at least, there is nothing beyond the text. Our findings with respect to the Adult Attachment Interview indicate, however, that both coherent (secure) and incoherent (dismissing, preoccupied, and unresolved) texts point beyond themselves. Indeed, each points to something external, predictable, and correspondent.

In sum, in developing the Adult Attachment Classification system, we broadened the "hermeneutic circle" by considering *behavior outside the text* as part of the hermeneutic whole. I believe that our findings with respect to the predictable relation between the interview and infant Strange Situation behavior—generated through a semihermeneutic methodology, emphasizing of coherence, and affirmed through a method of hypothesis—are in keeping with the reflections of Wallerstein as well as Blight and Holt.

The establishment of a systematic, predictable, and replicable correspondence between coherence in life narratives and behavior "outside the text" should not, however, conceal the irony of our findings with respect to the hermeneutic controversy:

i. Those parental narratives which best met the *hermeneutic* truth criteria of the greatest internal/linguistic coherence were exactly those predictive of/correspondent to the greatest (*external/behavioral*) security of attachment observed in the infant.

ii. Bowlby's instinct theory of attachment formed the background to these discoveries linking behavior and mental states. While findings made in a particular context do not validate that context (*post hoc ergo propter hoc*), we can nonetheless trace history accurately in reflecting that a discourse beginning in energics has contributed to a discourse of meanings.

REFERENCES

AINSWORTH, M. D. S., BELL, S. M. & STAYTON, D. J. (1971). Individual differences in strange-situation behavior of one-year-olds. In *The Origins of Human Social Relations*, ed. H. R. Schaffer. New York: Academic Press.
——— BLEHAR, M. C., WATERS, E. & WALL, S. (1978). *Patterns of Attachment: A Psychological Study of the Strange Situation*. Hillsdale, NJ: Erlbaum.
——— & EICHBERG, C. G. (1991). Effects on infant-mother attachment of mother's unresolved loss of an attachment figure or other traumatic experience. In *Attachment Across the Life Cycle*, ed. P. Marris, J. Stevenson-Hinde & C. Parkes. New York: Routledge, pp. 160–183.
BENOIT, D. & PARKER, K. (in press). Stability and transmission of attachment across three generations. *Child Devel.*
BLIGHT, J. G. (1981). Must psychoanalysis retreat to hermeneutics? Psychoanalytic theory in the light of Popper's evolutionary epistemology. *Psychoanal. Contemp. Thought*, 4:147–206.
BOWLBY, J. (1969). *Attachment and Loss, Vol. 1: Attachment*. New York: Basic Books.
——— (1973). *Attachment and Loss, Vol. 2: Separation*. New York: Basic Books.
——— (1980). *Attachment and Loss, Vol. 3: Loss*. New York: Basic Books.
BRETHERTON, I. (1985). Attachment theory: retrospect and prospect. In *Growing Points of Attachment Theory and Research*, ed. I. Bretherton & E. Waters. *Monogr. Soc. Res. Child Devel.*, 50:66–104.
——— & WATERS, E., Eds. (1985). *Growing Points of Attachment Theory and Research*. *Monogr. Soc. Res. Child Devel.*, 50.
BRUNER, I. (1990). *Acts of Meaning*. Cambridge, MA: Harvard Univ. Press.
CARLSON, V., CICCHETTI, D., BARNETT, D. & BRAUNWALD, K. (1989). Disorganized/disoriented attachment relationships in maltreated infants. *Devel. Psychol.*, 25:525–531.
CASSIDY, J. & BERLIN, L. (in press). The insecure/ambivalent pattern of attachment: theory and research. *Child Devel.*
CLYMAN, R. B. (1991). The procedural organization of emotions: a contribution from cognitive science to the psychoanalytic theory of therapeutic action. *J. Amer. Psychoanal. Assn.*, 39(Suppl.):349–382.
DOZIER, M. & KOBAK, R. R. (in press). Psychophysiology in attachment interviews: converging evidence for deactivating strategies. *Child Devel.*
EAGLE, M. N. (1984). *Recent Developments in Psychoanalysis: A Critical Evaluation*. New York: McGraw-Hill.
——— (1987). The psychoanalytic and the cognitive unconscious. In *Theories of the Unconscious and Theories of Self*, ed. R. Stern. Hillsdale, NJ: Analytic Press.
FONAGY, P., STEELE, H. & STEELE, M. (1991). Maternal representations of attachment during pregnancy predict the organization of infant-mother attachment at one year of age. *Child Devel.*, 62:891–905.
FREUD, S. (1914). Remembering, repeating and working through. *S. E.*, 12.
——— (1926). Inhibitions, symptoms and anxiety. *S. E.*, 20.
——— (1937). Analysis terminable and interminable. *S. E.*, 23.
GEORGE, C., KAPLAN, N. & MAIN, M. (1985). The Berkeley Adult Attachment Interview. Unpublished protocol, Department of Psychology, University of California, Berkeley.

GRICE, H. P. (1975). Logic and conversation. In *Syntax and Semantics: III. Speech Acts.* New York: Academic Press, pp. 41–58.

GROSSMANN, K. E. & GROSSMANN, K. (1991). Attachment quality as an organizer of emotional and behavioral responses in a longitudinal perspective. In *Attachment Across the Life Cycle*, ed. C. M. Parkes, J. Stevenson-Hinde & P. Marris. London: Tavistock/Routledge.

GRÜNBAUM, A. (1984). *The Foundations of Psychoanalysis: A Philosophical Critique.* Berkeley: Univ. California Press.

HINDE, R. A. (1982). Attachment: conceptual and biological considerations. In *The Place of Attachment in Human Behaviour*, ed. C. Parkes & J. Stevenson-Hinde. London: Tavistock.

HOLT, R. R. (1961). Clinical judgment as a disciplined inquiry. *J. Nerv. Ment. Dis.*, 133:369–382.

KAPLAN, N. (1987). *Individual Differences in Six-Year-Old's Thoughts about Separation: Predicted from Attachment to Mother at Age One.* Unpublished doctoral dissertation, Department of Psychology, University of California, Berkeley.

───── & MAIN, M. (1986). A system for the analysis of children's family drawings in terms of attachment. Unpublished manuscript, Department of Psychology, University of California, Berkeley.

KIHLSTROM, J. F. (1987). The cognitive unconscious. *Science*, 237:1445–1452.

LIOTTI, G. (1992). Disorganized/disoriented attachment in the etiology of the dissociative disorders. *Dissociation*, 4:196–204.

───── (in press). Disorganized attachment and dissociative experiences: an illustration of the developmental-ethological approach to cognitive therapy. In *Cognitive Therapy in Action*, ed. H. Rosen & K. T. Kuehlwein. San Francisco: Jossey-Bass.

LYONS-RUTH, K., REPACHOLI, B., MCLEOD, S. & SILVA, E. (1991). Disorganized attachment behavior in infancy: short-term stability, maternal and infant correlates, and risk-related subtypes. *Devel. Psychopathol.*, 3:397–412.

MAIN, M. (1981). Avoidance in the service of attachment: a working paper. In *Behavioral Development: The Bielefeld Interdisciplinary Project*, ed. K. Immelmann, G. Barlow, L. Petronovitch & M. Main. New York: Cambridge Univ. Press, pp. 651–693.

───── (1990). Cross-cultural studies of attachment organization: recent studies, changing methodologies and the concept of conditional strategies. *Human Devel.*, 33:48–61.

───── (1991). Metacognitive knowledge, metacognitive monitoring, and singular (coherent) vs. multiple (incoherent) models of attachment: findings and directions for future research. In *Attachment Across the Life Cycle*, ed. C. M. Parkes, J. Stevenson-Hinde & P. Marris. London: Routledge, pp. 127–159.

───── & CASSIDY, J. (1988). Categories of response to reunion with the parent at age six: predicted from attachment classifications and stable over a one-month period. *Devel. Psychol.*, 24:415–426.

───── & GOLDWYN, R. (1993). *Adult Attachment Scoring and Classification System.* Unpublished manuscript, Department of Psychology, University of California at Berkeley.

───── & HESSE, E. (1990). Parents' unresolved traumatic experiences are related to infant disorganized attachment status: is frightened and/or frightening parental behavior the linking mechanism? In *Attachment in the Preschool Years: Theory, Research and Intervention*, ed. M. T. Greenberg, D. Cicchetti, & E. M. Cummings. Chicago: Univ. Chicago Press, pp. 161–182.

――― ――― (1992). Disorganized/disoriented infant behavior in the Strange Situation, lapses in the monitoring of reasoning and discourse during the parent's Adult Attachment interview, and dissociative states. In *Attachment and Psychoanalysis*, ed. M. Ammaniti & D. Stern. Rome: Gius, Laterza & Figli.

――― ――― & VAN IJZENDOORN, M. H. (1993). Lapses in the monitoring of reasoning or discourse during the Adult Attachment Interview: related to dissociation, absorption, and difficulties with working memory. Paper presented at the biennial meeting of the Society for Research in Child Development, New Orleans, March 28.

――― KAPLAN, N. & CASSIDY, J. (1985). Security in infancy, childhood and adulthood: a move to the level of representation. In *Growing Points of Attachment Theory and Research*, ed. I. Bretherton & E. Waters. *Monogr. Soc. Res. Child Devel.*, 50:66–104.

――― & SOLOMON, J. (1986). Discovery of a new, insecure-disorganized/ disoriented attachment pattern. In *Affective Development in Infancy*, ed. T. B. Brazelton & M. Yogman. Norwood, NJ: Ablex, pp. 95–124.

――― ――― (1990). Procedures for identifying infants as disorganized/ disoriented during the Ainsworth Strange Situation. In *Attachment in the Preschool Years: Theory, Research and Intervention*, ed. M. T. Greenberg, D. Cichetti & E. M. Cummings. Chicago: Univ. Chicago Press, pp. 121–160.

――― & STADTMAN, J. (1981). Infant response to rejection of physical contact by the mother: aggression, avoidance and conflict. *J. Amer. Acad. Child Psychiat.*, 20:292–307.

――― & WESTON, D. (1982). The quality of the toddler's relationship to mother and to father: related to conflict behavior and the readiness to establish new relationships. *Child Devel.*, 52:932–940.

――― ――― (1982). Avoidance of the attachment figure in infancy: descriptions and interpretations. In *The Place of Attachment in Human Behavior*, ed. C. M. Parkes & J. Stevenson-Hinde. New York: Basic Books.

MAYNARD-SMITH, J. (1979). Games theory and the evolution of behavior. *Proc. Royal Soc.* London, 205:475–488.

MODELL, A. (1975). The ego and the id: 50 years later. *Int. J. Psychoanal.*, 56:57–88.

RADOJEVIC, M. (1992). Predicting quality of infant attachment to father at 15 months from prenatal paternal representations of attachment: an Australian contribution. Paper presented at the 25th International Congress of Psychology, Brussels, Belgium, 19–25 July.

RICOEUR, P. (1970). *Freud and Philosophy: An Essay on Interpretation.* New Haven, CT: Yale Univ. Press.

――― (1977). The question of proof in Freud's psychoanalytic writings. *J. Amer. Psychoanal. Assn.*, 25:835–871.

ROSENBERG, D. M. (1984). *The Quality and Content of Preschool Fantasy Play: Correlates in Concurrent Social-Emotional Personality Function and Early Mother-Child Attachment Relationships.* Unpublished doctoral dissertation, University of Minnesota.

SANDER, L. W. (1987). Awareness of inner experience: a systems perspective on self-regulatory process in early development. *Child Abuse & Neglect*, 11:339–346.

SOLOMON, J. & GEORGE, C. (1991). Working models of attachment of children classified as controlling at age six: disorganization at the level of representation. Paper presented at the biennial meeting of the Society for Research in Child Development, April, Seattle.

SPANGLER, G. & GROSSMANN, K. E. (1993). Biobehavioral organization in securely and insecurely attachment infants. *Child Devel.*, 64:1439–1450.

SROUFE, L. A. & WATERS, E. (1977). Heart rate as a convergent measure in clinical and developmental research. *Merrill Palmer Q.*, 23:3–27.

STEELE, R. S. (1979). Psychoanalysis and hermeneutics. *Int. Rev. Psychoanal.*, 6:389–412.

SUESS, G. J., GROSSMANN, K. E. & SROUFE, L. A. (1992). Effects of infant attachment to mother and father on quality of adaptation in preschool: from dyadic to individual organization of self. *Int. J. Behav. Devel.*, 15:43–65.

URBAN, J., CARLSON, E., EGELAND, B. & SROUFE, L. A. (1991). Patterns of individual adaptation across childhood. *Devel. Psychopathol.*, 3:445–460.

VAN IJZENDOORN, M. H. (in press). Attachment representations in mothers, fathers, adolescents and clinical groups: a meta-analytic search for normative data. *J. Clin. Consult. Psychol.*

——— & BAKERSMAN-KRANENBURG, M. J. (in press). Attachment representations in mothers, fathers, adolescents and clinical groups: a meta-analytic search for normative data. *J. Consult. Clin. Psychol.*

WALLERSTEIN, R. S. (1986). Psychoanalysis as a science: a response to the new challenges. *Psychoanal. Q.*, 55:414–451.

WARD, M. J. & CARLSON, E. A. (in press). The predictive validity of the adult attachment interview for adolescent mothers. *Child Devel.*

WARTNER, U. G., GROSSMANN, K., FREMMER-BOMBIK, E. & SUESS, G. (in press). Attachment patterns at age six in South Germany: predictability from infancy and implications for preschool behavior. *Child Devel.*

WATERS, E.; CROWELL, J.; TREBOUX, D.; O'CONNOR, E.; POSADA, G. & GOLBY, B. (1993). Discriminant validity of the Adult Attachment Interview. Paper presented at the 60th Meeting of the Society for Research in Child Development, New Orleans, LA.

PSYCHOANALYTIC AND EMPIRICAL APPROACHES TO DEVELOPMENTAL PSYCHOPATHOLOGY: AN OBJECT-RELATIONS PERSPECTIVE

PETER FONAGY, PH.D.

This paper outlines common ground between psychoanalytic ideas and recent work in developmental psychopathology. Research is described which examines the impact of the parents' internal working models of relationships on the child's quality of attachment. This work suggests that each parent's early attachment experiences contribute to a model of relationships, affecting all subsequent relationships including their capacity to respond sensitively to their child. This in turn crucially influences the child's security of attachment to each of them. However, this is only a partial explanation of the well-known continuities in attachment patterns across generations, particularly the transmission of abuse. It is clear that while certain individuals repeat adverse or abusive experiences with their own children, others are able to find a more adaptive resolution. It is suggested that what particularly distinguishes resilient individuals from those who remain damaged and damaging is a capacity to reflect on mental experience, perhaps allowing the child to modify negative working models in later relationships. In other cases, the capacity may be inhibited as a way of defending the developing self against the impact of malevolence and abuse. The phenomena of borderline personality disorder may be rooted in a distortion of this reflective capacity.

Freud Memorial Professor, University College London; Research Coordinator, Anna Freud Centre.

The author acknowledges his indebtedness to George Moran, the late Director of the Anna Freud Centre, whose work has inspired many of the ideas presented in this paper. The work reported was carried out in collaboration with Dr. Miriam Steele at the Anna Freud Centre, Dr. Howard Steele at University College London, and Drs. Tom Leigh and Roger Kennedy at the Cassel Hospital. Dr. Mary Target at the Anna Freud Centre and Dr. Elizabeth Spillius of The British Psycho-Analytical Society have made essential suggestions to the theoretical framework proposed. The author is also grateful to Dr. Robert N. Emde and Dr. Theodore Shapiro for extremely valuable comments on an earlier draft of this paper.

MODERN PSYCHOANALYSIS AND THE emerging field of developmental psychopathology (Cicchetti, 1990a) have in common a commitment to uncover the developmental course of psychological disorders of childood and adulthood. Increasingly, work in developmental psychiatry and psychology is focusing on the pathways through which internal representations of early experiences with the primary figures of childhood come to have an impact on the formation of relationships in later childhood and adulthood, and culminate in the types of relationship disorders and psychopathological conditions that appear across the lifespan (Emde, 1988a, 1988b; Cicchetti, 1990b). In this paper I intend to review studies in two related areas: (1) the effect of the mother's representation of interpersonal relationships on the child's attachment and (2) the intergenerational effects of maltreatment and abuse on these representational systems.

Using Bowlby's (1973) notion of "internal working models," research on the development and influence of attachment patterns has now moved quite close to object-relations theory, particularly as formulated by British theorists (see, e.g., Bretherton, 1987, 1990). Attachment researchers now assume that children develop expectations (models) regarding the nature of interactions between themselves and the attachment figure, based on representations that aggregate past experience (Bowlby, 1980). Integrated with these expectations are emotional experiences associated with past interactions. Out of such affect-laden expectations, mental models of the self and caregivers cohere.

Anna Freud and Dorothy Burlingham (1944) noted how some toddlers may respond to the mother with stony indifference following separation, as if the mother were a complete stranger, suggesting that separation had the power temporarily to alter the inner relationship between mother and child in such insecure infants. Ainsworth et al. (1978) observed how, upon reunion following a brief laboratory separation from the caregiver, some one-to-two-year-old children expressed relief while others indicated insecure attachments by remaining either inconsolable (resistant) or manifesting indifference (avoidant). Such observable differences may stem from the diversity of internal working models of relationships. Avoidant children appear disinterested, perhaps to forestall a further painful failure at communicating their emotional need. Working models are assumed to regulate children's behavior with the attachment figure and in due course organize their behavior in all significant relationships, including, eventually, their relationship with their own child. Psychoanalytic models and practice also suggest that parents respond to children's behavior and characteristics with expectations based on past experiences with their own primary caregiving figures (Freud, 1940; Fraiberg, 1980; Fraiberg et al., 1975).

"Internal working models," as elaborated by attachment theorists, correspond closely to certain psychoanalytic formulations of self- and object representations and internal object relations, in particular Sandler's ego-psychological model of the representational world (Sandler, 1960, 1990). The theories may differ in terms of the respective role given to fantasy and drives, but even here they agree in many fundamentals. The framework proposed by Sandler (1960, 1985) places the inborn wish to maintain safety at the center of the infant's motivational field in a manner analogous to Bowlby's (1958, 1969) emphasis on the innate propensity for attachment. Sandler and Sandler (1978) see mother-infant interactions as the context for the earliest formulations of self- and object representations. Critically, in both theoretical fields, the cognitive-affective structures of self- and other representation are assumed to regulate children's behavior with the caregiver, and in due course behavior in all important relationships.

Striking empirical support is provided for the transgenerational model by studies that demonstrate a strong association between the child's security of attachment measured at one or six years of age and an assessment of the caregiver's internal working model. These studies used Mary Main's remarkable structured assessment, the Adult Attachment Interview (George et al., 1985), as an indicator of the functioning of the internal working model. The interview is designed to elicit the individual's account of his or her childhood attachment experiences and evaluations of the effects of those experiences on present functioning. Ratings of emotional and cognitive features of the individual's representational world as revealed in the transcripts constitute the basis of a four-way classification scheme (Main and Goldwyn, 1991, unpublished; Bakerman-Kranenburg and Van Ijzendoorn, 1993). Broadly speaking, security is indicated by "undistorted" free/autonomous cognitive and emotional processes, insecurity by significant interference with cognitive or affective aspects of mental representations of self and other (splitting, derogation, and denial).

In the London Parent-Child Project (Fonagy et al., 1991a, 1991b, 1994; Steele et al., in press, in press 1994) we have found that expectant parents' mental models of attachment predicted subsequent patterns of attachment between infant and mother (75% concordance at 12 months) and infant and father (72% concordance at 18 months). Our work has confirmed that each parent transmits his or her internal working model independently of the actions of the other parent. For example, the security of the mother's internal working model apparently will not influence the child's security of attachment to the father at 18 months. Only the father's internal working model will have an association with this.

These results indicate that the adult's internal working model, at least as measured by Mary Main's Adult Attachment Interview, appears to identify the *propensity* to form secure as opposed to insecure relationships, and that children develop distinguishable sets of mental representations of relationship expectations with each of their caregivers for at least the first 18 months of life. The insulation of the internal working models of young children allows for the creation of a secure internal working model alongside one or more highly insecure ones.

Children who develop normally despite generally adverse circumstances frequently have in their object world a stable and responsive, even if relatively remote, figure (Werner, 1989).

Developmental psychology provides a heuristic model of the transgenerational process taking place in three stages: (1) the parent's attachment related experiences in childhood are embodied within a working model that (2) affects the development of the mental representation of the child and the parenting function underlying sensitive parental caregiving behavior with children which, (3) is the primary determinant of the child's quality of attachment to the parent (see Bretherton et al., 1989).

Despite experimental support, this heuristic model may be criticized on a number of grounds. First, the predictive power of maternal sensitivity, operationalized in these ways, is relatively weak (Field, 1987). Second, the observations upon which ratings of maternal behavior are made usually include the infant and therefore cannot be considered logically independent of the infant's characteristics (Kagan, 1987). Third, according to the model, as representations of past attachment experiences are likely to be fairly stable, all children of the same parent might be expected to manifest the same pattern of attachment—a prediction that is not supported by empirical evidence (Main and Weston, 1981).

From the psychoanalytic standpoint the heuristic model of transgenerational transmission of attachment based on sensitivity in mother-infant interaction is clearly inadequate. This is because operationalization in terms of maternal behavior confounds two independent psychic processes related to the development of the attachment relationship. The first pertains to the mother's attitude and behavior independent of the child's mental state. The second is the mother's capacity to envisage the infant as a mental entity, a human being with intentions, feelings, and desires. This can form the basis of her ability to mentally contain the baby (Bion, 1962; Winnicott, 1965) and to understand correctly and react appropriately to her infant's need in vocal or gestural communication, as well as in the provision of physical care. Yet this capacity calls upon mental processes of a different order from the first; it requires the mother to *reflect on the mental state of another human being*, and in this way goes beyond the demonstration of affection and concern.

Our investigations of the influence of what we termed *reflective self function*[1] (Fonagy et al., 1991b) have demonstrated that the capacity for making use of mental state constructs in discussing attachment relationships seemed to capture individual differences in parental sensitivity and provides a powerful prediction of the nature of the evolving relationship between infant and parent (Fonagy and Moran, 1991; Fonagy et al., 1993). Parents who were rated, on the basis of their AAI narratives, to be high in this capacity were three or four times as likely to have secure children than parents whose reflective capacity was rated as poor. This difference was not markedly affected when verbal ability and social class were statistically controlled for.

Internal working models that contain the representation of the mental states of self and other may be considered as "meta-models" which have the potential to activate representations of object relations not containing a reflective component. Assuming the parallel presence of alternative models of object relations, a reflective process may play a central role in determining which of the alternatives will be the *working* model in a particular relationship. The capacity to reflect upon human experience and take a mentalistic or "intentional" (Dennett, 1978) stance may therefore be crucial in forestalling the repetition of negative attachment experiences.

In the London Parent-Child Project, mothers who had experienced deprivation and neglect were significantly less likely

---

[1] The notion of reflective self originates from William James (1890). He used the term "reflective" in his description of the evolution of a self structure when the mental state of the individual becomes a subject of his own thought ("to think of ourselves as thinkers" p. 296). Freud (1900) discusses a similar idea in *The Interpretation of Dreams* (pp. 101–102), as does Rapaport (1951, p. 724). Joseph (1987) also uses the concept.

to transmit these to their children through insecure attachment if the narrative of their childhood experiences indicated high reflective self capacity (Fonagy et al., 1994).

A similar model is suggested by some recent findings from the analysis of Adult Attachment Interview data from a group of 97 nonpsychotic inpatients at the Cassel Hospital (Fonagy et al., 1992). Patients diagnosed as manifesting borderline personality disorder (J. G. Gunderson criteria) had low ratings on reflective self function. Although most patients in the sample reported experiences of early trauma or abuse, the borderline group was the only one to show a combination of unresolved trauma and inability to think about relationship experiences in mental state terms. On the basis of these findings, we hypothesized that individuals with experience of severe maltreatment in childhood who respond to this experience by an inhibition of reflective self functioning are less likely to resolve this abuse, and are more likely to manifest borderline psychopathology.

A Transgenerational Model of Borderline Pathology

These findings are in accord with a considerable body of research and theory which points to the intergenerational origins of child maltreatment. Mothers' descriptions of physical abuse and rejection by their parents during childhood have been related to mothers' reenactment of maltreatment with their own children. Kaufman and Zigler (1989), in their comprehensive review, estimate the risk of transgenerational transmission of abuse to be at least 30%, three times the risk of transgenerational concordance faced by the child of a schizophrenic parent.

Research has begun to document a specific link between the history of abuse and borderline personality disorder. Herman (1986) found 75% of patients meeting *DSM-III* criteria for borderline personality disorder (BPD) reported physical or sexual abuse. A number of independent interview studies found that sexual as opposed to physical abuse was specifically associated with a reliable diagnosis of BPD. Westen et al. (1990)

demonstrated that borderline patients tend to have a history of sexual abuse from multiple perpetrators and that the abuse typically occurs in a context of neglect and rejection by primary caregivers.

Notwithstanding the convergence of findings across studies, a number of questions remain unresolved. Although sexual and other forms of abuse are particularly prevalent in borderline patients, they are also common among general population samples. Approximately 20% to 25% of all women report a history of sexual abuse during childhood (Bickerton et al., 1991). The characteristics of the original experience of abuse or the psychological makeup of the individual that makes these individuals vulnerable to the experience and predisposed to BPD are unknown. I propose below that the availability of full reflective capacity may be critical in providing children with a measure of protection against the assault of destructive and inhumane parenting and culture which continues to characterize Western society.

In our view severe narcissistic and borderline states may be understood as involving dysfunctions of reflective self processes (Fonagy, 1989, 1991; Fonagy and Higgitt, 1989; Fonagy and Moran, 1991; Higgitt and Fonagy, 1992). We have proposed that an extreme defensive stance is adopted by some individuals exposed to early trauma. They cope with the intolerable prospect of conceiving of the mental state of their tormentors by refusing to recognize this, through a defensive disruption of the process of depicting feelings and thoughts. Consequently, their representations of themselves and others will lack accurate and detailed impressions of cognitive and affective content. This seems to me to be a crucial aspect of the clinical picture frequently referred to in the analytic literature as "borderline."

Borderline States and the Reflective Self

Our initial explorations in this area were inspired by Bretherton's pioneering work on the development of mental representations of mental states (Bretherton et al., 1981) as well as that of a number of British developmentalists on the so-called "theory of mind" (see Morton and Frith, in press; Baron-Cohen, 1993; Hobson, 1990a, 1990b). While I do not favor the term "theory of mind" (Whiten, 1991) to describe the capacity to use mental state concepts in social understanding, there is sufficient common ground between recent progress in cognitive developmental psychology and traditional psychoanalytic ideas to pursue the issue of individual differences in reflective self capacity.

I am proposing that a partial and dynamic inhibition of this aspect of mental functioning is a core feature of severe personality disturbance. Several aspects of pathological functioning characteristic of borderline organization may be understood in terms of such a deficit. First, the commonly noted difficulty in following the associations of borderline patients (e.g., Bion, 1957; Segal, 1975) may be understood as an external manifestation of a flawed representation of the mental state of the other. The failure to take into consideration the listener's current mental state may account for some of the phenomena previously described in the psychoanalytic literature in terms of "excessive projective identification" (Bion, 1957). Analysts may also find themselves internalizing the lack of mental functioning of their patients, involuntarily abandoning the capacity to attribute emotion through imagination, and reverting to an understanding of affect through affective resonance.

Second, numerous authors have noted that a difficulty in communicating emotional experience or subtle differences among inner sensations represents a hallmark of borderline functioning (e.g., Giovacchini, 1979). These observations seem consistent with the view that language functions that entail the capacity to represent mental processes are disturbed.

Third, one aspect of the desperate dependence borderline patients manifest in the transference (Searles, 1987) may well concern their difficulty in consistently maintaining the image of the analyst as a functioning mental entity (rather than, as is sometimes thought, the physical presence of the analyst). The analyst is desperately needed because the representation of the analyst who understands has little permanence.

This view has implications for interpretive work. Patients with limited reflective function may be able to think about mental processes as long as their primary representation of them is vivid, i.e., they are currently undergoing the experience referred to in an interpretation. Extratransference interpretations, particularly during the early stages of their treatment, may not be understood, can be experienced as an assault, and are probably of only very limited value to these patients.

Fourth, there is an often-noted absence of concern for the object which may manifest itself as remarkable cruelty (e.g., Kernberg, 1975). Although this may frequently be part of a disposition to excessive destructiveness, it may also, at least in part, be an indication that borderline functioning contains no compelling representation of pain in the object's mind. A critical source of moderation of the affective response is therefore absent.

Fifth, the representation of one's own ideas and desires forms the core of a coherent and mature identity. The relinquishing of the capacity to consider mental states thus inevitably brings with it a fear of disintegration. If the therapist's reflective capacity is used by the patient to support and maintain the latter's identity, the patient will be absolutely dependent on the therapist in maintaining a relatively stable mental representation of himself. Consequently, there will be an adhesive quality to the attachment to the therapist (Bick, 1968).

Sixth, a poorly functioning set of mental representations of mental functioning must interfere with social functioning. When unstructured social situations call upon his deficient capacity to predict the behavior of others on the basis of his model of their mental world, the patient may become extremely anxious and confused. The borderline patient's mental image of the object remains at the immediate context-dependent level of primary representation. It should not surprise us therefore that he manifests little capacity to mourn for absent or lost objects (Searles, 1986).

Finally, those working with such patients frequently note the absence of the "as-if" nature of the transference. The projection of the internal world onto the analyst is "for real" (Masterson, 1981). Winnicott (1971) eloquently described the stage of child development when feelings, thoughts, and objects may be played with, when pretend worlds may be created and inhabited. Pretence and the understanding of another's mental state have in common the need to be able to entertain a belief while at the same time knowing this to be false (Fonagy and Fonagy, 1992, unpublished). Psychoanalysis is a further context that requires the entertaining of such dual realities. The absence of reflective self function in borderline organization thus leads to a tendency to "act out" the transference because the ability to decouple mental representation from reality is vulnerable or absent.

Borderline and Normal Development

We assume that, in borderline individuals, there is a dynamic inhibition of reflective self function and a constriction of the representation of all relationship experiences to pragmatic forms. Individual differences in reflective self capacity emerge even within the normal range of parent-child relationships. We assume that mental representations ("frames") underpinning reflective self function are less likely to develop if the caregiver's own experiences of having been understood or reflected upon by an adult mind were limited or flawed. The frames where mental states predominate might be more common in the case of adults whose attachment experiences were positive. Preliminary findings from the five-year followup of the London Parent-Child sample indicate that narratives jointly created by mother and child contain more elaborations of mental states in the case of secure child-mother pairs than in the case of insecure dyads.

The importance of reflective self function for attachment is greatest when the hardship suffered by the parent places him or her at risk of recreating these negative experiences in the child. If the deprived caregiver's ability to create in her mind the infant's mental state of intent (wish, belief, or want) falters, the infant may well find himself confronted by quite a malevolent set of expectations encoded within the caregiver's internal working model ("So you don't want to be nice to Mommy," when the infant turns toward a new object of interest). Thus we see the parent's reflective self function as having the potential to prevent negative experiences from her past influencing her relationship with the child. This is the resilience process which we assume underlies the significant interactions observed in the London Parent-Child studies.

The concept may be helpful in considering aspects of resilience beyond the transgenerational process. The capacity to suspend the demands of immediate physical reality and contemplate alternative perceptions (yet retaining the distinction between what is fantasized and what is real) must offer a tremendous advantage in dealing with life's adversities. The willingness and capacity to plan and project alternative realities (Quinton and Rutter, 1988), to play and to amuse (Masten, 1982), are all rooted in reflective self function. They depend on decoupling immediate physical reality from an equally real internal state. A reliable capacity to reflect upon mental states enables the child to make optimal use of the individuals available to him, both through family (Quinton et al., 1984) and informal (Braithwaite and Gordon, 1991) relationships. Reflective self function is a critical component of autonomy (O'Grady and Metz, 1987) and a coherent sense of identity.

Reflective self function allows for the modification of unhelpful internal working models of relationships through encounters with new significant figures. It equips the individual with a sort of ballast, a self-righting capacity where working models may become the object of review and change. Such gradual and constant adjustments give rise to an internal world where the behavior of objects can be experienced as predictable and stable, where the need for splitting of incoherent mental representations of the other is minimized and new experiences can be readily integrated with past internal representations.

The seeds for such a capacity probably predate verbalized narratives, and are implied by the notion of the infant's mental containment by the mother (Bion, 1962, 1967). In receiving the child's primitive projections, and converting these to comprehensible mental states, the mother creates a frame for human understanding which later interactions can build upon and elaborate.

Clinical psychoanalysis commonly, and inevitably, deals with individuals whose past experience has left them particularly vulnerable to the repetition of past relationship experiences. Their difficulties are normally addressed in two ways: first in terms of identifying the defensive distortions in their internal working models, and bringing about schematic revisions, and second by imposing a nonpragmatic, elaborative, mentalistic stance that enhances the psychic resilience of the individual in a generic way, thus making the entire attachment system available for adaptation.

REFERENCES

AINSWORTH, M., BLEHAR, M. C., WATERS, E. & WALL, S. (1978). *Patterns of Attachment: a Psychological Study of the Strange Situation.* Hillsdale, NJ: Erlbaum.

BAKERMAN-KRANENBURG, M. J. & VAN IJZENDOORN, M. H. (1993). A psychometric study of the adult attachment interview: reliability and discriminant validity. *Devel. Psychol.*, 29:870–879.

BARON-COHEN, S. (1993). The development of a theory of mind: where would we be without the intentional stance. In *Developmental Principles and Clinical Issues in Psychology and Psychiatry*, ed. M. Rutter & D. Hay. Oxford, Eng.: Blackwell.

BICK, E. (1968). The experience of the skin in early object relations. *Int. J. Psychoanal.*, 49:484–486.

BICKERTON, D., HALL, R. & WILLIAMS, A. L. (1991). Women's experience of sexual abuse in childhood. *Public Health*, 105:447–453.

BION, W. R. (1957). Differentiation of the psychotic from the non-psychotic personalities. *Int. J. Psychoanal.*, 38:266–275.

—— (1962). Learning from experience. In *Seven Servants: Four Works by Wilfred R. Bion.* New York: Aronson, 1977, pp. 1–111.
—— (1967). A theory of thinking. In *Second Thoughts.* London: Heinemann, pp. 110–119.
BOWLBY, J. (1958). The nature of the child's tie to his mother. *Int. J. Psychoanal.*, 39:350–373.
—— (1969). *Attachment and Loss. Vol. 1: Attachment.* New York: Basic Books.
—— (1973). *Attachment and Loss. Vol. II: Separation, Anxiety, and Anger.* New York: Basic Books.
—— (1980). *Attachment and Loss. Vol. III: Loss.* New York: Basic Books.
BRAITHWAITE, R. L. & GORDON, E. W. (1991). *Success Against the Odds.* Cambridge, MA: Harvard Univ. Press.
BRETHERTON, I. (1987). New perspectives on attachment relations: security, communication and internal working models. In *Handbook of Infant Development,* ed. J. Osofsky. New York: Wiley.
—— (1990). Open communication and internal working models: their role in attachment relationships. In *Nebraska Symposium on Motivation. Vol. 36: Socioemotional Development.* Lincoln, NE: Univ. Nebraska Press.
—— MCNEW, S. & BEEGHLEY-SMITH, M. (1981). Early person knowledge as expressed in gestural and verbal communication: when do infants acquire a "theory of mind"? In *Infant Social Cognition,* ed. M. E. Lamb & L. R. Sherrod. Hillsdale, NJ: Erlbaum.
—— BIRINGEN, Z., RIDGEWAY, D., MASLIN, C. & SHERMAN, M. (1989). Attachment: the parental perspective. *Infant Ment. Health J.*, 10:203–221.
CICCHETTI, D. (1990a). An historical perspective on the discipline of developmental psychopathology. In *Risk and Protective Factors in the Development of Psychopathology,* ed. J. Rolf, A. Masten, D. Cicchetti, K. Nuechterlein & S. Weintraub. New York: Cambridge Univ. Press, pp. 2–28.
—— (1990b). The organization and coherence of socioemotional, cognitive, and representational development: illustrations through a developmental psychopathology perspective on Down syndrome and child maltreatment. In *Socioemotional Development: Nebraska Symposium on Motivation,* ed. R. Thompson. Lincoln, NE: Univ. Nebraska Press.
DENNETT, D. C. (1978). *Brainstorms.* Cambridge, MA: MIT Press.
EMDE, R. N. (1988a). Development terminable and interminable. I. Innate and motivational factors from infancy. *Int. J. Psychoanal.*, 69:23–42.
—— (1988b). Development terminable and interminable. II. Recent psychoanalytic theory and therapeutic considerations. *Int. J. Psychoanal.*, 69:283–286.
FIELD, T. (1987). Interaction and attachment in normal and atypical infants. *J. Consult. Clin. Psychol.*, 55:853–859.
FONAGY, P. (1989). On tolerating mental states: theory of mind in borderline patients. *Bull. Anna Freud Cnt.*, 12:91–115.
—— (1991). Thinking about thinking: some clinical and theoretical considerations in the treatment of a borderline patient. *Int. J. Psychoanal.*, 72:639–656.
—— & HIGGITT, A. (1989). A developmental perspective on borderline personality disorder. *Rev. Int. Psychopathol.*, 1:125–159.
—— & MORAN, G. S. (1991). Understanding psychic change in child analysis. *Int. J. Psychoanal.*, 72:15–22.
—— STEELE, M., MORAN, G., STEELE, H. & HIGGITT, A. C. (1991b). The capacity for understanding mental states: the reflective self in parent and

child and its significance for security of attachment. *Infant Ment. Health J.*, 13:200–216.

─────── ─── ─── ─── (1992). The integration of psychoanalytic theory and work on attachment: the issue of intergenerational psychic processes. In *Attaccamento e Psiconalis*, ed. D. Stern & M. Ammaniti. Bari, Italy: Laterza, pp. 90–91.

─── STEELE, M.; MORAN, G. S.; STEELE, H. & HIGGITT, A. (1993). Measuring the ghost in the nursery: an empirical study of the relation between parents' mental representations of childhood experiences and their infants' security of attachment. *J. Amer. Psychoanal. Assn.*, 41:957–989.

─── ─── & STEELE, H. (1991a). Maternal representations of attachment during pregnancy predict the organization of infant-mother attachment at one year of age. *Child Devel.*, 62:880–893.

─── ─── ─── HIGGITT, A. & TARGET, M. (in press). Theory and practice of resilience. *J. Child Psychol. Psychiat.*

FRAIBERG, S. (1980). *Clinical Studies in Infant Mental Health*. New York: Basic Books.

─── ADELSON, E. & SHAPIRO, V. (1975). Ghosts in the nursery: a psychoanalytic approach to the problem of impaired infant-mother relationships. *J. Amer. Acad. Child Psychiat.*, 14:387–422.

FREUD, A. & BURLINGHAM, D. (1944). *Infants Without Families. Writings*, 3. New York: Int. Univ. Press, 1973.

FREUD, S. (1900). The interpretation of dreams. *S. E.*, 4 & 5.

─── (1940). An outline of psychoanalysis. *S. E.*, 23.

GEORGE, C., KAPLAN, N. & MAIN, M. (1985). *The Adult Attachment Interview*. Privileged communication. Department of Psychology, University of California at Berkeley.

GIOVACCHINI, P. L. (1979). *Treatment of Primitive Mental States*. New York: Aronson.

HERMAN, J. L. (1986). Histories of violence in an outpatient population. *Amer. J. Orthopsychiat.*, 56:137–141.

HIGGITT, A. & FONAGY, P. (1992). Psychotherapy in borderline and narcissistic personality disorder. *Brit. J. Psychiat.*, 161:23–43.

HOBSON, P. (1990a). Concerning knowledge of mental states. *Brit. J. Med. Psychol.*, 63:199–214.

─── (1990b). On acquiring knowledge about people and the capacity to pretend: response to Leslie. *Psychol. Rev.*, 97:114–121.

JAMES, W. (1890). *Principles of Psychology*. New York: Holt.

JOSEPH, E. D. (1987). The consciousness of being conscious. *J. Amer. Psychoanal. Assn.*, 35:5–22.

KAGAN, J. (1987). *Psychological Research on the Human Infant: An Evaluative Summary*. New York: Wiley.

KAUFMAN, J. & ZIGLER, E. (1989). The intergenerational transmission of child abuse. In *Child Maltreatment: Theory and Research on the Causes and Consequences of Child Abuse and Neglect*, ed. D. Cicchetti & V. Carlson. New York: Cambridge Univ. Press.

KERNBERG, O. F. (1975). *Borderline Conditions and Pathological Narcissism*. New York: Aronson.

MAIN, M. & WESTON, D. (1981). The quality of the toddler's relationship to mother and to father: related to conflict behavior and the readiness to establish new relationships. *Child Devel.*, 52:932–940.

MASTEN, A. S. (1982). *Humor and Creative Thinking in Stress-Resistant Children.* Unpublished doctoral dissertation. University of Minnesota.

MASTERSON, J. (1981). *The Narcissistic and Borderline Disorders.* New York: Brunner/Mazel.

MORTON, J. & FRITH, U. (in press). Causal modeling: structural approaches to developmental psychopathology. In *Handbook of Developmental Psychopathology*, ed. D. Cicchetti & D. Cohen.

O'GRADY, D. & METZ, J. R. (1987). Resilience in children at high risk for psychological disorder. *J. Pediat. Psychol.*, 12:3–23.

QUINTON, D. & RUTTER, M. (1988). *Parenting Breakdown: The Making and Breaking of Intergenerational Links.* Brooksfield, VT: Gower.

────── & LIDDLE, C. (1984). Institutional rearing, parenting difficulties, and marital support. *Psychol. Med.*, 14:107–124.

RAPAPORT, D. (1951). Toward a theory of thinking. In *Organization and Pathology of Thought.* New York: Columbia Univ. Press, pp. 689–730.

SANDLER, J. (1960). The background of safety. In *From Safety to Superego: Selected Papers of Joseph Sandler.* London: Karnac, 1975, pp. 1–8.

────── (1985). Towards a reconsideration of the psychoanalytic theory of motivation. *Bull. Anna Freud Cntr.*, 8:223–243.

────── (1990). Internal objects and internal object relationships. *Psychoanal. Inq.*, 10:163–181.

────── & SANDLER, A.-M. (1978). On the development of object relationships and affects. *Int. J. Psychoanal.*, 59:285–296.

SEARLES, H. F. (1986). *My Work with Borderline Patients.* Northvale, NJ: Aronson.

────── (1987). The development in the patient of an internalized image of the therapist. In *The Borderline Patient: Emerging Concepts in Diagnosis, Psychodynamics and Treatment*, Vol. 2, ed. J. S. Grotstein, M. F. Solomon & J. A. Lang. Hillsdale, NJ: Analytic Press, pp. 25–40.

SEGAL, H. (1975). A psychoanalytic approach to the treatment of schizophrenia. In *The Work of Hanna Segal.* New York: Aronson, 1981, pp. 131–136.

STEELE, H., STEELE, M. & FONAGY, P. (in press). A snapshot of the internal working model of attachment: the factor structure of the adult attachment interviews. *Brit. J. Med. Psychol.*

────── ────── ────── (in press 1994). Associations among attachment classifications of mothers, fathers and their infants: evidence for a relationship-specific perspective. *Child Devel.*

WERNER, E. E. (1989). Children of the garden island. *Scient. Amer.*, April, pp. 106–111.

WESTEN, D.; LUDOLPH, P.; NISLE, B.; RUFFINS, S. & BLOCK, J. (1990). Physical and sexual abuse in adolescent girls with borderline personality disorder. *Amer. J. Orthopsychiat.*, 60:55–66.

WHITEN, A. (1991). *Natural Theories of Mind.* Oxford, Eng.: Blackwell.

WINNICOTT, D. W. (1965). *The Maturational Processes and the Facilitating Environment.* New York: Int. Univ. Press.

────── (1971). *Playing and Reality.* London: Tavistock.

DISCUSSION: CAN EMPIRICAL STUDIES OF DEVELOPMENT IMPACT ON PSYCHOANALYTIC THEORY AND TECHNIQUE?

Joseph D. Lichtenberg, M.D.

PSYCHOANALYTIC EXPERIENCE EXPLORES motivation; and motivation is understandable through empathic entry into an analysand's affects, cognition, and activity packaged in narrative form. Therefore, I look at the developmental studies in this issue to see how the problems they address and the findings they obtain can help to sense more deeply and effectively the experience of the partners in the clinical exchange. I approach these studies with the belief that the experiences of infancy, lived within the matrix of caregiver ministration, affects later psychological development. While this assumption requires empirical support, its implications cannot be ignored. Each of our analytic theories contains explicit and implicit assumptions about early development, and each account contains proposals that conflict with and contradict the others. But no single empirical study or even group of studies will resolve the issue of the pertinence of infantile experience to later development or to psychoanalytic technique. Too many factors come into play to be reduced to the design potential of an empirical study. We cannot hope to seek essential yes-no answers to the large questions. We *can* hope to obtain greater clarity about the significance of factors we hypothesize to be influential. For example, in studying a population of teen-aged mothers and their babies as reported by Osofsky, we can design studies to ask questions. One investigator might want to establish the salience of the mothers' being teenagers, believing the stage of life rather than early experience or psychopathology is a primary

---

Clinical Professor of Psychiatry, Georgetown University, Washington, DC.

determinant. Another investigator might center attention on the early experiences of the mother with her caregivers and how this affects her preparedness for child care. Other investigators might study conflicts of the mother focusing on the intrapsychic sources that led her to become pregnant at that time or on whether characterological pathology she might be found to have is key to understanding problems that occur with her baby. Some might focus on what place sociocultural factors occupy. I would add an assumption that is even harder to affirm empirically: the information gained from such studies would influence therapists' approach to their work with teen-aged mothers and their babies in subtle, difficult-to-specify ways.

Hobson begins with a central feature of empirical methodology. He states that in the mid-1970's when he first encountered autistic children, "It seemed to me that something was awry. On an *intuitive* level, one's own *experience of being in relation* with autistic individuals, the unearthly 'feel' of such relative nonengagement, must surely hold the key to this unique disorder" (*italics added*). In our field, ideally hypotheses to be tested originate from intuitions; intuitions are themselves based on experiences the intuiter has reflected on; the experiences that generally carry the greatest potential are those that arise in an emotionally evocative dyadic situation. Hobson reasoned that if the strange, unearthly nonengagement held the key, then other pertinent findings, such as a failure in the capacity for symbolization, develop as a consequence. The alternative hypothesis held by many is that because of cognitive impairments, autistic children are unable to process social stimuli. Working from Kanner's (1943) thesis that autism is a disorder of *affective* relatedness, Hobson set out to explore basic processes of affect perception and responsiveness. His aim is to use his study to learn about normal development as well as about autism.

We need proceed no further to recognize a significant problem: what does it avail us in our effort to understand normal or neurotic development to study autism (or other major psychopathological conditions)? This may seem an absurd question since the very essence of Freudian theory of development is based on reconstructions from psychopathological states. A defensible logic is that you study what something such as affective engagement does by examining what happens if you do not have it. This is the logic behind studying children without sight, hearing, mothers, fathers, etc. My point is that we have taken this approach so for granted that someone reading only the studies presented here might conclude that, as had been traditional, psychoanalytic development research must proceed in this manner—mapping pathology in order to map normality. Fortunately, in the last several decades, normal development has become a primary subject of study by many researchers (Lichtenberg, 1983; Stern, 1985; Emde, 1988a, 1988b, 1991).

Returning to Hobson, a thesis he wishes to explore is that an important step in the capacity to symbolize occurs when the infant relates to another person's reaction to visually shared objects and events. This developmental step, often conceptualized in terms of the onset of social referencing, marks an important change for infants. Rather than fixing on a pointing finger as an object of interest, children recognize that the finger (often accompanied by words), is a sign signaling an instruction and, furthermore, that a quick shift back to the caregiver's face will signal the emotion evoked by the object or event. Autistic children do not make the *affective* connection to read the safety or danger of the event from the caregiver's facial expression. Hobson's experiments prove autistic individuals are specifically impaired in their emotional sensitivity, perception, and understanding in comparison with control groups. As Hobson observes, a reader could say "there is nothing like proving the obvious." What is the significance for psychoanalysis of Hobson's demonstration that a failure in intersubjective contact may be a basis for failure in symbolic play and linguistic self representation? My answer is: only as a starting point to other questions. Has Hobson succeeded in establishing a *causal* relationship between intersubjective contact and failed symbolic development, or are they concomitant failures? How do we explain that the ordinary attachment behaviors of eye contact, seeking, cuddling and baby-talk communication are not missing (as vision is missing in the sightless), but emotionally aversive? Why is exploratory behavior such as the manipulation of a speck of dirt or a toy confined to a very narrow focus but within that restricted ritualistic range very helpful in ensuring a degree of emotional stability and pacification? Why do hard objects comfort more than soft (Tustin, 1988)? How is the surrounding environment, especially people's movements, being perceived despite the child's effort to neither acknowledge nor respond to the awareness? Main notes the *physical* location of attachment figures are constantly monitored. For autistic children the monitoring of others, often experienced as aversive intruders, is probably a function of peripheral vision. With each of these questions we might cross over a bit to the momentary "unearthly," uncanny dreads experienced in dreams, and in occasional regressive states during analysis. Hobson recognizes these further sources of inquiry when he states, "the peculiarities of autism may challenge us to rethink how biologically based and coherently organized capacities for emotional sensibility, responsiveness, and experience are necessary for or closely allied to primitive forms of object representation and psychological defense." We can also profitably turn this proposition upside down—we can understand the vicissitudes of a major disturbance in attachment motivation and in the motivation for exploration and assertion by a study of the normal development of these systems (Lichtenberg, 1989a, 1989b; Lichtenberg et al., 1992).

Hobson and Fonagy both present studies of borderline personality and both use Main's Attachment Interview for Adults. As Main notes, this remarkable instrument is the continuation of a series of developments that dramatically substantiate the value of observation and experimental research to verify or eliminate hypotheses. As is characteristic of our field, the saga begins with a controversy. Bowlby (1958, 1960) advanced the revolutionary proposal that seeking, following, and clinging are as inherent in the infant's repertoire for survival as sucking and feeding. One after the other, analysts committed to a psychosexual program of orality, infantile helplessness, and a belief that infants only search for mother as the result of an eroding purified pleasure rose to the attack (A. Freud, 1960; Schur, 1960; Spitz, 1960). Ainsworth, a psychologist impressed by Bowlby's ideas and outside the rhetorical struggle, decided to observe infants in another culture to confirm or disconfirm the role of neonatal attachment. Convinced of the soundness of attachment theory by her skilled anthropological data-gathering in Uganda, Ainsworth and her colleagues (1978, 1979) devised a standardized test for the attachment hypothesis that could be administered in laboratory situations in America and elsewhere. In this procedure one-year-old infants are exposed to a stressful situation in which they are confronted both by a stranger and by one or two brief departures of the mother, followed by a reunion. In a number of nonclinical groups selected for study, one-year-olds were found to reveal definitive well-established patterns of attachment manifest in reunions after maternal absences. These patterns were classified as secure, anxious-resistant, or avoidant. Mother-infant patterns of exchange were observed that conformed to reasonable expectations as sources of the different forms of attachment. The findings of this easily repeatable experimental design were then verified in samples from varying populations.

As Hobson notes, pattern categorization is only the beginning of further productive inquiry. While Bowlby's basic premise was substantiated, many questions remained that led to fruitful debate across theoretical lines. But most interesting from the standpoint of methodology are two further developments. First, the predictive capacity of the categories of attachment of the one-year-olds for later development, while strong, was less precise than the researchers hoped for. Just as the unexpected disappearance of bacteria in the moldy petri dish led Fleming to discover penicillin, here the surprised researchers looked for the source of their disappointment. A review of the findings led to recognition of a methodological flaw. While the original category classification was useful, observers forced by the design to restrict their choices to three patterns were overlooking a fourth group whose attachment responses on reunion were unorganized and without clear orientation. Once these responses were regarded as a separate grouping, the predictive potential of the remaining group of secure, ambivalent, and avoidant attachments for later patterning improved. Moreover, the newly discovered group proved to be extremely interesting as containing those infants most particularly at risk for later disorder.

The second development in this research is the finding that led to the instrument Hobson and Fonagy and many others have found so valuable. The styles of mothers in interviews were found to correspond to the nature of their attachments with their babies as categorized in the Strange Situation research. Particularly significant is the finding that those mothers whose accounting of their own life experience, whether reported to be positive or negative, showed strong evidence of being unresolved, disorganized, and disoriented tended most commonly to have illnesses that fall into the borderline diagnostic category. Hobson found that 10 of 12 borderline patients appeared confused, fearful, and overwhelmed in relating their past experiences with attachment figures. In contrast, despite roughly comparable severe actual trauma and abuse in their backgrounds, not one of a control group of dysthymic patients revealed a similar disorganized preoccupation. Hobson concludes that adult modes of representing early experience are intimately related to styles of intersubjective functioning, and that an incapacity to assimilate early experience within a coherent mental framework is a characteristic of borderline psychopathology. Main reports that some children in the disorganized, disoriented group exhibit a frozen trancelike expression. She associates this response to dissociative states and adds the intriguing finding of Liotti that these children are prone to respond to *subsequent* trauma with dissociation. Along with Liotti (1992), Lichtenberg et al. have suggested a relationship between this finding and multiple personality disorders (1992, pp. 164–168).

Fonagy places his emphasis on the relative absence of a self-reflective capacity as his prime candidate for the disturbance that leads to borderline conditions. In Fonagy's model, the transgenerational transmission of attachment derives from the mother's attitudes and behavior independent of the child's mental state and the mother's capacity to envisage the infant's own individuality, his or her desires, intentions, and feelings. For optimal functioning, the mother must be able to reflect both on her own state and the state of her baby. The capacity for making use of mental state constructs in discussing attachment relationships provided a powerful predictor—those high in reflective skills were three or four times more likely to have securely attached children than those with poor skills. Fonagy notes, as does Hobson, that trauma itself is not as significant a factor as the manner in which it is processed mentally. Mothers who experienced deprivation, neglect, and sexual and physical abuse were significantly less likely to transmit these to their children through insecure attachment if the narrative of their childhood experiences indicated high reflective self capacity. Fonagy's hypothesis is that the availability of full reflective capacity may be critical in providing children with a measure of protection against inhuman parenting and culture. In a related finding, children of depressed mothers who recognized and acknowledged their depression fared better than those of depressed mothers who either denied or were too unself-reflective to be aware of their state (Field, 1992).

Confused, disorganized narratives, inability to self-reflect, inability to sense the mental state of another—how do they relate to each other? Before tackling this question, I shall discuss another of Fonagy's findings. Mothers' mental models of attachment during pregnancy predicted the forms of attachment at 12 postnatal months with 75% concordance. The exciting finding is that *expectant* fathers models also showed a high

(72%) concordance with postnatal attachment patterns at 18 months. The security of the mother's model apparently did not influence the child's security of attachment to the father at 18 months—only the father's internal working model did. This attests to two premises: first, the working model of attachment of each primary caregiver is of major significance for the attachment to that caregiver; second, fathers are far more important in their own right than our mother-centered theory would indicate. Extensive recent research on the role of fathers (Brazelton, unpublished) and on alternative caregivers and figures in the child's environment confirms Fonagy's statement that children who develop normally despite adverse circumstances frequently have available a stable responsive person even if relatively remote. Resilience or the capacity to self-right, that is, innate adaptive qualities of temperament, can facilitate some children's seeking to and availing themselves of opportunities to thrive. But how does resilience in either a child or a parent become operative, or how are traumatic, unempathic childhood experiences passed on to the next generation?

Broussard (1970, 1976) reported a dazzlingly simple experiment. She had mothers assess their first-born babies as "better than average" or "not better than average" at the end of the babies' first month. Eighty-five of the children in the original sample were examined in a blind study at the age of four-and-a-half and at 10 or 11. At four-and-a-half years, 66% of those babies who had been rated as not better than average by their mothers had a degree of psychopathology warranting therapeutic intervention, as compared to 20.4% of those rated better than average. Broussard added a maternal judgment made at one or two days after delivery, to reveal better the mother's *initial* fantasy about her baby. Eighty-two percent of babies viewed as above average in both assessments were diagnosed as emotionally healthy at four-and-a-half, as compared to only 32% of those judged below average in both assessments. The predictive power of the mothers' initial fantasy of the worth of their infants continued when the children reached 10 or 11. Seventy-eight percent of the negatively viewed infants had diagnosable mental disorders in comparison to 49% of the others (astonishingly high figures in both instances!). Females were less vulnerable to their mothers' perception than were males. Broussard concluded that any male baby seen negatively by his mother in her initial fantasy, or as a result of her experience with him during the first month, is at high risk for future emotional difficulty. However, Broussard found, as have others (Appelbaum, 1982), that working with these mothers can affect their attitudes and facilitate significant changes from negative to positive assessments.

Fonagy tested expectant mothers and fathers and found that whether they could or could not be self-reflective about their attachment predicted attachment outcome. Broussard asked mothers to evaluate their neonates and found if they had a high or low opinion of them, this expectation predicted outcome. Main and Hobson found mothers who could not give a coherent account of their own attachment formed disorganized, disoriented attachments with their children. Incoherences within the narratives collected during the adult attachment interviews strongly suggest the effect of processes of warded-off awareness of aversive experiences. The adult attachment interview therefore provides a research tool that reveals a final outcome of dynamic processes, but the meaning of the processes and the specific lived experiences that underlie them are not open to a psychoanalytic inquiry.

For an analyst these questionnaire and interview findings represent a puzzling challenge. Mothers (and fathers) convey through *conscious* responses to questionnaires or interviews answers that have powerful predictive value over a most important and subtle relationship. Where are the *unconscious* fantasies, beliefs, motives that are the hallmarks of the factors we regard as prognostically significant? Clearly the research methods we are considering do not tell us the *how* of secure and pathological attachments. They permit no direct study of dynamic processes comparable to the way empathic perception during the clinical exchange helps us to uncover unconscious beliefs, fantasies, and motives and to understand symptoms and ways of relating in which we are participants. Winnicott (1963) suggested that being should be distinguished from doing and relating. Since disjointed narratives, poor opinions, lack of reflectiveness about self and others tell us little directly about doing and relating, let us speculate that they tell us about *being*, that is, that they communicate something significant about the state of the self. Disjointed narratives point to an individual's having a disturbed capacity for organizing information about the self (either deficit or dissociation) and/or a strong defensive need to perseverate (become preoccupied) and/or disavow (dismiss) the information. Lack of reflectiveness points in the same direction—cognitive-affective limitation and/or strong defensive avoidance of self-awareness. Low opinion points to low self-esteem and a pessimistic attitude. Put another way, the questions of the researchers involve eliciting responses comparable to a Rorschach inkblot or more precisely a TAT picture of a mother (or father) and child. This mother (or father) either seeing herself (or himself) with her mother or with her (or his) baby, responds, "I will not, I cannot, deal with that past or current image with any positive expectation." What can we presume is lacking in their being? I suggest they do not experience consciously (and especially unconsciously) *a fostering attitude or sentiment*. A fostering attitude combines an empathic appreciation of someone else's or one's own present state and struggles combined with the possibility in the future of taking a needed step to move successfully toward further development. Stern (1982, unpublished) noted the analogy between the developmental impetus of a mother's being in a dialogue with an infant as she imagines, guesses, wishes he or she will become, and an analyst's alignment with an analysand's potential state of being. Seen in the light of a fostering sentiment, "low opinion" parents may be revealing a lack of the capacity to envision a future in which they will be able to enhance the child's development or their relationship with the child. Parents who lack self-reflection are incapable of experiencing a present or future empathic evaluation of *themselves* and, by extension, their child. Parents who cannot organize a narrative accounting of their child-parent experiences have not been helped to overcome the disorganizing effect of persistent empathic failures, parental detachment, fright, and overt abuse during their development—an internal model of failed fostering, that is, of being locked in a pathological state rather than mastering it. As Main suggests, a specific form of incoherence in a parent's discourse predicts specific forms of insensitivity to selected infant signals—those that foster integration and growth.

In her paper, Osofsky presents a wide-ranging research strategy directed primarily toward discerning factors that influence pathological development: high psychosocial risk, negative emotions, intergenerational pattern repetition, and trauma associated with community violence. Her research confirms the now generally agreed-upon finding that many adolescent mothers have simultaneous difficulty in regulating their own affects and autonomy and the affects and assertiveness of their babies. They do well when the dyadic relatedness is pleasurable, but turn off when difficulties arise. An undesired outcome of their parenting style is that the developing child experiences little sense of having an influence on dyadic interactions. The main thrust of Osofsky's presentation is that the key to understanding development lies in the nature (dynamics) of the dyad centered on success or failure of affect regulation and emotional availability. She confirms the prevailing view of infant researchers that displays of aggression and negative affects are related to variations in adverse experience rather than to variations in intrinsic impulse discharge. She calls for a theory that emphasizes the affective exchange and "places less emphasis on either a drive model to explain aggression or a deficit model of self psychology that includes problems in self-object experience." She calls for a model centering in the dynamic interaction of the child-caregiver dyad.

At every point I find myself agreeing with Osofsky and wishing she would carry her ideas forward. The essential feature of displays of aggression and negative affects lies in aversive experiences, but each experience is a combination of many factors—expectations from prior experiences, innate and learned preferences and general proclivities, physiological changes such as hormonal upsurges, and the resilience of either parent or child to extract him- or herself from an unhappy dyadic interchange. Kohut's original (1971) model of deficits of self structure is, as Osofsky notes, unsatisfactory as a way to describe experience in affect-centered terms. But Osofsky speaks of deficits of emotional availability and, as the evidence demands, on the need for positive experiences of affect attunement and empathy. A main contribution of self psychology is to shift the emphasis in the exploration of dyadic interactions from the view of an external observer to the manner in which the individual *experiences* an exchange or event. Good-enough to someone else may be experienced as an empathic failure to the mother, the child, or both, and not-so-good may be experienced as enough of an empathic success for the attachment to remain secure. The problem inherent in most research, especially of the statistical variety, is that we obtain useful pooled data about, say, emotional regulation, or dyadic success in attachment, or empathic success in communication, without the moment-to-moment basis for individual developmental experience and for dyadic intersubjective experience.

Osofsky's call for a dyadic interactional model rings a strong resonate note in me. That has been the goal of my application of the full range of developmental studies. As I noted, I agree with each component she delineates, but I believe her focus to be too limited to attachment-relational experience. Somehow in deemphasizing drive and shifting emphasis to what I call an attachment motivational system, the influence of other motivations can be allowed to slip away. We fail to investigate the psychic regulation of such physiological needs as hunger, elimination, sleep, equilibrium, tactile and proprioceptive stimulation, and general health. We understate the role of exploration and assertion of skills and preferences when parent and child disengage from attachment interchanges. We emphasize aggression or, as I prefer, antagonism and fail to appreciate that responses to aversive experiences involve either antagonism or *withdrawal* or a combination. And as I found to my great surprise, we seem only rarely to attempt to investigate the normal predictable development of experiences of sensual enjoyment and sexual excitement.

I shall conclude by taking up the editor's charge to consider the limits and virtues for psychoanalytic clinical theory of empirical research on development. A virtue of empirical research is the rage of generalization it can encompass. As Osofsky recommends, you can do long-term prospective studies to determine outcome of children at risk—a contribution to epidemiology and social planning. You can do individual prospective studies as the Pavenstedt group has done and study the individual variations, including dramatically unexpected good outcomes, of some adults who as babies had horrendous relational experiences (V. Demos, unpublished; G. Stechler, unpublished). You can study a single factor such as cognitive capacities of neonates to respond differentially to their mothers and fathers (Brazelton, unpublished). But paradoxically, the range of generalization that empirical research must encompass is also an important limitation. The *general* statistics of more frequent depression of infants of depressed mothers (Field, 1992) fail in a clinical situation to tell us *how* it unfolds—only to be alert to it. Alternatively, a specific finding of great significance in an infant-mother dyad, such as eye aversion, may no longer be observable in an adult patient.

The greatest impact of developmental studies may not lie in the replacement of one theory by another, but rather in shifts of emphasis that are hard to link specifically to the research findings. I say that despite my own effort to offer a theory of motivational organization (Lichtenberg, 1989a, 1989b; Lichtenberg et al., 1992) that would replace the dual drive theory with a theory of systems and self. While I conceptualized the idea of shifting dominance of experience (and associations) by one or another of five motivational systems from clinical experience, I buttressed the plausibility of my hypothesis by evidence derived from the full range of empirical research on development. The type of more subtle shift I refer to is away from drive toward affect, away from old views of aggression toward aversive responses, away from a central preoccupation with sexuality toward attachment relatedness, and away from neutrality and abstinence toward empathy and communication. My colleagues and I (Lichtenberg et al., 1992) have begun to apply studies similar to those performed and reviewed by Fonagy, Hobson, Main, and Osofsky to principles of psychoanalytic and psychotherapeutic technique. For example, in employing *an empathic mode of perception* sensing the manner in which analysands' experiences unfold, we emphasize affects and intentions from the analysands' point of view. In assisting analysands to "fill the narrative envelope" by inquiring as needed about the who, what, when, where, and how of experiences, we promote a shared narrative organization in the exchange. This principle is coordinate with Main's contention that language is the central means by which individuals communicate with themselves, with one another, and "the only means in which incoherences can be expressed." By *following the interpretive sequence*, that is, by attending the sequence of responses the analysand makes to our interventions, we encourage reflective awareness and bring ourselves into the picture more solidly, thus opening the way to strongly felt expectations (transferences) recreated in the present but derived from generalized past experiences. Through the joint construction of *model scenes* that help to explain patterns of current and past interchanges, we utilize knowledge of significant developments and motivations exploiting information from research applied to the individual. By "the wearing of attributions," that is, accepting in an illusionary-actual realm the view analysands have of us, we open to joint construction the discovery of ourselves-with-the-analysand comparable to the way parents and child discover and in a fashion "create" each other. Seen through modifications of theory and technique, the findings of psychoanalytically oriented empirical studies of early development have and will have, I believe, a cumulative effect far greater than we have yet appreciated.

REFERENCES

AINSWORTH, M. D. (1979). Attachment as related to mother-infant interaction. In *Advances in the Study of Behavior*, ed. J. B. Rosenblatt, R. A. Hinde, C. Beer & M. Bushel. New York: Academic Press, pp. 1–51.

―――― BLEHAR, M. D., WATERS, E. & WALL, S. (1978). *Patterns of Attachment: A Psychological Study of the Strange Situation.* Hillsdale, NJ: Erlbaum.

APPELBAUM, H. (1982). Using the administration of the Brazelton Neonatal Assessment Scale to encourage the bonding of parents to their newborn babies. *Psychoanal. Inq.*, 1:643–657.

BOWLBY, J. (1958). The nature of a child's tie to his mother. *Int. J. Psychoanal.*, 39:350–373.

―――― (1960). Grief and mourning in infancy and early childhood. *Psychoanal. Study Child*, 15:9–52.

BROUSSARD, E. (1970). Maternal perception of the neonate as related to development. *Child Psychiat. Hum. Devel.*, 1:16–25.

―――― (1976). Neonatal prediction and outcome at 10/11 years. *Child Psychiat. Hum. Devel.*, 7:85–93.

EMDE, R. (1988a). Development terminable and interminable: 1. Innate and motivational factors from infancy. *Int. J. Psychoanal.*, 69:23–42.

―――― (1988b). Development terminable and interminable: 2. Recent psychoanalytic theory and therapeutic considerations. *Int. J. Psychoanal.*, 69:283–296.

―――― (1991). Positive emotions for psychoanalytic theory: surprises from infancy research and new directions. *J. Amer. Psychoanal. Assn.*, 39:5–44.

FIELD, T. (1992). Infants of depressed mothers. *Devel. Psychopathol.*, 4:49–66.

FREUD, A. (1960). Discussion of Dr. John Bowlby's paper. *Psychoanal. Study Child*, 15:53–62.

KANNER, L. (1943). Autistic disturbances of affective contact. *Nerv. Child*, 2:217–250.

KOHUT, H. (1971). *The Analysis of the Self.* New York: Int. Univ. Press.

LICHTENBERG, J. (1983). *Psychoanalysis and Infant Research.* Hillsdale, NJ: Analytic Press.

―――― (1989a). Model scenes, motivation, and personality. In *The Significance of Infant Observational Research for Clinical Work with Children, Adolescents, and Adults*, ed. S. Dowling & A. Rothstein. Madison, CT: Int. Univ. Press, pp. 91–107.

―――― (1989b). *Psychoanalysis and Motivation.* Hillsdale, NJ: Analytic Press.

——— Lachmann, F. & Fosshage, J. (1992). *Self and Motivational Systems: Toward a Theory of Technique.* Hillsdale, NJ: Analytic Press.

Liotti, G. (1992). Disoriented/disoriented attachment in the etiology of the dissociative disorders. *Dissociation,* 5:196–204.

Schur, M. (1960). Discussion of Dr. John Bowlby's paper. *Psychoanal. Study Child,* 15:63–84.

Spitz, R. A. (1960). Discussion of Dr. John Bowlby's paper. *Psychoanal. Study Child,* 16:63–84.

Stern, D. N. (1985). *The Interpersonal World of the Infant.* New York: Basic Books.

Tustin, F. (1988). Psychotherapy with children who cannot play. *Int. Rev. Psychoanal.,* 15:93–106.

Winnicott, D. W. (1963). Communicating and not communicating leading to a study of certain opposites. In *The Maturational Processes and the Facilitating Environment.* New York: Int. Univ. Press, 1965, pp. 179–192.

III. OUTCOME STUDIES

THE COLUMBIA RECORDS PROJECT AND THE EVOLUTION OF PSYCHOANALYTIC OUTCOME RESEARCH

Henry M. Bachrach, Ph.D.

> *The Columbia Records Project is one of the largest data base studies of psychoanalytic outcomes (and factors associated with outcomes) undertaken in modern times. Data were collected on hundreds of variables for 1,575 adult patients treated at the Psychoanalytic Clinic between 1945 and 1971. This paper presents a historical and critical overview of the methodology and findings of the project, and points toward promising directions for future research on psychoanalytic outcomes.*

SANDOR RADO, AS IT IS TOLD, strongly believed in the documentation of evidences for clinical inferences, and deplored those who "suck their theories out of thumbs." It was therefore not surprising that a climate of careful record keeping and empirical research rapidly became a value of the Psychoanalytic Clinic which he was a central figure in founding at Columbia University in 1945. In the Clinic's first decade, a wide range of studies germinated, from anthropology, childhood psychopathology, differential diagnostics, psychosomatics, to studies of the reliability of clinical inferences, and to the nature and prediction of clinical outcomes. Much of this work was interrelated, and a good sampling of the climate of the Clinic and its research efforts can be found in the early books it generated (e.g., Rado and Daniels, 1956; Goldman and Shapiro, 1966).

John Weber came to the Psychoanalytic Clinic in these early days fresh from conducting neurological research. Rado's hand fell upon this new candidate whose penchant for detail, documentation, tact, and research rapidly became evident. By the

---

Clinical Professor of Psychiatry, New York Medical College at St. Vincent's Hospital.

mid-1950's a research effort was taking shape in the mind of this young turk (along with Arnold M. Cooper, Aaron Karush, Ruth Easser, Bluma Swerdloff, Jack Elinson, Paul Bradlow and Leonard Moss, to name but a few). Since the inception of the Clinic, written case histories had been carefully collected in regular admissions and process notes for all persons applying to the Clinic for psychoanalytic treatment. Why not study this growing library of cases to determine their characteristics and the eventual fate of their treatments? Moreover, the facilities of the University even made it possible to code and store quantitative ratings about the characteristics of the cases on computer tape for the purposes of future, large-scale research which might be employed to test clinically derived analytic hypotheses. In essence, this became what was called the "Records Project." Under Weber's leadership, the Records Project became the most enduring of the early research efforts, and over the years evolved into a *data base* comprised of the largest number of psychoanalytic cases collected in the world!

Calls went out to the Clinic Faculty regarding their research interests and suggestions for variables to be included in the data base. This led to the collection of hundreds of variables which could be potentially applied to the individual cases. While many variables were drawn from the clinical lore regarding factors central to an understanding of the treatments and the reasons for the selection of patients for the treatments, many variables were also included to represent the specific research interests of the Faculty, e.g. demography, psychosomatics.

The project was officially begun in 1959 and was conceived as an exploratory study, utilizing a large number of written records on hand, aimed at studying change in "adaptation" among the patients treated by psychoanalysis and psychoanalytically oriented psychotherapy in the Clinic. Measures of change were then to be correlated with other information, such as the patient's background, predictive factors mentioned in the Clinic record at the beginning of treatment, ratings of the therapists, and information concerning the outcome of treatment subsequent to that recorded in the Clinic record. However, the study was not conceived as a controlled investigation of the effectiveness of psychoanalysis or a study of the therapeutic process itself. Indeed, it was to be preliminary to future studies, when methods were to become available for more refined, clinical-quantitative research.

One of the first efforts of the Project was the development of reliable scales for the measurement of adaptation (roughly equivalent to "ego strength"). By the mid-1960's an Adaptive Balance Profile had been constructed consisting of nine, clinically anchored, nine-point scales: Dependency, Pleasure-Frustration, Sexual Pleasure-Frustration, Affect, Defense, Emergency Emotion, Guilt, Pathology, and Social Integration Balance (Karush et al., 1964), and their clinical, psychometric, and predictive properties were studied. Suffice it to say the scales showed promise, and inter-rater reliability was found satisfactory and consistent with levels generally obtained in psychotherapy research (Cooper et al., 1966; Swerdloff, 1960; Weber et al., 1966).

By 1967 nine graduate analysts[1] had independently recorded information to the research protocol from the written records of 1,348 adult patients who ended treatment at the Clinic between 1945–1962. Of the total, 588 were seen in psychoanalysis four or five times a week, 434 judged initially as unsuitable for analysis by a candidate were seen in twice-a-week psychoanalytically oriented psychotherapy, and 326 were seen in twice-a-week psychotherapy on the psychosomatic service for physical complaints. Their *DSM II* diagnoses clustered in the neurotic range, with a correspondingly small proportion of patients considered more severely ill. A substantial proportion of these patients demonstrated favorable levels of change (Weber et al., 1967). Efforts to predict treatment outcomes based on the

[1] Drs. Andre Ballard, Paul Bradlow, Max Cohen, Seymour Jacobson, Peter Landerman, Leonard Moss, Alvin Shapiro, Josef Weistenberg, and John Weber.

data of initial evaluation, candidates', supervisors', and Clinic Chief's expectations were moderately successful (Weber et al., 1974), but these early findings were open to question, in part because of the idiosyncratic statistical treatment of the data, and because terminated as well as cases still in progress were combined in the data analysis.

Over the next 10 years data continued to be collected, but now by a modified method. Instead of employing independent judgments made by graduate analysts at the beginning and end of the Clinic record, data were obtained directly through questionnaires provided to the candidate analysts, supervisors, and patients. This added 112 more cases treated by psychoanalysis and an additional 125 cases treated by psychotherapy. In 1971, the investigators stopped collecting data and set about to reanalyze their data in the early 1980's employing newer methods developing in the broader psychotherapy research field.

The Final Form of the Project: An Overview

Here is a highly condensed overview of the data, methods, and findings of the Project in its final form (for details see Weber et al., 1985a, 1985b, 1985c; Bachrach et al., 1985). Between 1945–1971 approximately 12,000 patients applied to the Psychoanalytic Clinic for treatment, and 10% were accepted for analysis. The patients were all treated by candidate analysts under supervision, and until 1972, training in psychotherapy was also included in the curriculum of the Institute. Patients were assigned to psychoanalysis or psychotherapy generally on the basis of one screening interview by an experienced analyst after a history had been taken by a social worker, with the final determination being made by the Clinic Chief. First, a detailed demographic/sociological analysis of the patients was constructed (Weber et al., 1985a).

Next, the broad range of variables in the data bank was reduced to a smaller number of clinically meaningful dimensions which included evaluations by the nine graduate analysts on 38 demographic variables (including family, marital, occupational, educational, medical, and psychiatric history), 36 clinical variables (including diagnosis, social relations, work relations, nature and extent of symptomatic impairment), and the nine Adaptive Balance scales at the beginning of treatment *and* at termination, *or* the analyst's graduation (when the official Clinic record was closed), *whichever came first*. In those cases where treatment continued beyond the candidate's graduation, a 28-item questionnaire including rating scales was sent to the graduates for a retrospective assessment of their cases and their final outcomes. The questionnaire included assessments of clinical factors such as circumstances of termination, extent of change, motivation, psychological mindedness, personality integration, and object relations viewed from the perspective of termination. Seventy-three percent returned completed questionnaires.

The total sample of 1,585 cases was divided into two parts: (1) cases treated between 1945–1961 where data about outcomes were available from the graduate analysts' review of the Clinic record, and (2) cases treated between 1962–1971 where the information about outcomes was obtained from questionnaires completed by the treating analysts, supervisors, and patients. Similar measures and variables were employed in both samples, so that data of the second sample could be employed for partial replication of the findings of the first sample. In both samples final case *outcomes were judged according to measures of therapeutic benefit* (well represented in the original protocols) and *analyzability* (not represented in the original protocols, but now constructed from a combination of available variables).

Therapeutic Benefit was measured in three ways: (1) Circumstances of Termination judged according to a four-point scale (termination by mutual agreement that "maximum benefit" for *this* patient had been achieved; termination by mutual agreement that "maximum benefit" for *this* patient had *not* been achieved; Patient felt improved and terminated unilaterally;

Patient felt unimproved and terminated unilaterally, decompensated, or the analyst terminated the treatment because it seemed unsuitable), and (2) Direct Clinical Judgments of Improvement, i.e., the graduate analyst judges rated the cases terminating before the analyst's graduation on a three-point scale of Overall Improvement, and the treating analysts rated their privately terminated cases on four-point scales of Overall Improvement, Improvement in Principal and Secondary Areas of Disturbance. (3) Change scores[2] based on initial and final evaluation of Social Relations, Work Gratification, Principal and Secondary Areas of Disturbance, and the Adaptive Balance Scales—judged by the independent graduate analysts in the first sample, and the treating analysts in the second.

Analyzability was judged from a combination of three, four-point scales in the questionnaire completed by the treating analysts after termination, and therefore available *only* for those cases continuing beyond graduation: Handling of Psychological Data, Use of Resources at Termination, and Transference Manifestations During Treatment.[3]

---

[2]Change was measured from the beginning of treatment to the point at which the Clinic record was closed upon the candidate's graduation, which in many instances was before the cases were finally completed. Information about the qualities and fate of the treatments continuing beyond graduation was obtained directly from the treating analysts from the 28-item questionnaire, which included ego strength and other clinical rating scales. Simple measures of change were transformed into Residual Gain Scores which are statistically more reliable and the currently recommended measure of change in large-scale studies of psychotherapy. This transformation does not alter the clinical interpretation of the change score, i.e., how patients compare at the end of treatment with the way they were seen at the beginning.

[3]Cases were considered to have developed an analytic process when the analyst simultaneously gave the patient the highest rating on each of these scales following termination. Thus, a patient who was judged to have developed an analytic process would have been rated as follows: (1) "The patient brought psychological data into the treatment because he/she recognized it could be a source of understanding as well as relief." (2) "The patient recognized he/she had resources and learned to use these resources to achieve realistic adaptive growth as well as relief of personal suffering." (3) "The patient often used insights gained in the transference to plan and execute changes in his/her everyday life and interpersonal relations." A rating of any less on any one of these three scales would have excluded the patient from being categorized as having developed an "analytic process." For example, a

Predictions about clinical outcome were based on patient and analyst measures: 14 patient variables evaluated by the graduate analyst judges from the initial Clinic record (e.g., ego strength, social relations, previous treatment, primary areas of disturbance, range of ego weakness), 10 demographic variables (e.g., age, sex, occupation), 9 demographic variables about the analysts, and 14 variables about their clinical qualities obtained largely from supervisors' judgments. The Clinic Chief's expectation of outcome was also employed based on a four-point scale of optimism. Ten *retrospective* ratings of factors associated with outcome judged by the treating analysts after termination were also studied, based on the analyst questionnaire (e.g., personality integration, psychological mindedness, object relations), as well as related variables (e.g., treatment length).

With such an abundance of cases and variables, it was decided to adopt the most methodologically rigorous posture, and to include for study only those cases where there was complete and unequivocal information regarding circumstances of termination, and when analysts and clinical judges expressed considerable confidence about their assessments through confidence ratings.

Sample I: 1945–1961

The rigorous inclusion criteria regarding completeness and quality of data left 295 analyses, 172 analytic psychotherapies, and 114 psychosomatic patients treated by psychotherapy conducted between 1945–1961 available for study (Weber et al., 1985b). These patients were middle-class, well educated, and approximately equally distributed between sex and marital status. They ranged in age from 18 to 59, with a large majority

---

patient who might have been given a rating of "1" on each of the first two scales, but a "2" on the third ("Insights gained in the transference were often unclear and changes did not necessarily involve conscious planning by the patient.") would not have been categorized as having developed an analytic process. *The extent to which this measure captures what analysts typically mean by "analytic process" remains an open question.*

falling in the 20–34 range. Analytic patients were characterized as functioning within a neurotic range on initial examination, and patients referred for psychotherapy were considered more impaired in terms of motivation, psychopathology, and ability to participate in the work of analysis. One hundred fifty nine candidates conducted these analyses, with 98 treating one case, 54 treating two, and the rest between three and five. Among the psychotherapy cases, 105 candidates treated one case, 35 treated two, with the rest between three and five cases.

As can be seen in Table I, the highest levels of *therapeutic benefit* were found in the analyses continuing beyond the candidates' graduation (and therefore the longest, with the most advanced candidates for a portion of their analyses); 66% terminated by "mutual agreement that maximum benefit had been achieved," and 91% were judged "improved." In contrast, analyses terminating before the candidates' graduation (and therefore the shortest, with the least experienced analysts) showed least benefit. Only 26% terminated with maximum benefit; more than half terminated unilaterally with 44% unimproved. In some ways the clinical outcomes of this group resembled those of psychosomatic patients treated by psychotherapy, about half of whom terminated unilaterally as unimproved and were judged unchanged or worse by their therapists. Effect sizes[4] for the Clinic terminated analytic cases were, however, substantial (.40–.50 range), while Effect Sizes for the psychosomatic cases were more modest (.10–.30 range). There was also a group of 28 patients whose analysts "switched" the treatment from psychoanalysis to psychotherapy following graduation. These patients were largely judged improved (86%), with 41% terminating with "maximum benefit."

---

[4]Effect size is a statistical method of estimating the effect of interventions in a standardized manner that permits comparisons between different groups or interventions (Cohen, 1969). They are based on before-and-after differences, and were therefore only obtainable for patients terminating as Clinic cases in first sample where the graduate analysts' assessments were available. Anything less than .10 is considered small and over .40 substantial.

TABLE I
Selected Measures of Therapeutic Benefit: Sample I

	Psychoanalysis			Psychotherapy	
	End Private (N=77)	End Clinic (N=158)	Switch (N=28)	General (N=138)	Psychosomatic (N=96)
Rated Improvement					
1. Much Improved	(56%) ↘ 91%	(36%) ↘	(36%) ↘ 86%	61%	48%
2. Improved	(35%) ↗	56%	(50%) ↗		
3. No Change	5%	42%	7%	37%	45%
4. Worse	4%	2%	7%	1%	6%
Circumstances of Termination					
1. Maximum Benefit	66%	26%	41%	41%	23%
2. Not Maximum	21%	17%	23%	13%	17%
3. Improved	6%	16%	14%	9%	12%
4. Unimproved/Worse	7%	41%	23%	37%	48%

Overall, *analyzability* was modestly associated with all measures of therapeutic benefit, i.e., correlations in the .30–.40 range. However, 89% of the analyzable patients terminated with "maximum benefit," 78% were judged "much improved," and 91% were seen as functioning within a neurotic range. In contrast, only 47% of the patients who were not judged analyzable terminated with "maximum benefit," and only 40% were judged "much improved." Clearly, patients judged analyzable, according to the operational measure of analyzability, achieved greater therapeutic benefit than patients who were judged not to have developed an analytic process, but *only 43% of the patients who remained in analysis were characterized as having developed an analytic process at termination.* Neither analyzability nor therapeutic benefit turned out to be more than marginally predictable from the Clinic Chief's expectations (and there were four different senior analysts acting in this capacity during the time of the study), the patients' qualities evaluated at the beginning of treatment, rudimentary characteristics of the candidate analysts (e.g., demographic, faculty ratings), or combinations of these factors. But, it must be kept in mind that the cases were all highly selected for their suitability, thereby limiting the potentials for prediction within this narrow band; because potentially unsuitable cases were initially screened out, only the most promising cases were available for study. On the other hand, when the data were viewed retrospectively from the perspective of the treating analyst at termination, there was a more substantial relation between patient qualities (e.g., psychological mindedness, motivation, affect tolerances) and clinical outcomes, i.e., correlations in the .40–.50 range. *Treatment length was the only independently measured factor that was consistently correlated with analyzability and therapeutic benefit, i.e., correlations in the .30–.50 range.*

Sample II: 1962–1971

In the replication phase of the study (Weber et al., 1985c), 36 analyses and 41 psychotherapies conducted by 43 candidates between 1962–1971 were studied for which there were complete and reliable data following the rigorous inclusion criteria. These cases were similar to the first sample, though they were seen as functioning at slightly higher levels in initial evaluation. Detailed questionnaires, including rating scales, were distributed to candidates, patients, and supervisors; data about the analyst were obtained from Institute records and faculty ratings. Essentially the same variables were studied as in the first sample. The findings were similar. While the large majority of the analytic cases were considered improved according to their analysts (with one-third of all the analyses terminating with "maximum benefit" and another quarter terminating mutually but without maximum benefit), *only 50% of the analytic cases were judged to have developed an analytic process.* Analyzability was again associated with therapeutic benefit; 78% of the analyzable cases were judged "much improved" in contrast to 29% of the cases where an analytic process was judged not to have developed, and 75% terminated with maximum benefit, in contrast to 38% of the "unanalyzable" cases. Irrespective, the fate of these treatments was essentially no more than marginally predictable from the perspective of initial evaluation, either from the characteristics of the individual patient or analyst, or the direct predictions of supervisors (i.e., correlations in the .10 range), though the relationship between analyzability and therapeutic benefit was enhanced by the level of insight at termination (Bachrach et al., 1985). *Treatment length again was the only independent factor substantially related to analyzability and therapeutic benefit,* i.e., correlations in the .40–.70 range. The findings of the second sample completely confirmed those of the first, and are not only consistent with the accumulated body of psychoanalytic wisdom, but also with other formal, large-scale studies of psychoanalytic outcomes and their predictability. For example, Erle (1979) studied the fate of 40 terminated cases, Sashin et al. (1975) studied 130, and Kantrowitz (1987) studied 22; all found similar levels of therapeutic benefit among Psychoanalytic Clinic cases; Erle (1979), Kantrowitz (1987) and Wallerstein (1986) also found

TABLE II

Selected Measures of Therapeutic Benefit: Sample II

	Psychoanalysis		Psychotherapy	
	End Private (N=16)	End Clinic (N=20)	General (N=29)	Psychosomatic (N=12)
Rated Improvement				
1. Much Improved	60%	38%	33%	22%
2. Improved	40%	50%	33%	78%
3. No Change	0%	0%	33%	0%
4. Unimproved/Worse	0%	13%	0%	0%
Circumstances of Termination				
1. Maximum Benefit	56%	15%	28%	42%
2. Not Maximum	38%	15%	41%	33%
3. Improved	0%	35%	17%	17%
4. Unimproved/Worse	6%	35%	14%	8%

that fewer than half of their analytic cases developed an analytic process, despite meaningful therapeutic benefits. Further, Erle (1979), Erle and Goldberg (1984), Kantrowitz (1987), Kernberg et al. (1972), Sashin et al. (1975), and Wallerstein (1986) found analyzability and therapeutic benefit no more than marginally predictable from the data of initial evaluation among patients considered suitable for analysis. However, matters of definition and conceptualization complicate comparison of these findings with those of other investigators. Whether it is a working definition of psychoanalysis, or the meaning of analyzability, therapeutic benefit, or even circumstances of termination, all such designations exist only within varied conceptual and institutional frameworks. This limitation on the generalizability of the findings of the Columbia Project is of particular moment in the contemporary climate of proliferating psychoanalytic paradigms.

Commentary

The Columbia Project stands as a monument to the importance of systematic record keeping in outcome research, to the persistence of its investigators in anticipating the utility of newly evolving methods (e.g., computerization), and in continually maintaining its data base for a quarter-century. Its special merits included the large number of cases and clinically relevant factors studied from multiple perspectives, and employment of graduate analysts in providing independent judgments of clinical factors and outcomes, at least for some of the cases. Its main *clinical* contributions included documentation of range of outcomes among patients selected as suitable for psychoanalysis, the distinctions and relations between analyzability and therapeutic benefit, and the limited predictability of both when viewed from the perspective of initial evaluation. In this, its findings confirm rather than modify clinically derived knowledge, albeit on the basis of large numbers of cases spanning the experience of many individual clinical lifetimes.

At the same time the study had important limitations. These include the exclusive employment of novice analysts in the process of learning their craft, the relatively crude level of its scaling techniques and renderings of central psychoanalytic concepts applicable to the current praxis (a problem endemic to long-term research where concepts and methods inevitably change with time in concert with the accumulation of new knowledge). Provisions were also not made for independent study of the treatment process or the analysts' contribution to the final result in more than the most rudimentary ways, and the focus of the data was more descriptive than intrapsychic. The employment of patients seeking treatment at a low-fee clinic also introduced systematic biases. Thus, the project could only speak in the most general terms to central questions about the nature of psychoanalytic outcomes. Namely, its findings demonstrated that Psychoanalytic Clinic patients selected as suitable for analysis by a candidate achieved therapeutic benefits, and that seemingly more impaired patients treated by psychotherapy did not do as well under similar circumstances.

Paradoxically, it is the main strength of the project (i.e., the large number of variables studied among a very large number of diverse cases) which, in retrospect, raises questions about the viability of its methodology for making substantive contributions to an elaboration of the psychoanalytic theory of outcome. Namely, the employment of multivariate statistical methods for studying large numbers of cases requires preselection of categories for investigation on the basis of which all cases will be evaluated, results in a statistical averaging of findings, a sacrifice of the individuality specific to cases, and a loss of the kinds of qualitative distinctions which are the essence of psychoanalysis. This is precisely what concerned Freud (1933) about large-scale studies, and inspired Oberndorf (1943) to formulate the question of psychoanalytic outcomes in terms of what kinds of changes occur, in what kinds of patients, when treated by what kinds of analysts, with what kinds of techniques, to which one might add additional factors such as at what point in the developmental lives of both, and the nature of their environmental supports.

When the project first took shape, the large-scale multivariate method was considered the optimal design for studying outcomes from the perspective of the broader psychotherapy research community. Indeed, the method is well suited to studying overall trends, comparing the efficacy of "classes" of treatments, and useful for public health and planning purposes. Until recently most formal studies of psychoanalytic outcomes were built upon this model, and their findings have been highly similar, i.e., carefully selected patients benefit, but the nature of the benefits have been no more than marginally predictable from the data available at the beginning of treatment (Bachrach et al., 1991). One of the main contributions of the Columbia Project is a confirmation of this finding based on a patient population and collection of germane variables as large as all other studies combined. Such considerations point toward several directions for future research.

The first pertains to use of inexperienced analysts in attempting to further our understanding of psychoanalytic outcomes. In as complex an enterprise as psychoanalysis, where comprehension and clinical technique is so dependent upon experience, it seems only natural to study the work of practitioners sufficiently knowledgeable, skilled, experienced, and representative of the world of everyday analytic practice. This immediately points toward the need for studying the work of seasoned, graduate analysts with a broad range of cases in future outcome studies.

Second, the cumulative research yield (Bachrach et al., 1991) no longer commends large-scale multivariate designs as a singular method for deepening our understanding of psychoanalytic outcomes. One alternative promising research direction points toward an *amplification* of the traditional case study method. Systematic *individual case studies employing rigorous methods* provide opportunities for learning more about the specifically individual nature of change in psychoanalysis and the processes through which change emerges. The clinical followup method devised by Pfeffer (1959), anchored in a psychoanalytic understanding of transference, is an example that has contributed to modifications of theory, i.e., transference resolution is always incomplete. The stimulating findings of the Kris Study Group regarding borderline disorders (Abend et al., 1983) emerged from a rigorous application of the Study Group method to a specific type of individual case. The statistical methodology for even more rigorous, formal individual case designs has long been developed (e.g., Chassan, 1960), refined (e.g., Kazdin, 1992) and effectively applied in many fields (e.g., Yin, 1989), bringing us to a point where we may employ a variety of case-specific methods to similar questions about groups of individual cases selected according to specific criteria (e.g., psychopathology, outcomes), as Wallerstein (1986) has also proposed.

An allied promising research direction is the development of *clinically meaningful* methods for independently and reliably assessing core process variables (e.g., transference-resistance configurations, impact of interventions) in relation to the variegated nature of outcomes (e.g., alterations in the specific components of compromise formations and their case-specific durability). The CCRT (Luborsky and Crits-Christoph, 1990) is an example of one of the most promising methods, though many analysts believe it has not yet reached a point in its development where it fully captures the constructs it aims to measure, e.g., transference paradigms and unconscious fantasies.

We are now at a point where our field is beginning to address its research efforts to more intrinsically psychoanalytic questions, such as those adumbrated by Oberndorf (1943). But in this effort *we are still in the stage of method development*. Even the nature of the data or the units of measurement required for grappling with questions are not solved. Some researchers champion the utility of audiorecordings, while others continue to see our traditional clinical and study group methods as sufficient for expanding our knowledge. Clearly, an investigator's values are central to designing strategies, and since no single means of gathering and analyzing data is suited to answering all questions, the most appropriate method is the one that is best suited to answering specific questions in a reliable manner within one's domain of inquiry. As the manner in which one constructs an observational situation influences and partly determines the emerging data and the theory required to conceptualize the data (Rapaport, 1944), we must remain aware that the findings of our future research efforts will continue to be delimited by their methods. In an ideal world of the future, specific questions might be asked about the same individual cases, studied with different methods—e.g., rigorously conducted clinical study groups, audiorecordings or process notes employing clinically meaningful, reliable scales independently applied by experienced analysts—and the findings compared with a focus on understanding the reasons for the resulting similarities and differences.

In his final seminal contribution, Freud (1937) outlined the problems facing a psychoanalytic theory of outcome. He raised questions about the limits that interacting biological, intrapsychic, technical, and environmental factors place on change. This text, I believe, will continue to inform our future research efforts for some time to come. Once the questions raised in *Analysis Terminable and Interminable* have been significantly amplified by formal empirical research, we shall know that the psychoanalytic theory of outcome has truly undergone a systematic evolution.

REFERENCES

ABEND, S., PORDER, M. & WILLICK, M. (1983). *Borderline Patients: Psychoanalytic Perspectives*. Madison, CT.: Int. Univ. Press.
BACHRACH, H., GALATZER-LEVY, R., SKOLNIKOFF, A. & WALDRON, S. (1991). On the efficacy of psychoanalysis. *J. Amer. Psychoanal. Assn.*, 39:871–916.
—— WEBER, J. & SOLOMON, M. (1985) Factors associated with the outcome of psychoanalysis (clinical and methodological considerations): Report of the Columbia Psychoanalytic Center Research Project (IV). *Int. Rev. Psychoanal.*, 12:379–389.
CHASSAN, J. (1960). Statistical inference and the single case design. *Psychiat.*, 23:173–184.

COHEN, J. (1969). *Statistical Power Analysis for the Behavioral Sciences.* New York: Academic Press.

COOPER, A. M., KARUSH, A., EASSER, R. & SWERDLOFF, B. (1966). The Adaptive Balance profile and prediction of early treatment behavior. In *Developments in Psychoanalysis at Columbia University,* ed. G. Goldman & D. Shapiro. New York: Hafner, pp. 183–214.

ERLE, J. (1979). An approach to the study of analyzability and analysis: the course of forty consecutive cases selected for supervised analysis. *Psychoanal. Q.,* 48:198–228.

——— & GOLDBERG, D. (1984). Observations on the assessment of analyzability by experienced analysts. *J. Amer. Psychoanal. Assn.,* 32:715–737.

FREUD, S. (1933). New introductory lectures on psychoanalysis. *S. E.,* 22.

——— (1937). Analysis terminable and interminable. *S. E.,* 23.

GOLDMAN, G. & SHAPIRO, D., Eds., (1966). *Developments in Psychoanalysis at Columbia University.* New York: Hafner.

KANTROWITZ, J. (1987). Suitability for psychoanalysis. *Yearbook Psychoanal. Psychother.,* 2:403–415.

KARUSH, A., EASSER, R., COOPER, A. M. & SWERDLOFF, B. (1964). The evaluation of ego strength: a profile of adaptive balances. *J. Nerv. Ment. Dis.,* 130:332–349.

KAZDIN, A. (1992). *Methodological Issues and Strategies in Clinical Research.* Washington, DC: Amer. Psychol. Assn. Press.

KERNBERG, O. F. et al. (1972). Psychotherapy and psychoanalysis: final report of the Menninger Foundation Psychotherapy Research Project. *Bull. Menninger Clin.,* 36:3–275.

LUBORSKY, L. & CRITS-CHRISTOPH, P. (1990). *Understanding Transference: The CCRT Method.* New York: Basic Books.

OBERNDORF, C. (1943). Results of psycho-analytic therapy. *Int. J. Psychoanal.,* 24:107–114.

PFEFFER, A. Z. (1959). A procedure for evaluating the results of psychoanalysis: a preliminary report. *J. Amer. Psychoanal. Assn.,* 7:418–444.

RAPAPORT, D. (1944). The scientific methodology of psychoanalysis. In *Collected Papers of David Rapaport,* ed. M. M. Gill. New York: Basic Books, 1967, pp. 156–220.

RADO, S. & DANIELS, G. (1956). *Changing Concepts in Psychoanalytic Medicine.* New York: Grune & Stratton.

SASHIN, J., ELDRED, S. & VAN AMERONGEN, S. (1975). A search for predictive factors in institute supervised cases: a retrospective study of 183 cases from 1959–1966 at the Boston Psychoanalytic Society and Institute. *Int. J. Psychoanal.,* 56:343–359.

SWERDLOFF, B. (1960). *The Predictive Values of the Admission Interview.* Doctoral dissertation, Columbia University.

WALLERSTEIN, R. S. (1986). *Forty-two Lives in Treatment: A Study of Psychoanalysis and Psychotherapy.* New York: Guilford Press.

WEBER, J., BACHRACH, H. & SOLOMON, M. (1985b). Factors associated with the outcome of psychoanalysis: report of the Columbia Psychoanalytic Center Research Project (II). *Int. Rev. Psychoanal.,* 12:127–141.

——— ——— ——— (1985c). Factors associated with the outcome of psychoanalysis: report of the Columbia Psychoanalytic Center Research Project (III). *Int. Rev. Psychoanal.,* 12:251–262.

——— Bradlow, P., Moss, L. & Elinson, J. (1974). Predictions of outcome in psychoanalysis and analytic psychotherapy. *Psychiat. Q.*, 40:1–33.
——— Elinson, J. & Moss, L. (1966). The application of ego-strength scales to psychoanalytic clinic records. In *Developments in Psychoanalysis at Columbia University*, ed. G. Goldman & D. Shapiro. New York: Hafner, pp. 215–274.
——— ——— (1967). Psychoanalysis and change: a study of psychoanalytic clinic records utilizing electronic data-processing techniques. *Arch. Gen. Psychiat.*, 17:687–709.
——— Solomon, M. & Bachrach, H. (1985a). Characteristics of psychoanalytic clinic patients: report of the Columbia Psychoanalytic Center Research Project (I). *Int. Rev. Psychoanal.*, 12:13–26.
Yin, Y. (1989). *Case Study Research Design and Method.* Newberry Park: Sage Publications.

THE EFFECTIVENESS OF PSYCHOTHERAPY AND PSYCHOANALYSIS: CONCEPTUAL ISSUES AND EMPIRICAL WORK

ROBERT S. WALLERSTEIN, M.D.

The Psychotherapy Research Project (PRP) of the Menninger Foundation was a 30-year effort to follow the treatment careers and subsequent life careers of 42 patients, half in psychoanalysis and half in expressive and supportive psychoanalytic psychotherapies, in order to learn more about what changes take place in these therapies (the outcome question) and how those changes come about (the process question). A major conclusion from the project was that structural change, traditionally regarded as achievable only in insight-aiming expressive-analytic approaches, was also reached often via intrinsically supportive therapeutic modes, and that in fact much of the (structural) change reached in the expressive-analytic therapies—psychoanalysis included—was on the basis of noninterpretive, supportive means within those therapies. Overall, in almost every instance across the range of therapies, the treatment carried more supportive elements than originally intended, and these elements accounted for substantially more of the changes achieved than originally anticipated. A successor project in San Francisco (PRP-II) is designed to deal more definitively with these findings by defining underlying structural change (which is conceptualized differently within different theoretical perspectives in psychoanalysis) in terms of changes in experience-near observable "psychological capacities," on which adherents of all perspectives can agree, and then creating scales of these (mostly bidirectional) psychological capacities that will yield reliable measures of change over the course of therapy, that can then be more definitively correlated with the therapeutic modes (supportive or expressive-analytic) by which these changes are brought about.

ANY DISCUSSION OF THE EFFICACY of psychoanalysis and psychoanalytic psychotherapy as treatment modalities, as discernible upon treatment termination and/or followup, necessarily rests upon basic philosophy of science assumptions about

---

Professor Emeritus, Psychiatry, University of California, San Francisco; Training and Supervising Analyst, San Francisco Psychoanalytic Institute.

the nature of the psychoanalytic enterprise, and interlocks with a host of definitional, conceptual, methodological, and practical considerations that cover all the major theoretical and technical issues of the psychoanalytic therapies as treatment procedures. I shall therefore first state my own position on the nature of psychoanalysis as a science and profession, and then list the related considerations that interdigitate with the main focus of this presentation.

First, our assumptions about the nature of psychoanalysis. Holt (1981) put the question as follows: "Beneath all this diversity may be discerned some strikingly different positions on basic methodological issues: Is psychoanalysis a science or one of the humanities, like history? If a science, is it or can it be a natural or should it be a social-behavioral science, and what is the difference?" (p. 130). Or is it still another kind of "hermeneutic science" as Gill (1983) would have it, or a *unique* kind of science, "our science," as Harrison (1970) proposed, or simply no science at all, a hermeneutic discipline (one of the humanities) governed (according to Home, 1966) by a totally different logic and method. Home put it thus: "In discovering that the symptom had meaning . . . , Freud took the psycho-analytic study of neurosis *out of the world of science* into the world of the humanities, because a meaning is not the product of causes but the creation of a subject. This is a major difference; for the logic and method of the humanities is radically different from that of science" (p. 43; italics added). My own contrary position that psychoanalysis *is* (or can be) a science, governed by the usual canons of science at the level of its clinical (not its general or metapsychological) theory—i.e., the experience-near, "clinical" theory of resistance and defense, impulse and anxiety, transference and countertransference, conflict and compromise formation—has been spelled out (Wallerstein, 1986b, 1988a) and will not be repeated here.

The second set of considerations have to do with the related definitional, conceptual, methodological and practical issues that bear importantly on the research study of outcomes, i.e., of effectiveness, as a therapy. I quote this listing from an article on a related subject (Wallerstein, in press): "(1) the *goals* of these treatment modalities, both ideal and practical; (2) the issues of *treatability* as against *analyzability* which is not the same, though the two are often conflated; (3) the *indications and contraindications* for these treatments as these have evolved over time with increasing experience and expanding knowledge, including here the issues of *widening or narrowing scope* for analytic treatment and of so-called 'heroic' indications for analysis; (4) the role of the initial *diagnostic and evaluation procedures* in (*differential*) treatment planning (as against the view that only a trial of treatment can lead to proper formulation and prognostication); (5) the place then of *prediction* in relation to issues of outcome, of expectable reach and limitation; (6) the *theory of technique*, how treatment works, by what procedures it achieves its goals; (7) the *similarities and differences* between psychoanalysis and the dynamic psychotherapies, as compared from the viewpoint of different therapeutic goals projected for patients with differing illness pictures set into differing character organizations, determining through these differences the appropriate technical approaches from within the available range of psychoanalytically based psychotherapies; (8) the *criteria* for 'satisfactory' treatment termination; (9) the *evaluation of results*, a conceptual as well as technical issue, involving the issue of assessment of *therapeutic benefit* as against *analytic completeness* in terms of resolution of intrapsychic conflict and structural changes in the ego; (10) what theoretically constitutes the *ideal state of mental health* and the unavoidable impingement upon efforts at its empirical assessment by value judgments as well as by the vantage point and the partisan interests of the judge; (11) the place of *follow-up* as a desirable and feasible activity (or not) in relation to psychoanalytic therapies, for research and/ or clinical purposes; and (12) the place of the continuing accretion of knowledge by the traditional *case study method* innovated by Freud, as against the desirability or necessity for more *formal systematic clinical research*, by methods that are responsive of course to the subtlety and complexity of the subjectivistic clinical phenomena, while simultaneously loyal to the canons of empirical science" (pp. 1–2).

Within the limits of these epistemological assumptions, and the related conceptual and technical considerations, I shall lay out the overall conception, methods, and findings of the Psychotherapy Research Project (PRP) of the Menninger Foundation (Wallerstein, 1986a, 1988b; Wallerstein et al., 1956) as well as new directions being taken by successor research (Wallerstein, 1988c; DeWitt et al., 1991; Zilberg et al., 1991).

The intent of PRP was to follow the treatment careers and the subsequent life careers of a cohort of patients (42 in number), half in psychoanalysis, and half in other psychoanalytic psychotherapies—each in the treatment deemed *clinically* indicated—from the two-week period of comprehensive psychiatric evaluation, over the natural span of their treatments, however many years this might take, and then into followup inquiries, formally for several years after their treatment terminations and return to their home communities, and with as much open-ended followup thereafter as circumstance might make possible and as our span of interested observation might last. The cohort entered their treatments during the mid-1950's; their periods of treatment ranged from as short as a half-year, in the case of unanticipated disruptions, up to a full dozen years; they were all reached—100% of the sample—for formal followup at the designated two-to-three-year mark; and over a third could be followed for periods ranging from 12 to 24 years beyond termination, four of them still in ongoing treatment at the 30-year mark. Some of the observation spans are up to that 30-year point, the time of writing of my (1986a) book with its final accounting from that project.

The aim of PRP was to learn as much as possible about *what* changes actually take place in psychoanalysis and other psychoanalytically based psychotherapies (the outcome or effectiveness question) and *how* those changes come about, through the interactions of what factors in the patient, in the therapy and the therapist, and in the evolving life situation, that together determine those changes (the process question). In theory, process and outcome are inextricably interlocked, since any study of outcome, even if it only counts a percentage of cases "improved," must establish some criteria for "improvement," and these in turn derive from some conceptualization of the nature of illness and the process of change; similarly, any study of process, in delineating patterns of change among variables, makes, at various points, cross-sectional assessments which, if compared, provide measures of treatment change and outcome.

In practice, however, any given research project will throw more light on one or the other of these two domains. In this sense, the findings and conclusions from PRP were more decisive in the outcome realm, more inferential in the process realm (and the project is usually seen as a major outcome study). How PRP actually created and carried out a research program geared to try to answer those process and outcome questions to the best of its ability has been described in detail over the more than 30-year span of this research enterprise in six published books and close to seventy articles. Here I want only to iterate that we set up *three* treatment groupings—psychoanalysis, expressive psychotherapy, and supportive psychotherapy—in terms of the then-consensus in the psychoanalytic therapy literature on the characteristics of these therapeutic modes, together with differential indications for their deployment derived from the dynamic formulations of the patients' illness and character structure. These three therapeutic modalities were felt to (1) be indicated for different categories of patients, (2) work toward differing goals, and (3) lead to different results, different in scope and depth, and different in their promise of stability and duration, because they were (presumably) based on differing mechanisms of change.

Our expectations were to discern and specify in more accurate detail both the particular reach and limitation of the outcome for each kind of patient appropriately treated with each of the proffered therapeutic approaches. We were also interested in the more empirical elaboration of the psychological change mechanisms operative within both the uncovering and the "ego-strengthening" therapeutic modes. Given this intent, what can we say in summary of the treatment and followup findings from PRP that will throw light on the conceptual issues concerning the relations between psychoanalysis and the psychoanalytically derived psychotherapies, issues that had been debated in largely unaltered form over several decades? I have brought the overall PRP conclusions together as a series of sequential propositions regarding the efficacy, the reach, and the limitations of psychoanalysis (varyingly "classical" and modified) and of psychoanalytic psychotherapy (varyingly expressive and supportive) (Wallerstein, 1988b, pp. 144–149). I can condense those propositions as follows:

1. The changes reached via intrinsically supportive modes seemed often enough just as much "structural change" as the changes reached in our most expressive analytic cases. Therefore, in regard to the distinctions between "structural change," presumably based on the interpretive resolution of unconscious conflicts, and "behavioral changes" (or changes in "manifest behavior patterns" and symptoms) that are presumably all that can come out of all other noninterpretive change mechanisms, I now question strongly the continued usefulness of this effort to link the *kind* of change achieved so tightly to the intervention mode, expressive or supportive, by which it is brought about.

2. Therapeutically induced change will be at least proportional to the degree of achieved conflict resolution, though it emerged clearly that there can be significantly more change than there is true conflict resolution, change brought about on all the varying supportive (noninterpretive) bases adduced in the various PRP case studies.

3. Effective conflict resolution turned out *not* to be necessary for therapeutic change. An almost overriding finding was the repeated demonstration that a substantial range of changes was brought about via the more supportive therapeutic modes

cutting across the gamut of declared supportive *and* expressive therapies, and these changes were (often) indistinguishable from the changes brought about by typically expressive-analytic means.

4. Counterpart to the tendency to overestimate the necessity of the expressive treatment mode and of its operation via conflict resolution in order to effect desired change, has been the finding that the supportive psychotherapeutic approaches often achieved far more than initially expected and did so in ways that often represented indistinguishably "structural changes." Most of the treatments (psychotherapeutic and psychoanalytic alike) had been substantially altered during their course in varyingly supportive directions, and more of the patients (again, psychotherapeutic and psychoanalytic alike) had changed on the basis of designedly supportive interventions than had been expected beforehand.

5. Just as more was accomplished than expected with psychotherapy, especially in its more supportive modes, so psychoanalysis, as the quintessentially expressive therapeutic mode was more limited than had been predicted. This, of course, significantly reflected the patient population at the Menninger Foundation, considerably "sicker" than those in usual outpatient practice, often brought to the Menninger Foundation for intensive psychoanalytic treatment (within a protected sanatorium setting) on the basis of so-called "heroic indications." Certainly, these disappointing outcomes of analytic treatments with these sicker patients invite a repositioning of the pendulum in its swings around this issue, more in the direction of "narrowing indications" for (proper) psychoanalysis.

6. Put all together, the psychoanalyses and the expressive psychotherapies as a whole were systematically modified in the direction of introducing more supportive components in widely varying ways; they, by and large, reached more limited outcomes than promised and, as indicated, with a substantial amount of that accomplished by noninterpretive, i.e., supportive, means. The psychotherapies, on the other hand, often accomplished a good deal more than initially expected; however,

the admixture of intervention techniques was originally projected, with much of the change on the basis of more supportive techniques than originally specified.

Given this sequential statement of the overall conclusions from PRP, what can then be stated about the evolving and dialectically interacting relation of psychoanalysis and its derivative dynamic psychotherapies? This can be condensed as follows (Wallerstein, 1988b).

1. The treatment results, with patients selected either as suitable for psychoanalysis, or for varying mixes of expressive-supportive psychotherapies tended—with this sample—to converge, rather than diverge.

2. Across the whole spectrum of treatments, ranging from the most analytic-expressive, through the inextricably blended, onto the most singlemindedly supportive, in almost every instance the treatment carried more supportive elements than originally intended, and these supportive elements account for substantially more of the changes achieved than originally anticipated.

3. The supportive aspects of psychotherapy, as conceptualized within a psychoanalytic theoretical framework, and as deployed by psychoanalytically knowledgeable therapists, bears far more respectful specification than has usually been accorded it in the psychodynamic literature.[1]

4. When studying the changes reached by this cohort of patients, partly on an uncovering basis, and partly on the basis of the opposed covering-up varieties of supportive techniques, the changes themselves—divorced from how they were brought about—often seemed indistinguishable from each other, in terms of being structural changes in the ego.

In the light of the conceptual framework within which the Psychotherapy Research Project of the Menninger

---

[1] For a detailed exposition of the dozen differing supportive mechanisms delineated by PRP, see Wallerstein, 1986a (pp. 373–510); for an overall summary of these, see Wallerstein, 1988b (pp. 135–140).

Foundation was planned and implemented three decades earlier, there is, of course, real surprise to the overall project findings: that these distinctive modalities of psychoanalysis, expressive psychotherapy, supportive psychotherapy, etc., hardly exist in anywhere near pure form in the real world; that real treatments in actual practice are inextricably intermingled blends of more or less expressive and more or less supportive elements; that almost all treatments (including even presumably pure psychoanalyses) carry many more supportive components than are usually credited to them; that the overall outcomes achieved by those treatments that are more 'analytic' as against those that are more 'supportive' are less apart than our usual expectations would portend; and that the changes achieved in treatments from the two ends of this spectrum are less different than again is usually expected, and indeed can often not be easily distinguished [Wallerstein, 1988b, pp. 149–150].

I turn now to the question, "What are the new directions that result from this work?" Indeed, a successor project, which we have dubbed PRP-II,[2] has been launched in San Francisco, designed to deal more definitively with one of the most important findings of PRP, that the *kinds* of changes achieved by the range of psychoanalytic therapies, whether truly structural changes in personality or not, seemed *not* to be tied so directly to the *mechanisms* by which the changes were brought about, whether uncovering, leading via interpretation to insight and conflict resolution, or supportive, and "ego-strengthening"—designed to enable the existing ego organization to better manage the inner and outer pressures that had eventuated in illness and symptoms. This is, of course, at total variance with the prior conventional wisdom in the field, that it required

[2]This successor project is the work of a team, based at the Langley-Porter Institute in San Francisco, which also includes Daniel Weiss, Ph.D., Kathryn DeWitt, Ph.D., Saul Rosenberg, Ph.D., Nathan J. Zilberg, Ph.D., and Dianna Hartley, Ph.D.

interpretive-analytic techniques leading to resolution of unconscious conflicts to achieve truly structural changes in ego organization, and that other (supportive) techniques could only achieve symptom relief and improved functioning through changes in manifest behavior patterns that would enable the existing ego structure to better manage inner and outer conflict pressures.

The structure of PRP II has been designed to put the clinical impressionistic findings of PRP to more stringent empirical test. This has been described in detail elsewhere (Wallerstein, 1988c; DeWitt et al., 1991; Zilberg et al., 1991); here only a capsule summary can be given, beginning with the conceptual issues that frame the task. If one is to explore clinically or researchwise the proposition that the kinds of changes differ in the expressive analytic therapies from those that occur in the supportive therapies, then we need to have independent, consensually validated, and reliable indices of intrapsychic structures, and also a consensually validated, as well as reliable, metric, along which structural *change* can be assessed—e.g., a scale anchored to clear and concise description of scale points, preferably illustrated by clinical vignettes.

The first issue in approaching this problem from a research standpoint is that of definition. How shall we define structures in empirically meaningful ways, and how then will we be able to define structural change? To begin with, the structures of the mind are only useful explanatory *constructs*; they have no tangible substance. Also, they are theory-bound and, even within an overarching psychoanalytic framework, depend for their form on the psychoanalytic theoretical allegiance of the investigator. That is, structure is conceptualized within an ego-psychological framework in terms of impulse-defense configurations, within a Kleinian framework in terms of good and bad part objects (in the paranoid position) and ambivalently held whole objects (in the depressive position), within an object-relational framework in terms of self- and object representations and the affective valences that bind them, and within a self-psychological framework in terms of a varyingly cohesive or vulnerable bipolar self—this, despite the fact that the overarching theory within which all these constructs have meaning is declared to be (the same) psychoanalysis. And at this stage in the development of psychoanalysis, consensus on these concepts is not possible; in fact, this is probably the most salient dividing line among these presently alternative theoretical perspectives within psychoanalysis.

Therefore, rather than deciding on dimensions of intrapsychic structure and of structural change that reflect a particular theoretical position within psychoanalysis, our research group has sought to formulate assessable "psychological capacities" that adherents of *all* prevailing psychoanalytic perspectives will agree to be attributes that comprehensively describe personality functioning and that will necessarily shift if there is "underlying" change in intrapsychic structures, however those structures are conceptualized theoretically. That is, sustained change in these psychological capacities should be consensually accepted as reflecting underlying structural change, which may then be formulated differently by adherents of different theoretical positions in psychoanalysis.

To this point, 17 such psychological capacities have been elaborated by our group, descriptive in sum of the array of personality attributes that describe an individual's characteristic modes of functioning. They are intended to be comprehensive and nonoverlapping. They are designed to be low-level (experience-near) constructs, readily and reliably inferred from observable behaviors (interviews, anamnestic material, behaviors in the widest sense). In this they are in contrast to more abstract concepts—such as intrapsychic "structures" intended to represent the central elements of comprehensive personality theories. Not only are these underlying structures conceptualized differently within different theoretical perspectives, but, as compared with our psychological capacities, they are inevitably much more experience-distant and therefore much harder to *define consensually* and *assess reliably* when put to operational test.

The seventeen psychological capacities we have developed tentatively are designated as follows: hope, zest for life, attribution of responsibility, flexibility, persistence, commitment to standards and values, commitments to relationships, reciprocity, trust, empathy, affect regulation, impulse regulation, regulation of sexual experience, self-assertion, reliance on self and others, self-esteem, and self-coherence. Each is named for the "normal point" of a bidirectional scale, signifying the two directions of deviation from the point of optimal functioning, that of over- and that of underexpression. Since it is in the nature of psychological functioning that deviations can be in the "hyper" and "hypo" directions simultaneously (as in the rigidly controlled, affectively inhibited individual with periodic eruptions of explosive affect storms), the scales we have constructed are not stretched along a single dimension from hyper to hypo with an optimal midpoint, but are expressed with both deviating potentials strung out in a similar direction from the normal point. This makes it explicit that on any of the scales an individual can be placed on both of the deviating arms at the same time, and can progress toward health or normality along one or both of the subscales leading to it. For each subscale, we have created a simple metric (anchored with illustrative case vignettes) of just three nodal points away from the healthy—mild, moderate, and severe maladaptive deviations.

At this early point our tasks are still major in both the methodological and substantive realms. The tasks of method are, sequentially: to create and refine our 17 bidirectional scales, each scale pair having four points with one of the points (the normal) shared by each pair; to anchor these scale points in clear and concise clinical vignettes that will make the scales both congenial in spirit with, and easily usable by, the research-interested clinician; to establish the reliability of the scale assessments and of the assessment of changes along the scales consequent to therapy across a wide spectrum of psychopathological formations; and finally, to demonstrate that our scales reliably measure changes in psychological capacities (and hence in underlying psychic structures) that are separate from changes in just manifest behaviors or overt symptoms.

And beyond all these questions of method are our central questions of substance. Where symptom and behavior changes have occurred consequent to analytic therapy (psychoanalysis or psychoanalytically based psychotherapy), when does structural change, as defined and measured in the ways just indicated, also occur, and under what conditions? The crucial question here is whether such structural changes (as demonstrated by changes in psychological capacities) can or do come about concomitant with the symptomatic and behavioral changes, only in expressive analytic therapy, operating through the interpretive resolution of unconscious conflict, or whether they can and also do come about as a consequence of supportive therapeutic techniques geared not to the interpretation of resistance and defense, but to the bolstering of defenses and the restoration of the ego's faltering adaptive and coping capacities. Last, with adequate followup, we shall be able to discern the extent to which the instances of true structural change induced in supportive psychotherapies compare in stability, in durability, and in proof against future environmental vicissitude with the structural changes induced in the expressive and purely analytic modes.

A major methodological shortcoming of the original PRP resided in the limited success of the effort to come to grips with the issue of the definition of psychic structure and structural change. The project was also unable to create measures for them truly independent of measures of changes in behaviors and symptoms, and to ensure that the assessments of structural change could be applied to the treatment outcomes *independently* of the techniques (more expressive or more supportive) by which the changes had come about. This present research effort (PRP-II) is designed to tackle those next steps. Whatever success is achieved will help to further clarify the theoretical and clinical issues to which these research endeavors are addressed: what we mean by structure and structural change (the theoretical question), and how they are evident in the material of the treatment process (the clinical question)—and beyond all that, the complex empirical question of the relations among the kinds of changes induced by the treatments (true structural changes or not) and the mechanisms by which those changes have come about, expressive-interpretive or suppressive-supportive.

REFERENCES

DeWitt, K. N.; Hartley, D. E.; Rosenberg, S. E.; Zilberg, N. J. & Wallerstein, R. S. (1991). Scales of psychological capacities: development of an assessment approach. *Psychoanal. Contemp. Thought*, 14:343–361.
Gill, M. M. (1983). The point of view of psychoanalysis: energy discharge or person? *Psychoanal. Contemp. Thought*, 6:523–551.
Harrison, S. I. (1970). Is psychoanalysis "Our Science"? Reflections on the scientific status of psychoanalysis. *J. Amer. Psychoanal. Assn.*, 18:125–149.
Holt, R. R. (1981). The death and transfiguration of metapsychology. *Int. Rev. Psychoanal.*, 8:129–143.
Home, H. J. (1966). The concept of mind. *Int. J. Psychoanal.*, 47:42–49.
Wallerstein, R. S. (1986a). *Forty-two Lives in Treatment: A Study of Psychoanalysis and Psychotherapy*. New York: Guilford Press.
——— (1986b). Psychoanalysis as a science: a response to the new challenges. *Psychoanal. Q.*, 55:414–451.
——— (1988a). One psychoanalysis or many? *Int. J. Psychoanal.*, 69:5–21.
——— (1988b). Psychoanalysis and psychotherapy: relative roles reconsidered. *Annual Psychoanal.*, 16:129–151.
——— (1988c). Assessment of structural change in psychoanalytic therapy and research. *J. Amer. Psychoanal. Assn.*, 36 (Suppl.):241–261.
——— (in press). Outcomes of psychoanalysis and psychotherapy at termination and at followup. In *Textbook of Psychoanalysis*, ed. R. G. Kopff & E. Nersessian. Washington, DC: Amer. Psychiat. Press.
——— Robbins, L. R., Sargent, H. D. & Luborsky, L. (1956). The psychotherapy research project of the Menninger Foundation. *Bull. Menninger Clin.*, 20:221–278.
Zilberg, N. J.; Wallerstein, R. S.; DeWitt, K. N.; Hartley, D. E. & Rosenberg, S. R. (1991). A conceptual analysis and strategy for assessing structural change. *Psychoanal. Contemp. Thought*, 14:317–342.

OUTCOME RESEARCH IN PSYCHOANALYSIS: REVIEW AND RECONSIDERATIONS

JUDY L. KANTROWITZ, PH.D.

Twenty years after the start of the Boston outcome study of psychoanalysis, the author reviews the findings of this investigation. Twenty-two patients had been seen in four or five times a week supervised psychoanalysis by candidates at the Boston Psychoanalytic Institute. The underlying assumptions, on which this project and other outcomes studies were based, are reconsidered in light of contemporary understanding of the analytic process and the analytic relationship. The impact of the patient-analyst match on the outcome of treatment may help to explain why some seemingly suitable patients have unsuccessful outcomes and some seemingly unsuitable patients have favorable outcomes.

PSYCHOANALYSIS IS A DEMANDING endeavor that requires commitment and dedication, over many years, of both analysand and analyst. For the analysand, there must be a significant investment of time, financial resources, and emotional involvement. To justify such an investment, the efficacy of psychoanalysis must be established. Many of us within the profession recognize how much we have profited from psychoanalytic treatment and know that for many former patients psychoanalysis has fundamentally changed their lives. The subjective accounts of patients and the anecdotal reports of analysts regarding the benefits of treatment are not without merit or importance, but they are not objective or systematic examinations of treatment outcome. Most analysts would maintain that psychoanalysis can be a very powerful and effective treatment, but sometimes it is not. The question to be answered is how

---
Training and Supervising Analyst, Boston Psychoanalytic Society and Institute; Adjunct Associate Professor, Boston University; Faculty, Harvard Medical School.
    I thank Dr. Ann L. Katz for reviewing this paper and for her helpful suggestions.

can we understand which conditions lead to success and which lead to failure?

The evaluation of the outcome of psychoanalysis is very complex. Not only are there methodological difficulties; there are also conceptual issues that need to be addressed and clarified. Until the late 1970's, psychoanalysis was viewed as a one-person enterprise. The success or failure of the treatment was believed to depend solely on the personal characteristics and level of psychopathology of the patient. It was thought that if we could evaluate accurately the relevant patient qualities, we would be able to predict who would and would not benefit from this intensive treatment. Psychoanalytic literature and psychoanalytic teaching maintained that any well trained, reasonably skilled analyst would be able to treat any appropriately selected patient.

What we were told about ongoing analyses, however, revealed many differences in the process even when analysts were similarly trained. Anecdotes from analytic classmates about their experiences in training analyses conveyed the different levels of activity, tone, timing, and style of their analysts. In addition, reports of second analyses illustrated how dissimilar the treatment experience could be when working with a different analyst. Some of us also noticed that as analysts we were slightly different with different patients (A. Freud, 1954). The discrepancy between the more informal and personal clinical data and the formal reports in the literature and by most psychoanalytic instructors and supervisors was difficult to reconcile.

Our conceptual evaluation of an area determines our methods of investigation. Psychoanalytic researchers studying analyzability and outcome of psychoanalysis in the early 1970's explored the process defined by psychoanalytic theory available at the time. In designing their projects, they focused on the characteristics of the patient and put aside their clinical awareness that each analyst has a unique impact on the process.

Over the past few decades, efficacy studies of psychoanalysis conducted four or five times a week have documented the frequency of "success" and attempted to delineate which factors have led to "successful" outcomes and which factors have detracted from such beneficial results. Although consideration of the impact of the patient-analyst match was raised in discussion of postanalysis findings (Kantrowitz et al., 1989, 1990c; Wallerstein, 1986), no study built in an evaluation of this match in the initial design. There have been six systematic clinical-quantitative studies of terminated analyses over the past three decades. These studies have involved 550 patients treated in supervised psychoanalysis, four or five times a week, by 370 candidates at four different psychoanalytic institutes. Only two of these completed studies had a prospective design. A comprehensive review of these studies of psychoanalytic efficacy has recently been published (Bachrach et al., 1991). While these outcome studies varied in degree of comprehensiveness and rigor, their findings have been strikingly similar. Taken as a group, these studies found: (1) given a population preselected as suitable for psychoanalysis, that is, patients evaluated as having primarily neurotic difficulties who were motivated for analysis, almost all patients attained some therapeutic benefit following psychoanalysis; (2) only 40% of these patients demonstrated an analytic result, that is, development and at least partial resolution of the transference neurosis; (3) it was not possible to predict in advance either which patients would have a successful analytic result or which patients would retain their therapeutic gains over time (Bachrach et al., 1991). How can we understand this relatively small success in analytic outcome and this inability to predict who will achieve it? Conversely, if psychoanalysis can be of long-term benefit to 40% of the patients entering it, how can we understand their success?

To address these questions, we need to reconsider some of the fundamental assumptions on which the outcome studies were based. It was presumed that: (1) if a patient with primarily neurotic difficulties were motivated for analysis and the analyst were reasonably competent, the outcome would be successful (Freud, 1905; Panel, 1960; Kuiper, 1968; Żetzel, 1970); (2) it was possible to accurately assess the extent of the patient's psychopathology prior to beginning treatment (Bachrach and Leaf, 1978); (3) insight gained through interpretation of the transference neurosis was the primary curative factor in psychoanalysis; (4) psychoanalysts were reliably in agreement about the meaning of relatively abstract terms on which both the definition of suitability and criteria of outcome of psychoanalysis were based (Erle and Goldberg, 1984); (5) the analyst's evaluation of the outcome of the analysis accurately reflected the patient's change (with the exception of the Menninger project [Sargent et al., 1968] and the Boston project [Kantrowitz, 1987; Kantrowitz et al., 1986, 1987a, 1987b], which included patient's assessments and comparisons of pre- and postanalysis psychological tests, evaluation of treatment outcome had been exclusively the province of the treating analyst); (6) gains achieved in analysis would be stable and enduring unless untoward circumstances followed termination (Freud, 1905); (7) the capacity for self-analysis would ensure analytic gains; (8) analysts, with reasonable training and experience, were relatively interchangeable in terms of their impact on the process of analysis.

In other words, apart from the Menninger and Boston studies, reliability and objectivity of assessment had not been addressed in relation to analyzability or outcome of psychoanalysis. The psychological character dynamics and the level of psychopathology of the patient, independent of these attributes in the analyst, were believed to determine the course and outcome of analytic treatment. Psychoanalytic theories as presented in the literature through the 1960's, rather than the actual psychoanalytic experience of practicing psychoanalysts, dictated the design of these studies.

The Boston project, a prospective, longitudinal study of analytic suitability and outcome, begun in 1972, tried to remedy some of the problems in analytic outcome studies, but its design also suffered from the acceptance of some of these assumptions. The first phase of the study was designed to assess whether preanalysis evaluation of patients' characteristics would enable a prediction of which patients would benefit from psychoanalytic treatment (Kantrowitz et al., 1975). The second phase was designed to evaluate the stability of the outcome and the factors contributing to stability (Kantrowitz et al., 1990a). While the Menninger study had investigated questions parallel to the inquiries addressed in the Boston project, their patients were more severely disturbed than those usually accepted for institute analyses conducted by candidates (Wallerstein, 1986). Twenty-two patients were seen in four or five times a week supervised psychoanalysis. Although small for the purposes of generalizing and statistical inference, our sample was the first relatively large sample for a psychoanalytic study of relatively high-functioning patients who were evaluated prospectively for their analyzability. We sought data to specify which characteristics of the patients selected as analyzable contributed to or interfered with their successful engagement in the analytic work.

Using the current literature as our guide, we selected for evaluation the four variables most commonly agreed upon as essential qualities for analyzability (Freud, 1905; Panel, 1960; Kuiper, 1968; Zetzel, 1970). These were: reality testing, level and quality of object relations, affect availability and tolerance, and motivation for analysis. Both the analysts and the patients assessed the patients' changes on these attributes following the termination of treatment. In order to obtain a more objective view of the patients' changes, independent of the two participants, psychological tests administered before and after analysis were compared (Kantrowitz et al., 1975, 1986, 1987a, 1987b). To distinguish between therapeutic benefit and analytic result, we had clearly specified operational definitions of what constituted analytic process and psychological and behavioral change.

In the second part of the study, we wished to determine the extent and duration of psychological improvement and the factors contributing to its stability over time. While Freud

(1937) had suggested analysts themselves should have repeated analytic experience every five years because of the impact of patient's psychological conflicts on the analyst's unconscious, the implication had seemed to be that, for others, psychoanalysis provided a definitive treatment. We wanted to test this assumption. We wanted to know whether the functioning of patients at one year after termination would be predictive of their functioning over time.

Acquiring a self-analytic ability during analysis and continuing to employ this function after termination had been presumed to be an important feature in the maintenance of the stability of psychological gains (Freud, 1937; Gaskill, 1980; Hoffer, 1950; Kramer, 1959; Ticho, 1967; Novick, 1982; Pfeffer, 1959, 1961, 1963; Schlessinger and Robbins, 1974, 1975, 1983). We wished to assess the role self-analysis played for patients in this study after termination. We also wished to learn the frequency with which these patients had postanalytic contact with their former analysts, whether they sought further treatment with the original analyst or with someone else, and what determined these decisions. The first phase of the outcome study had suggested that the patient-analyst match played a role in the outcome of treatment (Kantrowitz et al., 1989); we wanted to know the extent to which the patients' perception of the analysts' impact on the treatment corresponded to the researchers' evaluations of the facilitating or impeding effect of the analysts' characteristics on the treatment. We were especially interested in the views of patients whose analysts had been assessed by researchers as having specific qualities that interfaced with their patients' central difficulties.

In the Boston study, post-termination evaluation of 22 patients revealed that none of the four psychological characteristics assessed prior to analysis either alone or in combination was predictive of the outcome of psychoanalysis (Kantrowitz, 1987). It is, of course, possible that either a larger or more diverse sample might have shown these variables to have more predictive power. In the Menninger project, where patients had a greater range of psychopathology, ego strength as measured on psychological tests was the single best predictor of treatment outcome (Appelbaum, 1977). In the Boston study, many patients were also discovered to have far more severe psychopathology than was assessed initially. Nonetheless, neither the initial level of psychopathology nor the number of years in analysis was related to the outcome of treatment. While as a group the patients showed therapeutic benefit in every area assessed following analysis, only 40% had a successful analytic result, based on the analysts' description of the treatment process. The only factor that seemed to be related to the analytic outcome was the presence of particular characteristics of the treating analysts which interdigitated with particular characteristics of patients when this correspondence in characteristics occurred in areas central to the patients' psychopathology. For example, when a creative but intellectualizing and narcissistically troubled patient was analyzed by a candidate analyst who highly valued creative and intellectual endeavors and whose own style tended toward intellectualization, areas of narcissism central to this patient's difficulties remained unanalyzed. Since the study had not been designed to assess the variable of patient-analyst match and these findings had emerged from a subtext assessment of the analyst interview, this aspect of the study was considered to be a pilot, and the conclusions drawn from it were considered tentative (Kantrowitz et al., 1989).

The evaluations made by the analysts and the patients based on their experience, and by the researchers from the comparisons of pre- and postanalysis psychological tests were not in agreement in their assessment of the outcome of treatment in regard to the extent of therapeutic benefit derived from analysis (Kantrowitz et al., 1986, 1987a, 1987b). Analysts, who made their evaluations based on their patients' functioning at the time of termination, tended to have the most optimistic view of the patients' therapeutic gains. The patients, who made their evaluations of themselves approximately one year after termination, while somewhat more guarded than their analysts in their estimate of their therapeutic success, nevertheless saw their outcomes as more positive than the researchers' assessments based on comparisons of pre- and postanalytic psychological test data. The postanalytic psychological tests were administered approximately one year after termination. The lack of agreement among patients, analysts, and researchers' psychological test evaluations about the extent of improvement in the four measured variables points to the importance of multiple perspectives when evaluating the outcome of analysis.

An exception to this finding was in the area of reality testing, where the evaluation made from the psychological test data was more sensitive in detecting both the initial levels of disturbance in reality testing and in the improvement in this dimension. None of the patients had manifested behavioral signs of psychosis prior to analysis. However, seven patients did show signs of severe disturbance in reality testing during analysis. Three of these patients were seen as improved in reality testing at the time of termination. This finding is at variance with another promulgated belief, that evidence of disturbance in reality testing is a contraindication for analysis. Those patients who had disturbed reality testing, but sufficient observing ego to stay within an analytic frame, were not only able to work analytically, but also had notable improvement in their reality testing following analytic work.

Five to ten years after termination of analysis, seventeen of the original 22 patients were reevaluated in individual followup interviews. While many patients retained their therapeutic gains and some showed further improvement over time, we were not able to determine any basis for predicting which patients would improve, remain stable in their gains, or deteriorate (Kantrowitz et al., 1990a). No psychological characteristic assessed prior to analysis alone or in combination predicted the stability of the analytic gains. The initial level of psychopathology, the length of treatment, and the outcome of the analysis as assessed one year after termination through patient and analyst interviews and psychological tests also were not predictive of the stability of outcome over time.

There was no evidence that attainment of a self-analytic function was related to the stability of therapeutic gains or the extent to which the transference neurosis had been resolved (Kantrowitz et al., 1990b). The majority of the patients reported developing the capacity for self-analysis. It is possible that the limited variability in the sample prevented any relation to the outcome from showing. Some patients described continuing their self-analytic work through analysis of dreams or in imaginary conversations with the former analyst or another imaginary listener, with the aim of acquiring further insight; others evoked memories of the analyst or another imagined listener to attain a sense of comfort or support.

Ten of these 17 patients returned for further treatment following termination. Six of these 10 patients returned initially to their former analysts, but three then went to different therapists for continued psychological treatment. Only two of the patients in this sample had sought a second analysis at the time of the five-to-ten-year followup interviews.

The preliminary finding in the one-year followup that the patient-analyst match had an important impact on the outcome of analysis was given support by 12 of the 17 patients in these later followup interviews (Kantrowitz et al., 1990c). Patients, with both successful and unsuccessful analyses in terms of developing, understanding, and resolving the transference neurosis, described characteristics of their analysts that corresponded to those characteristics researchers had independently identified through assessment of the followup interviews with these analysts. In unsuccessful outcomes, while some patients were aware of their own unresolved difficulties and others were not, all identified characteristics of their analysts, corroborated by the researchers, which overlapped with the patients' central problem areas. In the successful cases, the interdigitation of patient and analyst characteristics was often facilitating to the process in the early phases of analysis. Often the very same interfacing characteristics that had been beneficial initially proved to be an impediment in later phases of the analytic work. For example, a gentle, nonjudgmental analyst enabled a frightened patient, vulnerable to criticism, to engage in the analytic process. This initially successful work with the patient led to new anxiety-laden material where resistance developed, and the same gentle, accepting stance by the analyst then resulted in the analyst's failing to pursue what the patient was defending against. The data suggest that terminations often occurred when there was a patient-analyst impasse. These impasses were related to a lack of recognition of a difficulty stemming from the patient-analyst match. This blind spot sometimes resulted in unrecognized or unresolved transference-countertransference binds.

Since the analysts in this study were all candidates and, therefore, inexperienced, factors other than match may contribute to the limitations of the analysts' work with these patients. In this study, the data are based on the analysis of only one patient by each analyst. As a result, we cannot know whether similar facilitating or impeding characteristics would be manifest with other patients. Without a study of experienced analysts working with several patients, our conclusion about the importance of the match on the analytic process must remain tentative.

The findings of the Boston research project call a number of psychoanalytic assumptions into question. As indicated earlier, along with other studies of psychoanalytic outcome (Wallerstein, 1986; Erle, 1979; Erle and Goldberg, 1984; Weber et al., 1985a, 1985b), our findings indicate that, given a preselected sample of patients who enter psychoanalytic treatment, it is not possible to predict which patients will have a successful analytic outcome. In addition, our study supports the findings of the Menninger research that therapeutic benefit from psychoanalytic treatment may result from supportive techniques, not only from those techniques designed for insight. While transference neuroses did occur in 40% of the cases, there was no evidence to support the idea that even partial resolution of the transference neurosis was the curative element in the treatment.

Almost all the patients in this study had therapeutic benefit from their treatment, even when the transference neurosis was not fully developed, analyzed, or resolved. Since it is impossible to retrace our therapeutic steps and take a different path, we cannot know whether a less intense psychological treatment would have been as effective therapeutically for these patients. However, several of these patients had been in therapy previously without attaining these therapeutic gains.

Treating analysts' use of psychoanalytic terms and criteria for the assessment of change were not consistent. Only by employing clinically operational definitions was reliability in evaluations achieved. Assessments of change by patients and by psychological test measures were not always in agreement, and neither consistently concurred with the analysts' views of change.

By all methods of evaluation, however, it was found that the majority of the patients in this study changed psychologically, and some patients changed very substantially, following psychoanalysis. However, it still remains to be determined which factors are curative in psychoanalytic treatment. We have learned that the earlier assumption that development and resolution of the transference neurosis is the central mutative element is not sufficiently complex. Psychoanalysis is a two-person enterprise and it is necessary to consider contributing factors from both participants as well as their dynamic interaction over time when evaluating patients' psychological change.

The idea that psychoanalysis is a definitive treatment, leading to patients being able to weather the vicissitudes of life without subsequent therapeutic help, is also not supported by this study. Granted that the analysts in this project were all inexperienced, and analysts with greater skill and more experience might have conducted treatments with greater success and more enduring gains, we cannot minimize the fact that over half the patients interviewed in the second followup study had returned to treatment. Only two of these patients had had major life traumas in the intervening years to account for their need for help. While for some patients major difficulties had not been resolved by analysis, for other patients, even when the therapeutic benefit was considerable, issues resulting from later developmental stages led to the desire for more treatment. This finding is also similar to the Menninger study's findings where longitudinal followup showed that many patients returned for treatment throughout their lives (Wallerstein, 1986).

The role of a self-analytic capacity as it is developed in analysis and as a termination criterion also needs to be reevaluated. While almost all the patients in the Boston study valued self-understanding, whether these patients continued to employ a self-analytic process in their lives after termination was not predictive in determining the stability of therapeutic gains. For some former patients, continuing self-analytic work and accruing insight were of great emotional benefit; for some, the sense of well-being and comfort gained from reevoking their former analyst in fantasy at times of stress seemed far more important. For others, benefit came from a combination of acquiring insight into unconscious factors and maintaining a mental representation a supportive relationship, though there were few patients in this study who described this total process as having occurred.

While only a few patients had what is usually termed a transference cure, where the analyst remains an idealized figure and the negative transference has either not been addressed or not worked through, the stability of improvement was notable. Whether the sense of well-being achieved by these patients will remain stable over the years, we cannot know. What is clear, according to the reports of patients in this study, is that there are many different ways to attain improved functioning and to gain a sense of well-being through the use of the analytic process.

The most striking finding to emerge from the Boston study was the impact of the interface of personal characteristics of the analyst and the patient on the outcome of the analytic process. While the conclusions from this study need to be tentative due to the inexperience of the analysts and the sample of only one case for each analyst, the correspondence between the researchers' and patients' descriptions of the analysts' impact cannot be ignored. If the personal characteristics of the analyst are of central importance to the outcome of analysis, then it becomes understandable why preanalysis evaluations of the patient have been so limited in their predictive power. We have been viewing a two-person enterprise as if it were dependent on only one of the participants. While in their personal views of psychoanalysis, I do not think most analysts believe analysts are interchangeable, psychoanalytic literature and teaching, for the most part, purported this view until the late 1970's. As it happened, the findings in this study appeared at a time in the history of psychoanalysis when countertransference and the impact of the analyst in general on the analytic process were becoming a focus of attention in the analytic literature (Gill, 1982; Jacobs, 1983; McLaughlin, 1981; Sandler, 1976; Poland, 1984). This study provides data in support of the current clinical thinking and writing about the two-person nature of psychoanalytic work. If the match between patient and analyst is central to the outcome, it may explain why some patients who had appeared suitable for psychoanalysis have not had successful treatments and why other seemingly less suitable patients have had successful outcomes.

The findings of the Boston study are that it is not just the personal characteristics of the patient and the analyst that are important, but the match between them. The descriptions offered by patient-analyst pairs suggest that the impact of their similarities and differences over time is likely to be more important in terms of the outcome of analysis than characteristics of either patient or analyst which are recognizable at the outset. Over time, an analyst may be able to "see" in an area in which he or she initially is "blind" if a patient is able to persist enough. In other words, while there may be some characteristics of particular patients and analysts that seem to make them either well-or ill-suited partners from the outset, the dynamic aspect of their interactions, their resonances and dissonances, and their joint capacity or limitation in expanding the "blind spots" or bridging the differences that develop over the course of the analytic work are likely to be central to the outcome.

The relation of the patient-analyst match to the outcome of psychoanalysis is a new area of investigation which has emerged from the outcome study conducted in Boston beginning in 1972. In order to adequately assess the importance of the match, we would need to study analysts whose experience and skill were ascertained to meet rigorous standards. We would also need to view analysts' work with several cases, not just one. It would be essential that patients and analysts have comparable preanalysis assessments to evaluate the ways in which they are similar and different, and postanalysis assessments to study whether and to what extent these areas of interdigitation have changed following analytic work. It would be crucial, as in the present study, that there be independent, objective measures of change, as well as the data from the subjective reports of patients and analysts. In addition, we need a study of the impact of overlapping characteristics of patient and analyst on the actual analytic process. Such a study, focusing on the two-person process, could increase our understanding of variables that influence change.

REFERENCES

APPELBAUM, S. A. (1977). *The Anatomy of Change*. New York: Plenum.
BACHRACH, H. M., GALATZER-LEVY, R., SKOLNIKOFF, A. & WALDRON, S. (1991). On the efficacy of psychoanalysis. *J. Amer. Psychoanal. Assn.*, 39:871–917.
—— & LEAF, L. A. (1978). Analyzability: a systematic review of the clinical and quantitative literature. *J. Amer. Psychoanal. Assn.*, 26:881–920.
ERLE, J. B. (1979). An approach to the study of analyzability and analysis: the course of forty consecutive cases selected for supervised psychoanalysis. *Psychoanal. Q.*, 48:198–228.

―― & GOLDBERG, D. A. (1984). Observations on assessment of analyzability by experienced analysts: report on 160 cases. *J. Amer. Psychoanal. Assn.*, 32:715–737.
FENICHEL, O. (1945). *The Psychoanalytic Theory of Neurosis*. New York: Norton.
FREUD, A. (1954). The widening scope of indications for psychoanalysis: discussion. *J. Amer Psychoanal. Assn.*, 2:607–620.
FREUD, S. (1905). On psychotherapy. *S. E.*, 7.
―― (1937). Analysis terminable and interminable. *S. E.*, 23.
GASKILL, H. S. (1980). The closing phase of the psychoanalytic treatment of adults and the goals of psychoanalysis: 'the myth of perfectibility.' *Int. J. Psychoanal.*, 61:11–23.
GILL, M. M. (1982). *Analysis of the Transference, Vol. I. Psychol. Issues*, Monogr. 53. New York: Int. Univ. Press.
HOFFER, W. (1950). Three psychological criteria for the termination of treatment. *Int. J. Psychoanal.*, 31:194–203.
JACOBS, T. (1983). The analyst and the patient's object world: notes on an aspect of countertransference. *J. Amer. Psychoanal. Assn.*, 31:619–642.
―― (1986). On countertransference enactments. *J. Amer. Psychoanal. Assn.*, 34:289–308.
KANTROWITZ, J. (1987). Suitability for psychoanalysis. *Yearbook Psychoanalysis Psychotherapy*, 2:403–415.
―― KATZ, A. L.; GREENMAN, D.; MORRIS, H.; PAOLITTO, F., SASHIN, J. & SOLOMON, L. (1989). The patient-analyst match and the outcome of psychoanalysis: a pilot study. *J. Amer. Psychoanal. Assn.*, 37:893–920.
―― ―― & PAOLITTO, F. (1990a). Followup of psychoanalysis five to ten years after termination: I. Stability of change. *J. Amer. Psychoanal. Assn.*, 38:471–496.
―― ―― ―― (1990b). Followup of psychoanalysis five to ten years after termination: II. Development of the self-analytic function. *J. Amer. Psychoanal. Assn.*, 38:637–654.
―― ―― ―― (1990c). Followup of psychoanalysis five to ten years after termination: III. The relation of the transference neurosis to the patient-analyst match. *J. Amer. Psychoanal. Assn.*, 38:655–678.
―― ―― ―― SASHIN, J. & SOLOMON, L. (1986). Affect availability, tolerance, complexity, and modulation in psychoanalysis: followup of a longitudinal study. *J. Amer. Psychoanal. Assn.*, 34:529–560.
―― ―― ―― ―― ―― (1987a). Changes in the level and quality of object relations in psychoanalysis: followup of a longitudinal prospective study. *J. Amer. Psychoanal. Assn.*, 35:23–46.
―― ―― ―― ―― ―― (1987b). The role of reality testing in the outcome of psychoanalysis: followup of 22 cases. *J. Amer. Psychoanal. Assn.*, 35:367–386.
―― SINGER, J. & KNAPP, P. (1975). Methodology for a prospective study of psychoanalysis: the role of psychological tests. *Psychoanal. Q.*, 44:371–391.
KRAMER, M. K. (1959). On the continuation of the analytic process after psychoanalysis. *Int. J Psychoanal.*, 40:17–25.
KUIPER, P. C. (1968). Indications and contraindications for psychoanalytic treatment. *Int. J. Psychoanal.*, 49:261–264.
MCLAUGHLIN, J. (1981). Transference, psychic reality, and countertransference. *Psychoanal. Q.*, 50:639–664.

PANEL (1960). Criteria for analyzability. S. A. Guttman, reporter. *J. Amer. Psychoanal. Assn.*, 8:141–151.
NOVICK, J. (1982). Termination: themes and issues. *Psychoanal. Inq.*, 2:329–365.
OREMLAND, J., BLACKER, K. & NORMAN, H. (1975). Incompleteness in "successful" psychoanalysis: a followup study. *J. Amer. Psychoanal. Assn.*, 23:819–844.
PFEFFER, A. Z. (1959). A procedure for evaluating the results of psychoanalysis. *J. Amer. Psychoanal. Assn.*, 7:418–444.
——— (1961). Followup study of a successful analysis. *J. Amer. Psychoanal. Assn.*, 9:698–718.
——— (1963). The meaning of the analyst after analysis: a contribution to the theory of therapeutic results. *J. Amer. Psychoanal. Assn.*, 11:224–244.
POLAND, W. S. (1984). On the analysts' neutrality. *J. Amer. Psychoanal. Assn.*, 32:283–299.
SANDLER, J. (1976). Countertransference and role responsiveness. *Int. Rev. Psychoanal.*, 3:43–47.
SARGENT, H., HORWITZ, L., WALLERSTEIN, R. S. & APPELBAUM, S. A. (1968). *Prediction in Psychotherapy Research: A Method for the Transformation of Clinical Judgments into Testable Hypotheses*. Psychol. Issues, Monogr. 21. New York: Int. Univ. Press.
SCHLESSINGER, N. & ROBBINS, F. (1974). Assessment of followup in psychoanalysis. *J. Amer. Psychoanal. Assn.*, 22:542–567.
——— ——— (1975). The psychoanalytic process: recurrent patterns of conflict and changes in ego function. *J. Amer. Psychoanal. Assn.*, 23:761–782.
——— ——— (1983). *A Developmental View of the Psychoanalytic Process*. New York: Int. Univ. Press.
TICHO, G. (1967). On self-analysis. *Int. J. Psychoanal.*, 48:308–318.
WALLERSTEIN, R. S. (1986). *Forty-two Lives in Treatment: A Study of Psychoanalysis and Psychotherapy*. New York: Guilford Press.
WEBER, J. J., BACHRACH, H. M. & SOLOMON, M. (1985a). Factors associated with the outcome of psychoanalysis: report of the Columbia Psychoanalytic Center Research Project, II. *Int. Rev. Psychoanal.*, 12:127–141.
——— ——— (1985b). Factors associated with the outcome of psychoanalysis: report of the Columbia Psychoanalytic Center Research Project, III. *Int. Rev. Psychoanal.*, 12:251–262.
ZETZEL, E. (1970). Psychoanalysis and psychic health. In *The Capacity for Emotional Growth*. New York: Int. Univ. Press, pp. 271–290.

THE ERA OF MEASURES OF TRANSFERENCE: THE CCRT AND OTHER MEASURES

LESTER LUBORSKY, PH.D.
ELLEN LUBORSKY, PH.D.

Since 1976 a new genre of transference formulations has been developed with the Core Conflictual Relationship Theme (CCRT and then with other methods. This genre represents a formalization of clinical systems for transference formulation. For example, each CCRT formulation includes the wishes toward other people, expected responses of other people, and responses of the self. The use of these guided systems for transference formulation permits greater agreement among clinicians and more rapid formulation of transference. The discussion answers three key questions about the use of guided measures of transference: 1. Do they include unconscious aspects? 2. Do they include the context for the patient's major symptoms? 3. Do they inhibit or distort the natural sensitivity of clinicians in making transference formulations?

DYNAMIC PSYCHOTHERAPISTS have been formulating transference routinely in their practice of psychotherapy for almost 100 years, beginning with Freud (Breuer and Freud, 1895). Since the development of the Core Conflictual Relationship Theme (CCRT) method (Luborsky, 1976) there has been an era of steady growth of guided transference measures. These measures (a) help clinicians do better what they have already been doing and (b) give researchers a new tool to examine the concept. This review takes up (1) the usual process of

---

Lester Luborsky is at the University of Pennsylvania, Department of Psychiatry; Ellen Luborsky is at the Riverdale Mental Health Center, New York City.

Supported by the Research Scientist Award (to Lester Luborsky) from the National Institute of Mental Health MH40710–22, the National Institute on Drug Abuse Award DA0168–23A, and the Center for Psychotherapy Research, University of Pennsylvania Grant P50 MH45178 (to Paul Crits-Christoph). Tables 1, 2 and 3 were reprinted with permission from *Psychiatry* (Luborsky and Crits-Christoph, 1989). This paper is an expanded revision of the unpublished English version of Luborsky and Luborsky (1992).

formulating the transference, (2) the reasons for the new guided methods, (3) the procedures of the CCRT and other methods, (4) their clinical uses, and (5) their newly produced knowledge about the concept of transference.

How Clinical Transference Formulations Are Derived from Psychotherapy

Even though many volumes have been written about the nature of transference and the importance of interpreting it to the patient appropriately, not much has been learned about how the therapist usually infers the transference from the sessions. We only see that the therapist fashions a formulation, but how this is done is only glimpsed, like "looking through a looking glass darkly."

There is a wide variety of well-known definitions of transference that are intended to illuminate the concept. The essence of these definitions is expressed in this definition by Curtis (1983): "Transference is the revival in a current object relationship, especially to the analyst, of thought, feeling, and behavior derived from repressed fantasies originating in significant conflictual childhood relationships." Such definitions direct the therapist to find (1) a pattern of relationships with others, especially the early ones to parents, that parallels the relationship with the therapist and (2) a pattern with repressed aspects. But despite the varied definitions, the usual method followed by dynamic psychotherapists should be called "unguided" in the sense that each therapist is still free to follow his or her version of the definition and apply it to the data of the sessions.

Why Operational Measures of Transference Have Been Growing in Popularity

An operational measure is a guided measure. It is guided in the sense that the measure specifies some of the steps to be followed and the components to be used in the formulations of the transference. Not surprisingly, guided systems tend to be more reliable than unguided systems in showing agreement among judges (Holt, 1978). The biggest impetus toward moving to guided systems of transference comes from the recent startling realization that the commonly relied-upon unguided systems for formulating transference are unreliable—even expert experienced analysts do not agree with each other! Two main studies have revealed this unreliability, those of Seitz (1966) and DeWitt et al. (1983). Furthermore, the usual method of formulating transference is difficult to evaluate for its reliability because each therapist's formulations differ so much in language and components. In contrast, a guided method allows the therapists to use the same language and the same components.

How to Use the CCRT Measure

The oldest reliably guided system for deriving a central relationship pattern from psychotherapy sessions is the Core Conflictual Relationship Theme (CCRT) measure (Luborsky, 1977; Luborsky and Crits-Christoph, 1990). It will be briefly described here along with an example.

The CCRT method came about through self-conscious observations of the steps in formulating a central relationship pattern from psychotherapy sessions. In 1976 L. Luborsky inspected a set of psychotherapy sessions with this mental set. He noticed first that he was attending to the patient's narratives about the therapist and about other people. He was especially impressed by parts of the narratives that were recurrent across narratives. Within each narrative he saw three components that were prominent: what the patient wanted from the other people, how the other people reacted, and how the patient reacted to their reactions.

The method for extracting the CCRT from the narratives uses a two-phase guided system: Phase A is for locating and identifying the narratives (called relationship episodes) and Phase B is for reviewing the relationship episodes and extracting the CCRT from them (these phases are more fully described by Luborsky [1990c] and Luborsky and Schaffler [1990]).

An Example of the CCRT Derived from a Dynamic Psychotherapy

We will show through the example of Mr. Alton how the CCRT can be derived. Mr. Alton was diagnosed by *DSM-III* as having a social phobia; he engaged in a dynamic psychotherapy for 24 once-weekly sessions with a highly experienced psychoanalyst. The dynamic psychotherapy was similar to the time-limited supportive-expressive psychotherapy described by Luborsky (1984).

In his original family, Mr. Alton was the middle child of three; his parents were professionals. At the time therapy began, Mr. Alton was in his early 30's. He had been married for three years. His wife worked with him as a partner in their small design firm.

He hoped through the psychotherapy to overcome the moderately severe agoraphobic symptoms that were interfering markedly with his work and marriage. He was anxious and phobically restricted in travel, unfamiliar restaurants, and related situations. The phobic symptoms had started when he was in college while he was in a conflict with his fiancée, with whom he broke off the relationship.

The patient's father was persistently frustrated with his own professional career. Yet Mr. Alton often compared himself unfavorably with his father in terms of relative success; he also compared himself with his older brother in the same way.

It will be helpful in understanding the conflicts expressed during psychotherapy and captured in the CCRT, to read a brief account of session 17, which was a turning point in the treatment. The beginning of the session and some of the main relationship episodes in it are briefly described below:

P: Hello, how are you (slight laugh)?
T: Good; how are you today?
P: It's been a pretty difficult week. I didn't go on the airplane trip with my wife and partner. I feel I failed. I couldn't push myself to go, so I blamed myself. Also I'm using my fear as a weapon.

This abbreviated first narrative was about an event in which he was prevented by his phobia from going on an airplane trip; it is a relationship episode in which the main other person was the wife. As you review this relationship episode and the other four relationship episodes in Table 1, see whether you can identify the central relationship pattern within an episode and whether the central relationship pattern fits your own transference formulation.

The therapist of course was listening for the main relationship patterns and the conflicts within them, and trying to judge the degree to which they were reflected in the transference. Such formulations are usual in dynamic psychotherapy, and explain why it is so important to have ways to infer the central relationship pattern or transference.

We shall therefore continue our example from Mr. Alton and review relationship episode two which was about the therapist (RE #2). It will include some of the interpretations of the therapist based on the patient's central relationship pattern:

T: You feel resentful toward me and toward the situation. And one of the things you feel resentful about is the 60-minute structure.
P: Yea, I'm puzzled by it.
T: You're more than puzzled by it; you're irritated by it. Because it's *my* rules; the rules are being set by me, not by you.
P: Right?
T: I wondered in fact if in a way you were feeling toward me much as you did toward your father? He was kind of

Table 1
Abbreviated First Five Relationship Episodes (Mr. Alton, Session 17)

RE 1 *Wife*	I didn't go on the trip with wife and partner. Feel I've failed. I couldn't push self to go, so I blame self. Also I'm using my fear as a weapon.
RE 2 *Therapist*	I was uncomfortable since last session. We spoke of developing my own pace. But then the session ended at 60 minutes! I felt a quick temper and suspiciousness of you for ending it then. Maybe that's what you were supposed to do.
RE 3 *Father*	I relied on father's interpretation of what to do, but sometimes he didn't know what he was talking about. He said, to succeed, wear suits and ties. I was angry and confronted him. I didn't feel bad about what I said to him.
RE 4 *Fiancée*	The girl I almost married in college had a distinct concept of the role I was supposed to play in her life. It was the reason our relationship fell apart. It was the time in my life when I started feeling ill in restaurants so I stopped going. My work was a constant battle about what I was supposed to do.
Re 5 *Father*	I was living out what father taught us about success and careers. It is hard to rebel against father. The idea of "rebellion and trying to prove to him I can succeed" is a hard idea to hold on to. I'm scared of saying "I don't believe what you said"—it would be hurting him. He'd feel he'd failed because I'm in treatment.

pushing for success, and you were suspicious of his reasons for pushing you.

[Later in the same session:]

T: It was another instance [like the relationship to his fiancée] of somebody attempting to define for you what was good or bad.

P: Yes, it was really sort of after that [that the phobia developed].

T: And then you completely broke off and went off on your own path. There's an element of rebellion against your father as well as choosing something for yourself.

TABLE 2
NARRATIVES AND CCRT FOR MR. ALTON, SESSION 17

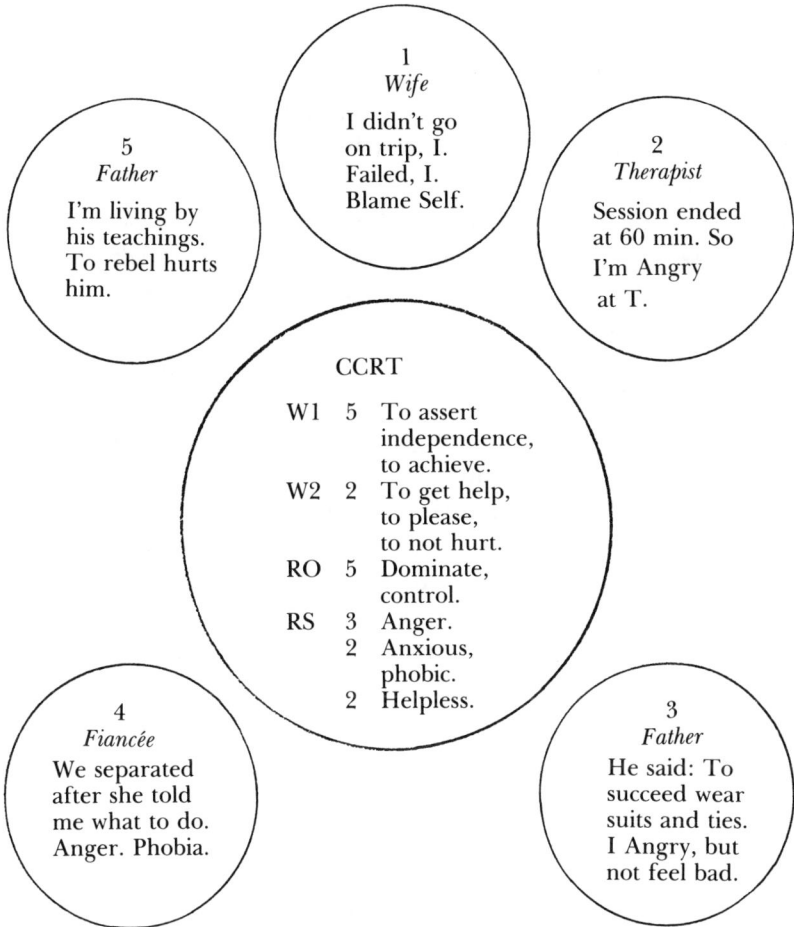

Number of narratives containing the component (pervasiveness)

It will be helpful to practice deriving the CCRT from the five relationship episodes from session 17 in Table 1. These episodes are given in even more abbreviated form in Table 2. Read them in clockwise order as they appeared in the session, and ask yourself for each one: what are the wishes, what are the responses from the other person and then what are the responses of the self. You can fill these in the central circle. The CCRT includes the most frequent of these types of components. Now in Table 3 you can compare your CCRT with the CCRT that is formulated by most clinicians who review the sessions of Mr. Alton. Similar results are given in Table 4, which is based on the standard categories that the clinicians who judge the episodes are trained to use (these results are based on the 10 relationship episodes from sessions 4 and 17 combined). The most frequent components are the wish *to assert independence and to achieve*. This wish conflicts with the wishes *to get help, to please, and to not hurt*. The patient's expected responses to his wishes are that the other person *tries to dominate and to control him*. His own responses are to become *angry, anxious, and phobic (his main symptom), and helpless*.

By now you know enough of the session to see that the therapist was pointing out the main theme in the session: the rebellious feelings toward the therapist that were like the feelings toward his father and toward his fiancée. It was after this session that the phobia began to decrease markedly. The therapy ended as planned after session 24, and the followup showed that the patient was able to function without impairment by the phobia. This brief example from Mr. Alton's psychotherapy has shown how the CCRT can help the therapist find the main theme and use it to focus interpretation.

A Sample of Other Central Relationship Pattern Measures

Since guided central relationship pattern measures were launched, a total of 15 such measures have appeared (Luborsky, 1990a; Luborsky, Popp et al., in press; Barber and Crits-Christoph, 1993.

The 15, in order of their appearance, are the following (with an "*" to note the 5 that are profiled in this paper): Luborsky,* 1976; Weiss et al.,* 1977; Benjamin, 1979; M. J. Horowitz,* 1979; Teller and Dahl, 1981; Carlson, 1981; Gill and Hoffman,* 1982; Schacht and Binder,* 1982; Grawe and Caspar, 1984; Kiesler et al., 1985; Bond and Shevrin, 1986,

Table 3
CCRT for Three Judges Using Tailor-Made Categories from 10 REs in Sessions 4 and 17 (For Mr. Alton)

Judge L ≐ RE[a]		Judge M ≐ RE[a]		Judge P ≐ RE[a]	
W 1. W To carry on in my own way; to oppose pressures from those I am close to.	7	W 1. W To do what I want without giving to other wishes	8	W 1. W To stand up for what I want; to not go along with other wishes.	9
W 2. W To please and not hurt the other.	4	W 2. To not hurt the other, so I try to live up to their expectations for me.	4	W 2. To be close to others; to communicate and share.	6
NRO: Controls me, pressures me, expects me to conform to their ideas.	6	NRO: Constrains me, cuts me off.	4	NRO: Unreceptive	3
		Expects me to do things his way.	3	Doesn't understand me.	3
				Leaves me.	3
NRS: Feel helpless	5	NRS: Angry, frustrated, resentful.	7	NRS: Not able to assert self, go along with others.	6
Phobic symptoms (anxiety, etc.)	4				
Self-blame	4	Nervous, upset, anxious	5	Anxious	5
PRO: Supportive and reassuring	5	PRO: Accepting, nonjudgmental	2	PRO: Understands me	1
				Likes me	1
				Receptive	1
PRS: Assertive, fight other's ideas	4	PRS: In control, not anxious	3	PRS: Do something about what I want (assert self)	4

a = The number of Relationship Episodes that show the CCRT category

unpublished; Maxim, 1986; Kiesler, 1987; Perry et al., 1989; L. M. Horowitz et al., 1989.

To qualify as a member of this class each transference-related measure must have certain properties: (1) It must be derived from a sample of relationship interactions taken from

TABLE 4
CCRT FOR THREE JUDGES USING STANDARD CATEGORIES FROM 10 RELATIONSHIP EPISODES (RE$_s$) IN SESSIONS 4 AND 17 (FOR MR. ALTON)

	No.[a]		Judges L #RE	M #RE	E #RE
W¹	23	To assert my independence and autonomy	7	7	10
W¹	18	To overcome other's domination; To be free of obligations imposed by others; To not be put down by others	7	7	9
W¹	22	To achieve, be competent, be successful	5	4	4
W²	12	To please the other person; To avoid hurting the other person	4	4	2
W²	13	To get help, care, protection and guidance from the other person	4	3	5
NRO:	20	Dominating, controlling, interfering, intimidating, intruding	6	5	3
NRS:	27	Anxious, tense, upset	5	7	10
	17	Helpless, less confident, ineffectual ("I do not know how to do things")	5	5	8
	20	Frustrated, disappointed	2	6	4
	21	Angry, resentful, hating	2	5	5
PRO:	3	Accepting, approving	3	2	2
PRS:	12	Assertive, expressive, self assertively gain control	4	5	6
	18	Gain self-esteem, feel affirmed, self-confident	3	4	4

# = The number of REs that show the CCRT category
W¹ = Assertive, independent wishes
W² = Submissive, dependent, affiliative wishes
a = The standard category number in Edition 2
(Luborsky and Crits-Christoph, 1990)

psychotherapy sessions or from evaluation interviews. The unit can be the whole session, the narratives, or the smaller thought units. The sample can also be based on behavioral enactments of the interactions of the patient and therapist in a session rather than only on narratives about interactions. (2) The measure must focus on the *central* conflictual relationship pattern, defined as the most pervasive pattern across episodes of relationship interactions. (3) The data base must be at least partly evaluated by clinical judgment rather than only by the patient's self-report. (4) The clinical judgment for making inferences about the pattern must be guided by a clinical-qualitative content analysis system. (5) The measure must have at least some preliminary reliability data to support it.

We have space here for a few brief descriptions of other central relationship pattern measures:

Plan Diagnosis method (Weiss et al., 1977). This method permits reliable and comprehensive formulations; it includes descriptions of these components: the patient's goals in the therapy (Silbershatz et al., 1989); the pathogenic beliefs that prevent the patient from obtaining the goals; the ways the patient is likely to test the therapist in terms of these beliefs; and the insights that would be helpful to the patient. Reliabilities are satisfactory for each of the components (Curtis et al., in press).

Configurational Analysis (M. Horowitz, 1979). This well-known method yields an encompassing Role Relationship Models Configuration. The data of psychotherapy sessions are examined from three points of view: states, relationship patterns, and information. The relationship pattern point of view has most in common with the CCRT.

The Patient's Experience of the Relationship with the Therapist (Gill and Hoffman, 1982). This system codes disguised allusions as well as explicit references to the relationship with the therapist. The system also focuses on the degree to which the therapist's interventions deal with the patient's experience of the relationship, both latent and manifest.

Cyclical Maladaptive Pattern (Schacht et al., 1984). This method has been integrated into the measurement system of the Structural Analysis of Social Behavior (SASB) which provides a scoring for each thought unit in the session. The scoring components include acts of self, expectations of others, consequent acts of others toward self, and consequent acts of self toward self.

Frame Method (Teller and Dahl, 1981). The method relies on sequences of events about wishes and beliefs as they are inferred from the person's actions, thoughts, perceptions, and emotions. (For descriptions of methods for finding and formulating the frame, see Teller and Dahl, 1992; Dahl et al., 1988; Dahl, 1992.) The frame is defined as the sequence of predicates. It is the sequence as the patient presents it that is followed exactly.

The various central relationship pattern measures are diverse, but they also have important commonalities: (1) The usual data base for these measures is the psychotherapy session, the narratives within the session, or the thought units within the session. (2) The scoring categories for each measure often include similar components to those in the CCRT, that is, wishes toward other people, the responses from other people, and the responses of the self. (3) The measures are based on pervasiveness of the components across sessions, narratives, or thought units.

Clinical Gains from the CCRT and Other Measures

As discussed below, the CCRT and other such measures offer a variety of gains for interclinician agreement, for clinical use to help focus interpretations, and for use to keep inpatient units treatment-oriented.

More Reliable Formulations

The formulation of the CCRT during each therapy session has much in common with the formulation of the transference; but the system for deriving the CCRT offers more explicit and precise guidelines. The therapist listens to the patient's communications, especially to each relationship episode, and notes the types of wishes and responses that are in common across the different episodes. The method as used clinically is no more complicated than this and does not require the rigorous scoring procedures described by Luborsky and Crits-Christoph (1990).

More Rapid Formulations for Use in Interpretations

The clinical use of the CCRT permits the therapist to make a rapid and accurate transference formulation (Crits-Christoph et al., 1990). Also, as illustrated by the example we presented from Mr. Alton, it offers a focus that can be helpful therapeutically for making interpretations.

More Focused Treatment in Residential Settings

An important clinical application of the CCRT in residential psychiatric treatment is being developed (Luborsky et al., 1993). The use of the method begins with a staff conference in which each member of the staff presents several accounts of his or her interactions with the patient. From these narratives of interactions with the patient, the CCRT is formulated. The effect of this formulation of the patient's central conflicts is to assist the staff to provide a more helpful response to the patient, one that is more generally shared among the staff members.

Research Gains from the CCRT and Other Measures

From about 1895 to 1937 Freud identified a broad spectrum of different qualities of his transference concept—22 in all (Luborsky, 1990b)! These almost entirely deal with aspects of his concept that Freud considered to be empirically based rather than only theoretically inferred; they came from Freud's own experiences in making inferences about patients' transference patterns. These observations deal with the origin, functions, and stimuli that activate the transference. Each of the guided clinical pattern recognition methods, especially the CCRT, have continued their research on these facets of the concept. As Table 5 shows, we have so far been able to examine the correspondence of Freud's observations with the data provided by the CCRT for 17 of Freud's 22 observations. For nine of these we found good correspondence (+): 1, 2, 5, 6, 12, 13, 15, 20, and 21. For seven other observations we found promising evidence (+?). For some of the others, we may eventually be able to work out operational measures and proceed with studies.

Several examples of studies of Freud's observations will show how vital these studies are for our field. One of these is observation 6: the early parental relationship pattern becomes expressed in the pattern with the therapist. It was this germinal observation that suggested to Freud the concept with the label of transference, which implies that elements of the early relationship are *transferred* to the later relationship. The first quantitative study of this observation was accomplished by Fried et al. (1990); it showed a significant parallel between the general pattern and the pattern to the therapist. The strength of the parallel was found to increase with a greater number of relationship episodes involving the therapist.

Another study is relevant to both observation 5, that the pattern originates in early parental relationships, and observation 12, that the pattern remains consistent over time. We have been examining narratives of young children loaned to us by H. Buchsbaum and R. Emde of the University of Colorado. Each of 25 children told 10 narratives at age three and again at age five (Buchsbaum and Emde, 1990). We have been able to establish the presence of a central relationship pattern at age three (Dengler, 1990). We have reexamined the same set of narratives more extensively and with more clinical judges both at age three and at age five (Luborsky et al., in press) and found high consistency at the two ages. We wish to follow these children through to maturity, but we may only be able to reevaluate them again at age eight.

TABLE 5
FREUD'S "TRANSFERENCE TEMPLATE" OBSERVATIONS AND THE CCRT EVIDENCE FOR THEM

Freud's Observation	CCRT Evidence*
1. Wishes toward people are prominent	+
2. Wishes conflict with responses from other and of self	+
3. Especially evident in erotic relationships	+?
4. Partly out of awareness	+?
5. Originates in early parental relationships	+
6. Comes to involve the therapist	+
7. May be activated by the therapist's perceived characteristics	R
8. May distort perception	R
9. Consists of one main pervasive pattern	+?
10. Subpatterns appear for family members	+?
11. Distinctive for each person	+?
12. Remains consistent over time	+
13. Changes slightly over time	+
14. Shows short-term fluctuations in activation	R
15. Accurate interpretation changes expression of pattern	+
16. Insight into pattern can benefit patient	+0?
17. Can serve as resistance	R
18. Symptoms may emerge during its activation	+?
19. Is expressed in and out of therapy	+
20. Positive vs. negative patterns are distinguishable	+
21. Is expressed in multiple modes (dreams and narratives)	+
22. Innate disposition plays a part	R

*Symbols used:
+   Study with positive results
+? Preliminary study with positive results
+0? Study with mixed results
R   Remains to be studied

A final example is for Freud's observation 21: the transference pattern is reexpressed in multiple modes. Freud's transference formulations for his own cases suggest that the pattern appears both in dreams and in narratives. Popp et al. (1990; in press) offer evidence for this observation.

It should be emphasized that in these studies we were not just looking for convergence with Freud's observations, but were open to whatever the data revealed both in terms of differences and in terms of totally unanticipated new findings. The same, we believe, is true of many of the studies of this type initiated after the publication of *Understanding Transference* (Luborsky and Crits-Christoph, 1990). There were so many studies that a *CCRT Newsletter* was started to keep track of them (Luborsky et al., 1992).

Key Questions and Answers About the Use of Guided Measures of Transference

We conclude by answering three of the most frequent questions that have been raised about the CCRT and similar guided systems: (1) Does the CCRT include unconscious aspects? (2) Does the CCRT include the context for the patient's major symptoms? (3) Does a guided system like the CCRT inhibit or distort transference judgments by clinicians?

Question 1

We start with Freud's observation 4 about his "transference template" that it is partly out of awareness. We have some converging evidence from the CCRT: some aspects of the CCRT are out of awareness or are in reduced awareness. Our view is further confirmed in a study by Crits-Christoph and Luborsky (1990) which compared the perspective of nonclinicians versus clinicians in the assessment of relationship themes. The nonclinicians were able to point to many of the same components that were pointed to by the clinicians, but they were not able to order the importance of the components in ways that corresponded to the order by the clinicians—the nonclinicians may have been less aware of the pattern. This result corresponds with clinical observations that the patient's recognition of a pattern of recurrent conflict tends not to occur until later in the therapy, and it is easier to be aware of single components than of their existence as a pattern (Luborsky, 1984, p. 125).

A more precise answer is being studied through special supplementary guides to the CCRT for identifying unconscious conflicts. Four guiding principles are offered for helping the clinician identify conflicts that are partly in reduced awareness. Principle 1 is: The opposites of the main CCRT components may be part of a set of unconscious conflicts. The main wish, for example, to be free of domination, is likely to have as its opposite a less conscious wish to submit to others. Principle 2 is: A wish that is frequently expressed might also have a less frequent version of that wish in reduced awareness. A patient might, for example, report feeling annoyed, and yet awareness of the annoyance might only be the tip-of-the-iceberg part of the anger. Principle 3 is: Instances of denial are likely to point to a content that is in reduced awareness, for example, "I did not feel angry" often suggests that the person *did* feel angry. Principle 4 is: An inference about reduced awareness is likely to be found for any content with which the patient has had a history of difficulty with awareness. One example where we know the principle was correctly applied was when a patient said, "I used to have a hard time with expressing anger toward my mother." With this patient there were many evidences of current difficulties of that kind.

A rating system for independent clinical judgments is being developed to apply these principles to the CCRTs. A sample of its application for Mr. Alton is given below.

Principle 1. The most frequent wish in Mr. Alton's CCRT was wish 1: "to assert my independence and autonomy." The opposite of this wish was often evident to clinical judges: "to show lack of independence, lack of autonomy."

Principle 2. Another of Mr. Alton's wishes was in his CCRT: "to please the other person and to avoid hurting the other person." There is much evidence that, especially in relation to his father, a stronger extension of this wish also appeared indirectly: to displease and to hurt the other person.

Principle 3. One example emerged when the patient described contradicting his father. The patient showed denial when he went on to say, "I didn't feel bad about doing it." The judges typically considered this an instance of denial and indicated that he did feel guilty for his behavior in relation to the father.

Question 2

Another question that is sometimes raised about the CCRT is the degree to which it provides a context that is helpful in understanding the patient's symptoms. It is commonplace for clinicians to assume that conflicts spawn symptoms; it is uncommon for systematic methods to be used to examine this assumption. Mr. Alton's CCRT suggests that his social phobia can be understood as a resultant of a conflict between opposed wishes. The more frequent and more expressed type of wish is part of the set of wishes labeled W^1 wishes, to be assertive and independent (Table 4). These wishes are in conflict with another simultaneously experienced but less expressed type of wish labeled W^2 wishes, "to be submissive or dependent." The CCRT lists both types of wishes. We infer that the clash of these opposed wishes sets the stage for the appearance of the phobic symptoms. The CCRT also reflects another direction of conflict, which is between the potential expression of these wishes and the expected responses from others; this conflict between CCRT components is the larger contributory context for the appearance of the phobic symptoms.

Question 3

The last question is the most basic: Is there a serious danger in imposing any guided system on a clinical inference? The question involves the more fundamental one of whether any guided method results in a transference formulation that is deficient in capturing the essential formulation for the particular patient. Clinicians already have their own guided systems. They derive these from Freud's (1912) recommendations or other expert clinicians' recommendations, but, as compared with the use of the CCRT, these clinical wisdom systems differ considerably from clinician to clinician. The CCRT only offers a set of guiding principles that permits a degree of agreement among clinicians. Our conclusion at this point is that the danger of using uniform principles is minimal and the gain is maximal.

A related version of the question is the extent to which the CCRT can be considered a measure of the clinical concept of transference. The main obstacle to coming to a conclusion on this form of the question is the absence of systematic studies of clinicians' individually guided transference formulations with clinicians' CCRT-guided formulations on the same sessions. We plan on doing a systematic study on this, but so far we have only a few cases on which we have both individually guided transference formulations and CCRT-guided ones. One of these is for Ms. Cunningham, described by Luborsky and Schaffler (1990); as expected, the clinical formulations showed relatively poor agreement while the CCRT formulations showed moderately good agreement.

This same question is also sometimes presented in terms of salience-based versus frequency-based inferences. "Salience" here means central or crucially meaningful. The claim is that the CCRT only relies on frequency of recurrence. Our thesis is that clinicians may think they are using salience in this restricted sense but that such salience is in fact associated with recurrent themes and therefore would be reflected in the CCRT. This thesis is easily illustrated in Tables 1 and 3 from Mr. Alton's five narratives in session 17. A clinician might understand Mr. Alton's argument with his fiancée in narrative four as a salient event—after his fiancée told him how he should behave, he became angry and developed his phobia. Yet each of the other narratives also contains a similar potentially salient event. That is what we mean by our thesis that salient themes are likely to be frequent themes.

We conclude with an apparent paradox about the acceptance of more exact methods of inferring and organizing the transference pattern. Why have clinicians generally not been searching harder for improvements in their method of transference formulation? One obvious reason for their lack of urgency may have been their unawareness of the limits of their formulations and of their differences with each other. Also, they tend to have confidence that they already know how to do this kind of formulation; if they do not see the transference at the moment, they need only to listen to the patient further. And there is an even more basic reason for some clinicians to be cautious about more exact methods: Clinicians are often concerned about tampering with the conventional method of formulation, fearing that any formal system will diminish or distort their natural sensitivity. But we have found that after some experience with the new methods, clinicians tended to be reassured. We and they came to see that the methods offer a common language and common conceptual domain for their formulations. So we and they have come to believe that the wine is still of high quality after its reliably recognized components have been distilled and reconstituted.

REFERENCES

BARBER, J. & CRITS-CHRISTOPH, P. (1993). Advances in measures of psychodynamic formulations. *J. Consult. Clin. Psychol.*, 61:574–585.

BENJAMIN, L. S. (1979). Use of structural analysis of social behavior (SASB) and Markov chains to study dynamic interactions. *J. Abnorm. Psychol.*, 88:303–319.

BREUER, J. & FREUD, S. (1895). Studies on hysteria. *S. E.*, 2.

BUCHSBAUM, H. & EMDE, R. (1990). Play narratives in 36-month-old children—early moral development and family relationships. *Psychoanal. Study Child*, 40:129–155.

CARLSON, R. (1981). Studies in script theory: 1. Adult analogs of a childhood nuclear scene. *J. Personal. Soc. Psychol.*, 40:501–510.

CRITS-CHRISTOPH, P., COOPER, A. & LUBORSKY, L. (1990). The measurement of accuracy of interpretations. In *Understanding Transference—The CCRT*

Method, by L. Luborsky & P. Crits-Christoph. New York: Basic Books, pp. 173–188.

―――― & LUBORSKY, L. (1990). The perspective of patients versus clinicians in the assessment of relationship themes. In *Understanding Transference: The CCRT Method* ed. L. Luborsky & P. Crits-Christoph. New York: Basic Books, pp. 197–210.

CURTIS, H. C. (1983). Toward a metapsychology of transference. Paper presented at the Annual Meeting of the American Psychoanalytic Association, New York, May.

CURTIS, J., SILBERSHATZ, G., SAMPSON, H. & WEISS, J. (in press). The plan formulation (PF) method. In *Seven Transference-Related Measures—Each Applied to the Interview with Ms. Smithfield*, ed. L. Luborsky, C. Popp, J. Barber, D. A. Shapiro & N. Miller. *Psychother. Res.*

DAHL, H (1992). Frames: how to find them and what they are good for. Presented at the Annual Meeting of the Society for Psychotherapy Research. Berkeley, CA.

―――― KÄCHELE, H. & THOMÄ, H., Eds. (1988). *Psychoanalytic Process Research Strategies*. Berlin: Springer.

DENGLER, D. (1990). Anwendung des zentralen Beziehungskonfliktthemas auf Narrative von dreijahrigen und suche nach zusammenhagen mit der Fahigkeit zur Problemlosung. Dissertation, Faculty for Clinical Medicine of the University of Ulm.

DEWITT, K. N., KALTREIDER, N., WEISS, D. S. & HOROWITZ, M. J. (1983). Judging change in psychotherapy: reliability of clinical formulations. *Arch. Gen. Psychiat.*, 40:1121–1128.

FREUD, S. (1912). Recommendations to physicians practicing psycho-analysis. *S. E.*, 12.

FRIED, D., CRITS-CHRISTOPH, P. & LUBORSKY, L. (1990). The parallel of narratives about the therapist with the CCRT for the people. In *Understanding Transference—The CCRT Method*, ed. L. Luborsky & P. Crits-Christoph. New York: Basic Books, pp. 147–157.

GILL, M. M. & HOFFMAN, I. (1982). A method for studying the analysis of aspects of the patient's experience of the relationship in psychoanalysis and psychotherapy. *J. Amer. Psychoanal. Assn.*, 30:137–167.

GRAWE, K. & CASPAR, F. (1984). Die plan Analyse als Konzept und Instrument für die Psychotherapie Forschung. In *Psychotherapie: Makro-und Mikroperspectiven*, ed. U. Bauman. Cologne, Germany: Hogrete.

HOLT, R. R. (1978). *Methods in Clinical Psychology: Vol. 2, Prediction and Research*. New York: Plenum.

HOROWITZ, L. M.; ROSENBERG, S.; URENO, G.; KALEHZAN, B. & O'HALLORAN, P. (1989). Psychodynamic formulation, consensual response method and interpersonal problems. *J. Consult. Clin. Psychol.*, 57:599–606.

HOROWITZ, M. J. (1979). *States of Mind: Analysis of Change in Psychotherapy*. New York: Plenum.

KIESLER, D. J. (1987). *Checklist of Psychotherapy Transactions—Revised (CLOPT-R) and Checklist of Interpersonal Transactions—Revised (CLOIT-R)*. Richmond: Virginia Commonwealth Univ. Press.

―――― ANCHIN, J. C.; PERKINS, M. J.; CHIRICO, B. M.; KYLE, E. M. & FEDERMAN, E. J. (1985). *The Impact Message Inventory: Form II*. Palo Alto, CA: Consulting Psychologists Press.

LUBORSKY, L. (1976). Helping alliances in psychotherapy: the groundwork for a study of their relationship to its outcome. In *Successful Psychotherapy*, ed. J. L. Claghorn. New York: Brunner/Mazel, pp. 92–116.

―― (1977). Measuring a pervasive psychic structure in psychotherapy: the core conflictual relationship theme. In *Communicative Structures and Psychic Structures*, ed. N. Freedman & S. Grand. New York: Plenum, pp. 367–395.

―― (1984). *Principles of Psychoanalytic Psychotherapy: A Manual for Supportive-Expressive (SE) Treatment*. New York: Basic Books.

―― (1990a). Alternative measures of the central relationship pattern. In *Understanding Transference—The CCRT Method*, ed. L. Luborsky & P. Crits-Christoph. New York: Basic Books, pp. 235–250.

―― (1990b). The convergence of Freud's observations about transference with CCRT evidence. In *Understanding Transference—The CCRT Method*, ed. L. Luborsky & P. Crits-Christoph. New York: Basic Books, pp. 251–266.

―― (1990c). A guide to the CCRT method. In *Understanding Transference—The CCRT Method*, ed. L. Luborsky & P. Crits-Christoph. New York: Basic Books, pp. 15–36.

―― & CRITS-CHRISTOPH, P. (1989). A relationship pattern measure: the core conflictual relationship theme. *Psychiat.*, 52:250–259.

―― ―― (1990). *Understanding Transference—The CCRT Method*. New York: Basic Books, pp. 1–313.

―― KÄCHELE, H., DAHLBENDER, R. & CIERPKA, M., Eds. (1992). *The CCRT Newsletter*. Philadelphia: Univ. Pennsylvania.

―― & Luborsky, E. (1992). Evaluation des phénomènes transférentiels par differentes méthodes dont celle du "thème rationnel conflictuel central." In *Recherches Cliniques "planifiées" sur les Psychotherapies*, ed. P. Gerin & A. Dazord. Paris: Institut National de la Santé et de la Recherche Médicale, pp. 35–53.

―― ―― DIGUER, L.; SCHAFFLER, P.; SCHMIDT, K.; DENGLER, D.; FAUDE, J.; MORRIS, M.; BUCHSBAUM, H. & EMDE, R. N. (in press). Is there a core relationship pattern at age 3, and does it remain at age 5? In *Development and Vulnerability in Close Relationships*, ed. G. Noam & K. Fisher. Hillsdale, NJ: Erlbaum.

―― & SCHAFFLER, P. (1990). Illustrations of the CCRT scoring guide. *Understanding Transference—The CCRT Method*, by L. Luborsky & P. Crits-Christoph. New York: Basic Books, pp. 51–81.

―― VAN RAVENSWAY, P.; BALL, W.; STEINMAN, D.; SPREHN, G. & BRYAN, C. (1993). How to use psychiatric hospital treatment—use of the CCRT-FIX method (focused inpatient treatment). *Prospettiva Psicoanalitichenel lavoro instituzionale*, 11:9–16.

―― POPP, C., BARBER, J. & SHAPIRO, D. (in press). Seven transference-related measures—each applied to the Ms. Smithfield interview. *Psychother. Res.* (special issue).

MAXIM, P. (1986). *The Seattle Psychotherapy Language Analysis Schema*. Seattle: Univ. Washington Press.

PERRY, J. C., AUGUSTO, F. & COOPER, S. H. (1989). Assessing psychodynamic conflicts: 1. Reliability of the Idiographic Conflict Formulation method. *Psychiat.*, 52:289–301.

POPP, C., LUBORSKY, L. & CRITS-CHRISTOPH, P. (1990). The parallel of the CCRT based on waking narratives with the CCRT based on dreams. In *Understanding Transference—The CCRT Method*, ed. L. Luborsky & P. Crits-Christoph. New York: Basic Books, pp. 158–172.
────── ────── DIGUER, L., MORRIS, M. & SCHMIDT, K. A. (1993). How similar are the central relationship patterns of dreams and waking narratives? Presented at the Annual Meeting of the Society for Psychotherapy Research, Pittsburgh, PA, June.
SCHACHT, T. & BINDER, J. (1982). *Focusing: A Manual for Identifying a Circumscribed Area of Work for Time-Limited Dynamic Psychotherapy* (TLDP). Unpublished manuscript, Vanderbilt University.
────── ────── & STRUPP, H. (1984). The dynamic focus. In *Psychotherapy in a New Key: A Guide to Time-Limited Dynamic Psychotherapy*, ed. J. Strupp & J. Binder. New York: Basic Books, pp. 65–109.
SEITZ, P. (1966). The consensus problem in psychoanalytic research. In *Methods of Research in Psychotherapy*, ed. L. Gottschalk & A. Auerbach. New York: Appleton-Century-Crofts.
SILBERSCHATZ, G., CURTIS, J. T. & NATHANS, S. (1989). Using the patient's plan to assess progress in psychotherapy. *Psychother.*, 26:40–46.
TELLER, V. & DAHL, H. (1981). The framework for a model of psychoanalytic inference. *Proceedings of the Seventh International Joint Conference on Artificial Intelligence*, 1:394–400.
────── ────── (1992). The characteristics, identification, and application of frames. Unpublished.
WEISS, J., SAMPSON, H., CASTON, J. & SILBERSCHATZ, G., Eds. (1977). *Research on the Psychoanalytic Process*. San Francisco: Psychotherapy Research Group, Department of Psychiatry, Mount Zion Hospital and Medical Center.

INTEGRATING EXPERIENTIALLY BASED CONCEPTS AND BEHAVIORAL OBSERVATIONS IN DEVELOPMENTAL AND INTERVENTION RESEARCH

CHRISTOPH M. HEINICKE, PH.D.

I argue for and illustrate a particular approach to the use of psychoanalytic knowledge in developmental and intervention research. To prove the validity of psychoanalytic concepts is less fruitful than posing research questions and then asking whether, in the conceptualization of the questions, collection and interpretation of the data, and/or defining the implications of the research, these concepts are useful. The emphasis is on using psychoanalytic theoretical concepts and clinical experiences that significantly enhance an effort designed to test hypotheses within a research design.

Within this broad research challenge, I focus on how experientially defined constructs such as the expectation of being cared for (trust) can be reliably rated in observation situations, and how such ratings can be meaningfully integrated with behavioral measures, such as frequency of crying. The nature of a research approach that has sought to integrate global-experiential ratings and specific behavioral observations is illustrated with four projects.

W<small>HEN I FIRST BECAME INTERESTED IN</small> expanding my research using interactional behavioral observation methodologies (Heinicke and Bales, 1953) by integrating more experientially based constructs, psychoanalytic theory and clinical practice had become a most exciting source of such concepts. Moreover, Robert Sears (1943), my research adviser, had already published a monograph reviewing the "objective basis for psychoanalytic concepts." His task was to provide an empirical basis for concepts generated primarily in the clinical treatment situation. To somehow prove the validity of various psychoanalytic concepts seemed to me less fruitful than posing

---

University of California, Los Angeles.

certain research questions and then asking whether in the conceptualization of the question, collection and interpretation of the data, and/or defining the implications of the research, these concepts were useful. That is, the emphasis is on using those psychoanalytic theoretical concepts and clinical experiences that significantly enhance an effort designed to test hypotheses within a research design.

Within this broad research challenge, I focused on how experientially defined constructs such as the expectation of being cared for (trust) could be reliably rated in observation situations and how such ratings could in turn be meaningfully integrated with behavioral measures like the frequency of crying. The nature of a research approach which has sought to integrate global-experiential ratings and specific behavioral observations is illustrated with four projects summarized briefly below.

Duration of Mother-Child Separation as an Influence on the Reversibility of Its Effects

Our first effort at the integration of psychoanalytically informed developmental concepts and sociobehavioral methodology was focused on the question of the impact on family development of two-year-old children being separated from their parents either into a residential or a day care setting. Observations in the day care setting was done to provide a contrast to the continuing separation in the residential nursery. Ten children were studied prospectively in each of these settings (Heinicke, 1956). They came from intact families, the fathers representing a range of occupations; all were Caucasian. Adequate care in terms of quality of staff and adult-to-child ratio characterized both settings. All children were of normal physical growth and health. They were not previously familiar with their caretakers. The day care was arranged to allow the mothers to work. Separation into the residential nursery occurred because the mother was temporarily unable to care for her child and home care was not available. The length of separation for the children in the residential setting was from three to twenty weeks.

The children were observed in the nurseries three times a week by a team of observers using a field unit category system. This allowed frequency counts of such behaviors as crying and hostility as well as reliability assessments of all observations. In addition, narrative accounts dictated by the observers in the nursery during separation and during the weekly home visits in the period of reunion made it possible reliably to rate global dimensions such as the "extent of ambivalence shown to the mother during reunion." Many such behavioral observations and global ratings were integrated to give a picture of the child's response to separation and reunion.

At the time of the conceptualization of our study of the effects of the two-year-old being separated from his parents (Heinicke, 1956), psychoanalytically informed thinking stressed among other things (1) the importance of the child's continuous relationship to a primary gratifying caretaker as an important influence on the development of trust (Erikson, 1950), and (2) the danger of the ongoing trauma of separation requiring defensive resolution of conflicts around longing and anger toward the mother that would in turn impede further progressive development (A. Freud, 1965). Controversy centered on whether the trauma was the event of separation itself or the nature of the relationships to the parents from which the child was separated (Klein, 1940). Bowlby (1951), in whose department this research was conducted, stressed the potential significance, especially of long-lasting separations, on later character development.

Although there was considerable consensus on the behavior seen when children are separated from their parents (Freud and Burlingham, 1944; Robertson and Bowlby, 1952; Heinicke, 1956) the theoretical interpretation of the nature of these responses differed greatly. Impressed by the profound reaction to the breaking of the mother-child tie, Bowlby (1958) reasoned that the intensity of the attachment could not be accounted for by a process whereby the child forms that attachment through being gratified by a primary caretaker.

Turning to ethology, he stated that the attachment of the twelve-month-old infant is made up of a number of component instincts that bind him or her to the mother. "To have a deep attachment for a person is to have taken them as the terminating object of our instinctual responses" (Bowlby, 1959, p. 13). The profound responses to separation were seen as "built into the organism," and adaptive from an evolutionary point of view; concepts such as internal working models and defense against affect were not included at the time.

With Bowlby's active encouragement, and with the help of Gill (Rapaport and Gill, 1959), I attempted my own integration of the behavioral observations, global ratings, and experiential processes set off by the trauma of separating parents from their two-year-old child (Heinicke and Westheimer, 1965).

Following Freud (1926), separation anxiety was understood in the context of the "intensification of need." It was hypothesized that anxiety is aroused when parents are no longer there to satisfy either the immediate or anticipated needs. Children whose relationship history was associated with the expectation of being cared for (trust) would tolerate more "tension due to need," but all two-year-olds would typically show some anxiety.

The next question became: what are those needs and "tensions due to need"? The need to be physically cared for and to experience a satisfying feeding experience was stressed. Equally important was the child's need to be loved and particularly so in relation to an emerging sense of self (Heinicke and Westheimer, 1965, p. 328). As a function of the separation, the main source of approval was removed. Although resisting any intimate contact in the first three days, the children soon desperately sought approval from the nursery staff.

As the separation continued, and the longing and associated anger increased, defensive adaptations came into play both to maintain the previous relationship and to prevent these intense feelings from overwhelming the contact with and approval from the visiting parents. The children's longing and anger could be seen in the way they devoured the candy that the parent brought, while the direct expression of feelings toward that parent were suppressed.

The conceptualization of three different forms of adaptation to the trauma of separation also integrated a psychoanalytically informed inference as to what the children were experiencing and the sequence of reliably observed responses. Thus, we inferred that during the first three days the children resisted every encounter with the alternate caregivers and were focused on retrieving their parents. From roughly the third to the twelfth day, regression in all phases of functioning characterized the effort of adaptation. After the twelfth day, which roughly coincided with the coming and going of the visiting parent and the associated intensification of longing and anger, the adaptation focused on the defensive suppression of all affects experienced toward those precious parents.

The longer the duration of the trauma of separation, the more likely was the occurrence of defensive adaptation. Moreover, the longer the separation, the longer was the period after reunion that the child expressed both anxiety about potential separations and provocative anger. To understand the provocative anger, it was assumed that in the "unsafe" environment of the nursery and the visiting parent, direct expressions of intense feelings could not occur and were presumably suppressed. In the safer environment of the continuing reunion in the family home, the child could express the anger and provocatively test whether the trauma of separation might occur again. This interpretation helped to understand why many mothers were driven to exasperation: "If he goes on like this I will take him back to the residential nursery." However, the research demonstrated that the harmful effect of even the longest separations in this sample of two-year-olds could be reversed. Without minimizing the impact of the trauma and the potential interaction with future events, the study also indicated the importance of the quality of the previous and ongoing relationship to the mother. Thus, the extent of the mother's affection previously expressed to her separated two-year-old was inversely related to the extent of avoidance of the observer (stranger) in the first week of separation. Moreover, if the sensitivity of the mother decreased after the separation, the child's response to reunion with the mother was also more avoidant (Heinicke and Westheimer, 1965). We recognized that prospective studies examining the impact of marital and parent personality variables on family development would have to be done. We were to return to such a project in subsequent years. However, our next effort at the integration of inferences about intrapsychic experiences and behavioral observations focused on studying the process and outcome of psychoanalytic treatment.

Frequency of Psychoanalytic Treatment as a Factor Affecting Outcome in Children

The interest in studying the impact of frequency of session on the outcome of the psychoanalytic psychotherapeutic treatment of children suffering from a failure to achieve at academic levels consistent with their IQ was based on the personal experience of treating some children once and others four times a week. The unfolding of the material, and particularly the specificity of the transference and its interpretation, was strikingly different. Even though current (1957) psychoanalytic thinking made clear that because of the striking differences in the potential for working through the emerging conflicts, the quality and the sustained nature of the outcome would also be strikingly different, reliable assessments of outcome were not available.

The measures chosen reflected an effort to integrate psychoanalytically informed diagnostic assessments with the multi-measurement approach of behavioral science (Heinicke and Ramsey-Klee, 1986). Our research design, data collection, and

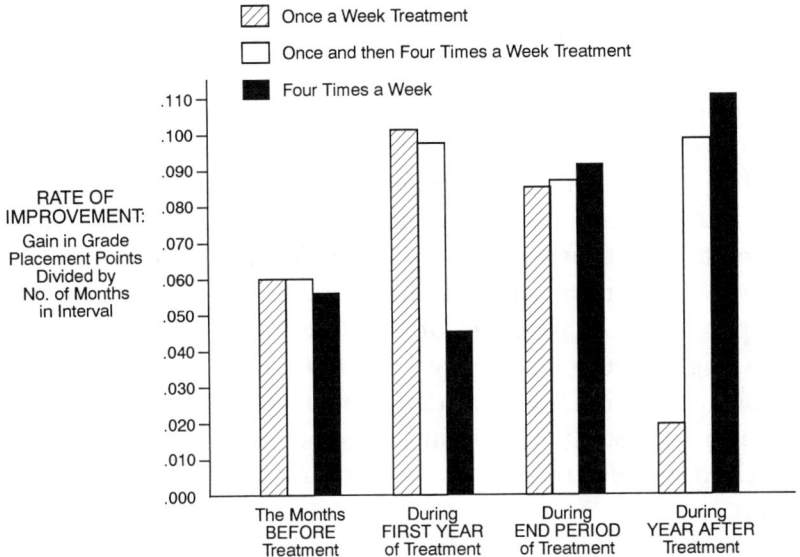

FIGURE 1. RATE OF IMPROVEMENT IN READING AS MEASURED BY WORD RECOGNITION TESTS.

data analysis again combined experientially focused global ratings based on clinical observations organized by the Anna Freud Diagnostic Profile (1965) with behavioral measures such as the count of the number of words that a child could recognize (The Wide Range Achievement Reading Test). Three frequency-of-session groups of eleven-year-old boys were compared. Experienced child therapists, all of whom had been trained at the Anna Freud Centre, were assigned randomly to either a once- or four-times-a-week group. A third group of children, diagnostically matched with the first two frequency groups was seen once-a-week for a year and was then seen four times a week by the same therapist until the end of treatment.

The results given in Figure 1 indicate that, as measured by the word recognition test, the rate of reading increased for the *less* frequently seen children in the first year, and was equivalent and at the normal level at the end of treatment. By contrast, the more frequently seen children showed a striking gain in the year following treatment (Heinicke and Ramsey-Klee, 1986). These findings were consistent with a psychoanalytic interpretation that the higher frequency permits more affect-laden working through both generally and specifically during the termination of treatment, and that the integration of intrapsychic changes and new modes of adaptation may not occur until after treatment. Content analysis of the therapeutic material of the intensive treatments revealed that major shifts in defensive organization were occurring. It was suggested that this psychic reorganization of the child and his daily transactions might well interfere with an immediate adaptive gain in the symptom area, i.e., "academic achievement." The findings are also consistent with many subsequent psychotherapy research projects stressing the importance of followup assessments.

Analysis of the clinical ratings further clarified what differential changes were taking place in the children of normal IQ referred for low levels of academic achievement (Heinicke and Ramsey-Klee, 1986). Cluster analysis of these ratings revealed four major domains: (1) effective adaptation, including self-esteem related to ego functioning; (2) capacity for relationships; (3) frustration tolerance and the ability to work; and (4) ratings indicating the capacity for flexible adaptation. The children seen more frequently showed more extensive positive gains *in all domains*, but the progressive development in ratings of the capacity for relationships and flexible adaptation were particularly striking at both the end of treatment and one year after treatment. Ratings of flexible adaptation suggest a greater balance in the defensive organization, expression of a variety of affects, modulation of aggression as opposed to the repression of it, and ability to elaborate an idea imaginatively.

The question arises why the more intensive treatment approach would not have a differential effect on ratings of effective adaptation such as ego integration. There are no doubt many factors involved, but the correlation of these ratings with IQ as measured at the beginning suggested the hypothesis that constitutionally based individual differences in ability may set limitations to the impact of a relationship therapy. Moreover, all those ratings significantly correlated with IQ showed no differential change as a function of frequency of treatment sessions.

While these findings suggested differential outcome of treatment as a function of the outcome indices used, and while the integration of other developmental research findings pointed to the potential role of the constitutionally determined variations in IQ and related adaptive functions, it was thought possible that certain of the ego functions, though correlated with IQ, such as task orientation, would also be influenced by the earliest relationship experiences. Given our emerging interest in early family intervention, we wanted to clarify what parent and child characteristics were most likely to respond to such a relationship intervention. Accordingly it was decided to study what parent personality and marital characteristics assessed before the birth of the first child affected the emerging post-birth parent-infant interaction and specifically variation in the two- to four-year-old child's IQ, sustained attention, task orientation (task persistence), verbal expressiveness, and aggression modulation. As documented above, these functions had shown a differential response to treatment.

Pre- and Post-Birth Antecedents of Attention, IQ, Verbal Expressiveness, Task Orientation, and Capacity for Relationships

In a series of longitudinal studies involving two samples of 46 families each, we have traced the impact of parent personality and marital characteristics on the emerging parent-infant transaction and child outcome in the first four years of life (Heinicke et al., 1986; Heinicke and Lampl, 1988; Heinicke and Guthrie, 1992). Both the review of the research literature and assumptions derived from psychoanalytic theory and clinical experience guided the formulation of a set of hypotheses expressed in the form of path analyses. For simplicity of exposition we

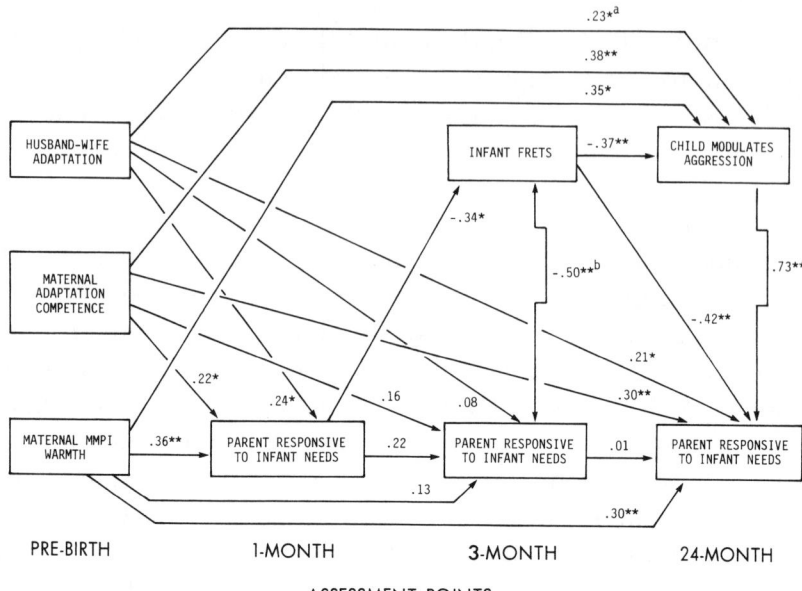

FIGURE 2. PATH ANALYSIS DIAGRAM FOR TWO INDEXES OF 24-MONTH POSITIVE PARENT-CHILD MUTUALITY: CHILD AGGRESSION MODULATION AND PARENT RESPONSIVENESS TO NEED ($N = 44$. *$p < .05$. **$p < .01$. [a]BETA WEIGHTS PLACED BY ACROSS TIME PATHS. [b]VERTICAL LINES INDICATE CROSS-SECTIONAL CORRELATIONS.).

shall focus initially on two of these, as displayed in Figures 2 and 3. Parental ego functioning, and the capacity for relationships including a partner relationship, were captured respectively by indices labeled adaptation-competence, warmth, and positive husband-wife adaptation (see left-hand side of Figure 2). To read Figure 2, when the coefficient next to a line (path) bears asterisks (* or **) it means that the prior variable influenced the later one, even when all the other influences listed in the figure were considered. For example, pre-birth husband-wife adaptation had a significant influence on the child's twenty-four-month modulation of aggression even when the influence of pre-birth maternal adaptation-competence and warmth and three-month infant fretting were taken into account.

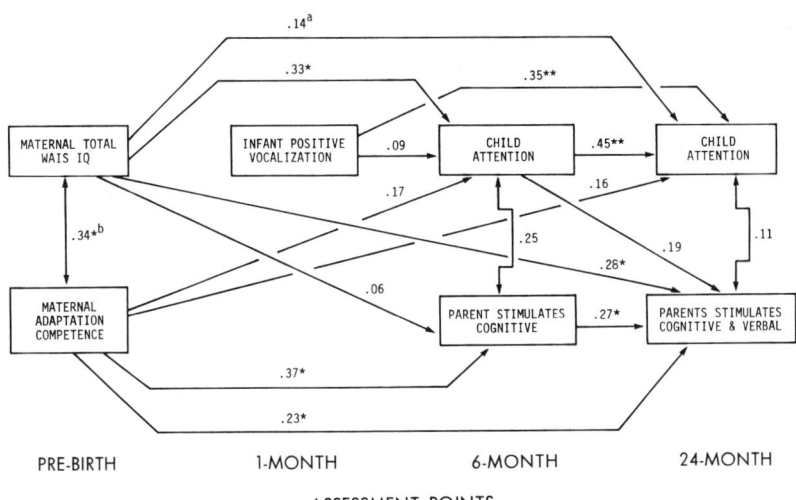

FIGURE 3. PATH ANALYSIS DIAGRAM FOR THE CHILD'S 24-MONTH ATTENTION AND THE PARENT'S STIMULATION OF COGNITIVE AND VERBAL EXPERIENCES ($N = 44$. $*p < .05$. $**p < .01$. [a]BETA WEIGHTS PLACED BY ACROSS TIME PATHS. [b]VERTICAL LINES INDICATE CROSS-SECTIONAL CORRELATIONS.).

As can be seen in Figure 2, measures of the mother's adaptive-competence, warmth, and marital quality were linked to variations in the parent's responsiveness to the needs of her one-month infant, which in turn associated with three-month infant fretting; and all of these factors were directly or indirectly related to the nature of the two-year-old positive parent-child mutuality as measured by the child's aggression modulation and the parent's continuing responsiveness (Heinicke et al., 1986). A model of the continuing mutual influence of parent characteristics, parent-infant transactions, and the child's development of a positive relationship and secure self emerged from followup studies of the same children at three and four years old (Heinicke and Lampl, 1988; Heinicke and Guthrie, 1992). The impact of the quality of the marital relationships on the development of the child's secure self was particularly striking (Heinicke and Guthrie, 1992).

By contrast, as seen in Figure 3, and as confirmed in further followup (Heinicke and Lampl, 1988), variations in the child's sustained attention and the parental stimulation of cognitive and verbal experience were anticipated by variations in the mother's pre-birth IQ and one-month infant positive vocalization. The predominance of a constitutionally based influence was suggested and is supported by much other research (Scarr, 1992). Specifically, Scarr (1985) also demonstrated that variations in the parent's stimulation of cognitive experiences is anticipated by variations in her pre-birth IQ. Task orientation was significantly linked to both pre-birth maternal IQ and the pre-birth and ongoing marital quality. That is, task orientation, a cognitive-motivational variable, may have been influenced both by inherent intellectual capacities and factors related to the developing positive parent-child relationship (Heinicke and Lampl, 1988).

The experiences outlined above, and a strong conviction that effective preventive interventions needed to be developed and evaluated, led us to our next and current project.

Our Current Early Intervention with At-Risk Families

In designing a study of how the initial characteristics of families at risk for neglecting and/or abusing their children interact with a home visiting intervention to affect outcome, our previous experience influenced us as follows.

We needed to define an effective relationship intervention such as home visiting that would link to other established research (Heinicke et al., 1988). Such a relationship intervention would be based on psychoanalytic knowledge, including the concept of transference and the positive working relationship. But the needs of the parents also required conceptualization of intervention based on cognitive-behavioral, social reinforcement, and advocacy principles (Heinicke, 1990). Our longitudinal etiological research had shown that effective intervention would have to be directed at various aspects of parent and marital functioning, at parent-infant functioning, and directly at child functioning. Psychotherapy research findings persuaded us to use an intensive (two-year) intervention and stressed the importance of followup after the intervention was terminated. Most important, our longitudinal studies suggested that a relationship intervention was most likely to make an impact on the parental context of responsiveness to child need and the associated development of the child's secure self. Using a multisituation, multirater model, the mothers and infants are being rated on dimensions relevant to the development of the secure self using time-sampled in-home observations and the Waters-Dean Q-Sort. The mothers and infants are also rated on these dimensions by the mother-infant group leader. Moreover, two test situations provide parallel information. One test is the Ainsworth Strange Situation (Ainsworth et al., 1978). The other is a brief mother-child separation followed by a period of mother-infant free play. In rating the responses to separation and the play sequences, we are again faced with the challenge of combining conceptions based on the empathic identification with the experience of the child and mother, and behavioral responses seen on the videotape recordings. For both settings (separation and play) we have achieved high levels of agreement in rating theoretically relevant dimensions, and we are also continuously expanding our conception of the caregiver context of the secure, competent, and separate self.

Concluding Remarks

The effort to integrate experientially based concepts and behavioral observations continues. Bretherton (1992) has written a most informative review of how the concepts of parent responsiveness to need and self-development were integrated into Bowlby's initial attachment formulations.

> If the attachment figure has acknowledged the infant's needs for comfort and protection while simultaneously respecting the infant's need for independent exploration of

the environment, the child is likely to develop an internal working model of self as valued and self-reliant [p. 767].

In outlining the future tasks for attachment theory, Bretherton calls for, among other things, the following directions:

> New theoretical treatments of defensive processes in the construction of internal working models of attachment need to be worked out in relation to insights from representational theories and research, and clinical attachment theory requires the development of an experiential language akin to that used by other psychoanalytic theories of interpersonal relatedness, such as Winnicott and Sullivan [p. 771].

Using my own clinical and research experiences, I have attempted to illustrate that both the validity and replicability of our findings are going to increase if the empathic understanding of an experience is captured by reliable global ratings and is combined with well-defined observations of behavioral sequences. We are currently returning to the study of the mother-child relationship to refine these approaches. For example, we find that raters with clinical and developmental experience can agree on the conceptualization of defensive processes in an infant's reaction to separation in the first year of life. Equally important, the continuing dialogue between the raters around what the infant is experiencing and what can be readily observed, is greatly expanding our definition of these defensive processes and the contexts in which they occur. We are hoping to develop more valid and varied outcome measures and at the same time to increase our knowledge of the development of the secure self.

Returning to Bowlby's (1958) earliest interest in the biological roots of attachment behavior, the task of formulating "a psychobiological theory of attachment" continues (Kraemer, 1992). I believe that in the study of parent-child separation and the larger issue of the attachment of caregiver and infant, constructs such as motives (to retrieve the relationship), affects (rage) and adaptation (suppression of affect) need to be part of a valid and testable theory of the development of the above transactions.

REFERENCES

AINSWORTH, M. D. S., BELHAR, M. C., WATERS, E. & WALL, S. (1978). *Patterns of Attachment.* Hillsdale, NJ: Erlbaum.
BOWLBY, J. (1951). *Mental Care and Mental Health.* Geneva: World Health Organization.
——— (1958). The nature of the child's tie to his mother. *Int. J. Psychoanal.,* 39:1–23.
——— (1959). Separation anxiety. *Int. J. Psychoanal.,* 41:1–25.
BRETHERTON, I. (1992). The origins of attachment theory. *Devel. Psychol.,* 28:759–775.
ERIKSON, E. H. (1950). *Childhood and Society.* New York: Norton.
FREUD, A. (1965). *Normality and Pathology in Childhood. Writings,* 6. New York: Int. Univ. Press.
——— & BURLINGHAM, D. (1944). *Infants Without Families.* New York: Int. Univ. Press.
FREUD, S. (1926). Inhibitions, symptoms and anxiety. *S. E.,* 20.
HEINICKE, C. M. (1956). Some effects of separating two-year-olds from their parents: a comparative study. *Human Relations,* 9:105–176.
——— (1990). Toward generic principles of treating parents and children: integrating psychotherapy with school-aged child and early family intervention. *J. Consult. Clin. Psychol.,* 58:713–719.
——— & BALES, R. F. (1953). Development of structure in small groups of men. *Sociometry,* 16:7–38.
——— BECKWITH, L. & THOMPSON, A. (1988). Early intervention in the family system: a framework and review. *Infant Ment. Health J.,* 9:111–141.
——— DISKIN, S. D., RAMSEY-KLEE, D. M. & OATES, D. S. (1986). Pre- and post-birth antecedents of two-year-old attention, capacity for relationships, and verbal expressiveness. *Devel. Psychol.,* 22:777–787.
——— & GUTHRIE, O. (1992). Stability and change in husband-wife adaptation, and the development of the positive parent-child relationship. *Infant Behav. Devel.,* 15:109–127.
——— & LAMPL (1988). Pre- and post-birth antecedents of 3- and 4-year-old attention, IQ, verbal expressiveness, task orientation, and capacity for relationships. *Infant Behav. Devel.,* 11:381–410.
——— & RAMSEY-KLEE, D. M. (1986). Outcome of child psychotherapy as a function of frequency of session. *J. Amer. Acad. Child Psychiat.,* 25:247–253.
——— & WESTHEIMER, I. (1965). *Brief Separations.* New York: Int. Univ. Press.
KLEIN, M. (1940). Mourning and its relation to manic-depressive states. In: *Contributions to Psycho-analysis 1921–1945.* London: Hogarth Press, pp. 1–416.

KRAEMER, G. (1992). A psychobiological theory of attachment. *Behav. Brain Sci.*, 15:493–541.
RAPAPORT, D. & GILL, M. M. (1959). The points of view and assumptions of metapsychology. *Int. J. Psychoanal.*, 40:1–10.
ROBERTSON, J. & BOWLBY, J. (1952). Responses of young children to separation from their mothers. Paris: *Courier of the International Children's Centre*, 2:131–140.
SCARR, S. (1985). Constructing psychology: making facts and fables for our times. *Amer. Psychol.*, 40:499–512.
—— (1992). Developmental theories for the 1990's: developmental and individual differences. *Child Devel.*, 63:1–19.
SEARS, R. R. (1943). *Survey of Objective Studies of Psychoanalytic Concepts*. New York: Social Science Research Council.

DISCUSSION: EMPIRICAL RESEARCH IN PSYCHOANALYSIS

OTTO F. KERNBERG, M.D.

THE PAPERS UNDER REVIEW might well be described as having been produced by two generations of researchers. The first generation's focus was mostly on outcome (the scientific evaluation of the effectiveness of psychoanalytic treatment); the focus of the second generation has been mostly on process (the extent to which outcome is determined by the interaction of the patient's psychopathology and personality, on the one hand, and the analyst's skills, personality, and particularly, his technical interventions, on the other). As a whole, these reports reflect both the progress and the present limitations and challenges of psychoanalytic research.

This first generation is perhaps best represented by the psychotherapy research project of the Menninger Foundation (to which Robert Wallerstein and Lester Luborsky contributed so importantly), a project that attempted to capture the central attributes of the patient, of the therapist and his technique, the psychosocial environment surrounding the treatment, and the treatment process itself.

Wallerstein summarizes the rationale of the Menninger Psychotherapy Research Project that began in 1954, its essential methodology, and appropriately concludes that " . . . the findings and conclusions from PRP were more decisive in the outcome realm, more inferential in the process realm (and the project is usually seen as a major outcome study)." As Wallerstein points out, while the Menninger Project's patient population was formally divided between patients treated by psycho-

---

Associate Chairman and Medical Director, The New York Hospital-Cornell Medical Center, Westchester Division; Professor of Psychiatry, Cornell University Medical College; Training and Supervising Analyst, Columbia University Center for Psychoanalytic Training and Research.

analysis and by expressive and supportive psychotherapy (with many being treated with a mixture of expressive and supportive psychotherapy), in fact the overall designation of the treatment modality for individual patients did not do sufficient justice to the subtleties by which expressive and supportive elements appeared throughout the entire spectrum of the patient population of the project.

Major findings of the Menninger Foundation's Psychotherapy Project included the importance of supportive elements influencing change, and the difficulty in differentiating specific "structural" change supposedly achieved by psychoanalysis alone from other changes achieved (Wallerstein, 1986). At a theoretical level, these findings pointed to the importance of reexamining the concept of structure and structural change in psychoanalysis. On a practical level, they pointed to the fact that outcome studies needed to be linked much more closely to the treatment processes. I shall return to this issue.

Henry Bachrach's report on the Columbia Records Project is another first-generation study—it had its inception in 1959. Again outcome is the focus. Bachrach concludes that the highest levels of therapeutic benefit were found in the analyses continuing beyond the candidates' graduation. Treatment length was the only independent factor substantially related to analyzability and therapeutic benefit. Patients judged "analyzable" achieved greater therapeutic benefit than patients who were judged not to have developed an analytic process; but fewer than half of the patients who remained in analysis were characterized as having developed an analytic process at termination. As Bachrach points out, provisions were not made for an independent study of the treatment process, nor for the analysts' contribution to the final result in more than rudimentary ways; the focus of the data was more descriptive than dynamic.

The criticism Bachrach makes of the Columbia Records Project might be directed equally at the Menninger Project, notwithstanding the latter's greater methodological sophistication, greater emphasis on process, and its independent evaluation of both process and outcome. Bachrach (referring to the Columbia Records Project) states: "Paradoxically, it is the main strength of the project (i.e., the large number of variables studied among a very large number of diverse cases) which, in retrospect, raises questions about the viability of its methodology for making a substantive contribution to an elaboration of the psychoanalytic theory of outcome. Namely, the employment of multivariant statistical methods for studying large numbers of cases requires preselection of categories for investigation on the basis of which all cases will be evaluated, results in a statistical averaging of findings, a sacrifice of the individuality specific to cases, and loss of the kinds of qualitative distinctions which are the essence of psychoanalysis."

Judy Kantrowitz also raises serious questions about outcome studies of psychoanalytic efficacy. In reviewing, as a group, studies of this kind, she concludes: "(1) Given a population preselected as suitable for psychoanalysis, that is, patients evaluated as having primarily neurotic difficulties who were motivated for analysis, almost all patients attained some therapeutic benefit following psychoanalysis; (2) only 40 percent of these patients demonstrated an analytic result, that is, the development and at least partial resolution of the transference neurosis; (3) in addition, it was not possible to predict in advance either which patients would have a successful analytic result or which patients would retain their therapeutic gains over time."

The Boston Project, a prospective, longitudinal study of analytic suitability and outcome begun in 1972, selected for evaluation the four variables most commonly agreed upon as essential qualities for analyzability, namely, reality testing, level and quality of object relations, affect availability and tolerance, and motivation for analysis. None of these four psychological characteristics assessed prior to analytic treatment either alone or in combination was predictive of the outcome of psychoanalysis. In the Boston Study, the only factor that seemed to be related to the analytic outcome was the presence of particular characteristics of the treating analysts which interdigitated with particular characteristics of patients when this correspondence occurred in areas central to the patient's psychopathology.

Again, as in the other studies Kantrowitz reviewed, almost all the patients in the study had therapeutic benefit from their treatment, even when the transference neurosis was not fully developed, analyzed, or resolved. At the same time, over half of the patients interviewed in the second followup study had returned to treatment (in fact, 10 of 17 patients seen at the followup time and of the 22 patients studied from the beginning of treatment).

Both the Columbia Clinic and the Boston studies evaluated the treatment conducted by psychoanalytic candidates, and thus, it might be argued, by therapists less than optimally skilled in carrying out psychoanalytic treatment. The Menninger Study included both candidates and graduates, and some senior analysts as well, and did indeed reveal influences of the therapist's skill on outcome (Kernberg et al., 1972). As Bachrach points out, the theoretical concepts that underlay the Menninger and the Columbia projects corresponded to psychoanalytic formulations that represented views no longer held at the time the projects ended and their data were evaluated. And, as Wallerstein notes, the concept of "structural change" utilized to evaluate specific effects of psychoanalysis is now considered quite problematic.

The foregoing considerations raise questions about the validity of the results achieved by these and other first-generation projects. But, these were the projects that permitted the formulation of the need for strategies of empirical research that have led to the second generation of empirical research on psychoanalysis, research characterized by a sharper focus on process, by efforts to link specific outcomes to specific process variables defined and evaluated in prospective studies, and by abandoning a "race" to discover which psychotherapeutic modality has a better general outcome.

This brings us to the dialectic of outcome studies carried out to evaluate, from a scientific viewpoint, efficacy of psychoanalysis and the factors it depends on, in contrast to responding to social pressures for "demonstrating" the efficacy of psychoanalysis as compared to other treatments. In the long run, I believe, the developing knowledge of what is specific about psychoanalysis, the processes and related outcomes that can be expected from psychoanalysis and not from other treatments, will provide a more significant contribution to both social and economic concerns, and to the development of psychoanalytic science itself than simplistic comparisons of alternative treatment methods applied to random patient populations.

Kantrowitz's report of the predictive value of interactional features of analyst and patient provides access to second-generation psychoanalytic research. It points to the importance of the psychoanalyst's personality features that permit him to "tune in" more sharply to certain of the patient's personality features, as well as potentially creating "blind spots" that might foster his entering into unconscious collusion with certain of the patient's problems. Kantrowitz points to the interesting observation that the same personality characteristics of the therapist that may foster therapeutic process at some point in the treatment may inhibit it at other points. Her focus is on countertransference and the importance of studies of transference-countertransference binds, which are increasingly occupying the attention of the entire psychoanalytic community (Kernberg, 1993).

She rightly underlines the importance of studying the treatment of different patients by the same analyst in order to more sharply differentiate the contributions of the analyst's personality and countertransference potential from the effects of the patient's transference developments. In this connection, I believe that empirical research on the patient's projective identification (which strongly influences the activating of countertransference) may prove helpful in expanding our knowledge about the means by which patients defensively attempt to free themselves of certain aspects of their own personality by successfully inducing similar personality characteristics in the analyst who is treating them. The analyst's "role responsiveness" (Sandler, 1976), in turn, needs to be examined in relation to his personality characteristics: paranoid patients may have real enemies at times, but more often create them in the process of projecting their own dissociated impulses and conflicts.

Heinicke provides a good example of how second-generation research focuses on attempts to link specific process and outcome features, and, in addition, developing new strageties that include naturalistic clinical observations as well as specifically designed test situations that lend themselves to empirical, controlled research. That Heinicke's work, in contrast to the other communications of this series, deals with a variety of interventions in infancy and early childhood also illustrates the importance of developmental infant research as a major testing ground for psychoanalytic hypotheses and the generation of new psychoanalytic knowledge.

Heinicke's research on separation anxiety revealed that children whose relationship history was associated with the expectation of being cared for (trust) were better able to tolerate traumatic separations than children whose past relationships were not so characterized. While reconfirming some of Bowlby's findings on attachment and separation, Heinicke found that the longer the duration of the separation trauma, the more likely defensive adaptations to this trauma occurred, particularly the defensive suppression of all affects. Again, the quality of the previous and ongoing relationship between infant and mother was related to the intensity of such defensive adaptation.

Heinicke also compared the treatment of a group of 11-year-old boys, selected on the basis of failure to achieve at academic levels consistent with their IQs, seen four times a week with another group seen only once a week. The children seen more frequently showed more extensive positive gains in their capacity for relationships, frustration tolerance, and ability to work. With regard to changes in self-esteem and ego integration, however, the differences between the two groups were smaller; outcome seemed significantly influenced by the child's IQ. The ratings correlated significantly with IQ showed no differential change as a function of the frequency of treatment sessions.

A third type of study reported by Heinicke includes the evaluation of the impact of parents' personalities and marital characteristics on the emerging parent-infant transactions and child development in the first four years of life. He found that the prebirth husband-wife adaptation had a significant influence on the two-year-old child's modulation of aggression, and that the impact of the quality of the marital relationship on the development of the child's secure self was particularly striking. The infant's task orientation was significantly linked to both prebirth maternal IQ and the prebirth and ongoing marital quality.

Heinicke concludes with a description of his current early intervention study with families at risk. The basic hypothesis of this work includes the assumption, derived from Bowlby, that when mother has acknowledged the infant's needs for comfort and protection while simultaneously respecting the infant's need for independent exploration of the environment, the child's internal sense of security and integration of self are enhanced, and that the child is better equipped to react to traumatic experiences of separation in the first year of life.

The common theme of Heinicke's research projects is the study of the impact of early object relations on psychological functioning, learning, social adaptation, and on resistance to trauma and separation. His studies seem to confirm the important consequences of the mother-infant relationship for the infant's resilience to separation as well as the influence of the psychoanalytic situation on overall improvement in a selected child-patient population. From the viewpoint of discussions regarding the importance of the frequency of psychoanalytic sessions, and the corresponding impact on the effects of psychoanalytic treatment, this latter finding is of real significance. The relation between frequency of sessions and outcome is, of course, already one component of the second generation of research on psychoanalysis, that is, an effort to link one process variable more tightly to outcome.

Returning now to Wallerstein's paper, his project addresses the issue of structural change from the viewpoint of change in patients' characterological patterns. Wallerstein outlines his present research effort to map out a complete set of "psychological capacities" that are experience-near constructs, readily and reliably inferred from observable behaviors. The 17 "psychological capacities" developed by his group should permit us to objectify the direction and degree of characterological change obtained with various modalities of psychoanalytically based treatment. Changes in these psychological capacities should help to clarify what we mean by structure and structural change, how these changes become evident in the material from the treatment process, and the relation between these changes and the mechanisms that have brought them about in the course of treatment.

Wallerstein crisply summarizes the different conceptualizations of structure (a) within an ego-psychological framework in terms of impulse-defense configurations, (b) within a Kleinian framework in terms of the nature of internalized object relations, and (c) within a self-psychological framework in terms of the cohesive or vulnerable bipolar self. With regard to this point, stimulated by Wallerstein's questions about structural change, I have suggested (1987) that an ego psychology-object relations theoretical framework may contribute to resolving the theoretical problems related to psychic structure and structural change. I have proposed that unconscious intrapsychic conflicts are always between certain units of self- and object representations under the impact of a particular drive derivative (clinically, a certain affective position reflecting the instinctual side of the conflict) and opposing units of self- and object representations and their respective affect dispositions reflecting the defensive side of the conflict. Unconscious intrapsychic conflicts are never simply between impulse and defense, but between internalized object relations through which both drive and defense find expression.

I have suggested (1987) that structural change resulting from psychoanalytic treatment is reflected in the development of significant shifts in predominant transference patterns, i.e., definite and enduring shifts in the therapeutic relationship as neurotic transference paradigms are resolved.

Accordingly, one central hypothesis linking psychoanalytic process to outcome is that significant shifts in dominant transference paradigms are preconditions and indicators of structural psychic change. In this connection, the work of Luborsky and his group on the Core Conflictual Relationship Theme (CCRT) now provides a well-tested instrument for empirical evaluation of dominant transferences and shifts in transference paradigms during psychotherapeutic treatments. Luborsky summarizes some of the salient findings with the CCRT methodology that confirm its value for assessing dominant transferences and transference change.

The method of evaluating the CCRT seems to me to be perhaps the most original and far-reaching contribution that Luborsky has made to the field of psychotherapy research, for it permits us to test individual transferences and to evaluate the therapist's capacity to become aware of them and to formulate them correctly in his interpretive interventions. Luborsky had demonstrated that the CCRT method is a useful system to guide clinical judgments of the content of the central relationship patterns in psychotherapy sessions.

This method permits us to rate the patient's narrative episodes about relationships that include the patient's principal wishes, needs, or intentions toward another person; the responses of that other person; and the patient's responses to the other person. This interactional frame for the definition of each relationship episode within the patient's narrative, carefully designed and successfully tested in a number of interconnected research efforts, is an excellent tool for diagnosing dominant themes in the transference, and evaluating the therapist's skill in diagnosing central transference patterns as evinced by the emergence of these core conflictual relationship themes in his interpretive interventions.

In earlier work, Luborsky and his coworkers (1988) were able to report that the congruence of the core conflictual relationship theme pattern and the content of interpretations correlates significantly with outcome of psychotherapy. Changes during psychotherapy in the pervasiveness of relationship conflicts as measured by the CCRT correlated significantly with changes in psychotherapy outcome. Now Luborsky and Luborsky, asking whether CCRTs include unconscious aspects, whether they include the context for the patient's major symptoms, and whether this method inhibits or distorts the natural sensitivity of clinicians in making transference formulations, conclude that the opposites of the main CCRT components may be part of a set of unconscious conflicts, that the clash of conflicting wishes as reflected in CCRTs indicates aspects of unconscious conflicts, and that CCRTs, relying on the frequency of occurrence of dominant themes, reflect a similar salience to that utilized by clinicians in diagnosing dominant transference themes.

The search for more precise process variables related to outcome of psychoanalytic treatment is still in progress. Luborsky and his group, in addition to developing the CCRT method as an instrument to evaluate dominant transference themes, also have constructed instruments to evaluate the therapeutic alliance, and the relation between positive transference and therapeutic alliance. Our own research group at the Department of Psychiatry of Cornell University Medical College and the Westchester Division of New York Hospital has developed a method for rating the extent to which interpretive as opposed to supportive techniques are being utilized by the therapist (Koenigsberg et al., 1993). We are now able to quantify the extent to which the treatment is truly interpretive in contrast to supportive (or combinations of these technical modalities) in each session.

These are some illustrations of the current trend of empirical research in psychoanalysis to link process research more closely to outcome research. They are way stations, I believe, on the road to specifying the essential ingredients of psychoanalytic treatment as contrasted to other psychotherapeutic methods, the specific effects of psychoanalysis as contrasted to the effects of other treatment procedures and to the "nonspecific" effects of all psychotherapeutic engagements. I hope that these efforts will contribute to new developments in psychoanalytic theory, psychoanalytic treatment, and the application of the psychoanalytic method to derived psychotherapies.

An early concern regarding the development of empirical research in psychoanalysis was that research methods that "invade" the clinical situation would unavoidably, and destructively, alter and interfere with the psychoanalytic process. The projects summarized in the papers of this section illustrate that empirical research is feasible and does not necessarily interfere with good treatment. To the contrary, findings derived from the projects reported in this section have had a positive influence on psychoanalytic technique as well as on the technique of psychoanalytic psychotherapy.

Another major concern regarding empirical research has been that operationalizing key psychoanalytic concepts would not do justice to their complexity, and would produce a tendency to oversimplified definitions and dilution of essential psychoanalytic concepts. Although it is true that operationalization of psychoanalytic concepts often does not do justice to their richness and ramifications, focused studies of specific aspects of psychoanalytic process and outcome may gradually be woven together and, at a later stage, restore a complexity to the research endeavor that does justice to the richness and complexity of the psychoanalytic situation. Perhaps a third generation of psychoanalytic research will bring together the strands of partial developments and openings in our field. The contributions of this section illustrate the road already traveled; new vistas have opened up, and have demonstrated the vitality of psychoanalysis as a developing science.

REFERENCES

KERNBERG, O. F. (1987). Psychic structure and structural change: an ego psychology-object relations theory viewpoint. *J. Amer. Psychoanal. Assn.*, 36(Suppl.):315–337.
——— (1993). Convergences and divergences in contemporary psychoanalytic technique. *Int. J. Psychoanal.*, 74:659–673.
——— BURSTEIN, E. D.; COYNE, L.; APPELBAUM, A.; HORWITZ, L. & VOTH, H. (1972). Psychotherapy and psychoanalysis: final Report of the Menninger Foundation's Psychotherapy Research Project. *Bull. Menninger Clin.*, 36, Nos. 1 & 2.
KOENIGSBERG, H. W., KERNBERG, O. F., APPELBAUM, A. H. & SMITH, T. (1993). A method for analyzing therapist interventions in the psychotherapy of borderline patients. *J. Psychother. Pract. Res.*, 2:119–134.
LUBORSKY, L., CRITS-CHRISTOPH, P., MINTZ, J. & AUERBACH, A. (1988). *Who Will Benefit from Psychotherapy?* New York: Basic Books.
SANDLER, J. (1976). Countertransference and role responsiveness. *Int. Rev. Psychoanal.*, 3:43–47.
WALLERSTEIN, R. A. (1986). *Forty-Two Lives in Treatment: A Study of Psychoanalysis and Psychotherapy.* New York: Guilford.
——— (1988). Assessment of structural change in psychoanalytic therapy and research. *J. Amer. Psychoanal. Assn.*, 36(Suppl.):241–261.

DISCUSSION: ON EMPIRICAL RESEARCH

Arnold M. Cooper, M.D.

Psychoanalysts have for some time comfortably debated the question of whether psychoanalysis is science or hermeneutics. The arguments on both sides have been stated clearly and frequently, and the controversy has been a useful one in helping us to understand the dimensions of psychoanalysis. However, to the extent that psychoanalysis lays claim to being a method of treatment, we are, for better or worse, drawn into the orbit of science, and we cannot then escape the obligations of empirical research. As long as we develop practitioners who are members of a profession and charge for their services, it is incumbent upon us to study what we do and how we affect our patients. As most of psychiatry has embarked on brain studies, psychoanalysts and our collaborators in the psychotherapies retain responsibility for the continuing study of mental processes.

Furthermore, while some psychoanalysts still believe that our activity is separate from, and unrelated to, advances in psychiatry, most analysts have come to appreciate that there are significant interactions between psychiatric empirical research and psychoanalysis that profoundly affect how we think about and practice our profession. It was not so long ago that psychoanalysts undertook to provide complete explanations of ticks, phobias, depression, obsessive-compulsive behavior, etc. Today we are quite aware that some of our explanations were simply wrong, while others were not wrong, but incomplete. We have learned that, contrary to our earlier views, some analyses can be conducted better, or only, if the analysis is combined

---

Stephen P. Tobin and Dr. Arnold M. Cooper Professor Emeritus in Consultation Liaison Psychiatry, New York Hospital-Cornell Medical Center; Training and Supervising Analyst, Columbia University Psychoanalytic Center for Training and Research.

with appropriate medication. Some disorders for which there was no treatment available other than analysis will, we now know, respond as well or better to varieties of treatments in addition to, or instead of, psychoanalysis or psychoanalytically derived psychotherapies. Like it or not, we are being powerfully influenced by empirical research.

The history of empirical research in psychoanalysis has not been a happy one. Beginning with Freud's contempt for American-style empirical research, many analysts have eschewed the methodology of empirical research, and few analytic institutes equip their candidates with the basic skills required either to conduct such research or to evaluate it intelligently. Ironically, it would seem that although, by the end of his life, Freud was far more interested in psychoanalysis as an investigative method than as a therapy, he did little to bring psychoanalysis into the orbit of empirical research. Over the past several decades a small group of determined and inspired psychoanalysts have sought to redress the paucity of empirical research in our field, and the five papers in this section are an exemplary sample of what has been accomplished. This set of papers illustrates the enormous advances of psychoanalytic empirical research, as well as some of the problems that beset the enterprise. Perhaps what is most striking is that empirical studies are being conducted in psychoanalysis with a degree of encouragement from the field that would not have occurred just a few years ago. When Karush and his group began, in the 1960's, to do empirical research on prediction of outcome using the Adaptive Balance Scale for patient ratings, none of the existing analytic journals would publish the paper, and the paper was published in the *Journal of Nervous and Mental Disease* (Karush et al., 1964). Although biases against empirical methods are still strong in our field, the publication of this supplement of the *Journal of the American Psychoanalytic Association* illustrates how far we have come. In 1990, The International Psychoanalytical Association, under Joseph Sandler's leadership, began a section on research, a significant portion of which is devoted to empirical research, and the American Psychoanalytic Association is now sponsoring an empirical research project on outcome.

What do we mean by empirical research? We can briefly define empirical research as the systematic study of any phenomena by a methodology that allows for some form of statistical analysis, simple or sophisticated, that gives a measure of confidence concerning the truth or falsity of the hypothesis under study, and that reports the phenomena and the tests applied to them in a way that allows others to attempt to replicate the experience. Both portions of this proposition have presented special difficulties for psychoanalysts. We have found many of our hypotheses difficult to cast in the form of a research question that would allow a test of the validity of the hypothesis, and we have found it difficult to describe our concepts so that we can be sure that someone else discussing the phenomenon is referring to the same thing. Wallerstein addresses this issue in his paper. As these papers show, empirical research may vary from the simplest tests of the reliability of an observation to complex experimental arrangements.

It is clear that psychoanalysis is not intrinsically unavailable for empirical research; rather, the culture of psychoanalysis and the failures of our educational system have inhibited the appropriate development of an appreciation of the importance of empirical research for the continued advance of the field. Without empirical studies we have no way ever to discard a hypothesis. Whether a particular presentation of the self, for example, is a result of deficit or conflict cannot be decided by argument alone, but will finally require some form of evidence. Many of the controversies in psychoanalysis endure not because the questions are philosophically unamenable to research scrutiny, but because we have not yet attempted to frame the research questions. Psychoanalysts have leaned heavily on clinical experience to give us confidence in our activities, although the history of medicine is replete with tenaciously held false beliefs based on clinical experience. We can be quite certain that eighteenth-century doctors using leeches had great confidence in their method, based on their clinical experience. They happened to be wrong.

Three of the five studies reported in this section began as outcome studies. It may be unfortunate that the greatest spur for empirical research in psychoanalysis is the need for efficacy (outcome) studies, not only to support our confidence in our treatment, but also to participate as a beneficiary of mental health funding. Clearly any rational health care system will increasingly, often incorrectly, demand efficacy data. While it seems entirely reasonable to demand evidence of effectiveness and safety, we are also aware that a large portion of every physician's time is devoted to activities that are untested and, in fact, are not clearly related to a diagnosable illness. Reassurance, encouragement, and all the aspects of transference that enter into a desirable doctor-patient relationship are largely untested. Furthermore, the majority of clinical treatments have never been subjected to rigorous clinical trial.

Although we urgently desire the information, psychoanalytic outcome data are probably the most difficult measure for which to achieve scientific reliability and validity; for psychoanalysis, therefore, to use its resources to demonstrate its effectiveness may be a serious misdirection of research capacities. The cost of a serious clinical trial seems overwhelming. Wallerstein's masterly review of the Menninger project reminds us how difficult outcome studies are. The three major students of analytic outcome reporting in this section, Wallerstein, Kantrowitz, and Bachrach, have each deviated from their original intent. Wallerstein is now more interested in studying how specific psychological capacities can be measured and how they change with a variety of psychotherapies, Kantrowitz is studying the effect on outcome of the match of therapist and patient, and Bachrach suggests that in place of large-scale multivariate outcome designs we return to scientific individual case examination and the pursuit of specific questions that are amenable to empirical research design. Each of them has given up broad outcome studies in favor of a different order of question. In addition, the odds that mental health policy makers are interested in funding psychoanalysis seems so unlikely that we may be better advised to pursue the empirical researches that are most promising rather than most expedient. Intellectually, the most interesting aspect of psychoanalysis is not its outcome but its process ideas. It may well be that from a public health vantage psychoanalysis is most valuable as the clinical and research field that has spawned the ideas and techniques of dozens of other therapies that, while less ambitious, are more easily studied and administered. Like most analysts, I have no doubt that psychoanalysis is efficacious and the treatment of choice for an important group of patients. I am dubious that proving this is possible with the resources that can be brought to bear.

Although each of the outcome studies reported here has significant problems, we must be struck by the consistency of the findings among the authors, using quite different methodologies. Our capacity to select cases for analysis is poor, with less than half of carefully selected patients ever experiencing an analytic process, however that is defined. Patients show improvement, but it cannot be demonstrated that the improvement is the result of the specific psychoanalytic components of the therapy, and there is excellent evidence that the reverse is true. Patients who see therapists more often and for longer periods do better, but this may only reflect that the patients whom the therapist likes and feels gratified by and are getting better are the ones he keeps in treatment, or perhaps that there are no clear endpoints to treatment, that we can all get better than we are, and therapeutic relationships are helpful. Wallerstein, who has dedicated his life to empirical research in psychoanalysis, is the most radical in accepting these findings.

I shall briefly review some of the major findings in each paper in this section.

Wallerstein is explicit in stating that within the limits of his study, the PRP, psychotherapy and psychoanalysis did not have clearly distinctive outcomes. Most important is his finding that within their use of the concept of structure, structural change was as likely with more supportive techniques as through interpretive insight-oriented techniques, and that conflict resolution was not necessary for deep and enduring psychic change. He concludes that we cannot tie the type of change to the mode of intervention, that the tie of theory to practice is poor, and that we are best advised in our studies of patient outcome to study capacities that can be behaviorally defined rather than structures that are not really subject to measurement. That structural change can be produced by noninterpretive means ought not to be surprising in the light of our changing views of the analytic process. For example, for many it has for some time seemed clear that the new experience with the new object is critical in the analytic process, and the relation of this new experience to interpretation and insight is not well understood (Cooper, 1989).

Wallerstein concludes that our differences of frame of reference preclude the possibility of consensus on broad concepts such as structure. His group has, therefore, abandoned the psychoanalytic conceptual perspective and has adopted a psychological perspective of capacities, describing 17 of them. (In passing, I note that this conceptualization is remarkably close to Karush's effort, but at a far more sophisticated level.) Wallerstein suggests that the capacities being measured—such items as hope, zest for life, flexibility, commitment to relationships, trust—are so clearly core aspects of character that one would accept that a change in these capacities reflects a change in underlying structures, no matter how defined. It may not be such a radical step to substitute capacities for structures for the purpose of research methodology, but it does raise the question of the value of our structural concepts. Unless one can show a clear derivation of these capacities from structural concepts, structure may become superfluous in analytic conception, and analysts might be advised to move closer to psychological schemas that better describe what it is we are interested in. Analysts are, I am sure, reluctant to speak a language of capacities and give up yet another piece of metapsychology. Wallerstein's research may be leading us in that direction. Psychologists such as Benjamin (1974) and others who have devised circumplex personality descriptions, may yet contribute greatly to our analytic thinking. It is always a pleasure to watch a brave thinker who follows his findings where they go, ready to abandon an idea when the weight of data against the idea becomes unbearably burdensome.

Kantrowitz, faced with the same problem of difficulty of broad outcome studies, has raised a different question about outcome. Outcome may be a variable dependent on the patient-analyst mix rather than on patient characteristics. She has evidence that certain characteristics of certain psychoanalysts foster some processes and inhibit others. In fact, the same characteristics may be desirable at one point in an analysis and undesirable at another. This brings up the topic of analytic style, the analyst's character (Cooper, 1982), and the analytic attitude. What is empathic at one stage of the treatment may not be at another. This is an important and interesting field of study attuned to our current recognition that psychoanalysis is a two- (at least) person system, rather than the observation of processes in a single individual. She, like Wallerstein, found that all patients in all treatments get better, and less than half of the patients ever engaged in an analytic process; that they were unable to relate outcome to any of the preassessment factors; and, that researchers and psychological testing found less improvement than doctors and patients claimed. Kantrowitz has shown that selecting by narrow rather than wider scope does not lead to better prediction of analyzability. Her evidence seems to contradict another analytic shibboleth, that the self-analytic function is an essential part of a successful analysis. In her data the self-analytic function seemed unrelated to therapeutic gains. Our inability to predict who will engage in and benefit from psychoanalysis must disturb us.

Bachrach's work, with the large data set of the Columbia Psychoanalytic Center, is concordant with that of the other authors in demonstrating that less than 50 percent of cases carefully chosen for psychoanalysis ever develop an analytic process. Bachrach is discouraged about whether outcome studies will tell us much, and considers the possibility that each treatment is unique and cannot be grouped with others, and that we will learn most from systematic individual case study.

Luborsky, another pioneer of empirical research in psychoanalysis, has shown that psychoanalytic propositions can be put in the form of researchable questions and elicit reliable and valid data relevant to the therapeutic process. Luborsky has done this with transference. Whether or not he has captured all the aspects of transference that are of interest psychoanalytically, he certainly has described aspects of the transference that all analysts would agree are central to the concept, and he has described how they can be specified in ways that allow for reliable and replicable empirical research about the phenomenon of transference. It is worth asking why so little use is made of the CCRT methodology for the elucidation of transference. Luborsky has shown that therapists can learn to identify the elements of the CCRT, and that if they do so, they are likely to conduct their therapies with greater efficacy. The data are good enough so that in most other health care fields, practitioners would feel an obligation to master and use the technique. While all therapeutic fields are slow to make use of research findings, there can be no doubt that psychoanalysis is by far the slowest. Analysts, to my knowledge, rarely consciously use the CCRT techniques as part of their ongoing analytic work. One part of the answer is in the intellectual climate of psychoanalysis. There is almost no formal encouragement from the analytic establishment to utilize instruments or objective criteria to check our formulations. Until recently, analysts were not encouraged to regard their technique as an objectifiable activity to be scrutinized by empirical methods. We are usually content to assure ourselves that our formulations are in accord with the theories we currently hold, whether explicit or obscure.

Psychoanalysts have the uneasy sense that while Luborsky may be able to objectify core aspects of transference, this is not entirely relevant to what we do when we are doing analysis. It is felt as a constriction of our capacity to think imaginatively and a constraint on our capacity to make further discoveries, continually deepening the transference. It is also likely that most analysts prefer to see themselves as closer to being artists than artisans. The idea of carrying out a manualizable, prescribable treatment is anathema to the majority of analysts. Furthermore, asking analysts to specify and bring full cognitive awareness to the analytic process may, for many analysts, seem to conflict with their desire to engage in freely hovering attention. While freely hovering attention is, of course, only a data-gathering method, the data of which should then be subjected to rigorous scrutiny, many analysts prefer to retain a vague open-endedness in their thinking.

Heinicke's work demonstrates the enormous value of analytic ideas in generating testable therapeutic propositions with practical consequences. He has proved the inestimable value of maternal empathy, and the great psychological repair capacities of the human infant. He shows us the distinctions between constitutional limitations and relational defects. While an empathic mother and a good marriage are very desirable for a child, so is a high I.Q. in both mother and child. Heinicke, like Wallerstein, concludes that a variety of techniques is essential in working with children—cognitive, behavioral, social reinforcement, and advocacy, as well as interpretation.

One of the consequences of empirical research is that we are required to give up favorite ideas, ideas we cherish and consider parts of ourselves. Empirical research now clearly shows that some old analytic shibboleths are untrue. For example, transference cures may be lasting; so-called structural change can occur without insight; conflict resolution is not necessary for change; and real treatments are not pure, and supportive measures are an integral part of analysis. The boundary between psychoanalysis and psychotherapy is fluid. Psychoanalysis is, clearly, much too important to be defined by such items as whether the patient is lying down or coming five or three times a week. Rather than continuing to devote so much attention and energy to finding ways to distinguish psychoanalysis from psychotherapy, we should consider embracing the various psychotherapies as our cherished offspring.

This set of papers sounds an alert for psychoanalysis. Empirical research methodology is developing rapidly. It will be applied to psychoanalytic propositions, and many of our favorite ideas will be shown to be wrong or what amounts to the same thing, not useful. Psychoanalysts should learn to entertain this prospect as good news rather than bad news. Psychoanalysis is still the treatment of choice in selected cases, as well as a superb training experience. New information will make us even more effective. Of even greater importance is that psychoanalysis provides a unique opportunity for studying unconscious and conscious mental processes, and continues to be an extraordinarily fruitful source of new ideas, able to incorporate within it the findings not only of its own studies, but of those of its neighboring fields—psychology and neuropsychology. Psychoanalysis is envigorated by the increase of our empirical research and by shedding concepts that no longer yield new knowledge. We are learning new things about our field and we are contributing enormously to our psychotherapeutic offspring, the variety of brief and supportive psychotherapies we have spawned. We pass a critical test for any healthy therapeutic field—we change as we gain new knowledge and experience. That change is likely to be increasingly rapid, and analysts dedicated to the preservation of a theory or a technique are likely to be left only with ideology.

REFERENCES

BENJAMIN, L. S. (1974). Structural analysis of social behavior. *Psychol. Rev.*, 81:392–425.
COOPER, A. M. (1982). Problems of technique in character analysis. *Bull. Assn. Psychoanal. Med.*, 21:110–118.
——— (1989). Concepts of therapeutic effectiveness in psychoanalysis: a historical review. *Psychoanal. Inq.*, 9:4–25.
KARUSH, A., EASSER, R., COOPER, A. M. & SWERDLOFF, B. (1964). The evaluation of ego strength: 1. A profile on adaptive balance. *J. Nerv. Ment. Dis.*, 139:332–349.

DISCUSSION: THE REWARDS OF RESEARCH

ROBERT M. GALATZER-LEVY, M.D.

I FIRST READ ABOUT AND BECAME fascinated with psychoanalysis in high school. It was presented like other disciplines I studied then—definitively. Planets orbited under gravity's force; the square on the hypotenuse of a right triangle equaled the sum of the squares on the other sides; sentences had subjects and predicates; symptoms expressed repressed unconscious forces; the working class would rise up.

I knew unfortunate people, mostly denizens of the land beyond the Hudson, did not appreciate these facts. But this was their problem. It had nothing to do with the truth of "facts" I was learning. Gradually, through college, graduate and professional school I learned that evidence could support, call into question, or refute important propositions. This normative process is especially clear in the sciences. I learned Pythagoras's theorem required Euclid's postulates, and the forces of physics changed with research. I discovered that otherwise reasonable people held different political positions. Perhaps the people beyond the Hudson were not such fools.

From the intellectual trends of the time and personal development, I learned that truth claims are contingent on method, that statements could only be evaluated within particular methodological contexts, and that different methods lead to different kinds of knowledge about the same subject. In most areas more sophisticated study brought increasingly clear statements of the bases of truth claims, including descriptions of the logic and data used in making those claims.

This association between more sophisticated content and concepts of method applied least to psychoanalysis. Personal

---

Training and Supervising Analyst, Chicago Institute for Psychoanalysis; Lecturer in Psychiatry, University of Chicago.

wishes and psychoanalytic literature supported a tolerance of ambiguity about its research methods. Psychoanalytic writings commonly contain authoritative statements that suggest empirical grounding, but finding those empirical referents is difficult or impossible.

In medical school, as I explored psychoanalysis more thoroughly, I found that the published empirical support for many of its ideas was extremely limited. I also discovered that it was difficult to even find clear descriptions of many psychoanalytic concepts. Through residency and analytic training, I was impressed with the richness of psychoanalytic thought, the obscurity of its bases, and the authoritative manner of its presentation. Analytic ideas applied well to clinical experience and cultural phenomena; they made sense of my personal experiences and, in analysis, provided relief from distress. This combination of powerful ideas, personal healing, and the wish to idealize limited my skepticism.

Other aspects of my situation did increase my doubts. Library searches continued to yield little empirical support of many analytic ideas, especially ideas about therapeutics. My teachers often provided little foundation for their assertions. This was particularly clear at the Chicago Institute for Psychoanalysis in the mid- and late 'seventies, when self psychology was coming into its own. Teachers with opposing views stated "facts" with equal authority and contempt for those who disagreed. Clearly views on psychoanalytic matters were determined by factors besides empirical evidence. Each of my institute classmates (including myself) adopted positions about controversies that were similar to those of our training analysts.

Similar phenomena are readily evident in other disciplines. Graduate students commonly irrationally adopt the advisors' viewpoints (LaTour and Woolgar, 1986). History shows that the need to idealize and affiliate commonly interferes with attention to empirical evidence (Jungnichkel and McCormmach, 1986; McCormmach, 1982; Thom, 1975). Furthermore, ideas presented clearly, vividly, with authority, or by personal friends carry more weight than they would otherwise. Such tendencies are universal in all scholarly pursuits. The self-denigration of analysts that comes from an overidealization of "real" scientists does not stand up to exposure to the history of science. However, in other disciplines, particularly the empirical sciences, there comes a point when a referent beyond personal opinion changes people's thinking.

Much of the confusion about the scientific status of psychoanalysis arises from rhetorical concerns. Having the status of science carries enormous prestige in our discourse. The idea that scientific rationality encompasses what is best, and most powerful, is a heritage many of us share with Freud. In this context, because only "scientific" beliefs are viewed as valid, psychoanalytic investigations are often cloaked in the mantel of empirical science. Yet much of what we know and of what most interests us lacks the support from systematic data. As a result, psychoanalytic discourse often carefully obscures its empirical referents, implying their presence and garnering the prestige of science while not submitting to the scrutiny customary in scientific discussion. Psychoanalytic data are rarely presented in ways that make it clear how they were collected, how they relate to conclusions, what information we have, and what information we lack. Clinical findings are rarely presented as the single or small number of instances they are, and the data supporting the finding are rarely described so readers can evaluate them (Klumpner and Frank, 1991). Clinical findings are overgeneralized. We implicitly borrow the authority of empirical science by mimicking its style and rhetoric. For example, we cite each other's opinions and limited clinical experiences as though the citations contained empirical evidence.

The pretense of empiricism in psychoanalysis has interfered with the appreciation of actual empirical investigations like those discussed in the preceding pages. When we pretend to have a solid empirical basis of psychoanalytic practice, and fear being clear about the bases we actually have, it is hard to attend to the specific value of actual empirical studies. Probably the most common informal objection heard to empirical studies is that the analyst-reader already knew the findings. Even when the reader's preexisting ideas are consistent with the empirical finding, such statements ignore the difference in the kind of knowing resulting from empirical investigation and other types of knowledge.

The problem is particularly great in the study of therapeutic efficacy. Unceasing pressure from our consciences, patients, and society encourages the assertion that the long, hard, and expensive work of psychoanalysis is predictably beneficial. We would like to assure all parties that, based on clear evidence, we can predict the therapeutic outcome with reasonable certainty. This is no empty hope. Any experienced analyst knows that some analysands benefit enormously from analysis. The temporal relation of change to the analysis and the logic of that change in terms of the analytic process convince us that psychoanalysis was the agent of change. But we also know that some patients benefit little from analysis, or change less than anticipated despite apparently good analytic work.

At first it would appear that empirical investigations of the type described in the preceding pages of this volume give us little solace. It is easy to find flaws in them. They variously suffer from such difficulties as uncertain means of measurement, unusual patient populations, small sample size, and the use of training cases. With the exception of the Menninger Study (Wallerstein) they fail to address issues with the depth of exploration customary in analytic discourse. Empirical research has not given us the answers we want. Nor has it validated the authority we desire.

This has led to another attitude toward empirical investigation besides the pretense of having done it. We often ignore or denigrate empirical investigations that are inconsistent with our preexisting beliefs. Rationalized by reference to the real methodological limitations of empirical investigation, analysts often see them as irrelevant to clinical practice. This is a pity, because empirical research has much to offer psychoanalysts.

Surprise and Empirical Investigation

What can research do for us? Because good empirical research carries the possibility of findings not previously believed by the researcher, it can surprise us. The findings of several studies reported in this volume are surprising. They differ from received analytic wisdom. This alone suggests their value.

A most important finding which is replicated in three of the studies reviewed in this volume (by Bachrach, Kantrowitz, and Wallerstein) is a negative result. At least within the range of patients ordinarily taken into analysis, neither experienced clinicians nor sophisticated psychological testing can predict analytic outcome based on the study of the patient alone.[1] Measures of overall sickness and health do predict outcome, but the fine-grained distinction about patients' dynamics that are common in discussions of analyzability are not good predictors of analytic results. The reasons for this failure are unclear. It may be, as Kantrowitz and others suggest, that the match of clinician and patient determines outcome. Possible pertinent dimensions of the patients' conditions are not tapped by current methods (Blatt et al., 1991). It may be that the range of patients and difficulty studied is so narrow as to make the expectation of differential prediction unreasonable. Whatever the cause, it is clear that the level of prognostic ability commonly asserted by practicing clinicians is contradicted by replicated empirical findings, and that many of the published statements regarding "analyzability" are not supported when researched empirically. This implies that the clinician may be better off looking at the patient's response to similar intervention than in formulating the patient's dynamics when recommending analysis (Horwitz, 1990).

[1] This finding is important for administrative situations where analysts try to predict the development of colleagues. From the selection process for candidacy to the appointment of training analysts, committees spend much time evaluating the dynamics of colleagues hoping to predict the analysts' functioning. If close evaluation of analysands cannot even predict their analyzability, how can we hope that similar data will predict the capacity to do analytic work except in the grossest way?

The researches reviewed in these reports have numerous other direct applications to current clinical practice. They show that many patients benefit from psychoanalysis. However, except for Heinicke's report, they say little about the comparison of psychoanalysis to other kinds of treatment. Together they suggest that therapeutic benefit and analytic process are not so closely linked as we have often believed.

Heinike's finding that target symptoms may remit *later* in analysis than in less intensive therapy, if replicated, has important implications. It suggests that the solution of a "trial of analysis," requires careful evaluations for its meaning for the future of an analytic undertaking. It also underlines how important it is to study parameters appropriate to psychoanalysis in investigating its efficacy. It might well be that in trials that compared the rapidity of symptom relief in analysis with alternative treatments, analysis would come out badly. Since the goals of psychoanalysis extend beyond symptom relief, findings such as these do not mean psychoanalysis is less effective than psychotherapy.

Another finding from these studies, especially in the Menninger study by Wallerstein, is that the probable mode of therapeutic action in many psychoanalyses is not through interpretation of unconscious conflict. Other factors, traditionally described as supportive elements in the treatment, do appear important. This surprising finding is important in planning investigations of what cures in psychoanalysis.

Finally, the finding that data can be systematically adduced that point to major psychoanalytic themes is important for research, practice, and teaching. Luborsky and his colleagues (this volume, and Luborsky and Crits-Christoph, 1990), along with a small dedicated group of other investigators (Bucci, 1985; Dahl, 1988, 1991; Gill, 1982) have shown that it is possible systematically to explore analytic data for convincing evidence of particular unconscious content and process (see Barber and Crits-Christoph, 1993, for a discussion of these methods). The authority of clinical wisdom is not the final arbiter of the presence or absence of material in the analytic situation, nor is nihilistic acceptance of a pseudo-egalitarian notion that reasonable people can see different things in the same clinical material an adequate response to divergent opinion. Data can be gathered that systematically bear on questions of unconscious content. This is a very important finding. Properly used, it means central controversies in psychoanalysis are open to empirical investigations and resolution through specific and clear methods. It also means that teaching is possible from clear evidence and, at least potentially, systematic study of material can provide an additional means of understanding unconscious content in the analytic setting.

The Value of Empiricism

Thus empirical investigations of the type summarized in this volume have given us psychoanalytically valuable information and promise to give us more such information. It is therefore desirable that psychoanalysis continue empirical investigations. This *pragmatic* consideration is different from the view that we should be empiricists because empiricism carries the authority of science. One might call the latter view imperialist empiricism. In this view there is a correct scientific method. Disciplines that do not abide by its "canons" are condemned as "unscientific" and denigrated for that reason. Grünbaum (1984, 1990) and Sulloway (1991) write in this mode. Well-done investigations of this kind can clarify epistemological issues. However, the idea that they form the "foundation" of the disciplines they study is mistaken.

Research can provide statements whose claim to truth is clearly laid out. This is not an exclusive merit of empirical investigation. Researchers using other points of view can also clearly document and spell out their methods. Bacon's (1620) ideal of publicly demonstrable methods requires that empirical investigation be reported with enough information so readers have a clear idea of how the researcher reached conclusions. Readers of the papers in this volume and the earlier publications upon which they are based, can easily find flaws in the investigations. For example, because its means of discovering unconscious thematic material are so clearly specified, it is readily apparent that the CCRT method would not be expected to tap a range of phenomena that do not correspond in form to its basic paradigm characterized by some psychoanalysts as transference (Bollas, 1987; Kohut, 1971). This ease with which such determinations can be made is a strong point of empiricism. Its methods and its reporting are designed to make visible the limitations of the investigation.

Empirical methods have been enormously effective in many disciplines. We as analysts can learn from these experiences. As discussed above, much is to be gained by explicitness about the nature of data and the process of inference. Most papers in empirical fields include "materials and methods" sections that spell out the research procedures. The logic of drawing and generalizing conclusions is also spelled out with particular attention to alternative interpretations of the data. Another feature of empirical science that psychoanalysts might emulate is the modesty of most empirical studies. Empirical investigators rarely address "big" questions. Most empirical study involves accretion of specialized information. Many psychoanalytic publications attempt to address large questions. They seldom focus on circumscribed problems, coming to a sharp conclusion about them.

The tactics of empirical investigation vary considerably. Approaches range from the collection of instances to hypothesis-testing experiments. Though a wide range of approaches has proved fruitful, physicist John Platt (1964) noted that certain sciences progress rapidly while others move ahead slowly. He attributed these differences to different styles of investigation. In the more rapidly moving sciences, studies were carefully designed to distinguish sharply among significant alternative possibilities, a process Platt called *strong inference*. In slower-developing sciences, studies tended not to sharply address specific questions. In much psychoanalytic investigation we "explore," "investigate." Our data suggest possibilities, but seldom sharply distinguish among them. Strong inference is more difficult in dealing with complex situations where variables cannot be manipulated at will. Psychoanalysis is inherently complex, and we are constrained by its therapeutic intent. Nonetheless, despite their merits, a recurrent weakness of the type of study reported in this section is the failure to address well-formulated questions in ways that provide sharp answers. Attempts to formulate empirical investigations using strong inference may prove fruitful in moving our discipline forward.[2]

Much of the discomfort with empiricism is that it seems far from the core of psychoanalytic interests. Most analysts are primarily interested in explaining the psychology of people in depth, and derive their principal reward from the detailed description of how particular people function psychologically. Studies like those described by Bachrach, whatever their other merits, do not even address such concerns. Several factors bring contemporary empirical investigation closer to the central concerns and methods of psychoanalysis.

Shifting Visions of the "Facts"

The background understanding of scientific investigation that I share with most of my psychoanalytic colleagues includes several important epistemological assumptions that are now widely questioned. These assumptions should be made explicit and some of them should be discarded.

The first of these assumptions relates to the nature of order. We have assumed that any orderly system is characterized by predictability similar to that of classical physics. Given enough information about a system at one moment, we expect to know its evolution thereafter. Waelder (1963) appreciated that these conditions do not apply to the human mind and attributed this to the complexity of human psychology. Over

---

[2]Note that Platt's *heuristic* recommendation is not a philosophical standard of scientific status. It is simply a way to approach empirical investigation that has proven particularly fruitful in many sciences.

the past quarter-century it has become apparent that the orderly picture of the world suggested by nineteenth-century physical sciences is largely an artifact of our means of appraising that world. Because scientists lacked theoretical tools to deal with ordinarily complex systems, research focused on artificial or simple systems that could be managed with available mathematical tools (Thom, 1975). As means emerged to explore more complicated and realistic systems associated with ideas like chaos theory (Stewart, 1989), catastrophe theory (Thom, 1975), and complexity theory (Kauffman, 1993), the pictures of the ordinary possibilities for the world and the kinds of predictions that are expectable in that world have changed dramatically. The goal of predicting the value of a particular variable at a particular time is gradually shifting to descriptions of qualitative features of evolving systems. Current research on the solar system tends not so much to address questions of predicting planetary position, as questions about whether the system is stable over time. These shifts in the vision of an adequate theory in the physical sciences are likely to shape our picture of adequate psychoanalytic theories. They provide models of more realistic and complex systems than older ideas of the physical sciences did (Spruiell, 1993).

But it is likely that psychoanalytic theory cannot be modeled on the theories of physical science. A major shift that characterized the scientific revolution was the abandonment of the goal to understand natural phenomena in terms of meanings and motives (Dijksterhuis, 1950; Lewis, 1964). Nineteenth-century researchers extended this shift first to biology and then to the study of people. Freud's attempts to operate within the framework of physicalist science resulted in a systematic confusion of clinical findings with metapsychological theorizing (Klein, 1976). In recent years psychoanalysts have shown an ever-increasing interest in and commitment to a hermeneutic stance focused on people's meanings and motives (Galatzer-Levy and Cohler, 1990). This interest reflects a wide-ranging philosophical and practical critique of the study of people in the spirit of the physical sciences (Ricoeur, 1970, 1977; Rorty, 1989; Rouse, 1991; Roth, 1991; Taylor, 1971).

A principal objection to the hermeneutic approach has been its seeming lack of rigor and a means by which its propositions could be consensually evaluated. This contrast with the methods of modern science is *not* a necessary feature of the hermeneutic approach. Several investigators have shown that hermeneutic methods can be highly explicit and approached with epistemological clarity. This is both generally the case (Hiley et al., 1991) and has been shown for psychoanalysis in particular (Ricoeur, 1970, 1977; Cooper, 1993; Spezzano, 1993; Geha, 1993). Research methods can, for example, differentiate the extent to which interpretation results from the material being interpreted as opposed to the analyst's preexisting implicit theory (Caston, 1993; Caston and Martin, 1993). Luborsky's CCRT method is an essentially interpretive methodology based on an extension of Freud's ideas of transference (Luborsky, 1990). It permits, with significant but explicit limitation, a consensually validatable methodology for extracting transference materials from transcripts of interactions. As his paper in this volume shows, the yield from such methods can be enormous, demonstrating, for example, the relation between accuracy of transference interpretation and therapeutic progress.

The Single-Case Study Method

Part of the vision of true science that I and those of my generation received was that quantitative knowledge is valuable, while qualitative knowledge is unsatisfactory. This idea pervades physical sciences, but it is most strongly avowed by social scientists. An altered version of Kelvin's dictum to this effect is emblazoned in the stonework of the University of Chicago's social science building (Merton et al., 1984).

In the social sciences and medicine, quantitative methods were most satisfactorily applied to populations rather than individuals. Starting in the nineteenth century, it became possible to make precise quantitative statements about groups of people, though such statements could not be made about individuals (Hacking, 1990). For example, while it remains impossible to predict the death of a particular individual, highly accurate actuarial tables are available that predict longevity and cause of death in large populations. The prestige of statistical methods grew to the point where they became a mandatory part of many medical and social science researches whether they added to the investigation or not (Cohen, 1990). Though many readers and authors retained an insecure notion of their exact meaning, concepts like random sampling, control groups, statistical significance, and notation that $p<.05$, became essential to legitimate investigations of therapeutics (Salsburg, 1985). Proper assessment of therapeutics required comparing two statistically identical representative samples of a population, one treated, the other not, observing the results, and calculating the likelihood of that observed difference resulted from chance.

Problems arise when this method is applied to complex interventions for complex problems as we are doing in studying the efficacy of psychoanalysis. Meeting criteria for adequate statistical studies becomes essentially impossible in such circumstances. As the number of pertinent variables increases, the size of the sample needed to identify the effects of each variable increases dramatically. Failure to appreciate the consequences of this process can easily lead to statistically invalid conclusions (Hsu, 1989). Simply measuring the many pertinent variables over an adequate time to be psychoanalytically meaningful becomes a huge task, as demonstrated by the enormous amount of work involved in the Menninger study (Wallerstein, this volume.) Furthermore, psychoanalysis is by its nature interactive and changing across the course of the treatment. It is not well conceptualized as a discrete intervention applied at a moment in time. Statistical methods that treat it as such miss the ordinary happening that analyst and patient change the nature of the intervention in response to observed effects within the analysis. As a result of these difficulties, statistical methods, instead of providing a tool for learning more about important problems, often become a means to attack investigations that do not measure up to their supposed authority. They can be used against entire fields, like our own, which cannot provide adequate statistical studies. As is clear from Bachrach's, Kantrowitz's and Wallerstein's presentations of their very extensive research efforts, existing investigations of psychoanalysis, viewed as clinical trials, have many serious limitations. None of these studies involve a sample that can be regarded as meaningfully representative (in the statistical sense) of a larger population. The samples studied by Kantrowitz and Wallerstein are too small to allow meaningful statistical analysis, while the methods used in the study described by Bachrach do not use valid and reliable means of data collection. Not only do these limitations apply to all existing studies of psychoanalytic outcome (Bachrach et al., 1991), there is good reason to believe that satisfactory investigations in the form of clinical trial research *are not possible* in psychoanalysis.

A radical possibility is to abandon empirical investigation in psychoanalysis. Unfortunately, this solution seems to have been widely, though quietly, adopted by much of the psychoanalytic community. Another approach is to note that statistical methods are tools for finding out what we want to know, not authorities about correctness. We can then look for appropriate tools for exploring psychoanalysis.

Fortunately, investigators in many fields have become increasingly interested in methods for exploring the evolution of complex phenomena over time. Powerful tools are emerging to study such situations. These tools should be particularly attractive to psychoanalysts because they extend and refine the traditional method of psychoanalytic research, the detailed study of the single case. Essentially single-case research methodology involves a variety of ways to make explicit the kinds of inferences that can be legitimately made from longitudinal observations of a single case. Both philosophical and data-analytic problems in the study of single cases are being addressed with increased sophistication (McCleary and Welsh, 1992). These methods are being applied in ways that come increasingly close to addressing core psychoanalytic concerns (see, e.g., Hillard, 1993; Jones et al., 1993; Spence et al., 1993; Silberschatz and Curtis, 1993). For example, extending Luborsky's application of the CCRT method of investigating the effects of CCRT-consistent interpretations on the progress of psychotherapy to psychoanalysis, we could empirically explore the validity such propositions as Strachey's (1934) assertion that analysis works through interpretation of the transference to the analyst. These methods hold great promise for extending the traditional methods of psychoanalysis into systematic investigation.

Conclusion

I began this discussion by reviewing how my own adolescent enthusiasm for ideas gradually grew, as I believe it ordinarily does in those engaged in intellectual pursuits, to an appreciation of the centrality of method in thinking about ideas. Psychoanalysts, partly out of wishes for certitude, partly because their interests often lie elsewhere, partly because of the intrinsic difficulty of the task, and partly because methodological discussions have so frequently been used to attack psychoanalysis, have been slow to invest their intellectual energies in finding ways to systematically explore psychoanalysis as therapy. When I look at psychoanalysis as a field rich in opportunity for systematic investigation with its many challenges to discover appropriate methods to study its central questions, I cannot help but feel the same enthusiasm that stimulated my initial adolescent interest in the field. Systematic investigation of the outcomes of psychoanalysis can be undertaken in several different spirits. The tools of research can be seen in various ways. Many of our implicit ideas of research have grave disadvantages. They tend to view research methodologies as in themselves authoritative rather than as tools for discovering things about psychoanalysis. They often represent images and explanations that are not consistent with what we appreciate and are interested in as clinicians. As a result, the relation between psychoanalysis and systematic research has been less than satisfactory.

The investigations summarized in this section show that traditional research methods can yield important findings about psychoanalysis. They also demonstrate the difficulties of systematic investigation. They suggest some limitations of these investigative methods. Several developments in research methods and ideas about the nature of knowledge can inform future research. It is important that these developments be made explicit because they are at variance with what we learned to think of as scientific. These newer viewpoints include the appreciation of meaning and motives as explanatory in the sciences of man, the nature of prediction and description of complex and nonlinear systems, and the methods of research appropriate for the study of complex idiosyncratic processes like psychoanalysis.

REFERENCES

BACHRACH, H., GALATZER-LEVY, R. M., SKOLNIKOFF, A. & WALDRON, S. (1991). On the efficacy of psychoanalysis. *J. Amer. Psychoanal. Assn.*, 39:871–916.

BACON, F. (1620). *Novum Organum*, ed. T. Fowler. Oxford, Eng.: Oxford Univ. Press, 1889.

BARBER, J. & CRITS-CHRISTOPH, P. (1993). Advances in measures of psychodynamic formulations. *J. Consult. Clin. Psychol.*, 61:574–585.

BLATT, S., WISEMAN, H., PRINCE-GIBSON, E. & GATT, C. (1991). Object representations and change in clinical functioning. *Psychother.*, 28:273–283.

BOLLAS, C. (1987). *The Shadow of the Object*. New York: Columbia Univ. Press.

BUCCI, W. (1985). Dual coding: a cognitive model for psychoanalytic research. *J. Amer. Psychoanal. Assn.*, 33:571–607.

CASTON, J. (1993). Can analysts agree? The problems of consensus and the psychoanalytic mannequin: I. A proposed solution. *J. Amer. Psychoanal. Assn.*, 41:493–511.

——— & MARTIN, E. (1993). Can analysts agree? The problems of consensus and the psychoanalytic mannequin. II. Empirical tests. *J. Amer. Psychoanal. Assn.*, 41:513–548.

COHEN, J. (1990). Things I have learned (so far). *Amer. Psychol.*, 45:1304–1312.

COOPER, S. (1993). Interpretive fallibility and the psychoanalytic dialogue. *J. Amer. Psychoanal. Assn.*, 41:95–126.

DAHL, H. (1988). Frames of mind. In *Psychoanalytic Process Research Strategies*, ed. H. Dahl, H. Kächele & H. Thomä. New York: Springer, pp. 51–66.
────── (1991). The key to understanding change: emotions as appetitive wishes and beliefs about their fulfillment. In *Emotion, Psychotherapy and Change*, ed. J. Safran & L. Greenberg. New York: Guilford Press.
DIJKSTERHUIS, E. (1950). *The Mechanization of the World Picture*. London: Oxford Univ. Press, 1961.
GALATZER-LEVY, R. M. & COHLER, B. (1990). The developmental psychology of the self: a new world view in psychoanalysis. *Annual Psychoanal.*, 18:1–43.
GEHA, R. (1993). Transferred fictions. *Psychoanal. Dialog.*, 3:209–243.
GILL, M. M. (1982). *Analysis of Transference. Vol 1: Theory and Technique. Psychol. Issues*, Monogr. 53. New York: Int. Univ. Press.
GRÜNBAUM, A. (1984). *The Foundations of Psychoanalysis: A Philosophical Critique*. Berkeley, CA: Univ. California Press.
────── (1990). "Meaning" connections and causal connections in the human sciences: the poverty of hermeneutic philosophy. *J. Amer. Psychoanal. Assn.*, 38:559–577.
HACKING, I. (1990). *The Taming of Chance*. Cambridge, Eng.: Cambridge Univ. Press.
HILEY, D., BOHMAN, J. & SHUSTERMAN, R., Eds. (1991). *The Interpretive Turn*. Ithaca, NY: Cornell Univ. Press.
HILLARD, R. (1993). Singe-case methodology in psychotherapy process and outcome research. *J. Clin. Consult. Psychol.*, 61:373–380.
HORWITZ, L. (1990). Psychotherapy as a trial for psychoanalysis. *Psychoanal. Inq.*, 10:43–66.
HSU, L. (1989). Random sampling, randomization, and equivalence of contrasted groups in psychotherapy outcome research. *J. Consult. Clin. Psychol.*, 57:131–137.
JONES, E., GHANNAM, J., NIGG, J. & DYER, F. (1993). A paradigm for single-case research: the time series study of a long-term psychotherapy for depression. *J. Clin. Consult. Psychol.*, 61:381–394.
JUNGNICHKEL, C. & MCCORMMACH, R. (1986). *Intellectual Mastery of Nature: Theoretical Physics from Ohm to Einstein*. Chicago: Univ. Chicago Press.
KAUFFMAN, S. (1993). *The Origins of Order: Self-organization and Selection in Evolution*. New York: Oxford Univ. Press.
KLEIN, G. S. (1976). *Psychoanalytic Theory: An Exploration of Essentials*. New York: Int. Univ. Press.
KLUMPNER, G. & FRANK, A. (1991). On methods of reporting clinical material. *J. Amer. Psychoanal. Assn.*, 39:537–551.
KOHUT, H. (1971). *The Analysis of the Self*. New York: Int. Univ. Press.
LATOUR, B. & WOOLGAR, S. (1986). *Laboratory Life: The Construction of Scientific Facts*. Princeton, NJ: Princeton Univ. Press.
LEWIS, C. (1964). *The Discarded Image: An Introduction to Medieval and Renaissance Literature*. Cambridge, Eng.: Cambridge Univ. Press.
LUBORSKY, L. (1990). The convergence of Freud's observations about transference in the CCRT evidence. In *Understanding Transference: The Core Conflictual Relationship Theme Method*, ed. L. Luborsky & P. Crits-Christoph. New York: Basic Books, pp. 251–266.
────── & CRITS-CRISTOPH, P. (1990). *Understanding Transference: The Core Conflictual Relationship Theme Method*. New York: Basic Books.

McCleary, R. & Welsh, N. (1992). Philosophical and statistical foundation of time-series experiments. In *Single-Case Research Design and Analysis: New Directions of Psychology and Education*, ed. T. Kratochwill & J. Levin. Hillsdale, NJ: Erlbaum.

McCormmach, R. (1982). *Night Thoughts of a Classical Physicist.* Cambridge, MA: Harvard Univ. Press.

Merton, R., Sills, D. & Stigler, S. (1984). The Kelvin dictum and social science: an excursion into the history of an idea. *J. Hist. Behav. Sci.*, 20:319–331.

Miller, N., Luborsky, L., & Barber, J., Eds. (1993). *Psychodynamic Treatment Research: A Handbook for Clinical Practice.* New York: Basic Books.

Platt, J. (1964). Strong inference. *Science*, 146:347–353.

Ricoeur, P. (1970). *Freud and Philosophy.* New Haven, CT: Yale Univ. Press.

——— (1977). The question of proof in Freud's psychoanalytic writings. *J. Amer. Psychoanal. Assn.*, 25:835–872.

Rorty, R. (1989). *Contingency, Irony and Solidarity.* Cambridge, Eng.: Cambridge Univ. Press.

Roth, P. (1991). Interpretation as explanation. In *The Interpretive Turn*, ed. D. Hiley, J. Bohman & R. Schusterman. Ithaca, NY: Cornell Univ. Press, pp. 179–196.

Rouse, J. (1991). Interpretation in natural and human science. In *The Interpretive Turn*, ed. D. Hiley, J. Bohman & R. Schusterman. Ithaca, NY: Cornell Univ. Press, pp. 42–56.

Salsburg, D. (1985). The religion of statistics as practiced in medical journals. *Amer. Statistician*, 39:220–223.

Silberschatz, G. & Curtis, J. (1993). Measuring the therapist's impact on the patient's therapeutic progress. *J. Clin. Consult. Psychol.*, 61:403–411.

Spence, D., Dahl, H. & Jones, E. (1993). Impact of interpretation on associative freedom. *J. Clin. Consult. Psychol.*, 61:395–402.

Spezzano, C. (1993). A relational model of inquiry and truth: the place of psychoanalysis in human conversation. *Psychoanal. Dialog.*, 3:177–208.

Spruiell, V. (1993). Deterministic chaos and the sciences of complexity: psychoanalysis in the midst of a general scientific revolution. *J. Amer. Psychoanal. Assn.*, 41:3–44.

Stewart, I. (1989). *Does God Play Dice.* London: Blackwell.

Strachey, J. (1934). The nature of the therapeutic action of psychoanalysis. *Int. J. Psychoanal.*, 15:127–159.

Sulloway, F. (1991). Reassessing Freud's case histories: the social construction of psychoanalysis. *Isis*, 82:245–275.

Taylor, C. (1971). Interpretation and the sciences of man. In *Philosophy and the Human Sciences. Philosophical Papers, 2.* Cambridge, Eng.: Cambridge Univ. Press, pp. 15–57.

Thom, R. (1975). *Structural Stability and Morphogenesis: An Outline of a General Theory of Models.* Reading, PA: Benjamin.

Waelder, R. (1963). Psychic determinism and the possibility of predictions. In *Psychoanalysis: Observation, Theory, Application*, ed. S. A. Guttman. New York: Int. Univ. Press, 1976, pp. 283–307.

EPILOGUE: A BEGINNING—RESEARCH APPROACHES AND EXPANDING HORIZONS FOR PSYCHOANALYSIS

Robert N. Emde, M.D.

SCIENTISTS TEND TO BE HARSH critics of their endeavors. They point to limitations in method and inference and they often voice frustrations about the slow rate of knowledge acquisition and the acceptance of new discovery by others. The voices of the clinician investigators of this volume are no exception. Empirical approaches for psychoanalysis are still at an early state of development. And many criticisms are voiced, not only about the limitations of research findings, but about the limitations stemming from a psychoanalytic culture that has not heretofore encouraged scientific thinking or work. There are signs, however, that the culture of our field may be changing. Moreover, the research programs summarized in this volume represent substantial accomplishments.

This epilogue allows an opportunity to draw some general conclusions from these programs. The conclusions cut across the three domains of research: psychoanalytic process, development, and outcome studies. The conclusions also serve to connect psychoanalysis with a wider world of contemporary scientific inquiry. I shall address each general conclusion and its linkages separately, and then turn to a perspective on nondeterministic science and psychoanalysis.

Conclusion 1. Psychoanalysis is as much an interpersonal psychology as it is an intrapsychic one.

Professor of Psychiatry, University of Colorado Health Sciences Center, School of Medicine, Denver, Colorado.

Clinical theory in psychoanalysis has centered on the activation and resolution of the transference neurosis within the context of the analyst-analysand relationship. While many have been reluctant to give emphasis to the interpersonal aspects of psychoanalytic theory, recent clinical discussions have emphasized transference-countertransference relations. The conclusion that psychoanalysis is as much an interpersonal psychology as it is an intrapsychic one pervades the results of all three domains of empirical programs summarized in this volume.

Our first compelling line of evidence for this conclusion comes from outcome studies, and in particular the Boston outcome study summarized by Kantrowitz, where a major significant factor in outcome was determined by the match between personal characteristics of the analyst and patient. In the words of Kantrowitz, "the most striking finding to emerge from the Boston study was the impact of the interface of personal characteristics of the analyst and the patient on the outcome of the analytic process. . . . It is not just the personal characteristics of the patient and the analyst that are important, but the match between them." The author goes on to take a critical view of psychoanalysts for too long viewing "a two-person enterprise as if it were dependent on only one of the members," and argues for expanded research on the relation of the patient-analyst match to the outcome of psychoanalysis. (The findings about match, by the way, are similar to those reported earlier in a controlled study of brief psychodynamic and other therapy by Luborsky and his colleagues, 1985.)

All three outcome studies in this volume comment on the low predictability of outcome from initial assessments of analyzability. They also point to the surprising extent to which supportive techniques (i.e., those that are noninsight and interactively based) contribute to therapeutic change. As Wallerstein writes, summarizing the results of the Menninger psychotherapy research project, "An almost overriding finding was the repeated demonstration that a substantial range of changes was brought about via the more supportive therapeutic modes, cutting across the gamut of declared supportive *and* expressive therapies, and these changes were [often] indistinguishable from the changes brought about by typically expressive-analytic means." The Boston study echoes the findings that therapeutic benefit from psychoanalytic treatment may result from supportive techniques. Their findings, along with the findings from the Columbia records project summarized by Bachrach, lead to the conclusion that there are many routes to improvement. Moreover, there is no tight linkage of outcome to resolution of a transference neurosis. The implications of these findings seem straightforward: increased attention needs to be paid to the study of the interpersonal aspects of psychoanalytic psychology.

As startling as this first general conclusion may seem from a traditional perspective, it is not so surprising from another angle. The idea of studying and expanding our psychology in the interpersonal sphere is quite consistent with some other recent trends in psychoanalysis. These include the study of "intersubjectivity" in developmental work (e.g., Hobson) as well as in self psychology approaches, the extensive literature concerning object relations, the literature on countertransference, and some discussions on narrative textual approaches to psychoanalysis—all of which focus our attention on interpersonal actions as well as on intrapsychic representations.

Our second line of evidence for the above general conclusion stems from both psychoanalytic process studies and developmental studies. Determining the unit of observation is a crucial strategy in research, for both practical and theoretical reasons. One must find a unit that different observers can agree upon reliably; it must be pervasive, and it must be meaningful theoretically, since all else will build upon it. Both process and developmental domains of research reviewed in this volume seem to agree on this strategic decision. *Relationship units are fundamental and heuristic psychoanalytic units.* The studies of psychoanalytic process, whether of Core Conflictual Relationship Themes (Luborsky), Role Relationship Model Configurations

(Horowitz), Fundamental Repetitive and Maladaptive Emotion Structures (Dahl and Teller) or any of a host of other central relationship pattern measures—nicely summarized for us in the essay by Luborsky and Luborsky—all choose a central unit for investigation and knowledge-building that is a relationship unit. More significantly, these units are both represented (i.e., intrapsychically) and observed over time in interactions with the therapist (i.e., interpersonally). Jones also makes explicit use of such a unit in tracing changing representations as well as interpersonal interactions over the course of treatment by using a Q-sort methodology. The Ulm research program, summarized by Kächele and Thomä, also makes explicit use of repetitive relationship patterns and offers opportunities to contrast several different measurement schemes of such units.

Relationship units are also found fundamental in psychoanalytically oriented developmental studies. This is not surprising since, from much earlier times, such studies have involved observations of early parent-child interactions. Thus, Heinicke, Hobson, and Osofsky, in each of their research programs, focus on the caregiver-child relationship, as represented in each of the partners—sometimes referred to in terms of "internal working models," a construct introduced by John Bowlby—and as directly observed in behavioral interactions. Hobson, moreover, studies the "intersubjective domain" with respect to both intrapsychic and interpersonal manifestations that occur in development and psychopathology. And Osofsky calls for a "dynamic interactional model" to guide her studies of intergenerational repetitions of maladaptive patterns of behavior with respect to teenage pregnancy and parenting.

Perhaps the most dramatic instantiation of relationship units as fundamental and of their being equally important at the interpersonal and intrapsychic levels, comes from the series of investigations reporting crossgenerational patterns of attachment. Main summarizes how Bowlby's evolutionary theory of attachment, based in part on object-relations theory, became translated into research terms and was operationalized into the

Ainsworth "Strange Situation" paradigm. The latter is a laboratory playroom situation for assessing one-year-olds in observed interactions with their mothers (or other caregivers). Inferences about secure and insecure attachment categories are based on such interpersonal interactions, and a generation of studies is summarized. The most recent phase of attachment research, referred to as the "move to representation," includes the Adult Attachment Interview, by Main. Relations have been found, and replicated across different settings and investigators, that link represented caregiving relationships in parents to observed interpersonal behaviors in infants who interact with parents at a later time. Such crossgenerational findings, again using an attachment relationship unit, are taken even further by Fonagy and colleagues. Using the Adult Attachment Interview, based on psychodynamic principles and administered separately to mothers and fathers *prior to birth*, the Fonagy team finds independent predictive relations between the quality of attachment representations measured antenatally and the postnatal classifications of attachment security/insecurity. Most striking is that these relations hold for one-year-old infants interacting in the Strange Situation with their respective parents. In other words, the relationship unit is organized specific to a given caregiving relationship and has a relative degree of independence, even as early as at one year of age. The current work of the Fonagy group relates the intrapsychic and interpersonal in still another way. Assessments of reflective self function in parents (intrapsychic level) are found to be related to later security of attachment as manifest in the behavior of infants with their parents (interpersonal level). Fonagy is now following these infants to preschool age to see if predictive longitudinal relations will be found in children's representations as expressed through narratives (i.e., at the intrapsychic level; personal communication). These followup studies reveal yet another virtue of the empirical approach—one can test and retest the relations between earlier findings as recorded in later states if there is a longitudinal followup.

Conclusion 2. There is a wider zone of nonconscious mental activity than we have been used to thinking about.

This general conclusion may be less apparent to the reader of this volume than the first one mentioned above. Still, I believe it is an important conclusion, and it is relevant both for the intrapsychic and interpersonal aspects of psychoanalytic theory.

The wider zone of nonconscious mental activity supplements what psychoanalysis has heretofore conceptualized as the dynamic unconscious and the preconscious modes of functioning. There is a major amount of nonconscious mental activity that is neither preconscious (i.e., readily accessible to consciousness using recent or working memory) nor defensively excluded (i.e., involving repressed memories or isolated affects). Such mental activity includes schematic and scripted functioning (Horowitz), the nonconscious operation of goals and plans (Weiss) and, more generally, a variety of organized automatically functioning procedures and rules for guiding behavior in particular contexts. Procedural knowledge has been defined as that kind of information underlying a skill that need not be represented in consciousness in order for one to manifest the skill (Cohen and Squire, 1980). Procedural mental activity, or procedural knowledge, can be illustrated by our acquisition and use of grammatical rules in our primary language, even though we may not be able to represent or "declare" such rules. A similar illustration concerns our acquisition and use of complex rules concerning social interactions, including rules governing reciprocity and automatically functioning aspects of moral behavior (for a review of this topic see Clyman, 1991, and Emde et al., 1991). Still another illustration comes from our psychoanalytic work: a skilled clinician may make an intervention based on years of cumulative experience even though the decision about it may occur outside of awareness. Recent research in the cognitive neurosciences has not only shown the extent of such nonconscious mental activity, but has also modeled it through a form of artificial intelligence known as "parallel distributive processing." The modeling has shown us that rules need not be represented explicitly in order to govern behavior, but can emerge from the interaction of units. (For reviews of procedural mental activity and related topics, see Kihlstrom, 1987.)

The above wider zone of nonconscious mental activity can be inferred from the theory of John Bowlby and finds expression in the work of Main and Fonagy. One learns from the behavior of smoothly operating procedures (especially in secure attachment) as well as from their interruptions (which may be occasioned by dynamically represented intrapsychic configurations). Like the rules of grammar, most of the rules governing discourse in the adult attachment interview operate silently and are presumably governed by procedural activity.

I believe an interpersonal level of procedural nonconscious mental activity is implied by the contributions of the volume. Reiss (1989) points out that there are "practicing modes" of behavior that are manifest interpersonally, such as in groups or families during times of ritual. Not only will individuals in the family be unaware of important aspects of what is transmitted across generations in family rituals, for example, but the holistic aspects of such activity and knowledge will not be contained or represented within any one of the individuals. The configuration of mental activity and knowledge takes place only during such rituals when the individuals come together in a particular circumstance. Cultural anthropologists have come to emphasize that much of what is valued and considered important by a culture can only be known by a field worker if he or she becomes immersed in the everyday practices of a people over a period of time. In other words, much of what is important is implicit, nonconscious, and can only be known interpersonally through actions and interactions. A new interdiscipline known as "cultural psychology" (Shweder, 1991) conceptualizes domains of "interintentionality" and various forms of shared meaning at both intraindividual and interpersonal levels.

This is in many ways a new world for psychoanalysts, who even after Heinz Hartmann (1939) are used to thinking of nonconscious mental activity, chiefly, and often exclusively, in traditional psychodynamic terms. In many ways, it is even a more dramatic new world for behavioral scientists in general. Many questions are raised, e.g.: To what extent are aspects of procedural automatic mental activity influential in the unique dyadic arrangements of psychoanalysis and psychotherapy? To what extent are interpersonal practices and "rituals" influential? Do such influences contribute in a substantial way to determining the "match" between personality styles and thus contribute to outcomes in psychoanalysis? This is a vast new territory for thinking and research.

Conclusion 3. There are useful empirical approaches for understanding individuality, psychopathology, and the search for meaning.

I would hope that readers of this volume would agree with this straightforward conclusion. There are aspects of the conclusion, however, that seem worthy of reflection. Psychoanalysis is in a privileged position. Unlike the rest of psychology which typically investigates individuality in terms of individual differences (i.e., searching for consistent differences on the average among a large group of individuals—for a discussion see Emde, in press), psychoanalysis investigates individuality through intensive, intimate exchanges with an individual patient over a long period of time. And in carrying out such investigation, psychoanalysts deal with a polarity. On the one hand, we are dealing with *uniqueness*, with "singularities" in human experiences, with understanding the coursing through a life that is not only existentially unique but is in some ways ineffable and unknowable by another, even when words are supplemented by transference phenomena and nonverbal expressions. On the other hand, we are dealing with what is *commonly human*, and what we understand empathically by virtue of our humanity and value as such. In our clinical work, we continually readjust our perspectives in order to formulate our interpretations and guide our actions; to do this we need multiple views at any given time and across time. We then share what seems useful with our patients and with each other.

The empirical work of the volume illustrates similar principles to the clinical way of working. In investigating individuality, and in coming to grips with the above polarity, multiple contexts of observation must be used, whether dealing with transcripts, chart data, psychological assessments, or followup interviews. Not only is it important to apply methods and hypotheses iteratively within single cases, but they must be applied repeatedly across intensively studied cases.[1] It is also important that empirical work be done in different cultural contexts, since individuality—what is shared empathically as part of our humanity and what is valued individually—differs in vital ways as part of one's culture.

The research of our contributors illustrates that the investigation of individuality and psychopathology can make productive use of narrative and coconstructed data. Thus, the work of Fonagy and of Main, using the adult attachment interview, shows that the coherence or incoherence of the parental narrative can not only be understood on its own terms, but has predictive consequences for observed security of attachment of infants interacting with those parents. Hence the dichotomy set up by some—of hermeneutic interpretation of narratives *versus* science—may be rejected as artificial. Main finds a basis for this in Freud's 1914 essay on "Remembering, Repeating, and Working-through," in which it is pointed out that what is forgotten and repressed is expressed in action. Her words use Freud to frame the scientific findings that link narratives to other behaviors of importance: " . . . by action, we refer both

---

[1] As Spence points out, the transcript of one treatment, that of Mrs. C., has been studied by many investigators; this has the advantages of applying the contexts of many different methods to the transcript; but such methods now need to be applied to other cases.

to the violations of coherence and collaboration found in discourse during the adult attachment interview, and also behavior exhibited toward the infant."

That there are useful empirical approaches for psychoanalysis does not mean that there are not many methodological issues that concern us. There are. Programmatic research is difficult, often tedious, and even more often laden with the researcher's painful awareness of the limitations of one's methods and findings. For reasons of space, the editors did not encourage the researcher authors of the volume to discuss limitations in their work, nor did we encourage their strongly critical comments about the state of research in psychoanalysis compared to that in other disciplines. Our commentators, however, take up such matters. I would like to highlight three methodological issues in this epilogue that will lead up to its own conclusion. The first concerns the issue of replicability. All commentators touch on this issue. Although it is true in a sense that one cannot step in the same river twice, as Heraclitus put it, the accumulation of knowledge in science requires that practitioners seek replication. A discovery of a particular pattern of behavior or of a proposed general relation between phenomena needs to be seen in more than one context on different occasions. Spence discusses the need for replicability of findings from transcripts by research groups other than those who have invested in research with FRAMES, CCRTs, RRMCs, or the process methods described by Weiss, Jones, Caston, or Kächele and Thomä. This brings up a related issue that is not often discussed among researchers, i.e., the "exportability" of our research methods. Because we wish to encompass complex patterns of behavior in our search for meaning, our methods are frequently expert-based, requiring intensive training and therefore difficult to export. When new groups of raters need to undergo intensive training by the original designers of the observation system, the likelihood of "hidden assumptions" and biases, reflecting the operations of the procedural nonconscious, is strong. We all have assumptions and biases in our work; the problem in replication is that these are unknown and can lead to false conclusions. The goal for the researcher is to simplify and specify our expert-based systems of observation; the challenge is enormous and this issue seems worthy of more attention. The technique of having independent judges discern stereotypical patterns or "mannequins" from case material, based on selected propositions, as devised by Caston, is a promising approach to such problems in that its goal is to find the extent to which there can be agreement not based on a prior interpretive set of observers contributing to the case record.

Another major issue for empirical approaches to psychoanalysis concerns single-case versus multiple-case methods. This issue is addressed directly by Jones in his discussion advancing the single-case method and the Q-sort. How can we infer beyond the single case? Correspondingly, how can we make generalizations across cases when so much of what we investigate is unique. Uniqueness stems not only from the individuality of conflicts and adaptations in our patients, but also from the coconstructive circumstances of each analytic relationship. The issue is no less challenging than that of replicability (and in fact is related to it). In addition to the necessity of repeating our studies and observations in multiple contexts (both within the psychoanalytic situation, and outside of it) there is a strong necessity to expand our methods applicable to single cases. We have barely approached this strategic scientific issue.

A related concern is the question of what is "scientific" for psychoanalysis. There are many views on this philosophical topic, but I believe that the contributors to this compendium indicate it is best not to take an extreme position. We can appreciate that there are many contexts of observation and that multiple methods are needed to address any problem. Every method has its shortcomings in addition to its advantages; hence each method gives a partial and distorted view of phenomena. Patterns of meaning in narrative, for example, can be shown to have influences in other domains of an individual's functioning. Thus, the investigation of narratives is a legitimate area for science. But such findings need to be appreciated according to their contextual limitations and what we mean by "influences." It is also worth remembering that in thinking about what is "scientific" for psychoanalysis, we are no longer guided by a *Zeitgeist* that contains expectation of determinism and strict predictability, as was the case in the days of Freud. This leads us to our ending topic.

Postmodern Nondeterministic Science and Psychoanalysis

"Postmodern" is a phrase that has received currency as a way of emphasizing the philosophical view of today's scientific approaches according to which we are no longer able to accept a faith in determinism. This is so for at least three reasons. First, the Heisenberg principle has made us appreciate that the observer, or the technique of observation, always influences what is observed. This brings added emphasis to themes we have discussed above, such as the need for cultural pluralism being accounted for in multiple contexts of observation. It also gives emphasis to an additional topic we have not discussed, namely, the importance of understanding and being open about the values that necessarily enter into our work—a recognition that is just as true in the basic behavioral sciences (see Emde, in press, for developmental sciences, and Sperry, 1993, for cognitive neurosciences) as it is for the clinical sciences such as psychoanalysis.

A second reason for an attitude for nondeterminism in today's science has to do with our appreciation of the influence of random events. It stands to reason that we cannot predict (or replicate) the influence of random events on an individual's life.

A third reason for nondeterminism stems from our appreciation of creativity in development. Modern biology has been characterized as the biology of organized complexity, and modern developmental biology is that of increasingly organized complexity. Increasingly organized complexity across development brings with it transformations and new modes of operation. And creativity in development, with a formation of new structures and new modes, occurs as a result of the coaction of individual initiative and environmental influence (and opportunity).

Because of the above factors, the best that scientists can say is that there is "probabilistic determinism" that can be described under very limited circumstances of what we refer to as "controlled observation," i.e., those observational circumstances that are artificially constrained. We should emphasize that the "postmodern" attitude is not pessimistic. Far from it, it brings a new respect for personal initiative and responsibility and it brings more openness about what is possible. Practically speaking, the programmatic psychoanalytic researchers herein represented describe the patterns of phenomena they see within the context of their particular method's place and time. They realize they can never "predict" with any certainty or "account for all the variance" in their observations.

A final point concerns all psychoanalytic clinicians who, like the empiricists of this volume, are pragmatists. Clinicians who are developmentally oriented cannot afford to take extreme philosophical positions, or be much preoccupied with them. Psychoanalysts are in the business of helping particular people in particular circumstances, not just for the purposes of discourse, but for the purposes of "getting on with their lives." It is hoped that the work summarized in this volume opens our eyes to new ways of thinking, new directions, and knowledge that may be applied.

REFERENCES

CLYMAN, R. B. (1991). The procedural organization of emotions: a contribution from cognitive science to the psychoanalytic theory of therapeutic action. *J. Amer. Psychoanal. Assn.*, 39(Suppl.):349–382.

COHEN, N. J. & SQUIRE, L. R. (1980). Preserved learning and retention of pattern-analyzing skill in amnesia: dissociation of knowing how and knowing that. *Science*, 221:207–210.

EMDE, R. N. (in press). Individuality, context, and the search for meaning. *Child Devel.*
——— BIRINGEN, Z., CLYMAN, R. B. & OPPENHEIM, D. (1991). The moral self in infancy: affective core and procedural knowledge. *Devel. Rev.*, 11:251–270.
FREUD, S. (1914). Remembering, repeating and working-through. *S. E.*, 12.
HARTMANN, H. (1939). *Ego Psychology and the Problem of Adaptation.* New York: Int. Univ. Press, 1958.
KIHLSTROM, J. F. (1987). The cognitive unconscious. *Science*, 237:1445–1452.
LUBORSKY, L.; MCLELLAN, A. T.; WOODY, G. E.; O'BRIEN, C. P. & AUERBACH, A. (1985). Therapist success and its determinants. *Arch. Gen. Psychiat.*, 42:602–611.
REISS, D. (1989). The represented and practicing family: contrasting visions of family continuity. In *Relationship Disturbances in Early Childhood: A Developmental Approach*, ed. A. J. Sameroff & R. N. Emde. New York: Basic Books, pp. 191–220.
SHWEDER, R. A. (1991). *Thinking Through Cultures: Expeditions in Cultural Psychology.* Cambridge, MA: Harvard Univ. Press.
SPERRY, R. W. (1993). The impact and promise of the cognitive revolution. *Amer. Psychol.*, 48:878–885.

NAME INDEX

Abend, S., 294
Adelson, E., 173, 200–201, 247
Ainsworth, M. D. S., 188, 195, 209–210, 214, 215–216, 218, 219, 220, 224, 231–232, 246–247, 265, 365
Alavarez, W., 72
Albani, C., 123
Anchin, J. C., 336
Andrews, G., 182
Appelbaum, A., 372, 379
Appelbaum, H., 269
Appelbaum, S. A., 316, 319
Arlow, J. A., 63, 143
Auerbach, A., 378, 412
Augusto, F., 75, 337
Azim, H. F. A., 85

Bachrach, H. M., 93, 282, 285, 288–289, 293, 315, 316, 322, 370–371, 372, 384–385, 388, 397, 401, 405, 413
Bacon, F., 399–400
Bakersman-Kranenburg, M. J., 228–229, 248
Bales, R. F., 353
Ballard, A., 281n
Barber, J., 46n, 336, 398
Barnett, D., 222
Baron-Cohen, S., 175, 253
Beck, A., 183
Beckwith, L., 364
Beeghley-Smith, M., 252–253
Beermann, S., 122
Bell, S. M., 218, 219
Benjamin, L. B., 79
Benjamin, L. S., 336, 387
Benoit, D., 230
Berlin, L., 220
Berry, J., 21, 34, 39, 123
Bick, E., 254
Bickerton, D., 252

Binder, J., 46n, 336, 339
Bion, W. R., 169, 179, 185, 249, 253, 257
Bird, B., 79
Biringen, Z., 249, 416
Blatt, S., 397
Blehar, M. C., 188, 195, 210, 214, 218, 219, 220, 246–247, 365
Blight, J. G., 237, 240
Block, J., 95, 251–252
Bohman, J., 403
Bollas, C., 400
Bond, M., 85–86, 87, 336
Bowlby, J., 124, 180, 184, 187–188, 197, 203–204, 209–210, 212–215, 219, 231, 235, 240, 246, 247, 264–265, 355–356, 365–366, 374, 375, 414–415, 417
Bradley, S., 179
Bradlow, P., 280, 281n, 282
Braithwaite, R. L., 256
Braunwald, K., 222
Brazelton, 268, 273
Brenner, C., 63
Bretherton, I., 204, 211, 246, 249, 252–253, 365
Breuer, J., 72, 329
Brierly, L. M., 173
Brim, G., 26
Broitman, J., 18, 19, 20, 24
Broussard, E., 268–269
Brown, L., 180, 182
Brown, R., 173–174
Brumer, S., 13–14, 15–16
Bryer, J., 179
Bucci, W., 36, 41–42, 69, 71, 72, 73, 74, 85, 398
Buchsbaum, H., 342
Bugas, J. S., 20
Burlingham, D., 246, 355
Burstein, E. D., 372
Bush, M., 17–18, 136

Calamari, G., 186
Campos, J., 172, 186
Carlson, E. A., 217, 230
Carlson, R., 336
Carlson, V., 222
Caspar, F., 336
Cassidy, J., 211, 216, 217, 220, 223, 224
Caston, J., 16–17, 18, 56, 59, 60, 62, 75, 136, 138–139, 140, 149, 157, 159, 161–162, 336, 339, 403, 420–421
Chassan, J. B., 53, 105, 294
Chirico, B. M., 336
Churchill, D. W., 168
Cicchetti, D. V., 171, 187, 222, 246
Cierpka, M., 344
Clippinger, J., 122
Clyman, R. B., 214, 416
Cohen, D. J., 187
Cohen, J., 286n, 404
Cohen, M., 120, 281n
Cohen, N. J., 416
Cohler, B., 402
Colby, K. M., 110
Compton, A., 111
Cooper, A. M., 280, 281, 341, 382, 386, 387
Cooper, S., 85–86, 87, 403
Cooper, S. H., 75, 337
Corley, R., 186
Coyne, L., 372
Crits-Christoph, P., 41, 79, 294, 331, 336, 341, 342, 343–344, 378, 398
Crowell, J. A., 185, 229
Cumming, J. D., 91, 97
Curtis, D., 69, 71, 72, 73, 74, 85
Curtis, H. C., 330
Curtis, J., 18, 19, 20, 46n, 406
Curtis, J. T., 102, 339

Dahl, H., 12, 31, 32, 33–40, 43, 46n, 91, 100, 101, 102, 112, 120n, 123, 131, 133, 135–136, 137, 138, 140, 147–148, 154–155, 155–156, 161, 336, 340, 398, 406, 414
Dahlbender, R., 123, 344
Daniels, G., 279
Danzger, B., 193
Davies, J., 37
Davilla, L., 18, 19
de Rivera, J., 33, 161
DeFries, J., 186
Demorest, A., 79
Demos, V., 273
Dengler, D., 123, 342
Dennett, D. C., 250
DeWitt, K. N., 69, 82, 84, 302, 307n, 308, 331
Diguer, L., 342
Dijksterhuis, E., 402
Diskin, S. D., 361, 363
Dozier, M., 226
Dreher, A. U., 111
Drews, S., 111
Dunn, L. M., 177
Dyer, F., 406
Dyer, J. F., 91, 99, 101, 104

Eagle, M. N., 214, 237
Easser, R., 280, 281, 382
Eberhart-Wright, A., 193, 194, 197, 198, 199, 202, 203
Eckert, R., 123
Edelson, M., 99, 101
Edelstein, S., 21, 24
Eells, T., 75, 81
Egeland, B., 217
Ehlers, W., 111
Eichberg, C. G., 224
Eissler, K. R., 47
Eldred, S., 289–291
Elinson, J., 280, 281, 282
Emde, R. N., 172, 186, 194, 195, 196–197, 199–200, 246, 263, 342, 416, 418, 422
Endicott, N. A., 115, 119
Erikson, E. H., 355
Erle, J. B., 289–291, 316, 322

Ewert, M., 69, 71, 72, 73, 74, 75, 77, 80, 81, 85
Ewing, J. A., 53

Faude, J., 342
Federman, E. J., 336
Feinman, S., 172
Feldman, S. S., 185
Ferenczi, S., 171
Field, T., 249, 267, 273
Fink, G., 115, 119
Fodor, J. A., 51
Fonagy, P., 101, 102, 163, 185, 198, 199, 203, 230, 248, 250, 251, 252, 255, 264–265, 266–268, 269, 274, 415, 417, 419
Fosshage, J., 264, 267, 273–274
Fraiberg, S., 173, 197–198, 200–201, 247
Frank, A., 395
Fremmer-Bombik, E., 216, 223
Fretter, P., 18, 19, 20, 24, 102
Freud, A., 246, 265, 314, 355, 359
Freud, S., 1, 3, 7–8, 10–11, 11–12n, 33, 72, 113, 146, 153–154, 231, 234–236, 247, 250n, 292, 295, 300, 301–302, 316–318, 329, 341–344, 347, 356, 382, 402, 403, 419–420, 422
Fridhandler, B., 69, 71, 72, 73, 74, 78, 80, 81, 85–87
Fried, D., 342
Friedman, S. H., 79
Friedrich, F. J., 79
Frith, U., 253
Fulker, D. W., 186
Fürstenau, P., 114

Galatzer-Levy, R. M., 93, 293, 315, 402, 405
Galenson, E., 198
Gaskill, H. S., 318
Gassner, S., 13–14, 15–16, 17–18, 136
Gatt, C., 397
Gedo, J. E., 36, 83–84

Geha, R., 403
George, C., 180, 188, 211, 218, 223, 224, 247–248
Gergen, K. J., 113
Ghannam, J. H., 72, 75, 77, 81, 91, 99, 101, 104, 406
Gianino, A., 195, 202
Gill, M. M., 41, 45, 113, 115, 119, 300, 325, 336, 339, 356, 398
Giovacchini, P. L., 253
Glymour, C., 63–64
Golby, B., 229
Goldberg, A., 83–84
Goldberg, D., 291, 316, 322
Goldman, G., 279
Goldman, R., 60, 62
Goldstein, K., 173
Goldwyn, G., 201
Goldwyn, R., 181, 185, 224, 248
Gordon, E. W., 256
Gottman, J. M., 102
Goudreau, D., 187
Gould, J., 173
Grawe, K., 336
Grebel, J., 24
Greenberg, R. P., 120
Greenman, D., 92, 315, 318, 319
Greenson, R., 144
Greenspan, S. I., 195
Grice, H. P., 224, 235
Grossmann, K., 216, 217, 219, 223
Grossmann, K. E., 217, 219, 220, 222, 235
Grünbaum, A., 93, 154, 237, 399
Grünzig, H., 101, 117, 120–121
Gunderson, J. G., 251
Guthrie, O., 361, 363
Guttman, S. A., 316, 317

Hacking, I., 404
Hall, R., 252
Hall, S. A., 95
Hamlyn, D. W., 175
Hanly, C., 111
Hann, D. M., 193, 194, 197, 199, 202

Harrison, S. I., 300
Hartley, D., 69, 71–75, 77, 79, 81, 85, 307n
Hartley, D. E., 302, 308
Hartmann, H., 418
Heinicke, C. M., 353–356, 358, 360, 361, 363, 364, 374–376, 389, 414
Henderson, A., 182
Henry, W., 45
Herman, J. L., 179, 251
Hermelin, B., 168
Hertzig, M. E., 186
Hesse, E., 185, 222, 224, 225, 227, 228, 235n
Higgitt, A. C., 199, 250, 251, 252
Hiley, D., 403
Hilliard, R., 100, 406
Hinde, R. A., 232
Hobson, R. P., 169, 172–180, 253, 262–267, 269, 274, 413, 414
Hoffer, W., 318
Hoffman, I. Z., 45, 113, 336, 339
Hohage, R., 120
Holt, R. R., 41, 239, 240, 300, 331
Hölzer, M., 34, 37–39, 111, 121–123
Home, H. J., 300
Hook, S., 154
Hornstein, G. A., 92
Horowitz, L. M., 46n, 316, 337, 372, 397
Horowitz, M. J., 12, 41, 43, 45, 46n, 69–87, 91, 97, 139, 147, 149, 155–156, 159–160, 331, 336, 339, 413–414, 416
Houben, A., 109–110
Hsu, L., 404
Hubbs-Tait, L., 198, 202, 203

Isaacs, S., 110

Jacobs, T., 325
Jacobson, E., 75
Jacobson, S., 281n
James, W., 250n
Jones, E. E., 37, 91, 92, 95, 97–102, 104, 133, 136–138, 149, 151, 156, 160–161, 171, 406, 420, 421
Jordan, D., 69, 71, 72, 73, 74, 81, 85
Joseph, E. D., 250n
Joyce, A. S., 85
Jungnichkel, C., 394

Kächele, H., 37, 42, 43, 110–111, 113–118, 120–124, 138, 154–155, 158, 340, 344, 414, 420
Kagan, J., 186, 249
Kalehzan, B., 337
Kaltreider, N., 69, 71, 73, 331
Kanner, L., 168, 175, 262
Kant, I., 57
Kantrowitz, J. L., 92, 120, 289–291, 315–321, 371–374, 384–385, 387–388, 397, 405, 412
Kaplan, B., 170
Kaplan, N., 180, 188, 211, 217, 218, 220, 223, 224, 247–248
Karush, A., 280, 281, 382
Katz, A. L., 92, 315–321
Kauffman, S., 402
Kaufman, J., 251
Kazdin, A. E., 100, 294
Keats, J., 144
Keeler, W. R., 173
Kelly, T., 20
Kerig, P. K., 92
Kernberg, O. F., 75, 169, 179, 185, 197, 199, 254, 291, 372, 373, 377, 379
Kiesler, D. J., 336, 337
Kihlstrom, J. F., 214, 417
Klein, G. S., 41, 402
Klein, M., 171, 174, 355
Klinnert, M. D., 172
Klumpner, G., 395
Knapp, P. H., 120, 317
Kobak, R. R., 226
Koch, D., 186
Koenigsberg, H. W., 379
Kohut, H., 118, 179, 185, 197, 199, 200, 204, 272, 400
König, H., 124

Kraemer, G., 366
Kramer, M. K., 318
Krol, P., 179
Krupnick, J. L., 69, 71, 73, 92
Kubie, L., 112
Kuiper, P. C., 316, 317
Kyle, E. M., 336

Lachmann, F., 264, 267, 273–274
Lampl, 361, 363, 364
Landerman, P., 281n
Langer, S. K., 171
LaTour, B., 394
Leaf, L. A., 316
Lee, A., 176, 177
Leichtman, M. L., 193
Leslie, A. M., 171
Leuzinger-Bohleber, M., 120, 121, 122
Lewis, C., 402
Lichtenberg, J., 263, 264, 267, 273–274
Liddle, C., 256
Linsner, J. P., 20
Liotti, G., 234n, 267
Lolas, F., 121
Loss, L., 280
Luborsky, E., 342, 378, 414
Luborsky, L., 12, 36, 41, 43, 45, 46n, 53, 79, 96, 100, 102, 120–123, 155–156, 294, 302, 329, 331, 332, 336, 341–344, 347, 369, 377–379, 388–389, 398–399, 403, 412–414
Ludolph, P., 251–252
Lyons-Ruth, K., 222

Mackinnon, A., 182
Mahler, M. S., 171, 174
Main, M., 180–181, 185, 188, 199, 201, 210, 211, 213, 216–226, 228, 232, 233, 235, 237, 239, 247–248, 249, 264, 266–267, 269, 271, 274, 415, 417, 419
Malan, D. H., 98
Manghan, B., 169, 179–180
Mark, D., 79

Marmar, C., 69, 71, 73, 82, 84
Martin, E., 56, 59, 75, 403
Maslin, C., 249
Masten, A. S., 256
Masterson, J., 255
Maxim, P., 337
Mayer, L. C., 133
Maynard-Smith, J., 232
McCallum, M., 85
McCleary, R., 406
McClure, M. M., 60, 62
McCormmach, R., 394
McLaughlin, J. T., 104, 325
McLellan, A. T., 412
McLeod, S., 222
McNew, S., 252–253
Meissner, W. W., 110
Mergenthaler, E., 43, 69, 71–74, 85, 115, 121, 122
Merluzzi, T. V., 72, 75, 77, 81
Merton, R., 403
Metz, J. R., 256
Meyer, A. E., 112, 117, 118, 124
Milbrath, C., 69, 71–74, 81, 85
Miller, J., 179
Miller, S., 37
Minter, M., 173–174
Mintz, J., 378
Modell, A., 215
Moran, G. S., 101, 102, 198, 199, 203, 250, 251, 252
Morris, H., 92, 315, 318, 319
Morris, J., 46
Morris, M., 342
Morton, J., 253
Moss, D., 40, 123
Moss, L., 281, 281n, 282

Nathans, S., 339
Nelson, B., 179
Neudert, L., 120
Nigg, J. T., 91, 99, 101, 104, 106
Nisle, B., 251–252
Norville, R., 19–20
Novick, J., 318

Oates, D. S., 361, 363
Oberndorf, C., 292–293, 294
O'Brien, C. P., 412
O'Connor, E., 229
O'Connor, L., 21
O'Connor, N., 168
O'Grady, D., 256
O'Halloran, P., 337
Oppenheim, D., 416
Osofsky, J. D., 193, 194, 197, 198, 199, 202, 203, 261–262, 271–273, 274, 414
Ouston, J., 176, 177

Paolitto, F., 92, 315–321
Parens, H., 197, 203
Paris, J., 179
Parke, L. A., 91, 95, 98
Parker, G., 180, 182
Parker, K., 230
Patrick, M., 169, 179–180
Paul, I. H., 115, 119
Paul, R., 187
Pearlman, C. H., 120
Peebles, C. D., 194
Perkins, M. J., 336
Perry, J., 46n, 179
Perry, J. C., 75, 85–86, 87, 337
Pfeffer, A. Z., 294, 318
Piper, W. E., 85
Platt, J., 400–401
Plomin, R., 186
Pokorny, D., 123
Poland, W. S., 325
Popp, C., 79, 336, 343
Porder, M., 294
Porges, S. N., 195
Posada, G., 229
Prince-Gibson, E., 397
Pulos, S. M., 91, 97, 98
Pulver, S. E., 112

Quinton, D., 256

Radloff, L. S., 194

Rado, S., 279
Radojevic, M., 230
Ramsey-Klee, D. M., 358, 360, 361, 363
Rapaport, D., 250n, 295, 356
Redington, D., 69, 71–74, 80, 81, 85
Reidbord, S., 69, 71–74, 81, 85
Reiss, D., 417
Repacholi, B., 222
Reznick, J. S., 186
Richard, I. A., 51
Richardson, E., 209n
Ricoeur, P., 237, 403
Ridgeway, D., 249
Robbins, F., 318
Robbins, L. R., 302
Robertson, J., 355
Robinson, J., 186
Rorty, R., 403
Rosenbaum, R., 69, 82, 84
Rosenberg, D. M., 218
Rosenberg, S. E., 18, 302, 307n, 308, 337
Rosenblatt, B., 75, 204
Roth, P., 403
Rothmann, E., 173
Rouse, J., 403
Ruberg, W., 117
Rubinstein, B., 40
Ruffins, S., 251–252
Rutter, M., 168, 170, 256
Rycroft, C., 171

Salovey, 81
Salsburg, D., 404
Sampson, H., 8, 13–16, 18, 41, 45, 52–53, 75, 96, 100, 102, 157, 158–159, 336, 339
Sander, L. W., 216, 236
Sandler, A.-M., 247
Sandler, J., 75, 111, 112, 202, 204, 247, 325, 374, 382–383
Sargent, H. D., 302, 316
Sashin, J., 120, 289–291, 315–319
Scarr, S., 364
Schacht, T., 45, 46n, 336, 339

NAME INDEX

Schaer, 201
Schaffler, P., 79, 332, 342, 347
Schaumberg, C., 120, 121, 122
Scheerer, M., 173
Schinkel, A., 118
Schlessinger, N., 318
Schmidt, K., 342
Schmieder, B., 118, 120
Schnekenburger, S., 123
Schopler, E., 170
Schors, R., 121
Schur, M., 265
Schwartz, R., 34
Searles, H. F., 253, 255
Sears, R. R., 353
Segal, H., 171, 253
Seitz, P., 52, 157, 331
Shapiro, A., 281n
Shapiro, D., 279, 336
Shapiro, T., 186
Shapiro, V., 200–201, 247
Shashin, J., 92
Sherman, M., 186, 249
Shevrin, 336
Shusterman, R., 403
Shweder, R. A., 417
Silberschatz, G., 15–16, 18, 19, 20, 46n, 61–62, 102, 136, 336, 339, 406
Sills, D., 403
Silva, E., 222
Silverman, L. H., 92
Simon, H., 36
Simon, J., 115, 119
Singer, J. L., 69, 71–74, 81, 85, 317
Skolnikoff, A., 93, 293, 315, 405
Smith, T., 379
Solomon, J., 199, 201, 210, 218, 221, 222, 223
Solomon, L., 92, 315–319
Solomon, M., 282, 285, 288–289, 322
Sorce, J. F., 172
Spangler, G., 220, 222, 235
Sparrow, S. S., 187
Spence, D. P., 41, 91, 101, 102, 110, 120n, 133, 137, 138, 406, 419n, 420–421
Sperry, R. W., 422
Spezzano, C., 403
Spitz, R. A., 265
Spruiell, V., 402
Squire, L. R., 416
Sroufe, L. A., 195, 217, 219
Stadtman, J., 219
Stayton, D. J., 218, 219
Stechler, G., 273
Steele, H., 185, 199, 230, 248, 250, 251
Steele, M., 185, 199, 230, 248, 250, 251
Steele, R. S., 237
Stengel, B., 33, 36
Stern, D. N., 186, 195, 204, 263, 270
Stewart, I., 402
Stigler, S., 403
Stinson, C. H., 69, 71–75, 77–78, 81, 85, 115
Stoller, R. J., 110
Stone, L., 79
Strachey, J., 406
Strenger, C., 110
Strupp, H. H., 41–42, 45, 53, 339
Suess, G., 216, 217, 223
Sullivan, H. S., 366
Sulloway, F., 399
Swaan, A. de, 114
Swerdloff, B., 280, 281, 382

Target, M., 198, 203, 251
Taylor, C., 403
Teller, V., 32, 36, 37, 40, 43, 46n, 123, 131, 135–136, 154–156, 161, 336, 340, 414
Thom, R., 394, 402
Thomä, H., 37, 42, 43, 46, 109–110, 111, 113–118, 124, 138, 154–155, 158, 340, 414, 420
Thompson, A., 364
Thorne, A., 92
Ticho, G., 318
Trabasso, T., 34
Treboux, D., 229
Tronick, E. Z., 195, 202

Trujillo, M., 40, 123
Tunis, S. L., 81
Tupling, H., 180, 182
Tustin, F., 174–175, 264

Urban, J., 217
Ureno, G., 337

Vaillant, G. E., 85–86, 87
Van Amerongen, S., 289–291
van der Kolk, B., 179
Van Ijzendoorn, M. H., 228–229, 239, 248
Volkmar, K. R., 187
Voth, H., 372
Vygotsky, L. S., 170

Waelder, R., 144, 401–402
Waldron, S., 93, 293, 315, 405
Wall, S., 188, 195, 210, 214, 218, 219, 220, 246–247, 365
Wallerstein, R. S., 26, 42, 69, 71, 73, 85, 93, 236–239, 289–291, 294, 300–302, 304–309, 315–317, 322, 324, 369–370, 372, 376–377, 384–385, 386–387, 396, 397, 405, 412–413
Ward, M. J., 230
Ware, L. M., 193, 194, 197, 198, 199, 202, 203
Wartner, U. G., 216, 223
Waters, E., 188, 195, 210, 211, 214, 218, 219, 220, 229, 246–247, 365
Watson, D. D., 91
Weber, J. J., 279–280, 281, 282, 285, 288–289, 322
Weeks, S. J., 177

Weiss, D. S., 69, 82, 84, 307n, 331
Weiss, J., 13–16, 18, 21, 41, 45, 52–53, 75, 96, 100, 102, 136–137, 147, 157, 158–159, 336, 339, 420
Weistenberg, J., 281n
Welsh, N., 406
Werner, E. E., 249
Werner, H., 170
Westen, D., 251–252
Westheimer, I., 356, 358
Weston, D., 219, 249
Whetton, C., 177
Whiten, A., 253
Williams, A. L., 252
Willick, M., 294
Wilner, N., 69, 71, 72, 73
Windholz, M., 37, 91, 99, 100, 136, 138
Wing, L., 173
Winnicott, D. W., 249, 255, 270, 366
Wirtz, E. M., 121
Wiseman, H., 397
Wittgenstein, L., 168
Wittig, B. A., 188
Wolf, E. S., 179, 185
Woody, G. E., 412
Woolgar, S., 394
Wynne, M. F., 91

Yeates, S. R., 173
Yin, Y., 294

Zahn-Waxler, C., 186
Zeig-Frank, H., 179
Zetzel, E., 316, 317
Zigler, E., 251
Zilberg, N. J., 82, 302, 307n, 308
Zimmermann, V., 123
Zoppel, C. L., 92

SUBJECT INDEX

AAI. *See* Adult Attachment Interview
Academic achievement, 359–360
Adaptation, 36
  changes in, 280–281, 284
  flexible, 360–361
  scales for measuring, 281, 284
  separation trauma and, 355–358
Adaptation-competence, 362
Adaptive Balance Scale, 283, 382
Addiction, 34
Adelphi University, Derner Institute, 41–42
Adolescent mothers, socioemotional development with, 193–205
Adult Attachment Classification system, 240
Adult Attachment Interview, 180–184, 188, 211, 223–230, 248–249, 269, 415, 419
  avoidant, ambivalent patterns in, 235
  in borderline patients, 264–265
  classification and scoring system of, 228–229
  data from, 251
  predicting infant strange situation behavior, 229–230
  tasks of, 225
Affect. *See also* Emotional availability; Emotions
  availability and tolerance of, 317
  reciprocal management of, 204
  regulation of, 195, 271–273
  source of moderation of, 254
Affective connectedness, 175–176, 262, 263–264
Affective core of self, 199–200
AFH. *See* Automatic functioning hypothesis
Aggressive behavior
  defensive response to, 198
  modulation of, and parent-child mutuality, 362–364

negative emotion and, 196–198, 272–273
positive emotions and, 196–198
Agoraphobia, 332–336
Ah-ha reaction, 144
Ambivalent/resistant behavior, 220–221
  intergenerational transmission of, 234–235
American Psychoanalytic Association
  Fund for Psychoanalytic Research of, 45
  multisite research program of, 42
  outcome research project of, 383
Analyst. *See also* Patient-analyst match
  factors in limitation of, 322
  individual differences in, 314
  interchangeability of, 316
  mental functioning of, 143–146
  patient's testing of, 20, 23, 55, 61–62, 96, 135, 136–137
  personality of, 373–374
Analytic concepts, 111
Analytic conversation, 131–132
Analytic interaction, 111
Analytic process
  study of, 93–97
  theory of, 9–10
Analytic result. *See also* Outcome; Therapeutic benefit
  predictability of, 322–323
  versus therapeutic benefit, 317
Analyzability, 284, 301, 370
  predictability of, 387–388, 397
  qualities for, 317
  therapeutic benefit and, 288, 289–291
Anna Freud Diagnostic Profile, 359
Anti-plan insight statements, 23–24
Anti-plan interventions, 18, 19–20
  efficacy of, 62
Anxiety, 159. *See also* Separation anxiety
  computer-assisted measurement of, 121–122

433

expectations and, 234–235
Artificial intelligence model, 122
As-if behavior, 255
Assumptions, 36
   about efficacy, 299–312, 322–324
   hidden, 420–421
   in outcome studies, 315–317, 322–324
Attachment
   ABCD classification of, 216–223
   with adolescent mother, 194–195
   classification of, 265–267
   focused, 213–214
   formulations for, 365–366
   hermeneutic/constructivist controversy and, 236–240
   implications for psychoanalysis of, 209–240
   individual differences in, during infancy, 210–211, 215–223
   insecure, 210, 212, 246–247
   instinct theory of, 240
   intensity of, and mother-child separation, 355–356
   intergenerational transmission of, 233–236
   monitoring of, 214
   mother's representation of relationships and, 246–257
   parental states of mind and, 223–230
   patterns of, 210–211
   reflective self and, 256–257
   roots of, 366–367
   separation trauma and, 374–375
   strength of, 214
   survival and, 214–215
   transgenerational model of, 247–248
Attachment behavioral systems, 210–211
   environment and, 212–215
   intersubjective contact and, 264
Attachment motivational system, 272–273
Attachment-related experience, in borderline personality, 180–185
Attachment relatedness, 274
Attachment-separation reactions, 187–188
Attachment theory
   borderline personality and, 183–184
   emotional availability and, 199
   evolutionary, 212–215, 414–415
   testing of, 265
Attention
   biologically guided, 214
   control of, 231–233
   pre- and post-birth antecedents of, 361–364
Attentional/representational states, 230
   organized, 233–236
Audiorecordings, 110, 115–117
   usefulness of, 294–295
Autism, early childhood, 168, 170–171
   capacity to symbolize in, 171–174
   cognitive and linguistic theories of, 168
   empirical studies of, 185–187, 262–263
   monitoring of others and, 264
   object-relational structures, 168–169
   personal relatedness in, 174–178
Automatic functioning hypothesis, 10, 134, 138–139, 147
   versus control mastery model, 158–159
   repression and, 13–14
   testing of, 12–13
   transference and, 14–16
Avoidance, 233
   intergenerational transmission of, 234–235
Avoidant children, 247

Beck Depression Inventory, 183
Behavioral change, 304
Behavioral observations, 353–367
Behavioral strategies, conditional, 232–233
Beliefs, emotions as, 34

SUBJECT INDEX

Berkeley Psychology Research Project, 91–106
  early focus of, 92
  study methods of, 92–93
Borderline personality disorder, 178–185
  developmental exploration and, 169
  DSM-III criteria for, 251
  empirical studies of, 264–267
  Kris Study Group findings on, 294
  versus normal development, 255–257
  reflective self and, 252–255
  transgenerational model of, 251–252
Borderline self-and-other schematization, 84
Boston outcome project, 313–326, 371–372
  design of, 316–317
  findings of, 412–413
  post-termination evaluation in, 318–321

Mrs. C case, 132–135, 139, 159
Calm and safe state, 78
Case formulation, 68, 71–72
Case studies, 68, 118, 280. *See also* Single-case studies
  in empirical studies, 156–157
Catastrophic fantasies, 223
Causal effects, 101–105
CCRT. *See* Core Conflictual Relationship Theme
CCRT Newsletter, 344
Character formation, 67
Child abuse, 197–198
  borderline personality and, 184, 251–252
  intergenerational effects of, 246, 251–257
Clinic follow-up method, 293–294
Clinical data, as accessible knowledge, 131–141
Clinical experience, 394
  dependence on, 383–384
  versus scientific data, 394–396

Clinical hypothesis testing, 59–64
Clinical inference, guided systems and, 346–348
Clinical outcome predictions, 285
Clinical phenomena, 93–94
Clinical practice
  analytic models in, 162–163
  growth of, 1–2
Clinical studies, 93, 419
  findings of, 163–164
  groups of, 295
  scientific status of, 51–64
Clinical theory
  interpersonal psychology in, 412–415
  limits of, 273
Clinical transference formulations, 329–330. *See also* Core Conflictual Relationship Theme; Transference, measures of
  derivation of, 330
  reasons for popularity of, 330–331
Clinical trial research, 405
Clinical wisdom, 131–132, 347
  authority of, 398–399
Clinically meaningful methods, 294–295
Clinician, versus scientist, 153–164
Cognitive development
  in autism, 170–171
  intersubjective experience and, 169
Cognitive processes
  in control process, 85–86
  free/autonomous, 248
Coherence theory, 237, 240
Columbia Records Project, 279–295, 370–372
  final form of, 282–291
  findings of, 388, 412–413
  viability of methodology of, 292–293
Complexity theory, 402, 422–423
Compromise behaviors, 153–154
Compromising role-relationship models, 76
  problematic and adaptive, 78
Computer, 150–151

in empirical studies, 123–124, 146–147
Computer (content) text analysis, 33, 43, 120–122, 132–133, 161
Computer dictionary categories, 33
Conceptual issues, 314
  of efficacy, 300–312
  of psychoanalysis as science, 300
Conditional behavior strategies, 230, 231–233, 235–236
Configurational analysis, 71–72, 339
  control and self regulation in, 85–87
Conflict resolution, 304–305, 390
  defensive, 355
Conflictedness, 54
Constructivist theory, 237–240
Containment, failures of, 179
Content analysis. See Computer (content) text analysis
Control frame, 38
Control mastery hypothesis, 52, 138–139, 157
  domains of, 54, 55
  efficacy of, 62
  efficacy of intervention in, 60
  reliability of, 53–57
  testing of, 158–159
Control-process language, 86–87
Control processes, 68–69, 85–87
  cognitive operations in, 85–86
Controlled observation, 423
Cooperative research projects, 42–44
Core Conflictual Relationship Theme, 36, 53, 122–123, 147, 156, 413–414
  applications of, 406
  categories in, 337–338
  clinical gains from, 340–341
  evaluation of, 377–379
  example of, from dynamic psychotherapy, 332–336
  interpretive nature of, 403
  limitations of, 400
  methodology of, 388–389
  reliability of, 294

research gains from, 341–344
versus role-relationship model configuration, 79
in transference measure, 329–348
transference template observations and, 343
use of, 331–332, 344–348
Corrective emotional experience, 26
Correspondence theory, 237
Couch-lab intersect, 63–64
Countertransference
  future research on, 123–124
  syntax choice and, 40
Critically-friendly frame prototype, 38, 39
Cultural anthropology, 417
Cultural group
  caregiving and, 203
  socioemotional development and, 195–196
Cultural pluralism, 422
Curriculum, 46
Cyclical maladaptive patterns, 36–37, 40, 67–68, 147, 155, 161, 339–340

Data banks, redundancy in, 46
Decision theory, emotions, 33
Decontextualized process, 98
Defense-impulse configurations, 54
Defenses, 10
  FRAMES and, 36
  functions of, 34
  in role-relationship model, 75
Defensive adaptation, to mother-child separation, 356–358
Defensive control
  of states of mind, 73–74
  styles of, 72
Defensive processes
  attachment and origins of, 233–236
  development of, 231–233
  treatments of, 366
Delay frame, 38
Desired role-relationship models, 76, 78

Developmental concepts, 353–367
Developmental psychopathology, 167–189
　emotional availability and affect regulation in, 271–273
　object-relations perspective on, 245–257
Developmental studies
　experiential concepts and behavioral observations in, 353–367
　interpersonal relations in, 413–414
Discourse monitoring lapses, 226–228
Discourse rules, 417
Discovered hypotheses, 63
Dismissing behavior, 226, 235–236
Disorganized/disoriented personality, 181, 221–223
Displacement transference, 59
Distraught sadness state, 78
Dreaded role-relationship models, 76, 78
Drive function, 51
Dyadic interactional model, 272–273
Dynamic interactional model, 193–205, 414
Dynamic psychotherapy, 160, 329–330
　CCRT from, 332–336
Dyselaboration, 73
　verbal, 85
Dysthymia, 182
　attachment capacity in, 183–184
　DSM-III-R criteria for, 183

Ecological validity, 111
Effect size, 286
Efficacy
　conceptual issues and, 299–312
　empirical studies of, 315, 396, 398
　outcome studies of, 371, 373, 384–385
Ego
　early modifications of, 212
　integration of, 360–361
　strength of, 307, 319
　tasks of, 11–12n

Ego psychology
　framework of, 308, 376
　theory and, 10–11
Emotion theory, 43
Emotion words, 33–34
Emotional availability, 271–273, 317
　in high psychosocial risk infants and parents, 199–200
　in mother-infant unit, 194–195
Emotional coloration, 73
Emotions
　classification scheme for, 35, 39–40
　communication of, in borderline personality, 253
　dysregulation of, 197, 199–200, 204–205
　empirical research on, 33–36
　FRAMES and, 36
　free/autonomous processing of, 248
　leakage of, 73
　positive and negative, 196–198
　recognition of, in autism, 177–178
　stability of, 264
Empathy, 26, 274
Empirical research
　areas of focus in, 32–40
　clinicians and, 153–164
　clinician's view of, 143–152
　concerns about, 379–380
　definition of, 383
　on developmental psychopathology, 245–257
　effectiveness of psychotherapy and psychoanalysis issues in, 299–312
　historical context of, 40–44
　impact on psychoanalytic theory and technique, 261–275
　knowledge from, 381–390
　multilevel observational strategy and, 117–122
　need for, 31–47
　pretense of, 394–396
　on process, 7–27
　prospects of, 44–46

SUBJECT INDEX

in psychoanalysis, 369–380
redundancy in, 45–46
rewards of, 393–407
shifting visions of "facts" and, 401–403
surprise and, 397–399
tactics of, 400–401
in understanding individuality, psychopathology and search for meaning, 418–422
validity of, 110
value of, 399–401
Empirical science, 1–3
Enduring attributes, 75–76
Epistemological assumptions, 301–302
Ethnicity, 195–196
Evolutionary attachment theory, 212–215, 414–415
Experiential concepts, 353–367
Expressive psychotherapy, 84–85, 303
effectiveness of, 305
psychoanalysis and, 306–307
Eye aversion, 273

Fact, shifting vision of, 401–403
Families, at-risk, 364–365
Father, caregiving role of, 268
Fears, 75
Feedback system, 34–36
Field research, 92–93
Followup interviews, 320–321
Followup studies, 301
findings of, 323–324
Fragmented self-and-other schematization, 84
FRAMES, 36–40, 43, 135, 147, 155–156, 161
findings of, 135–136
prototype, 38–39
in relationship pattern measure, 340
reliability of, 140–141
stabilization of, 123
Frequency-based inferences, 347–348
Freudian psychology, 153–154
Fund for Psychoanalytic Research, 45

Fundamental Repetitive and Maladaptive Emotional Structures. *See* FRAMES
Funding opportunities, 44–45

Generalizability, 105
Gratification seeking, 14–16
Guided clinical judgment procedures, 120
Guided transference measures, 329–348
danger of, 346–348
focus of, 341
reliability of, 340–341
Guilt, mourning and, 73–74

Habitual interactions, 157–158
Hermeneutic/constructivist controversy, 236–240
Hermeneutic interpretation, 402–403, 419–420
Hermeneutic science, 300
Heroic indications, 301, 305
Heuristic transgenerational model, 248–250
Higher mental functioning hypothesis, 10–11, 134, 138–139, 147
automatic functioning hypothesis and, 12–13
repression and, 13–14
transference and, 14–16
Historical linkages, 54–55
HMFH. *See* Higher mental functioning hypothesis
Hostile destructive affect, 197
Husband-wife adaptation, 362
Hypothesis
generation of, 117
testing of, 158–159

Ideas, 51
Identification phenomena, 70
Improvement
criteria for, 303
extent and duration of, 317–318

overall, 284
Impulses, 10
Impulsivity, 201–202
Individuality, empirical approaches to, 418–422
Infant
   abuse and neglect of, 197–198
   attachment behavior and environment of, 212–215
   attachment behavior differences in, 215–223
   primary attachment figure of, 213
   survival skills of, 265
Infant-mother dyad. *See also* Mother-child separation; Mother-infant relationship
   with adolescent mothers, 193–205
   attachment patterns in, 210–211, 215–223, 265–266
   dynamic interactional model for, 202–205
   emotional availability and, 271–273
   emotions and aggression in, 196–198
   regulation in, 216–217
   self development with high psychosocial risk, 199–200
Infantile helplessness, 265
Insecure/ambivalent attachment pattern, 234–236, 246–247
Insecure/avoidant behavior, 218–220, 246–247
   intergenerational transmission of, 234–236
Insecure infant attachment, 210, 212
Insight, 316
   in brief psychotherapies, 21–24
   structural change and, 389–390
Insight Scale, 24
Instinct theory, 240
Intellectualization, 319
Interactional behavioral observation, 353–367
Interdisciplinary perspective, 32–33
Interintentionality, 417
Internal consistency, 238–239

Internal working models, 246–250
International Psychoanalytic Association, 46
   research section of, 382–383
Interpersonal psychology, 411–415
Interpersonal relationships, autistic, 174–178
Interpretation, 403
   benefits of, 26
   effects of, 25
   extratransference, 254
   immediate effects in brief psychotherapy, 17–19
   long-term effects of, 19–20
   objective, 148
   pro-plan vs. anti-plan, 23–24
   research on, 109–110
   validity of, 148–149
Interpretive techniques, 378–379
Intersubjective contact, symbolic capacity and, 263–264
Intersubjective development
   in borderline personality, 178–185
   disruption of, 174–178
Intersubjective psychological processes, 167–189, 413–414
Interventions
   effects of, 51, 60–62
   efficacy of, 60–62
   experiential concepts and behavioral observations in, 353–367
   narrow-focus, 87
   testing efficacy of, 53
   testing hypotheses about, 60–62
Intrapsychic conflict, unconscious, 376–377
Intrapsychic structure, 308–309
Intuition, 144
Investigational methods, 44
IQ ratings, 358–359, 360–361, 389
   achievement and, 374–375
   pre- and post-birth antecedents of, 361–364
IT emotions, 34

Kleinian framework, 376
Kris Study Group, borderline disorder findings of, 294

Laboratory-based research, 92
Language, in process evaluation, 121
Large-scale multivariate method, 292–293, 384–385
Life events, 145
Linguistic variables, 161
London Parent-Child Project, 248, 250–251, 255–256
Longitudinal studies, 163, 371–372
  followup, 324
Loss, unresolved, 184

MacArthur Foundation, 45
Maladaptive behavior patterns, 36, 67–68
  cyclical, 36–37, 40, 67–68, 147, 155, 161, 339–340
  intergenerational repetition of, 200–201
Maladaptive beliefs, 8–9
Maladaptive personality structures, 34
Marital relationships
  child development and, 362–364
  intervention for, 364–365
Mastery, wish for, 11. *See also* Control mastery hypothesis
Maternal separation, borderline personality and, 179
ME emotions, 34
Meaning, search for, 418–422
Menninger Project, 85, 316, 369–370, 372, 384–385, 396
  findings of, 302, 398, 412–413
  methodology of, 404–405
  post-termination evaluation in, 318–319
Mental activity, nonconscious, 416–418
Mental functioning, 381
  automatic vs. higher, 10–11, 12–13
  higher vs. automatic, 134, 138–139
  rules of, 153–154

Mental representations
  adult, 185, 187–188
  in autism, 169, 176–178
  dual code system of, 36–37
  poorly functioning, 254–255
Mental structures, 308–309
Methodology, 145–146, 292–295, 382
  quantitative vs. qualitative, 403–406
  replicability of, 420
Mind, theory of, 253
Mirroring, 200
Mother
  adaptation-competence of, 362–363
  conditional behavior strategies of, 232–233
  infant fantasy of, 268–269
  mental representations and infant attachment, 267–268
  sensitivity of, 194–195
  warmth of, 362–363
Mother-child relationship, 246–257
Mother-child separation
  attachment behavior and, 374–375
  duration of, 354–358
Mother-infant relationship, 246–247, 374–376. *See also* Infant-mother dyad
Motivation, 261
  for analysis, 316, 317
  psychoanalytic model of, 34–36
Mt. Zion group research, 11–24
Mourning
  phenomena of, 70–71
  states of mind in, 73–74
Multilevel observational strategy, 117–122

Narcissistic states, 252
Narcissistically vulnerable self-and-other schematization, 83
Narrative patterns, 421–422
Narratives, hermeneutic interpretation of, 419–420
Narrowing indications, 301, 305
Natural selection, 232

SUBJECT INDEX

Need, intensification of, 356
Negative result, 397
Neurosis
  expressive technique in, 84–85
  successful analytic result in, 315
Neurotic character structure, 68
Neurotic self-and-other schematization, 83
NIMH grants, 44
Nondeterminism, 422–423
Normal self-and-other schematization, 83

Object relations, 414–415
  alternative models of, 250
  in autism, 168–169, 171–174
  early, psychological functioning and, 375–376
  language of, 157
  level and quality of, 317
  primitive, traumatic, 201–202
Object relations theory
  biological bases of, 187
  borderline personality and, 183–184
  in developmental psychopathology, 245–257
  framework of, 308–309
Object representation, primitive, 263–264
Objectivity, 148–150
Obligatory script, 76
Observation, controlled, 423
Obstructions, degree of, 55
Operational transference measures, 330–331
Operationalization, 379–380
Orality, 265
Organizational Level of Self and Other Schematization (OLSOS), 83–84
Others
  organizational level of schema for, 82–85
  roles and traits of, 76
Outcome
  classifications of, 283–284
  effectiveness of, 300–312
  evolution of research on, 279–295
  follow-up study of, 302–303
  frequency of psychoanalytic treatment and, 358–361
  patient-analyst match and, 321–322, 325–326, 387–388
  predictability of, 322–323, 371–372, 382–383
  process variables in, 378–379
  protocols for evaluating, 281–282
  in psychoanalysis, 313–326
  reality testing and, 320
  successful, 315
Outcome studies, 369–371
  assumptions of, 315–317
  conceptual issues in, 314–315
  consistence of findings of, 385–390
  data from, 384–385
  dialectic of, 373
  interpersonal relations and, 412–413
  questions about, 371
  validity of, 372–373
Outline (Freud), 11
Overprotection, 182

Papers on Technique (Freud), 8
Paradigm formulation, 53–54
Parallel distributive processing, 416–417
Parent. *See also* Father, role of; Mother
  frightening behavior of, 222–223
  idealized, 180–181
  low opinion, 270–271
  reflective self function in, 415
  responsiveness of, 362–363
  states of mind of, and predicted attachment behavior, 223–230
Parent-child interaction, 210. *See also* Mother–child relationship; Infant–mother dyad
Parent-child mutuality, 362–364
Parent-infant function, 364–365
Parental Bonding Instrument, 180–184
Parenting figures, borderline personality and, 179–185

Pathogenic beliefs, 8–9, 11, 25
  analysis to disprove, 16–17
  transference demands and testing of, 14–16
Pathological beliefs, 55
Patient
  goals of, 55, 62
  testing of analyst by, 20, 23, 55, 61–62, 96, 135, 136–137
Patient-analyst interactions, habitual, 157–158
Patient-analyst match, 318, 387–388
  impact of, 325–326
  importance of, 321–322
Patient-analyst relationship, 373–374
  analysis of, 133–134
  patient experience of, 339
Peer play, 37
Person schemas
  defensive control of, 67–87
  definition of, 67–68
  organizational levels of, 82–85
  phenomena of, 159
  as role-relationship models, 75–80
Personal relatedness, 174–178
Physical science research, 401–402
Plan concept, 21–24
Plan Diagnosis method, 339
Plan formulation, 25–26
Pleasure principle, 10
Post-traumatic stress disorder (PTSD), 72–73
Postmodern nondeterministic science, 422–423
PQS method, 106
Preanalysis evaluation, 316, 317
Preconscious mental activity, 416–418
Preoccupation, 233
Preoccupied behavior, 226–227, 235–236
Pro-plan insight statements, 21–24
Pro-plan intervention, 17–18, 19–20
  efficacy of, 60
Probabilistic determinism, 423
Problematic role-relationship models, 76
Process, 111
  conceptualized, 98–99
  decontextualized, 98
Process-to-outcome equation, 84–85
Progressive effects scales, 61
Projective identification, excessive, 253
PRP. *See* Psychotherapy Research Project
Psychiatric research, 381–382
Psychic change, 311–312
Psychic forces, 10
Psychoanalysis
  aesthetic phase of, 143–144
  applied, 193–205
  assumptions about, 300
  attachment and, 230–240
  benefits of research to, 393–407
  cognitive phase of, 144
  in developmental psychopathology, 245–257
  to disprove pathogenic beliefs, 16–17
  dynamic interactional model of, 193–205
  efficacy of, 299–312, 315
  empirical research on, 1–3, 31–47, 143–152, 369–380, 382–390
  empirical studies effect on, 261–275
  FRAMES in, 36–40
  hermeneutic/constructivist controversy in, 236–240
  immediate effects of interpretation during, 17–18
  interpersonal and intrapsychic nature of, 411–415
  limitations of, 305
  mainstream domains of, 54
  nature of, 25–26
  nondeterministic science and, 422–423
  outcome research in, 279–295, 313–326
  psychotherapy and, 390
  research approaches for, 411–423
  scientific nature of, 421–422

self-study of, 91–106
  as two-person system, 323, 325–326, 387–388, 412
Psychoanalytic mainstream, domains of, 59
Psychoanalytic Clinic, 279–280
  research of treatment outcomes of, 282–295
Psychoanalytic formulations
  agreement studies of, 52–57
  reliability of, 161–162
Psychoanalytic framework, 308–309
  relevance of, 162–163
Psychoanalytic mannequins, 52, 161, 421
  construction of, 58–59
  studies of, 57–60
Psychoanalytic process
  empirical studies of, 7–27
  Freudian view of, 113–114
  interactive foundation of, 112–114
  new understandings of, 131–141
  research methods and achievements with, 109–124
  research on, 369
  scientific approach to, 153–164
Psychoanalytic technique, 261–275
Psychoanalytic terms, 323
Psychoanalytic training, reform of, 124
Psychodynamic formulations, 71
Psychodynamic technique, 97
Psychological capacities, 309–310
Psychological change, 369–370
  assessment of, 323
  conditions of, 311–312
  kinds of, 307–308
  mechanisms of, 304
  process of, 302–303
  treatment modality and, 304–312
Psychology, cultural, 417
Psychometric properties, 228–229
Psychopathology
  developmental, 167–189, 245–257
  empirical approaches to, 418–422
  severity of, 319

theory of, 8–9
Psychosocial risk
  emotions and aggression in, 196–198
  in infants and adolescents, 193–205
  maladaptive behavior and, 200–201
  self development and, 199–200
Psychotherapy
  brief, 18–19, 21–24, 26
  clinical transference formulations from, 330
  dynamic, 329–330, 332–336
  effectiveness of, 299–312
  levels of insight in, 21–24
  plan formulation in, 26
  psychoanalysis and, 306–308, 390
Psychotherapy Process Q-set (PQS), 94–95, 132–133, 135, 137
Psychotherapy Research Project, 369–370
  findings of, 304–312, 372, 386–387
  methodological shortcoming of, 311–312
  part II, 307–312
  purpose of, 302–303

Q-set, 94–95, 132–133, 135, 137
Q-sort methodology, 94–95, 101–102, 105–106, 149, 160–161, 365, 414, 421
  single-case research and, 97–105
  time sampling and, 95–96
  unite of observation and, 96–97
Qualitative methods, 403–406
Quantitative knowledge, 403
Quantitative studies, 93, 95–107
Quasi-adaptive compromises, 75

Rage, outbursts of, 198
Reality testing, 317, 320
Record-keeping, 145–146
Recurrent maladaptive patterns. *See* Repetitive maladaptive behavior patterns
Reflective self function, 250, 415
  attachment and, 256–257

borderline states and, 252–255
Regressions, deepening cycles of, 69
Regressive behavior, 20
Relationship intervention, 364–365
Relationship patterns, 76, 333–336, 386–387, 413–415
  CCRT and, 377–379
  measures of, 336–340
Relationship schemas, 68
Relationships
  configurations of, 159–160
  pre- and post-birth antecedents of capacity for, 361–364
Repetitive behavior patterns, 159–160
  maladaptive, 36–37, 40, 67–68, 147, 155, 161, 339–340
Repetitive structures, 45–46
Replicability, 420–421
Representations, 211
Repressed mental contents, spontaneous emergence of, 13–14
Repressions, unconscious control of, 11
Research, 400. *See also* Empirical research
  approaches in, 411–423
  experiential concepts and behavioral observations in, 353–367
  implications of, 24–27
  levels of, 138
  nonanalytic, 167–189
  on psychoanalysis outcomes, 313–326
  on psychoanalytic process, 109–124
  rewards of, 393–407
  on theory of process, 11–24
Research Center for Mental Health (RCMH), 41
Resistant children, 247
Rituals, 417–418
Role-relational models, 72, 156, 159–160
  person schemas as, 75–80
Role Relationship Model Configurations, 139, 147, 413–414
  reliability and validity of, 80–82
Role responsiveness, 374

Roles, 75–76
RRMC. *See* Role Relationship Model Configurations

Safety, 11
Salience-based inferences, 347–348
San Francisco Psychotherapy Research Group, 41
Science, postmodern nondeterministic, 422–423
Scientific beliefs, 394–395
Scientists, clinicians and, 153–164
Secure attachment behavior, 217–218
Secure/autonomous behavior, 225–226
Self
  internalized views of, 75–80
  organizational level of, 82–85
  reflective, 250, 252–255
  schemas for, 67–68, 75–76
Self-acceptance, 70
Self-analytic capacity, 316, 318, 321, 324
Self-criticism, 70
Self development, 199–200
Self-organization
  continuity of, 67–68
  during mourning, 71
Self psychology
  deficit model, 202–203
  framework of, 376
Self-reflective function
  absence of, 267–268
  in mothers and fathers, 268–271
Self-regulation, 85–87
Self-righting capacity, 256–257, 268
Separation
  infant response to, 246–247
  mother-child, 354–358
Separation anxiety, 356–358, 374–375
Sessions
  audiorecording of, 115–117
  frequency of, and outcome, 358–361, 375
  recording of, 146–147, 294–295
  retroreporting of, 124
  verbatim records of, 118–119

SUBJECT INDEX 445

Sexual abuse, borderline personality and, 179, 184, 251–252
Shameful worry state, 78
Sharing, mother-infant, 196–197
Signal anxiety, organized attentional/representational states and, 233–236
Single-case studies, 110, 156–157
 advantages of, 293–294
 analysis of, 160–161
 causal effects and, 101–105
 generalizability of, 105, 162–163
 method of, 403–406
 versus multiple-case studies, 421
 Q-technique and, 97–105
Social behavior, structural analysis of, 147–148
Social development, autism and, 170–171, 186–187
Social experience, early childhood, 188–189
Social interactions, 416–417
 attachment and, 213–214
Social referencing
 autism and, 172–173
 blindness and, 173–174
 symbolization capacity and, 263–264
Social stimuli, 170
Socioemotional development, 193–205
Somatic appetites, 34
States of mind, 68–69
 analysis of, 72
 cycles of, 69
 defensive control of, 67–87
 emotional coloration of, 73
 phenomena of, 159
 predicted attachment behavior and, 223–230
Statistical methods, 404
Stereotypic view, 58
Stereotypical templates, 52
Strange Situation paradigm, 188, 210–211, 215–216, 217, 218–223, 231–232, 365, 415
 classification in, 224–225
 predictability of, 229–230
 response to, 235, 238, 239, 266–267
Stress response syndromes, 72–73
 resolution of, 73–74
Strong inference, 400–401
Structural Analysis of Social Behavior (SASB), 339–340
Structural change, 305, 370, 376–377, 386–387, 389–390
 conditions of, 311–312
 definition of, 308–309
 scales for, 310
Structure, conceptualization of, 376–377, 386–387
Subjectivity, 155
SUNY Health Science Center, 41
Support frame, 38
Supportive psychotherapy, 303, 308, 378–379
 changes with, 304–305
 psychoanalysis and, 306–307
 therapeutic benefit from, 322–323
Surprise, 397–399
Symbolization
 autism and, 171–174
 capacity for, 263–264
Symptoms, 346
Syntax choice, 40
Systematic clinical research, 92–93, 118–119, 301–302

Task orientation, 361–364
Tavistock Clinic Psychopathology Research Unit, 168–189
Tensions due to need, 356
Termination, circumstances of, 283–284
Testing, of analyst, 20, 23, 55, 61–62, 96, 135–137
Theory, 8–11
Therapeutic alliance construct, 96–97
Therapeutic benefit, 319, 370, 372
 versus analytic results, 317
 analyzability and, 288, 289–291
 empirical study of, 396

levels of, 286
measures of, 283–284, 287, 290
from psychoanalysis, 315
stability of, 323–324
with supportive techniques, 322–323
Therapeutic interventions, efficacy of, 151
Therapist. *See* Analyst
Thing-in-itself, 57
Time sampling, 95–96
Time-series analysis, 102–104, 160–161
Togetherness frame, 38
Topic Index method, 119
Transference
as-if nature of, 255
beliefs vs. gratification seeking in, 14–16
borderline personality and, 253–254
countertransference and, 112–113
definitions of, 330
displacement, 59, 162
measures of, 54, 329–348
negative, 324
objectification of, 389
patterns of, 377
phenomena of, 69
prediction of, 81–82
recurrent patterns in, 79–80
relationship patterns and, 333–336
themes in, 378
Transference/countertransference issues, 119
Transference neurosis, 37, 372
interpretation of, 316
intrapsychic conflicts in, 113
occurrence of, 322–323
resolution of, 315, 321
Transference template, 343, 344
Transgenerational developmental process, 248–250
of borderline pathology, 251–252
Trauma
community violence and, 201–202
conflict and, 72–73
early, 210

parental, 222–223
unresolved, 184
Treatability, 301
Treatment frequency, 358–361, 375
Treatment length, 288, 289
Treatment modalities
outcome and, 303–312
psychic and structural changes and, 311–312
Treatment outcomes. *See* Outcome
Trial actions, 11
Trust, caretaker relationship and, 355
Truth, 393

Ulm process model, 43–44, 111–124
Ulm Research Program, 154–155, 414
new directions and questions for, 122–124
psychoanalytic rationale of, 109–114
research approach and findings of, 114–122
team in, 138
Ulm Textbank, 43, 114–117, 158
Unconscious collusion, 373
Unconscious conflict, 376–377
in CCRT, 344–346
Unconscious mental processes
phenomena derived from, 72–73
theory of, 8
Unconscious mind, 10
Unconscious role expectancies, 112–113
Understanding Transference (Luborsky, Crits-Christoph), 344
Unfeeling state, 78
Unit of observation, 96–97
University of California, San Francisco, Program on Conscious and Unconscious Mental Processes, 41
University of Pennsylvania Psychotherapy Research Group, 41
University of Ulm, Department of Psychotherapy, 42–44. *See also* Ulm Research Program
Unresolved/disorganized individual, 227

SUBJECT INDEX

Validation, 110
Vanderbilt University psychology department, 41–42
Variables, artificial tying/untying of, 96
Verbal expressiveness, 361–364
Verbatim analytic text, 58
Violence, chronic community, 201–202
Visual cliff test, 172
Vocabulary assimilation patterns, 122
Voice Stress Measure, 20

Warding-off behavior, 85
 aggressive behavior and, 198
Warmth, maternal, 362–363
Well-being, sense of, 324
Wide Range Achievement Reading Test, 359
Wish-fear dilemma, 76
Wished-for response, 204
Wishes, 75
 structures of, 55
Word recognition tests, 359–360